The Status of
Seabirds
in Britain
and Ireland

The Status of Seabirds in Britain and Ireland

by

Clare Lloyd, Mark L Tasker and Ken Partridge

ILLUSTRATED BY
Keith Brockie

Published for
THE NATURE CONSERVANCY COUNCIL
and
THE SEABIRD GROUP

T & A D POYSER

LONDON

© Nature Conservancy Council and The Seabird Group 1991
All map outlines Crown copyright © 1991

First published in 1991 T & A D Poyser Ltd
24–28 Oval Road, London NW1

United States Edition published by
ACADEMIC PRESS INC.
San Diego, CA 92101

Text set in Baskerville
Typeset by Phoenix Photosettings, Chatham, Kent
Printed and bound in Great Britain by
Mackays of Chatham PLC, Chatham, Kent

British Library Cataloguing in Publication Data
Lloyd, Clare
The status of seabirds in Britain and Ireland.
1. Great Britain. Marine birds. Distribution
I. Title   II. Tasker, M.L. (Mark L)   III. Partridge, Ken
598.2941

ISBN 0–85661–061–5

Contents

Foreword by Mike Pienkowski   xi

Introduction   xv

Part 1:   Seabird Biology and the Seabird Colony Register

Seabirds and their Breeding Populations   3
The Reasons for Change in Seabird Numbers   13
The Methods used for the Collection and Analysis of Seabird Counts   25

Part 2:   The Species Accounts

Fulmar: *Fulmarus glacialis*   37
Manx Shearwater: *Puffinus puffinus*   53
Storm Petrel: *Hydrobates pelagicus*   60
Leach's Petrel: *Oceanodroma leucorhoa*   68
Gannet: *Sula bassana*   73
Cormorant: *Phalacrocorax carbo*   82
Shag: *Phalacrocorax aristotelis*   96
Arctic Skua: *Stercorarius parasiticus*   108
Great Skua: *Catharacta skua*   116
Black-headed Gull: *Larus ridibundus*   125
Common Gull: *Larus canus*   136
Lesser Black-backed Gull: *Larus fuscus*   144
Herring Gull: *Larus argentatus*   155
Great Black-backed Gull: *Larus marinus*   172
Kittiwake: *Rissa tridactyla*   182
Sandwich Tern: *Sterna sandvicensis*   194
Roseate Tern: *Sterna dougallii*   204
Common Tern: *Sterna hirundo*   216
Arctic Tern: *Sterna paradisaea*   226
Little Tern: *Sterna albifrons*   234
Guillemot: *Uria aalge*   243
Razorbill: *Alca torda*   258
Black Guillemot: *Cepphus grylle*   269
Puffin: *Fratercula arctica*   278
Rare Breeders   290

Appendices

I.   Numbers of seabirds breeding on different parts of the coast of UK and Ireland in 1985–87   293
II.   Contributors since 1980 to the Seabird Colony Register   294
III.   Instructions and recording forms used for the Seabird Colony Register between 1985 and 1988   298

IV. Seafarer instructions and Sample Count Card 307
V. Scientific names of vertebrate and invertebrate animals mentioned in the text 317

References 321

Gazetteer 343

Index 351

List of Figures

1   Main seabird colonies.

2   County and district boundaries in Britain and Ireland and sections of coast not adequately surveyed between 1985–87.

3   Fulmar colonies.

    a)   Fulmar colonies in Shetland.

    b)   Fulmar colonies in Orkney.

4   Overall changes in Fulmar numbers, 1969–87.

5   Changes in Fulmar numbers at six colonies, 1969–87.

6   Manx Shearwater colonies.

7   Storm Petrel colonies.

8   Leach's Petrel colonies.

9   Gannet colonies.

10   Cormorant colonies.

11   Overall changes in Cormorant numbers, 1969–87.

12   Changes in Cormorant numbers in four colonies, 1969–87.

13   Cormorant nests at The Lamb and Craigleith.

14   Shag numbers at Canna and the Isle of May.

15   Shag colonies.

16   Overall changes in Shag numbers, 1969–87.

17   Arctic Skua colonies.

18   Great Skua colonies.

20   Common Gull colonies.

    a)   Common Gull colonies in Orkney.

21   Lesser Black-backed Gull colonies.

22   Overall changes in Lesser Black-backed Gull numbers, 1969–87.

23   Herring Gull colonies.

    a)   Herring Gull colonies in western Scotland.

24   Overall changes in Herring Gull numbers, 1969–87.

25   Great Black-backed Gull colonies.

    a)   Great Black-backed Gull colonies in Shetland.

26   Overall changes in Great Black-backed Gulls, 1969–87.

27   Kittiwake colonies.

28   Overall changes in Kittiwake numbers, 1969–87.

29   Sandwich Tern colonies.

30   Overall changes in Sandwich Tern numbers, 1969–87.

31   Roseate Tern colonies.

32   Common Tern colonies.

33   Arctic Tern colonies.

34   Little Tern colonies.

35   Guillemot colonies.

36   Overall changes in Guillemot numbers, 1969–87.

37   Change in median colony size of Guillemots, 1969–70 to 1985–87.

38   Razorbill colonies.

39 Black Guillemot colonies.
40 Puffin colonies.
41 Changes in Puffin numbers at seven colonies.

List of Plates

1   Guillemots, Kittiwakes and Gannets, Noss, Shetland
2   Dividing the catch of Fulmars, St Kilda 1880.
3   Razorbill caught in fishing net
4   Dead Guillemots and Fulmar, victims of oil pollution
5   Fulmars feeding behind fishing vessel
6   Gulls following trawler
7   Counting seabirds nesting on St Kilda
8   The cliffs of Hirta, St Kilda
9   Fulmars nesting in an old Raven's nest
10 Storm Petrel
11 Gannet colony on Les Etacs, Alderney
12 Cormorant colony at Braewick, Shetland
13 Shag on nest, Farne Islands
14 Shag colony, Isle of May
15 Great Skuas
16 Black-headed Gull colony
17 Black-headed Gulls feeding behind tractor
18 Common Gull colony, Co. Galway
19 Lesser Black-backed Gull and chick
20 Herring Gulls, St. Ives, Cornwall
21 Nesting Kittiwake, St Johns Church, Lowestoft
22 Sandwich Tern colony
23 Common Terns at nest, Co. Wexford
24 Arctic Tern at nest site, Isle of Man
25 Little Tern on nest
26 Guillemot colony at Sumburgh Head, Shetland
27 Guillemot colony, Isle of May
28 Black Guillemots, Bangor, Co. Down
29 Puffin with sandeel, North Rona
30 Puffins on Boreray, St Kilda

List of Tables

1   Seabird numbers in Britain and Ireland, in Europe and in world range.
2   Inland and coastal seabirds.
3   How seabirds die.
4   Numbers of seabirds fed by fishing activities.
5   Chick diet and breeding success on Foula.
6   British and Irish Fulmars.
7   World Fulmars.
8   Fulmar increase.
9   World Manx Shearwaters.
10   British and Irish Manx Shearwaters.
11   World Storm Petrels.
12   British and Irish Storm Petrels.
13   World Leach's Petrels.
14   British and Irish Leach's Petrels.
15   World Gannets.
16   British and Irish Gannets.
17   World Cormorants.
18   British and Irish Cormorants.
19   World Shags.
20   British and Irish Shags.
21   World Arctic Skuas.
22   Scottish Arctic Skuas.
23   World Great Skuas.
24   Scottish Great Skuas.
25   World Black-headed Gulls.
26   British and Irish Black-headed Gulls.
27   Coastal and inland Black-headed Gulls.
28   World Common Gulls.
29   British and Irish Common Gulls.
30   World Lesser Black-backed Gulls.
31   British and Irish Lesser Black-backed Gulls.
32   Firth of Forth Lesser Black-backed Gulls.
33   World Herring Gulls.
34   British and Irish Herring Gulls.
35   Firth of Forth Herring Gulls.
36   World Great Black-backed Gulls.
37   British and Irish Great Black-backed Gulls.
38   World Kittiwakes.
39   British and Irish Kittiwakes.
40   Changes in Kittiwake numbers.
41   Trends in Kittiwake numbers.
42   World Sandwich Terns.
43   British and Irish Sandwich Terns.

44   World Roseate Terns.
45   British and Irish Roseate Terns.
46   World Common Terns.
47   British and Irish Common Terns.
48   British and Irish Common/Arctic Terns.
49   World Arctic Terns.
50   British and Irish Arctic Terns.
51   World Little Terns.
52   British and Irish Little Terns.
53   World Guillemots.
54   British and Irish Guillemots.
55   Guillemot trends.
56   World Razorbills.
57   British and Irish Razorbills.
58   Razorbill trends.
59   World Black Guillemots.
60   Pre-breeding censuses of Black Guillemots.
61   British and Irish Black Guillemots.
62   World Puffins.
63   British and Irish Puffins.

Foreword

Mike Pienkowski
Assistant Chief Scientist, Nature Conservancy Council

Breeding seabirds require marine feeding areas and land relatively nearby on which to nest and rear young. The archipelago of Britain, Ireland and the adjacent islands provides both nesting sites and complex mixing of different water bodies in extensive, shallow, productive seas. Thus the area is of quite exceptional international importance to seabirds.

The international responsibility to safeguard these breeding populations depends on sound information about their distributions, population trends and factors affecting these. A pioneering start to this task was the Seabird Group's "Operation Seafarer" in 1969–70. Despite its great value, this suffered the inevitable consequence of innovative work: the identification of methodological problems which needed solving. In the years since then, many of these have been solved—although major difficulties remain in respect of hole-nesting species, especially nocturnal ones. The need to update "Seafarer" and to apply widely these improved methods led in 1984 to the Nature Conservancy Council (NCC) and the Seabird Group planning the Seabird Colony Register.

We intended to establish a database for breeding seabirds in Britain and Ireland which could be readily updated in future. At the same time, we planned to arrange for the filling of gaps by new surveys. Thanks to the efforts of the large number of mostly amateur observers almost complete coverage of British coastal colonies was achieved within the main survey period (1985–87), and results of the various surveys undertaken since "Seafarer" were compiled. This magnificent result is a tribute to the cooperation which was achieved by combining volunteer efforts of skilled observers, brought together by the Seabird Group, with professional organisers, employed by NCC. Without this combination, it would have been impossible to obtain such a complete picture of seabird breeding numbers.

Although NCC and the Seabird Group were able to give some support for the observers' expenses, particularly for visits to remote areas, the costs and time contributed by the volunteers were immense, and we hope that this book and the other products of the study go some way to expressing our thanks for their hard work and commitment. They can be assured that the results will be—and already have been—put to good use.

Although NCC's statutory remit relates to Great Britain, we were anxious to treat the natural area as completely as possible, as the conservation of such mobile animals depends on coordinated action over wide areas. We were, therefore, delighted to receive the enthusiastic cooperation of colleagues throughout Ireland, as well as in the Isle of Man and the Channel Isles, and to be able to provide an integrated service for all these. This was facilitated greatly by the recruitment of Dr Clare Lloyd as the project officer. Clare's experience of seabird work included work in the Republic of Ireland as well as the United Kingdom, and this greatly enhanced contacts with the many participants.

Most of us see seabirds mainly at their breeding sites, but it would be a serious omission to ignore the crucially important marine feeding areas of these birds. Survey of these was not part of the Seabird Colony Register project. However, concurrently with this, NCC has operated its Seabirds at Sea Team (SAST), which is funded also by the oil industry and relevant government departments. This surveys the distribution of seabirds at sea throughout the year in all the waters around Britain. These results are reported separately, but use is made of them also in this book in order to paint a more complete picture and place the colony counts in context. The coordination of these different and complementary facets of seabird studies has benefited greatly from the presence in NCC's Aberdeen office of our Seabirds Team, within the Chief Scientist Directorate. This has also enabled the sufficiently wide view necessary to put the work on the national and international scale required for these wide-ranging birds of a mobile environment.

Apart from its major use in providing updated information on total numbers and distributions throughout Britain and Ireland, another major application of the results is in identifying trends. Some provisos are important here. First, the lack of suitable methods for some species in the earlier complete survey prevents detailed comparison. With the benefit of the new methods whose development was stimulated by "Seafarer", our new survey will provide a baseline for future comparisons for further species.

Second, single counts at intervals of many years are subject to all sorts of methodological problems in interpretation. The authors outline these in an early chapter and draw attention to the relevant provisos in each species description. This will go a long way to helping readers interpret the results. I must, however, emphasise that further detailed analyses of these data require the expertise of persons qualified to do so and with full experience of the methodologies. NCC's Ornithology Branch and the Seabird Group are able to advise here.

As the authors explain, the most practicable way to follow trends in breeding populations of most species is by combining annual counts and, where possible, breeding productivity assessments at sample plots with less frequent single-count, complete surveys, such as those reported here. Several organisations have undertaken sample counts of breeding seabirds at various locations over recent years. These include NCC and its contractors, as well as the Royal Society for the Protection of Birds (RSPB) and the Shetland Oil Terminal Environmental Advisory Group. Reference to the results of such work is included in the texts where relevant and available. NCC, in cooperation with these other organisations, is attempting to integrate and make these monitoring results more available as part of its Seabird Monitoring Programme. These results, together with the counts of breeding terns coordinated by the RSPB, will be reported annually in future.

This work forms part of NCC's duty to monitor populations and environments. Amongst other programmes, one of particular relevance to seabirds is the national bird-ringing scheme operated by the British Trust for Ornithology (BTO). The results of this are vital in assessing survival rates and movement patterns of birds, including seabirds.

Apart from the crucial importance of these seabird studies for the conservation of our internationally important seabird populations, they provide one of the few ways we have of monitoring the broader marine environment. In effect, these wide-ranging birds are acting as our sampling agents. As human impact on the seas increases, whether directly by exploitation of resources or marine pollution, or less directly by factors such as global warming, early indications of changes are vital. Thus, our surveys are even more useful if they are designed to give clues to the causes of changes observed, thereby enabling investigative studies to be well targeted.

In the case of our work on seabirds, this is often best achieved by ensuring that standard methods are used over a sufficiently large study area to allow geographical comparisons. Several examples of the benefits of this are evident in this book. Perhaps the best known relates to the breeding failures of seabirds in Shetland in recent years. The comparative information noted here allows these to be placed in a wider context, showing for example, that failures were not solely in areas of sandeel fisheries, so that fishermen and birds may have been suffering from a common cause, rather than one being the source of the other's difficulty. The differences in effects on seabirds of different foraging methods have also helped focus the attention of biologists on the aspects requiring most study. Some other geographic differences identified in this book are also certainly worthy of further study. For example, is the decline of auks in northwest Ireland connected with fishing activities in those areas? In all parts of Britain, except the major salmon-farming areas, the Cormorant population has grown; is this coincidence or not? Why have Herring Gulls declined so greatly in all areas except around the northern Irish Sea and Clyde?

Some human activities appear to have had far less effect on seabird population than was once feared. Oil production activities are one such case. The close level of consultation between our Seabirds Team and the industry has undoubtedly helped this. However, eternal vigilance is important to maintain this, especially as the location and timing of oil-spills is generally more important than the quantity of oil involved. Those problems that have arisen come mainly from the transportation side of the industry. Some consequential, fairly long-term local impacts on Black Guillemots and Puffins are noted in relevant sections of this book.

Also evident throughout the text are the interactions of the many different features which can influence the birds' numbers. Both the protection from persecution, which was an early success of the embryonic RSPB 100 years ago, and the increase in fish offal, rubbish and other food sources saved several gull species from local extinction and led to the vast population increase in many. It is less clear why some, notably the Herring Gull, are now declining markedly. The importance of maintaining long-term monitoring programmes is evident for such long-lived species, where trends are slow to become clear.

What are the concerns for current attention evident from the results in this book? It is clear that interactions with food supply is the dominant element in most situations. We would do well therefore to develop current initiatives in working alongside fisheries biologists in order to examine the consequences of changes in these systems, whether natural or man-induced—or increasingly a combination of both. It is important to note, however, that changes in human behaviour in relation to direct or indirect persecution can also have major and very rapid effects. There are many cases in which human introduction of ground-predators to islands has caused at least local extinction of seabird species, and precautionary measures should be taken. Prevention is the solution here, rather than attempts at cure. For example, the arrival of one pregnant rat is potentially enough to create havoc on St Kilda, the North Atlantic's major seabird colony and a World Heritage Site.

Direct persecution by humans is no longer a general problem, but we should be wary of some developments, such as the increasing seabird deaths in some areas due to drift-nets. Other workers have also expressed concern about killing of breeding skuas because of their "nuisance" value. We remain unsure as to whether killing of Roseate Terns in their winter areas is a cause of the major problems with this species.

The interest in seabirds—other than as objects for killing—came a little late for one of our most fascinating seabirds, the Great Auk (unless DNA manipulation makes further major strides). The studies reported here should enhance our interest in the biology of seabirds, particularly with a view to conserving these spectacular creatures which we hold in trust.

I would like to congratulate the authors and all the many people who contributed their time and effort on the production of what will become both a major reference work, and a starting point for many future studies.

Introduction

This book owes its existence to the Seabird Group and the Nature Conservancy Council, who were responsible for creating the Seabird Colony Register as a single source of information on breeding seabirds in Great Britain, Ireland, the Isle of Man and the Channel Islands (collectively referred to as Britain and Ireland in this book unless otherwise specified). It summarises the information collated for the Seabird Colony Register, in particular a complete survey made in 1985–87 when the Register was established. The book also reports changes in seabird numbers since 1969–70. It would have been impossible to describe these changes without the counts made during the Seabird Group's Operation Seafarer survey in 1969–70 now included in the Register.

Operation Seafarer was the first complete survey of coastal seabird colonies in Britain and Ireland and was an admirable achievement. It was carried out largely with untrained observers, using the best counting methods available at the time and without access to a computer for storage or analysis of results, yet it succeeded in providing a comprehensive set of data on seabird numbers. Its published results (Cramp *et al.* 1974), including a review of the changes in seabird numbers earlier this century, have provided an invaluable source of reference for nearly 20 years. Research in the intervening years has improved, but not perfected, techniques for counting seabirds in this type of large-scale survey and has established relatively accurate methods for monitoring breeding populations, based on sample counts in a few selected colonies.

The Seabird Colony Register was established in 1984 by the Seabird Group and the Nature Conservancy Council, and a repeat survey of the whole coastline of Britain and Ireland was organised in 1985–87 (with some counts in 1988). The results of this survey and the changes which have occurred since 1969–70 form the basis of this book. The Seabird Colony Register also holds most counts of breeding seabirds made in Britain and Ireland between 1970 and 1985 and since 1987, so that it now provides a single source of reference for current and past estimates of seabird numbers.

The information in the Seabird Colony Register has been put to various uses. First, the up-to-date population totals permit an assessment of the importance of British and Irish seabirds in an international context (Table 1). The numbers of both the Gannet and Manx Shearwater are of major international importance as over 70% of the world breeding population of both are found in Britain and Ireland. At least half of the world's Great Skuas and Storm Petrels, and 10–50% of the world's Lesser Black-backed Gulls, Shags, and Razorbills also breed in these islands.

Current estimates of the size of seabird breeding populations are needed to allow both the United Kingdom and the Republic of Ireland to fulfil their obligations under law and international agreements. The data from the Seabird Colony Register have been used by the Nature Conservancy Council in Britain and the Wildlife Service in Ireland to identify Special Protection

Table 1. *Approximate total numbers of seabirds (pairs) in Britain and Ireland compared with those in Europe and in the relevant biogeographical area for each species (see text).*

Species	British and Irish	European	Biogeographical	Comments
Fulmar	571,000	5,840,000	7,540,000	North Atlantic *F. g. glacialis*
Manx Shearwater[a]	275,000	306,000	294,000	*P. p. puffinus*
Storm Petrel[a]	160,000	247,000	257,000	World
Leach's Petrel[a]	55,000	60,600	955,000	North Atlantic
Gannet	187,700	223,600	263,000	North Atlantic
Cormorant	11,700	86,000	41,200	*P. c. carbo*
Shag	47,300	125,000	125,000	*P. a. aristotelis*
Arctic Skua	3350	17,500	30,000	North Atlantic
Great Skua	7900	13,600	13,600	World
Black-headed Gull	233,000	1,200,000	1,650,000	Europe to Urals
Common Gull	71,400	488,000	530,000	Europe to Urals
Lesser Black-backed Gull	88,500	187,000	124,000	*L. f. graellsii*
Herring Gull	206,000	978,000	940,000	*L. a. argenteus* and *argentatus*
Great Black-backed Gull	23,400	83,100	140,000	Northeast Atlantic
Kittiwake	544,000	1,740,000	3,170,000	*R. t. tridactyla*
Sandwich Tern	19,000	54,700	132,000	*S. s. sandvicensis*
Roseate Tern	650	750	1770	Eastern Atlantic
Common Tern	16,100	91,400	122,250	Eurasian *S. h. hirundo*
Arctic Tern	81,200	278,000	900,000	World
Little Tern	2800	18,400	67,700	*S. a. albifrons*
Guillemot[b]	806,100	3,000,000	2,250,000	East Atlantic *U. a. albionis* and *aalge*
Razorbill[b]	122,000	612,000	575,000	*A. t. islandica*
Black Guillemot[c]	20,200	100,000	39,200	East Atlantic *C. g. arcticus*
Puffin[c]	467,000	6,890,000	901,000	*F. a. graba*

The mid-points of all population estimates taken: this may lead to considerable inaccuracies.

Biogeographical populations are either the whole range of a subspecies, or the limits of the range that the British and Irish breeding population appears to interact with. In some cases these are best guesses within the limits of existing studies. For sources, see each species account.

[a] Very speculative figures.

[b] Numbers of individuals multiplied by 0.67 to obtain pair estimates.

[c] Numbers of individuals multiplied by 0.5 to obtain pair estimates.

Europe as used here excludes USSR, Svalbard, Jan Mayen, Greenland and Macronesian islands.

Areas required by the EC Directive on the Conservation of Wild Birds 1979; also for assessment of the Ramsar Sites established following the Convention on Wetlands of International Importance Especially as Waterfowl Habitat in 1971; and in Britain, under the Wildlife and Countryside Act of 1981 and later amendment, seabird counts have been provided for existing and potential Sites of Special Scientific Interest. Information from the Register has also proved useful to several academic studies, to seabird ringers, in the preparation of environmental impact statements and the assessment of possible threats from oil spills. Assessments of trends in numbers of birds are important, not least for identifying needs for further investigation of possible causes of any changes.

The text of this book is divided into two parts. The first chapter of Part 1 describes something of the fascination that seabirds and their breeding colonies hold for professional and non-professional ornithologists alike and why Britain and Ireland are so important for them. With the comparable information collected by Operation Seafarer, we now have as good a baseline of data on seabird numbers as we could expect in view of the enormous difficulties in counting them—or even in reaching some of their more remote colonies. The reasons why seabird numbers changed in the way and at the speed they did between 1969–70 and 1985–87 are usually far from clear, however.

The role of the birds' food supply and some of the other factors possibly contributing to change in numbers are discussed in the second chapter. A description of the methods used to count seabirds and of the biases and limitations involved is given in the third chapter. This is aimed more at the specialist reader who may be interested in repeating some of the counts in future, but it also provides an explanation of how the counts, past and present, have been interpreted. Scientific names of all birds, mammals and invertebrates mentioned in the text are given in Appendix VI.

In the second part of the book we cover in turn each of the 24 species of seabirds which breed commonly in Britain and Ireland. Information on their current breeding distribution and numbers throughout the world are given so that totals for Britain and Ireland can be put into an international perspective. For each species, some of the special problems encountered during 1985–87 and previous surveys in finding colonies and censusing breeding birds are explained, with a discussion of how errors in counting can be minimised. The distribution and size of colonies in different parts of Britain and Ireland is described and attempts are made to assess changes in numbers that have occurred since 1969–70. Each chapter in Part 2 ends with a review of possible causes of change in the size of the species' breeding population.

ACKNOWLEDGEMENTS

Over 600 people helped to collect information for the Seabird Colony Register between 1981 and 1988 (Appendix II). Without them this book could not have been written. We are also especially grateful to the Regional Organisers and others who helped to coordinate the surveys: S. Angus, N.K. Atkinson, J.S. Armitage, R.W. Arnold, C. Badenoch, A. Blackburn, D. Browne, S. Casey, L.V. Cranna, A. Currie, P.J. Dunn, M.M. Elliott, J.G. Greenwood, M. Heubeck, M.G. Hill, D.B. Johnson, B.M. Lynch, E.R. Meek, O.J. Merne, A.S. Moore, G.P. Mudge, J. Stafford, M. Stentiford, S.J. Sutcliffe, R.L. Swann, A. Webb, J. Watson, B. Zonfrillo.

The Executive Committee of the Seabird Group and M.W. Pienkowski provided us with useful advice and much encouragement. The planning and execution of the 1985–87 survey and the book's text were greatly improved by the generous help and criticism of M.P. Harris and S. Wanless. Others who helped referee parts of the text were N. Aebischer, M. Brooke, J.C. Coulson, E.K. Dunn, G.M. Dunnet, P.G.H. Evans, P.J. Ewins, R.W. Furness, H. Galbraith, R. Macdonald, O.J. Merne, P. Monaghan, P.H. Oswald and B. Zonfrillo; M.G. Wilson translated appropriate parts of the new handbook of Soviet Union birds. M. Avery prepared the texts for the five tern species. E.K. Dunn, M.W. Pienkowski and P.M. Walsh also read the entire text and the latter helped to compile and checked many of the tables. The authors, of course, absolve the reviewers for any remaining errors.

We have been fortunate to have the help of S. Hiscock who, with P.M. Walsh, drafted the maps, using colony totals compiled by P.M. Walsh. S. Wallace drew most of the figures. C.A. Lloyd input much of the data sheets to the computer. Trevor Poyser, Andy Richford and David Atkins provided much help and guidance.

W.R.P. Bourne is thanked for keeping the original Operation Seafarer cards safe. These are now held at NCC's Aberdeen office, and have been microfiched free of charge by Britoil plc.

Finally we should like to thank colleagues in the Nature Conservancy Council (NCC) and elsewhere for use of unpublished data and information, and those colleagues in NCC's Aberdeen office for their help, encouragement and tolerance.

The Seabird Colony Register was funded mainly by the NCC under the Chief Scientist Directorate Research Programme; additional funding was provided by the Seabird Group. In addition, many counters contributed their time and travel. Without this combination of resources, the project would have been impossible.

PART 1

*Seabird Biology and the
Seabird Colony Register*

Seabirds and their Breeding Populations

Every summer many millions of seabirds use the coasts of Britain and Ireland for breeding. Some arrive after long migratory journeys from as far away as Newfoundland, Brazil and the Antarctic; others spend their whole life within 50 km of the colony where they were born. However, we know far more about some species than others. The distribution and size of many breeding colonies of the nocturnal petrels are still a mystery but, at the other extreme, every Gannet colony in the world has been counted several times within the last 80 years. Everyone is familiar with the gulls which are a noisy and sometimes troublesome addition to city life, nesting untidily on buildings and thronging rubbish tips and reservoirs. Fewer people may be aware of the truly marine birds which gather in vast numbers to nest in remote parts of Britain and Ireland. In June, seabird colonies on the cliffs, sandy spits, rocky islets and coastal moorland around these shores teem with birds and echo to their cries.

Britain and Ireland have about 2–2.5 million auks and 2.5–3 million pairs of other species (Appendix I). Twenty-four different seabirds nest regularly, out of a total of about 275 species worldwide. Guillemots, Fulmars and Kittiwakes are the most numerous, and the Roseate Tern the rarest. In terms of international status, this seabird community is collectively of considerable importance. However, despite the enormous numbers of seabirds in Britain and Ireland, they are outnumbered by some of the commoner species of land birds. For example, seven million pairs of Blackbirds have been estimated to breed in Britain and Ireland (Sharrock 1976).

WHAT IS A SEABIRD?

Seabirds are a group of birds which depend mainly on the sea, beyond the tide-line for their food. The group includes some species which often breed and feed inland, such as the Black-headed and Common Gulls, but excludes other species which spend only part of the year at sea (e.g. divers, seaducks, phalaropes). The adaptations to life at sea summarised in this chapter address the species which live in Britain and Ireland; for a fuller, worldwide appraisal see, for example, Nelson (1980). Although seabirds share a broadly common lifestyle, they are evolutionarily quite diverse. The species which breed regularly in Britain and Ireland belong to seven taxonomic Families:

Procellariidae—four species of petrel (Fulmar, Manx Shearwater, Storm Petrel, Leach's Petrel)

Phalacrocoracidae—two species of cormorant (Cormorant, Shag)

Sulidae—one species (Gannet)

Stercorariidae—two species of skua (Great Skua, Arctic Skua)

Laridae—six species of gull (Herring Gull, Common Gull, Black-headed Gull, Lesser Black-backed Gull, Great Black-backed Gull, Kittiwake)

Sternidae—five species of tern (Sandwich Tern, Roseate Tern, Common Tern, Arctic Tern, Little Tern)

Alcidae—four species of auk (Guillemot, Razorbill, Black Guillemot, Puffin)

Like many water birds, seabirds have webbed feet and a well-developed preen gland situated at the base of the tail, from which the bird secretes a waterproof oil which is smeared onto feathers during preening. A seabird is able to rid its body of excess salt which it cannot help accumulating through ingesting seawater and food. A highly concentrated salt solution is secreted from the salt gland in the nasal passages and trickles out of the bird's nostrils. It can sometimes be seen dripping off the tip of the bill.

Seabirds feed generally on fish and marine invertebrates which are high in energy in relation to volume and weight. This diet is a necessary adaptation for a lifestyle which requires long periods of flying when bulky or heavy food in the digestive system would be a disadvantage. Thus no seabird relies upon a diet entirely of plants since this would require the consumption and digestion of bulk food.

Many seabirds spend most of their life in the air and their wings are adapted to the type of flight most often used. The petrels are specialised for a flap-and-glide flight-style and the gliding component approaches perfection in their close relatives, the albatrosses. The Fulmar, for example, has long narrow wings which can carry it for great distances using the winds at the sea's surface without the need for energetic, flapping flight. Among seabirds, petrels perform some of the longest migrations and are also able to forage far from the colonies during the breeding season. The Gannet and terns have long, pointed wings also adapted for long-distance flight and providing the terns with aerial manoeuvrability. Both the Gannet and terns plunge-dive after fish and undertake long migrations. By comparison, the cormorants, which dive from the surface and swim underwater, have shorter, rounded wings. The auks' short, stiff wings are the smallest in relation to body size of any existing northern hemisphere seabird group, and are adapted for high-speed propulsion underwater, the feet and short stiff tail serving as rudders and stabilisers.

Petrels, which forage over huge areas of sea, are unusual amongst birds in that they have a finely developed sense of smell. This enables them to detect from afar the presence of oily foods, such as offal or the oil from surface shoals of fish. The habit has been turned to advantage by birdwatchers who throw loads of "chum" (mixtures of fish-oil and offal) from boats at sea in order to attract rare petrels. Petrels are also unique in their ability to store oils in their stomachs. This gives them a slowly digestible food source which provides more energy for its weight than body fat does. It is a vital adaptation for long-distance foraging in adults and for helping chicks to survive periods without food.

The Gannet is a plunge-diving specialist, with thickened bone in the front of its skull which absorbs the impact of plummeting into the water. Air trapped in the thick body-plumage provides buoyancy to help the bird to surface after a dive. Birds which dive underwater from the surface have the opposite problem. Cormorants have to overcome their natural buoyancy in order to reach food on the bottom of the sea. Accordingly, they have a poorly developed preen gland so that their plumage is barely waterproof and unable to hold much air. After a diving session, the birds need to dry their waterlogged feathers and, to this end, are often seen resting on a prominent perch with outspread wings.

For underwater swimming, cormorants—like auks—have a streamlined body and dense plumage which traps little air. The two largest skeletal parts, the breast bone and pelvic girdle, are relatively narrower and longer than in other seabirds, lending the body a torpedo-like shape. The cormorants' large feet and particularly sturdy legs are set far back on the body and are used as paddles; the wings are kept folded underwater.

SEABIRD FEEDING AND BREEDING

Seabirds feed in many different ways and are able to exploit most marine sources of food as well as some of those on land (e.g. Ashmole and Ashmole 1967). Some seabirds feed mainly at night when organisms which are out of reach in deep water during the day migrate to the surface. The gulls are particularly opportunistic when foraging and adapt their diet accordingly. They are equally at home feeding behind fishing boats at sea, on estuarine mudflats and rocky shores, inland behind a plough or on a rubbish tip, and by hawking for aerial insect swarms.

The petrels and the Kittiwake take food from the surface and from shallow depths; the smaller species do so whilst still in flight. The Storm Petrel and Leach's Petrel are particularly adept at flitting just over the waves picking up planktonic food or scraps of offal. The largest petrel, the Fulmar, usually flops down onto the surface and plunges its head underwater to grasp a food item. To reach another patch of food, it often runs over the surface of the water, flapping its wings rather than bothering to fly.

Other seabirds exploit generally deeper water layers. All five species of terns hover and plunge head first after fish and crustaceans. The momentum of the dive brings them into contact with their prey without the need for underwater swimming. The depth of the dive depends on body weight so that the Little Tern, for example, feeds largely in surface waters. The Gannet also fishes by plunge-diving and its dives are often higher and more precipitous than those of the terns. Both Gannets and Manx Shearwaters can, if necessary, swim underwater and accordingly they feed at greater depths than any of the terns.

The Cormorant, Shag and the four species of auks dive from the surface and descend into comparatively deep water (see species chapters) or to the bottom of the sea to collect food. The gulls and skuas are opportunistic feeders. They feed on the surface of the sea and just below it, by stealing from other birds, by scavenging behind fishing boats and on land, or by direct predation of other seabirds' eggs and chicks, occasionally killing even adults. Among the gulls, the Kittiwake feeds furthest offshore, the large species forage mainly in inshore waters and on rocky shores, whilst the Common and Black-headed Gulls are estuarine and inland feeders. The skuas feed mainly by fishing and scavenging at sea, by predation on other seabirds and especially by stealing food from them.

Seabirds can survive and breed only if they are able to find the right kind of food, of a suitable size and at an accessible depth. The continental shelf off northwest Europe provides particularly favourable conditions for fish, supporting both commercial fisheries and a rich seabird community. However, food for seabirds is not evenly distributed over the shelf. Instead, many invertebrates and fish (or their larval and juvenile forms) are concentrated at spawning or feeding grounds and at distinct boundaries where different water masses meet (Cushing 1982). For example, water depth and bottom sediments in the English Channel, Irish Sea, North Sea and the firths of the Scottish coast are such as to provide ideal spawning grounds for many commercial fish stocks, including important seabird foods such as Herring and sandeels. Until oceanic change and fishing pressure reduced their numbers, large shoals of Herring used to feed in the North Sea where their distribution mirrored that of their chief plankton prey *Calanus* (e.g. Cushing 1952). The North Sea still supports a large commercial fishery for a range of whitefish and flatfish.

The boundary between water of contrasting temperature or salinity is known as a front and these areas can be particularly attractive to fish. Deep water layers of the sea tend to be colder and more saline than surface waters, which are warmed by the sun and diluted by fresh water running off the land. In shallow water near land, the wind and tides mix these layers together. The fronts which occur most commonly around Britain and Ireland are those formed at the boundary between the layered offshore and mixed inshore water masses. These fronts are typified by an abundance of nutrients brought up from the deep water into the sunlit surface waters where phytoplankton can make use of them, the resulting increase in production of plankton attracting fish and seabirds (Brown 1980). The productivity and scale of the front depends on the strength of the forces mixing the water masses together. They may be relatively constant, or may change, for example, seasonally or tidally. The number of birds at a front seems to depend on its strength and persistence, with the weak or intermittent fronts less likely to attract seabirds (Schneider *et al.* 1987).

Breeding seabirds have two main requirements. They need a supply of food near enough to the breeding colony to be within their foraging range and a safe place with suitable habitat in which to nest. They are able to use a wide variety of different nesting habitats from urban rooftops to the most isolated and inhospitable offshore islands, from cliffs of over 300 metres to low-lying shingle banks which change shape, or even disappear, with each winter's storms. The thousands of kilometres of indented coastline and islands surrounding Britain and Ireland seem to offer abundant nesting sites for seabirds. Nearby are rich fishing grounds which normally provide a dependable food supply.

Most seabirds nest on the coast or within sight of it, either on offshore islands or a little way inland. Only six species have 5% or more of their breeding population in truly inland colonies (Table 2) and the habit varies regionally and between species. On the islands of Shetland and Orkney, for example, where nowhere is very far from the open sea, many gulls and terns, skuas and Fulmars nest away from the coast on lochs, moorland and ruined buildings. The majority of Black-headed and Common Gulls breeding in Britain and Ireland, and of Lesser Black-backed Gulls in Ireland, nest inland.

Table 2. *Approximate numbers of seabirds (pairs) breeding inland and on the coast in Britain and Ireland.*

	Britain			Ireland		
	Coast		Inland	Coast		Inland
Cormorant	6200	11%	800	4200	11%	500
Black-headed Gull	74,600	55%	90,000	6800	90%	59,000
Common Gull	14,800	78%	53,000	900	75%	2700
Lesser Black-backed Gull	63,500	24%	20,000	2200	58%	3000
Herring Gull	146,100	9%	15,000	44,200	1%	500
Sandwich Tern	14,000	0%	0	4400	4%	200
Common Tern	12,000	7%	900	2700	13%	400
Arctic Tern	77,700	1%	500	2500	4%	100

Percentages show proportion of British or Irish total inland. Small numbers of Fulmars, Arctic Skuas and Great Black-backed Gulls also nest inland; these are <1% of the total for each species.

Seabirds are generally colonial breeders although some colonies of Fulmars, Shags and Black Guillemots are very dispersed with nests at low densities. Often several species of seabirds with similar habitat requirements nest side by side. Mixed tern and gull colonies are common, skua territories are often found near tern colonies and many cliffs hold a mosaic of Fulmars, Shags, Kittiwakes

Plate 1.   Charlies Holm, Noss, Shetland, showing Guillemots, Kittiwakes and Gannets occupying differing parts of the cliff (Dr M.P. Harris)

and auks. Each species in these mixed colonies has a preferred type of nesting habitat, but some nest-site competition, both within and between species, is common. The main benefits of colonial breeding are safety in numbers from predators and possibly the chance of sharing information on the whereabouts of locally variable food supplies. Disadvantages include the attraction of predators to a conspicuous concentration of birds, competition for nest sites, and the increased chance of disease and cannibalism (see Furness and Monaghan (1987) for further details).

HOW SEABIRD NUMBERS VARY

Seabirds are long-lived birds with high survival rates among adults. However, they produce relatively few young each year when compared with many species of land birds in which multiple clutches and large broods are common. The seabirds in Britain and Ireland attempt to breed at most only once a year. The maximum number of young produced annually by a breeding pair varies from one for most of the auks, to four or five for the Shag. Seabirds do not usually breed in their first summer of life and, although a few do so in their second summer, most wait at least another two or three years before attempting to breed.

In order to ensure clarity later, a "population" is defined in this book as all of the birds belonging to the same species living in a specified geographical area. The term is used to refer, for example, to all of the Fulmars in northwest Europe or Britain. A population of birds includes immature individuals and those capable of breeding. Not every bird old enough to breed succeeds in finding a mate and a nest site, and in becoming physically fit enough, to breed every year. The proportion of non-breeding adults in a population of seabirds is large (relative to that in passerines, for example) and usually varies from year to year in ways which are inadequately understood. Many seabirds, such as the Shag, Fulmar and Puffin for instance, occasionally take a year or more off from breeding so that, although the size of their colonies may decline, the number of birds in the breeding population remains unchanged.

In general, numbers of seabirds are limited by natural regulating factors to a level which can be supported by their environment. In a stable breeding population of seabirds, recruitment (birds surviving to breed) and immigration (birds entering the breeding population from outside) exactly balance mortality (birds dying) and emigration (birds moving out of the breeding population).

In seabirds, the number of young produced by each pair per year is low, and the period of immaturity long. Adult mortality rates are also relatively low. This rate must stay low for the seabird breeding population to remain stable. A series of seasons with low breeding productivity or even complete breeding failure may have a relatively insignificant effect on the size of the breeding population (assuming other factors remain unchanged). For example, Puffins on the Norwegian island of Røst produced almost no fledged chicks from 1975 onwards, yet the colony size remained nearly unchanged for many years (Lid 1981). Years in which one or more species of seabirds are unable to breed successfully also occur in Britain. In the late 1980s, the inability of some seabirds in the Shetland islands to find enough food for their chicks led to large-scale breeding failure among Kittiwakes, Arctic Terns, skuas and some Razorbills and Puffins (Heubeck 1989a, see also following chapter).

By contrast, a small change in adult mortality rate is enough to have a large effect on the size of a breeding population. For example, in a stable colony of 50 pairs of breeding Razorbills, about ten adults die each year (Lloyd and Perrins 1977). The death of 15 birds in a year rather than ten represents a 50% increase in the mortality rate which, in turn, would lead to a 5% decline in the numbers of breeding birds. Annual mortality in the Robin, by comparison, results in the deaths of 62 birds per 50 pairs (Lack 1948), and in order for the mortality rate to increase by 50%, as many as 93 birds, instead of 62, would have to die. The same argument applies to a decrease in annual mortality (i.e. increased survival) among seabirds, with the result that some breeding populations are able to grow fast if conditions are favourable. The number of Guillemots breeding in Britain and Ireland, for example, more than doubled, from about 500,000 to over a million birds, between 1970 and 1987 (see Part 2).

The level of mortality among immature birds is also important, but it has a less critical effect upon population size because immature mortality is generally higher than that in adults. Average annual mortality of immature Razorbills is about 30% (Lloyd and Perrins 1977). Using the example quoted above, the death of five extra immature birds in one year would represent an increase in annual mortality of only 17% (cf. 50% in adults).

Most seabirds return to their natal colony to breed although some emigration and immigration occur. Ringing and colour marking of chicks of several species, including the Manx Shearwater, Fulmar, Shag, Razorbill and Puffin, have shown that some immature birds may visit other colonies and a few may even settle to breed in a colony other than their natal one; but once a bird has bred in a particular colony, it is unlikely to move to another (Potts 1969, Harris 1972, 1976b, Lloyd and Perrins 1977, Dunnet et al. 1979). Some birds are prevented from returning to the same colony site from year to year. Species like terns and some gulls, which nest in habitat liable to sudden changes, or Cormorants, which are often persecuted, show the least attachment to a colony or colony site. If conditions become unfavourable, for example when a nesting island is flooded by rising water levels, the colony may break up and its members breed elsewhere. Seabirds which nest in relatively stable habitat, such as offshore islands and cliffs, are mostly faithful to their breeding colony.

Several different hypotheses have been proposed for the regulation of seabird numbers. Lack (1966) argued that starvation outside the breeding season, due to density-dependent competition for food (i.e. the intensity of competition varying with population size) was the most important factor. Alternatively, density-dependent mortality may occur during the breeding season through competition for food; this may be critical in determining numbers of tropical seabirds (Ashmole 1963) and, possibly, also of northern temperate species (Furness and Birkhead 1984, Hunt et al. 1986). Shortage of suitable nest sites may also sometimes be involved in regulating numbers (Potts et al. 1980). Wynne-Edwards (1962) suggests that seabirds regulate their numbers through social interactions and at a level below that imposed by food supplies. Whatever the controlling mechanism, natural changes in the environment will alter the numbers of birds that can be supported and, hence, the size of breeding populations. Thus seabird numbers can be expected to show both long- and short-term changes and rarely to be exactly stable.

MONITORING SEABIRD NUMBERS

Clearly any changes in the size of seabird breeding colonies are of major concern to conservationists especially if they are accompanied by increased adult mortality or decreased production of young. A wide range of factors are known to influence seabird numbers breeding in Britain and Ireland, but the way, if any, in which they determine population levels are poorly understood. Factors currently regarded as threats include variations in food availability, especially those which may be associated with over-fishing. Oil spills and toxic chemical pollution at sea seem to be having relatively little effect on seabird populations at the moment, but complacency is dangerous. A single oil spill during the breeding season near one of the many major colonies, or off northeast Britain during autumn when auks have gathered to moult, could swiftly wipe out a significant part of the breeding populations of several species (Tasker and Pienkowski 1987). Mammals introduced onto islands with nesting seabirds represent a considerable threat; for example, St Kilda, the largest seabird colony in Britain and Ireland, could easily be invaded by rats from boats bringing supplies from the mainland (Tasker *et al.* 1988). Accidental drowning in netting and shooting seriously affect some seabirds, mostly in winter; much of this could be prevented by law since the countries concerned are members of the European Community. Other threats are described in the following chapter and elsewhere (e.g. Evans 1984, Evans and Nettleship 1985).

Seabirds are usually counted when they are in their breeding colonies, mainly because this is the only time when a majority of the population can be seen on land. Total counts of occupied nests give an estimate of the current year's breeding numbers but an unknown proportion of the breeding population, namely the birds which did not attempt to nest, is excluded from these censuses. On the other hand, for species with often inaccessible nest sites, such as the Razorbill, Guillemot and Black Guillemot, there is no alternative to counting birds rather than nests in the breeding colonies, and census totals then include a proportion of the non-breeding adult and immature birds in the population.

The changes that have occurred in seabird numbers in Britain and Ireland are probably among the best documented of any in Europe. One of the earliest seabird censuses was carried out in the first decade of this century by J. H. Gurney who surveyed all the Gannet colonies. He estimated that the eight colonies then in Britain and Ireland held about 75,000 birds (Gurney 1913). Regular complete surveys have been conducted since for the Gannet, Fulmar and Kittiwake. Other breeding seabird surveys since 1969 have included roof-nesting gulls in Britain (Monaghan and Coulson 1977); terns (Whilde 1985) and Cormorants (Macdonald 1987) in Ireland, Black Guillemots (Ewins and Tasker 1985), and terns (Bullock and Gomersall 1981) in Shetland and Orkney, terns on many nature reserves in Britain (Thomas 1982, Thomas *et al.* 1990), Black-headed Gulls in England and Wales (Gribble 1976), skuas (Meek *et al.* 1985, Ewins *et al.* 1988), and Puffins (Harris 1984a).

The first complete census of all seabirds breeding on the coasts of Britain and Ireland was organised by the Seabird Group (Cramp *et al.* 1974). The survey was named Operation Seafarer and was carried out mainly in the summers of 1969 and 1970. The census was repeated again in 1985–87.

The results of these two national surveys provide start and end points for changes in numbers between 1969 and 1987. Far less is known about how the size of most seabird colonies altered in the intervening years. However, from 1971 onwards, an annual seabird census at a sample of colonies was organised by the Seabird Group and the Royal Society for the Protection of Birds (RSPB) and later by the Nature Conservancy Council and others. This monitoring scheme was restricted to Fulmars, Kittiwakes, Guillemots and Razorbills, with study colonies spread through Britain and in the west of Ireland (Stowe 1982).

In each colony, one or more study plots were selected. These were sample cliff faces or sections of the area occupied by seabirds, with clearly defined boundaries. Birds, nests or nest sites were counted annually. Auk counts were repeated on at least five days in June, where possible, in order to avoid the bias caused by variations in colony attendance (Lloyd 1975, Evans 1980). The two national censuses, carried out mostly on a single visit to each colony, are known to have provided no more than estimates of the breeding populations and hence measure only large-scale changes. By contrast, the sample monitoring counts are considered sufficiently accurate to have detected relatively small, short-term population trends, although use of non-random sample areas within a colony may have biased the data (details in Wanless et al. 1982, Harris et al. 1983).

Monitoring of seabird populations by NCC's Seabird Monitoring Programme has recently expanded to include monitoring of breeding productivity (Walsh 1990) and may in future include a measure of changes in mortality rate, derived from ringing returns and recoveries. The monitoring of breeding productivity can provide an easy and relatively sensitive way of monitoring the health of a seabird population. As explained above, the long immaturity and low adult mortality rate of seabirds means that any changes affecting seabirds will take some time to show themselves in the adult population. It may be too late to study any changes if only adult numbers are monitored.

The Reasons for Change in Seabird Numbers

There are several factors which influence seabird numbers (see preceding chapter) and it is clear that unlimited increase or decrease does not occur. However, if for any reason, the approximate balance between the numbers of birds starting to breed and those dying is destroyed, numbers can decline to extinction. Several species of seabirds breeding in Britain and Ireland have increased in numbers for a decade or more of the present century, but in most cases growth has been followed by a period when it slowed, or halted, or even reversed. Examples of this are the Fulmar, whose numbers increased nearly five times as quickly earlier this century (13–19%) as they did in 1969 to 1987 (3–4%); and the Guillemot, which more than doubled in numbers during the 1970s and early 1980s; an increase which has now stopped or, in some areas, reversed. This chapter reviews some of the natural and artificial factors which affect seabird numbers.

Seabirds may be killed directly by man. In contrast to some other factors affecting seabirds, there is plenty of information on the extent of this influence. For example, statistics from ringing recoveries or shooting bags provide an indication of the geographic distribution and amount of mortality. In the nineteenth century, enormous numbers of seabirds were killed at their breeding colonies, variously for sport, food, or feathers. Stuffing and mounting dead birds and hoarding large collections of their eggs were among the fashions for "nature study" which swept Victorian Britain (Lloyd 1985). The hair-raising behaviour of the "eggers" and "climmers" on the seabird cliffs of Flamborough and Bempton (Yorkshire) and the quantities of eggs collected and birds killed there and elsewhere (e.g. Fisher and Lockley 1954) are difficult to believe by today's standards of legally enforced bird protection. A team of three climbers at Flamborough Head were reported to be able to collect 200–300 Guillemot eggs a day for up to five weeks of the year, with as many as four teams working the cliffs (Bourne and Vauk 1988).

In most countries of northern Europe, especially Iceland, the Faroes, Svalbard and Novaya Zemlya, seabirds have been (and in some places, still are) exploited extensively as a source of food, feathers and oil (e.g. Williamson 1948, Belopol'skii 1957). In the remote parts of the west of Scotland and Ireland, harvesting of seabirds and their eggs was vital for the subsistence economy, especially in times of famine, and for the survival of island communities. One of the best documented examples is St Kilda, 150 km west of the Scottish mainland and still Britain's largest seabird colony. Up to 12,000 Fulmar chicks and 89,600 Puffins are estimated to have been taken annually during the late 1800s (Harris and Murray 1978). Exploitation of seabirds on St Kilda and elsewhere, including Bempton and the Faroe Islands, was organised according to traditional rules designed to prevent decline in breeding birds (e.g. Nørrevang 1986). Indeed the harvesting of some seabirds on the Faroe Islands and of Gannets on Sula Sgeir off northwest Scotland has continued to the present with no apparent decrease in colony size.

Plate 2. Dividing the catch of Fulmars, St Kilda 1880 (from the G.W. Wilson collection, Aberdeen University Library)

Generally, however, the persecution of seabirds in the last century was carried out without regard for its effect on numbers. Seabirds such as gulls and terns, which were mostly not in inaccessible or remote colonies, were especially vulnerable to persecution. Great Auks were large flightless seabirds which once bred on islands on both sides of the North Atlantic including Orkney, Shetland and St Kilda. This species suffered the most extreme consequence of persecution, being driven to extinction in 1844 (e.g. Fisher and Lockley 1954). Towards the end of the last century, public opinion in Britain began to turn against the killing of wild birds. Seabirds were among the early beneficiaries of new wildlife conservation laws. The first legislation to affect non-game species was the Protection of Sea Birds Bill in 1869. Organisations, such as the Royal Society for the Protection of Birds (founded 1889), campaigned for the increase and enforcement of laws to prevent birds and their eggs being exploited by man. Much of the growth in seabird numbers earlier in the present century may have been due to the legal protection which seabirds and their eggs received.

Most seabirds are now protected by law in Britain and Ireland, but large numbers are shot legally in other countries or taken with bait on fishing lines, usually for sport, in areas where they winter inshore (Table 3). For example, ringing has shown that among tens of thousands of seabirds shot off Norway each winter in the 1970s were breeding birds from Britain, Ireland and the Faroe Islands, as well as those from northern Norway (e.g. Baillie and Mead 1982). This affected mainly immature birds which wintered in areas where shooting of seabirds was common practice. In recent years, hunting of auks off Norway has become illegal, but numbers now being caught accidentally in fishing nets in the same area has increased dramatically (Mead 1989).

Table 3.   *Causes of death reported in ringed seabirds (after Potts 1969, Flegg and Morgan 1976 and Mead 1974, 1989).*

Species	Oiled	Shot	Netted	Sample Size
Shag	5%	11%	5%	696
Black-headed Gull	4%	5–13%[a]	—	?
Common Gull	—	3–4 %[a]	—	?
Lesser Black-backed Gull	11%	14–27%[a]	—	?
Herring Gull	13%	4–9 %[a]	—	?
Great Black-backed Gull	17%	4–20%[a]	—	?
Kittiwake	58%	10–39%[a]	—	?
Guillemot (to 1970)	28%	22%	5%	504
Guillemot (late 1980s)	15%	5%	37%	662
Razorbill (to 1970)	18%	23%	6%	611
Razorbill (late 1980s)	15%	2%	26%	144
Puffin	19%	10%	3%	176

Most birds are reported as "found dead" or "dying" etc. More of the ringed birds which die from artificial causes, like netting and shooting, will be reported than those which die from causes unassociated with man, such as old age or starvation.

[a] Varies with age, percentage usually highest in first year birds.

Seabirds nesting on offshore islands or inaccessible cliffs are generally safe from disturbance by man or ground-predators, and from destruction of their nesting habitat. Elsewhere, disturbance and predation by foxes and stoats have adversely affected breeding seabirds, especially gulls and terns, to the extent of causing considerable changes in numbers (Lloyd *et al.* 1975, Thomas 1982, Thomas *et al.* 1990). Seabirds nesting on islands which would otherwise be free from ground-predators are particularly vulnerable to mammals introduced by man such as rats and feral cats, ferrets and mink. The burrow-nesting Puffin, Manx Shearwater and Storm Petrel are most at risk from introduced predators. Several Puffin and Manx Shearwater colonies in Wales and Scotland are known to have been severely reduced by rats in the past (Harris 1984a, Brooke 1990). In areas with introduced ground-predators, Black Guillemots nest at low density or on inaccessible cliffs. Their largest and densest colonies are on offshore islands free from such predators (Ewins and Tasker 1985). Evidence of the destruction of Black Guillemot colonies in Iceland and Scandinavia by escaped mink (Asbirk 1978a, Petersen 1981) was part of the reason for the refusal of planning permission for similar fur farms in Orkney and Shetland during the 1970s (Evans 1984).

Fishing nets and traps also provide a hazard to seabirds, which can become entangled in them and drown. This has been responsible for the death of many wintering seabirds, particularly off Iberia, including Gannets, Shags and auks (Nelson 1978, Galbraith *et al.* 1981, Castro 1984, Teixeira 1985). In the north and northwest of Ireland, netting also affects breeding birds. Drift-

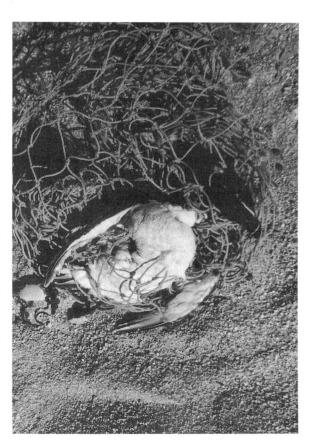

Plate 3.   Razorbill caught in fishing net (Dr M.P. Harris)

nets for salmon are set at the surface and often close inshore from May to July. These may catch thousands of seabirds a year (Bibby 1971, Melville 1973, Whilde 1979, O. J. Merne *in. litt.*). Numbers of breeding Puffins, Razorbills and Guillemots have declined recently in many colonies from Galway to Donegal, contrary to the trend elsewhere in Ireland and Britain (see Part 2). Using evidence from ringing recoveries, Mead (1989) considered that modern fishing techniques, particularly the use of plastic monofilament nets, are now the main cause of unnatural death among auks, especially in the seas around Britain and off Iberia.

Plate 4. Victims of oil pollution, Guillemots and a Fulmar washed up on a strand line on a beach in South Devon, winter 1988 (Jeff Stratford)

Pollution of the sea by oil from ships can kill huge numbers of seabirds. The auks are especially vulnerable because they spend much of their time on the sea surface. Accidental oil spills in the past have caused enormous and much-publicised seabird mortality (e.g. "Torrey Canyon", Cornwall 1967; "Amoco Cadiz", Brittany 1978; "Esso Bernicia", Shetland 1979), but chronic pollution resulting from ships illegally dumping oil or washing out tanks at sea probably has a greater impact on seabirds (Bourne 1976, Andrews and Standring 1979). Pesticide residues and other toxic chemicals have been found, sometimes at high concentrations, in almost all seabirds and seabird eggs examined, but their effect, if any, upon survival, breeding performance or population size, is unclear (see NERC 1983). Toxic chemicals have been heavily implicated in a crash in numbers of breeding terns in the Netherlands (Duinker and Koeman 1978).

Probably the most important factor currently affecting seabird numbers is the quality and abundance of their food. These determine how successfully a seabird species can breed, how many chicks reach breeding age, and the annual mortality among adult birds. These in turn control the size of the breeding population at any given time. Unfortunately, relatively little is known about what seabirds eat. Most information on diet comes from observing or sampling meals fed to young; information on what the adults eat, at any time of the year, is scarce. In addition, almost nothing is known about the processes regulating the fish stocks upon which many seabirds depend.

It has been argued that the effects of food supply around colonies during the breeding season may be the most critical factor controlling seabird numbers (e.g. Furness and Birkhead 1984), but this is impossible to demonstrate experimentally. Seabirds breeding in Britain and Ireland depend on a range of vertebrate and invertebrate foods. Fish, especially Herring, Sprat and sandeels, are the mainstay of most species in coastal colonies during the breeding season. Information on the abundance and location of fish is often difficult to obtain, although some information on seasonal and annual changes in abundance can be obtained from fishery records. This has its disadvantages, for although the foraging range of many seabirds includes areas where commercial fishing fleets operate, the species and size of fish caught for market are usually not the same as those eaten by seabirds. Data on sandeel stocks, for example, which would be of use in the study of seabird diets, are not well represented in fishery records.

Furness and Monaghan (1987) summarised historical changes in fishing methods and in fish stocks in the North Sea in relation to food available for seabirds. The introduction of steam power for fishing boats and their winches from the 1870s onwards was accompanied by an expansion of the whitefish industry which eventually began to reduce stocks of species like Plaice and Whiting. In the 1920s and 1930s, fishing boats turned from coal to oil as a source of power enabling them to fish far from land. The advent, in the 1950s, of purse seining, stern trawling and freezer holds increased the amount of fish caught even further. Over-fishing was partly responsible for the collapse of the North Sea Herring fishery in the 1970s.

The expansion of commercial fishing in the North Sea and elsewhere off Britain and Ireland had three main effects upon seabird food stocks (Furness 1987). First, the loss of Herring from the North Sea and other inshore waters took away what may have been an important winter food source for some seabirds. Secondly, the removal of large quantities of predatory fish may have increased the food available to seabirds in the breeding season. Stocks of sandeels and Sprat, upon which the predators would have fed, increased. Whitefish also increased in abundance, perhaps because predation on their larvae was reduced by the removal of Mackerel and Herring. Fishing for sandeels, Norway Pout and Sprat in the North Sea expanded during the 1970s early 1980s, but it remains to be seen what effect this will have on seabird numbers.

Thirdly, there has been a significant increase in another major source of food for seabirds, that provided by fishing boats (Table 4). Fish below the legal size limit, non-commercial species, and offal are discarded in great quantities after a catch is brought to the surface, particularly by trawlers for whitefish and Norway Lobster. This provides food which would otherwise remain out of reach to most seabirds and is especially important to species such as Great Skuas, Gannets and Great Black-backed Gulls during the breeding season (Hudson and Furness 1988). The amount of fish discarded at sea has grown as the fishing industry expanded; it was estimated that in the 1980s roughly two

Table 4. *Numbers of seabirds that could be supported by fishery offal and discards around Britain and Ireland in the early 1980s (after Furness et al. 1988).*

Fishing ground	Number of 1000g seabirds supported	
	by offal	by discards
North Sea (3 areas)	1,300,000	625,000
Northwest Scotland	172,000	220,000
Irish Sea	58,000	153,000
Western Ireland	25,000	31,000
English Channel (2 areas)	49,000	13,000
Bristol Channel	15,000	8000
Southwest Approaches	67,000	84,000
All areas	1,686,000	1,134,000

Plate 5.   Fulmars feeding behind fishing vessel. Fulmars dominate in the scramble for offal discarded from trawlers around Shetland (Dr Anne Hudson)

Plate 6.   Gulls following trawler off south coast of Ireland (Richard T. Mills)

and a half million seabirds could survive on the offal and discards from fishing boats around Britain and Ireland (Furness *et al.* 1988).

Seabirds are affected indirectly by various factors which control the abundance of their prey. Climatic changes play a significant but poorly understood role in determining the numbers and distribution of fish in the northwest Atlantic (Cushing 1982). Climatic change (on a scale of interest to biologists) caused a general warming of air and sea temperatures between the end of the nineteenth century and about 1940. This was followed by a period of stability and then temperatures cooled from about the 1960s onwards, a trend which is thought to have lasted until the mid 1980s.

These fluctuations in sea temperature have been accompanied by considerable and well-documented changes in plankton and fish stocks. For instance, during the period of warming, various southern species, like the Portuguese Man O'War jellyfish, Goose Barnacles and the Loggerhead Turtle, extended their range northwards to the coasts of France, Britain and Ireland, whilst fish such as the Cod invaded the waters around Greenland. With the more recent cooling, the Cod fishery off Greenland collapsed and the ranges of several barnacles, which had extended northwards up the English Channel, retreated south again. Several European seabirds also expanded their breeding ranges during the climatic cooling, but their response was varied. Since 1940, four new Gannet colonies have been established in Iceland, five (or six) in Norway, five in Scotland, one (and in 1989, another) in Ireland and one (possibly two) in the Channel Islands. These new colonies mark a pronounced northward extension of the species' east Atlantic range (Wanless 1987). Other species colonised southern Europe during the same period of cooling; these included the Cormorant, Black-headed and Lesser Black-backed Gulls and Kittiwake.

The relationship between seabird food, fish populations and climate is complicated by large variation in the scale of annual recruitment to fish breeding stocks. Many fish are long-lived; in theory, Herring have a lifespan of 10 to 20 years and Cod may live for 20 to 25 years. Annual recruitment may vary naturally by up to two orders of magnitude. This means that the number of young fish entering the breeding stock may be anything up to a hundred times higher or lower than in the previous year. The average annual variation is one order of magnitude (Cushing 1982). Cushing suggested that environmental factors associated with climate, such as wind, temperature, sunlight and salinity, affect survival of larval and juvenile fish and hence recruitment to the breeding stock. Year-classes within a fish population have been shown to vary widely in their resilience to climatic change. Different fish species also respond in different ways; mid-water, pelagic fish such as the Herring tend to react faster to climatic change than do bottom-dwelling species like Cod.

Several studies have linked food resources to breeding productivity in seabirds (e.g. Furness and Ainley 1984, Monaghan *et al.* 1989). Over-exploitation of Herring off northern Norway during the 1960s coupled with climatic change led to a decline in Herring stocks; fishing for sandeels, which would have been a possible alternative food for local seabirds, increased at the same time. From 1975 to the late 1980s there was repeated, almost total breeding failure among Puffins on the Lofoten Islands. Breeding success was also reduced in Kittiwakes, Razorbills and Guillemots (Lid 1981, Barrett and

Vader 1984). The same thing may have occurred in Newfoundland Puffin colonies following over-fishing of Capelin (Brown and Nettleship 1984b). In the Pacific, breeding success in seabirds as far apart as the Bering Sea and southern California has been influenced by abundance of their local food supplies (Anderson et al. 1980, Schaffner 1986, Springer et al. 1986). Thirty-one years of study at a Kittiwake colony at North Shields in northeast England showed how various population parameters changed during a period when an important source of the birds' food (Herring) outside the breeding season became steadily less abundant (Coulson and Thomas 1985).

Seabirds faced with critical decline in one food stock can switch to another more abundant prey if available. Puffins on the Isle of May, for example, fed their chicks on sandeels, Sprat and Herring between 1973 and 1982 (Hislop and Harris 1985). Stocks of Sprat near the island declined during 1978–82 and their range shifted southwards. At the same time, Herring stocks, as measured by overwinter survival of larval fish, appeared to have increased near the Isle of May. The diet of young Puffins reflected this change with a gradual replacement of Sprat by Herring. However, a change of diet forced on seabirds when their preferred foods are scarce or unavailable can affect breeding productivity. In years when Puffins on St Kilda fed their chicks largely on Whiting rather than Sprat, fledging weights were depressed (Harris and Hislop 1978). Sprats are rich in oil and provide more energy than Whitings for young Puffins. A diet of Sprat enabled the chicks studied by Harris and Hislop to grow faster and reach fledging age at heavier weights, compared with the chicks fed on Whiting. The failure to breed by many seabirds in Shetland in the 1980s (Table 5) has

Table 5. *Data from nearly 30 years of study of seabirds on Foula, showing chick diet and adult breeding success (after Furness 1989).*

Species	Breeding success[a]				% of sandeels in chick diet		Main species in chick diet
	1960–80	1986	1987	1988	1971–80	1988	1988
Fulmar	Good	Good	Good	Poor	97	17	Butterfish
Gannet[b]	?	Good	Good	Good	90	6	Herring/Mackerel
Shag	2.2	2.4	—	2.3	100	100	Sandeels
Arctic Skua	1.1	—	<1	0.04	100	100	Sandeels
Great Skua	1.2	—	0.7	<0.01	82	5	Discarded fish
Great Black-backed Gull	2.2	—	—	2.3	—	—	
Kittiwake	1.3	0.9	Low	0.0	100	67	Sandeels
Arctic Tern	0.5	0.0	0.0	0.0	100	19	Young gadids
Guillemot	Good	Good	Good	Good	100	97	Sandeels
Razorbill	Good	Good	Good	Poor	100	43	Young gadids
Black Guillemot	0.9	—	—	0.0	60	6	Butterfish
Puffin	Good	—	Poor	0.0	96	39	Young gadids

[a] Breeding success measured as mean values of chicks reared to fledging or nearly full grown, or given as subjective assessment.
[b] After Martin (1989) from Hermaness (Shetland); first food sample was in 1981.

illustrated several features of seabird biology and conservation. In 1980, large variation in breeding success amongst Arctic Terns in different colonies in Shetland was noticed (Bullock and Gomersall 1980) and by 1985 extensive breeding failure was being recorded (Monaghan and Uttley 1989). Nesting success also declined in many colonies of Kittiwakes, Fulmars and skuas in Shetland between 1986 and 1988. Desertion of nests and the presence of starving chicks suggested that the birds were having difficulty finding food, especially enough sandeels. The seabirds (Guillemots and Shags) that dive deep to catch larger sandeels or other fish, and species (Gannets) which can change their diet to take other larger fish fared better than these others which fed on smaller sandeels close to the surface.

Several studies have shown the importance of sandeels in the diet of Shetland's seabirds and on Foula, Furness (1989) showed that the proportion of sandeels in the diet of most species (except the kleptoparasitic skuas) declined steeply during the 1980s (Table 5). There was no evidence of similar major breeding failures elsewhere in Britain, but Harris and Wanless (1990) showed that Kittiwake breeding productivity in the mid 1980s increased steadily with decreasing latitude in the western North Sea. There was also evidence that the proportion of sandeels in the diet of seabirds breeding on the Isle of May had decreased during the same period, and had been replaced by Sprat and small Herring. Such replacement would not be possible around Shetland as numbers of small Herring and Sprat are low. These studies illustrate the importance of food availability in controlling the breeding success of seabirds and also the importance of alternative prey should one type decline.

The reasons behind the decline in the availability of sandeels around Shetland have caused considerable debate. The sandeel stock is exploited by the fishermen of Shetland, not for direct human consumption, but for conversion to fishmeal and oil for use in such products as agricultural feedstuffs and salmon feed. The fishery started in 1974 and landed 8000 tonnes; it peaked in 1982 when 52,600 tonnes were landed and since then landings have declined to 4800 tonnes in 1988 (Goodlad 1989). These changes in fish landings partly reflect the fall in the size of sandeel stocks as assessed by the Department of Agriculture and Fisheries, Scotland (DAFS) but also reflect changes in the economics of various fisheries around Shetland. The sandeel fishery has been seen by some as a possible cause of the decline in the availability of sandeels to seabirds.

The abundance of sandeels of different ages has been monitored in the catches landed by fishing vessels (Kunzlick 1989). Although there are sandeel fisheries in other parts of the North Sea, the Shetland sandeel fishery is more dependent on small immature sandeels (0-group fish, locally called "needles") than are the offshore fisheries. The needles first appear in the catches in June, and are fish which have hatched from eggs during the previous winter. By July almost the entire catch is composed of needles, and about two-thirds of the annual catch (by weight) in Shetland (and in the North Minch fishery based at Stornoway) is made up of immature fish less than two years old (0- and 1-group fish).

As far back as 1982, DAFS scientists were concerned about the reliance of the fishery on these immature fish (Bailey 1983). This could mean that two successive years of poor production of needles would result in a big decrease in stock abundance, and hence in the productivity of the fishery (Bailey 1983) and in the breeding success of seabirds dependent on it. Bailey considered that the most effective way to reduce this exploitation of immature sandeels would be to close the fishery in the middle of the summer when they first appear in the catches; however, there was no evidence of any problem in 1983 so no controls were introduced.

However, decreasing catches of sandeels in Shetland waters from 1983 onwards led to widespread concern among fishermen who feared that reduction in sandeel numbers would also affect numbers of predatory fish, such as Haddock, in the waters around Shetland. In 1987 the Shetland Fishermen's Association introduced voluntary restrictions on the landing of small sandeels. These measures proved inadequate and it was not until 1989 that statutory restrictions, including the cessation of sandeel fishing after 1 July, were introduced. It remains to be seen if these restrictions will have any effect on numbers of needles available to seabirds.

The difficulty with blaming the fishery for the fall in sandeel stocks is that there is strong evidence that numbers of small fish maturing from eggs fell dramatically prior to the decline in the mature fish stock. The mature fish stock at the time of this decline in immature fish production was apparently large; thus the problem affecting sandeels appeared to occur in the first few months of their lives rather than after they begin to be caught by the fishery.

There have been other changes in the marine environment which may have affected numbers and availability of sandeels. Harris and Wanless (1990) have pointed out that the surface temperature of the northern North Sea has warmed by 2°C in the 1980s, which is a large increase in marine terms. In addition, the widespread evidence of decline in seabird breeding performance away from areas actually fished for sandeels indicates that the problem is not localised to the Shetland sandeel fishery area. The recovery of the Herring stock in the northern North Sea may also be affecting sandeels by direct predation on sandeel larvae or competition for adult food. A similar situation existed in the western Atlantic, where studies have shown changes in sandeel and Herring abundance have occurred at approximately the same time as similar shifts in the eastern Atlantic (Sherman et al. 1981). There is, however, scant evidence (due in part to a lack of research) to support these hypotheses and no-one can be sure of the causes underlying the shortfall in sandeels.

If the low availability of sandeels is due to a factor other than over-fishing, then the Shetland sandeel fishery, and many of Shetland's seabirds are destined to experience hardship until that factor changes again. However, if the fishery has caused or greatly contributed to the lack of sandeels then the controls on fishing intensity, particularly on the 0-group fish, should hopefully allow the situation to improve.

Further research into the problems facing both Shetland's seabirds and sandeel stocks is proposed in the future. The role of natural and man-made factors in changing seabird numbers elsewhere is also far from clear. Recent events in Shetland have confirmed the close link between food availability during the breeding season and reproductive success. Clearly further study is required before the trends in numbers of breeding seabirds throughout Britain and Ireland can be correctly understood and the effects on seabirds of future actions by man predicted.

The Methods Used for the Collection and Analysis of Seabird Counts

The distribution and numbers of each seabird and the changes that have occurred since 1969 are discussed in Part 2, based on analysis of data in the Seabird Colony Register. This chapter explains what information is held in the Register and how the data were collected and analysed. This is particularly important for anyone wishing to use the data in specialised studies, or for those in future who may need to compare the 1985–87 results with more recent surveys. General readers, however, may prefer to turn directly to Part 2. It must be stressed that all counts in the Register are only as accurate as the observers concerned were able to make them and it was assumed that observers had followed the instructions provided. The authors would welcome information on any errors detected by readers or by users of the Seabird Colony Register data.

COLLECTION OF DATA

Information in the Seabird Colony Register comes from four main sources:

1. The Seabird Group's Operation Seafarer survey, 1969–70.
2. The NCC/Seabird Group's repeat survey in 1985–87.
3. Published and unpublished records for 1971–84.
4. Counts made since 1987.

The NCC and the Seabird Group intend to keep the Register as far as possible up to date until and beyond the next complete survey. For this reason, they would like to receive counts of breeding seabirds made at any colonies in Britain or Ireland.

The Seabird Colony Register is at present held on computer in NCC's Aberdeen office. Readers who wish to consult the Register are welcome to write to the Register coordinator at NCC, 17 Rubislaw Terrace, Aberdeen, Scotland, or c/o Seabird Group, The Lodge, Sandy, Bedfordshire, England. A small charge may be levied to offset costs of data abstraction, and to build up a fund to help carry out future counts.

Over 600 volunteer observers helped with the surveys for the Seabird Colony Register, mainly between 1985 and 1987 (Appendix II) and without them this book could not have been written. Grants towards expenses, such as travel and boat hire, were provided by NCC and the Seabird Group. Potential contributors to the Seabird Colony Register were contacted amongst the Seabird Group membership and NCC staff, through appeals for help in ornithological publications and personal contacts. As a result, almost all observers had previous experience in ornithological survey work and a majority of them had been involved in seabird censusing before. Twenty regional organisers were appointed for different areas of Britain and Ireland; they recruited counters, distributed instruction sheets and recording forms, and collected completed forms after the seabird breeding season was over. The organisers also ensured that overlap in coverage of the coastline by different observers was kept to a minimum.

Almost all the coastline of Britain was surveyed between 1985 and 1987; most remaining gaps were covered in 1988. The areas not visited were negligible (Figure 1). Separate pre-breeding surveys of Black Guillemots were carried out in 1985–87 in much of Scotland, and in the Isle of Man. Similar data collected in 1983–84 in Orkney and Shetland (Ewins and Tasker 1985)

Figure 1 (opposite).   Main seabird colonies mentioned in the text; see Appendix V for complete list of other sites.

Circles indicate sections of coastline with no counts of seabirds for the period 1982–88, with the exception of terns and Cormorants (Ireland) and Black Guillemots (Scotland).

1. Hermaness	16. Flannans	31. Bass Rock	46. St Bees Head
2. Ramna Stacks	17. St Kilda	32. St Abb's Head	47. Calf of Man
3. Foula	18. Clo Mor	33. Farne Islands	48. Rathlin Island
4. Fetlar	19. Handa	34. Coquet	49. Copeland Islands
5. Noss	20. Shiants	35. Bempton–Flamborough	50. Strangford Lough
6. Sumburgh Head	21. Canna	36. Scoll Head	51. Rockabill
7. Fair Isle	22. Rhum	37. Orfordness	52. Lambay
8. Papa Westray	23. Berneray/Mingulay	38. Needs Ore Point	53. Lady's Island Lake
9. Westray	24. Treshnish Islands	39. Lundy	54. Great and Little Saltee
10. Marwick Head	25. Ailsa Craig	40. Skokholm	55. Bull and Cow Rocks
11. Hoy	26. Scar Rocks	41. Skomer	56. Skelligs
12. Sule Skerry	27. Caithness cliffs	42. Grassholm	57. Blaskets
13. Sule Stack	28. Troup Head	43. Carreg y Llam	58. Cliffs of Moher
14. North Rona	29. Fowlsheugh	44. Bardsey	59. Stags of Broadhaven
15. Sula Sgeir	30. Isle of May	45. South Walney	60. Horn Head

and in 1988–90 in the Western Isles and western Scotland (Tasker and Webb in prep.) are also included here. Other sources of information on breeding seabirds used to supplement the counts made in 1985–87 included the 1984–85 Gannet survey (Wanless 1987), the Shetland and Orkney tern survey in 1980 (Bullock and Gomersall 1980, 1981) and unpublished data collected from 1984 onwards by the NCC Moorland Bird Survey Team in north and west Scotland. Throughout this book, unless otherwise stated, all of these recent counts are described as 1985–87, despite some occurring in years either side of the period.

Coverage in 1985–87 was less complete in Ireland. Virtually the whole coast of Northern Ireland was covered between 1985 and 1987, and a separate survey of Black Guillemots was carried out there in April 1987. Breeding terns had been censused thoroughly in 1984 by the All Ireland Tern Survey (Whilde 1985) and no effort was made to obtain complete coverage of tern colonies again during 1985–87. Almost all important seabird breeding areas in the Republic of Ireland were visited between 1985 and 1988 but, because of lack of resources, many parts of the west coast and some parts elsewhere, thought to be without major seabird colonies, were not surveyed (Figure 1). These sections were estimated to have held about 25% of the Irish population of such ubiquitous species as Fulmar and Herring Gull, but less than 5% of Kittiwakes and Guillemots. A special effort is being made in 1990 to fill these gaps, but for the purposes of this book, estimates have been made for the missing colonies. These estimates were made by calculating the percentage change for each species in those colonies counted in both 1969–70 and 1985–87 for each of the four regional divisions of Ireland (Figure 2). This percentage change was assumed to have occurred also at those colonies not counted in 1985–87, so that an estimate of the total numbers of each species could be made for Ireland.

Instructions used by observers for the recent surveys (see Appendix III) were prepared by the Censusing Committee of the Seabird Group after consultation with relevant specialists for each seabird species. The methods recommended for counting Razorbills and Guillemots were those outlined by the Seabird Group (Evans 1980). The coastline of Britain and Ireland was divided up into 10 km Ordnance Survey squares and the observer for each square was asked to map the presence or absence of seabird colonies on a card provided (10 km Summary Card). Nearly 1200 of these cards were completed, covering the whole coastline of Britain and Ireland and a few inland areas. There were up to 48 seabird colonies on each card and less than 50 of the cards received had no seabird colonies at all.

Many seabird colonies were also entered on a Colony Register Form which requested general details about the site. These included its name, location, Ordnance Survey references for its limits and central point, the observer's name and address, a brief description of the habitat type, details of ownership and access, breeding seabirds present and their status, if known, and a bibliography of any published and unpublished information about the site. In practice, Colony Register Forms were only used for the larger colonies or those of particular interest to observers and less than 500 of them were completed.

A third recording form, the Data Sheet, was used for the counts made at the colony in each year. If two observers made separate counts of the same colony in one year, their results were combined onto a single summary Data Sheet (see below). The information recorded on the Data Sheets included the observer's name, the date of the count, numbers of seabirds counted, unit and method used for each species and its breeding status (Appendix III). About 10,600 Data Sheets were used for the Seabird Colony Register up to 1987, the majority completed by observers during the surveys in 1985–87; these contained nearly 32,000 seabird counts.

It was not possible to count all birds with the same level of accuracy. Some species were easier to census than others (see Part 2) and, in many colonies, birds and nests furthest away from the counting point or under overhanging rock or in caves were difficult (or impossible) to see and their numbers could only be estimated. The proportion of birds which could be seen well enough for an accurate count varied from one colony to another. The Data Sheet enabled observers to record separately the birds counted accurately and those for which only a minimum and maximum estimate could be made. The accurate counts were combined with the estimated counts during data analysis to provide the best estimate of total numbers for each species breeding in the colony (see Appendix III).

Completed recording forms for the Seabird Colony Register were returned, usually via regional organisers, to NCC in Aberdeen where the information from the Data Sheets was entered into a computerised database. This enabled a

Plate 7.   A telescope and great care are needed to count accurately the huge number of seabirds nesting on the cliffs of St Kilda (Peter Moore)

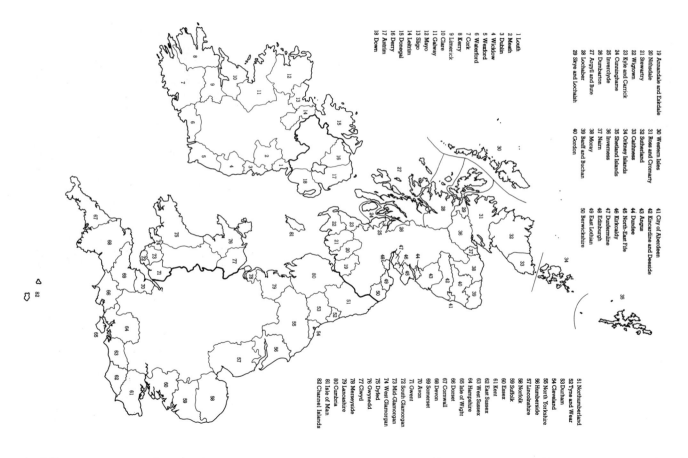

1 Louth
2 Meath
3 Dublin
4 Wicklow
5 Wexford
6 Waterford
7 Cork
8 Kerry
9 Limerick
10 Clare
11 Galway
12 Mayo
13 Sligo
14 Leitrim
15 Donegal
16 Derry
17 Antrim
18 Down

19 Annandale and Eskdale
20 Nithsdale
21 Stewartry
22 Wigtown
23 Kyle and Carrick
24 Cunninghame
25 Inverclyde
26 Dumbarton
27 Argyll and Bute
28 Lochaber
29 Skye and Lochalsh

30 Western Isles
31 Ross and Cromarty
32 Sutherland
33 Caithness
34 Orkney Islands
35 Shetland Islands
36 Inverness
37 Nairn
38 Moray
39 Banff and Buchan
40 Gordon

41 City of Aberdeen
42 Kincardine and Deeside
43 Angus
44 Dundee
45 North-East Fife
46 Kirkcaldy
47 Dunfermline
48 Edinburgh
49 East Lothian
50 Berwickshire

51 Northumberland
52 Tyne and Wear
53 Durham
54 Cleveland
55 North Yorkshire
56 Humberside
57 Lincolnshire
58 Norfolk
59 Suffolk
60 Essex
61 Kent
62 East Sussex
63 West Sussex
64 Hampshire
65 Isle of Wight
66 Dorset
67 Cornwall
68 Devon
69 Somerset
70 Avon
71 Gwent
72 South Glamorgan
73 Mid-Glamorgan
74 West Glamorgan
75 Dyfed
76 Gwynedd
77 Clwyd
78 Merseyside
79 Lancashire
80 Cumbria
81 Isle of Man
82 Channel Islands

Figure 2 (opposite).   County and district boundaries in Britain and Ireland; groupings of counties and districts used to calculate percentage change in seabird numbers.

COUNTY/DISTRICT	REGION FOR % CHANGE MAPS
Shetland, Orkney, Nairn, Moray, Banff and Buchan, Gordon, City of Aberdeen, Kincardine and Deeside	NE Scotland
Western Isles, Caithness, Sutherland, Ross and Cromarty, Inverness, Skye and Lochalsh, Lochaber	NW Scotland
Angus, City of Dundee, Northeast Fife, Kirkcaldy, Dunfermline, City of Edinburgh, East Lothian, Berwickshire	SE Scotland
Argyll and Bute, Dumbarton, Inverclyde, Cunninghame, Kyle and Carrick, Wigtown, Stewartry, Nithsdale, Annandale and Eskdale	SW Scotland
Northumberland, Tyne and Wear, Durham, Cleveland, North Yorkshire, Humberside, Lincolnshire	NE England
Norfolk, Suffolk, Essex	E England
Kent, East Sussex, West Sussex, Hampshire, Isle of Wight	SE England
Dorset, Devon, Cornwall, Isles of Scilly, Somerset, Avon, Gloucestershire, Channel Islands	NW England and Channel Islands
Merseyside, Lancashire, Cumbria, Isle of Man	NW England and Isle of Man
Gwent, South Glamorgan, Mid Glamorgan, West Glamorgan, Dyfed, Gwynedd, Clwyd	Wales
Derry, Antrim, Down	NE Ireland
Meath, Louth, Dublin, Wicklow, Wexford, Waterford	SE Ireland
Cork, Kerry, Limerick, Clare	SW Ireland
Galway, Mayo, Leitrim, Sligo, Donegal	NW Ireland

relatively swift and easy analysis of population totals and comparison of data for different years.

The counting methods which were used during the 1969–70 survey (Appendix IV) were not exactly the same as those recommended for the 1985–87 survey, but in most cases direct comparison of counts was possible. Volunteer observers for Operation Seafarer were recruited by appeals for help both in ornithological circles and from the general public, with the result that only about half the 400–500 contributors seem to have had previous experience in counting seabirds. Including some lengths of coastline surveyed in 1968 and 1971, coverage was almost complete during Operation Seafarer. Counts for Foula and east Caithness were considered incomplete by the organisers and those for Horn Head, Clo Mor, Westray and Papa Westray were also regarded as "weak areas" (W. R. P. Bourne *in litt.*) Observers completed a single record card giving the numbers of seabirds counted in each colony that they visited during the survey.

The figures from the 3000 or so record cards completed during Operation Seafarer were collated by species during analysis of the survey's findings. Copies of "species lists" were deposited in libraries and research institutions around Britain and copies of the lists referring to Irish colonies were given to the Irish Wildbird Conservancy in Dublin (Perrins 1975). The data were published in summary form, as totals for each county in Britain and Ireland (Cramp *et al.* 1974).

The original record cards were not available for further analysis until 1986 when the counts were entered on the Seabird Colony Register database. Differences between totals presented here for 1969–70 and those in Cramp *et al.* (1974) are due mainly to differences in interpretation of the original record cards. Also, county/district boundaries have changed since 1969 and a few errors (almost all of minor importance) have been corrected. Where a colony was visited by more than one observer in one year, or was visited in both 1969 and 1970, several counts were available for each species censused. During the present analysis, a strict set of criteria was used to select a single count from those available (see below) since only one count per colony would be included in species totals. For example, counts in the recommended unit and at the recommended date were selected in preference to others available. Cramp *et al.* (1974) did not record how they selected counts. During the present analysis, every attempt has been made to maintain consistency with Cramp *et al.* (1974); where this has proved impossible, we apologise to readers for any confusion caused.

ANALYSIS OF DATA

The exact definition of a seabird "colony" can be difficult; for example, in species such as the Black Guillemot which sometimes nests at low density, or where seabirds breed along an entire cliff face for many kilometres, or cover a large island with their nests. During surveys for the Seabird Colony Register, observers were asked to treat two groups of nests as separate colonies if they were more than 100 metres apart and if it was possible to stand between them without disturbing breeding birds in either group, a definition first proposed by Bullock and Gomersall (1981) for Arctic Tern colonies. For convenience, some very large colonies were subdivided by observers; and some small colonies were combined during analysis for comparison with counts made in earlier years. The extra detail available in the Seabird Colony Register database and files about the exact distribution of seabirds on different parts of the cliff in 1985–87 can be used for comparison with the results of future censuses.

The main surveys for the Seabird Colony Register were carried out during three summers and a few colonies were visited twice or more, sometimes in the same year. This was also true, but to a lesser extent, of the Operation Seafarer data. Thus, in some cases, several counts were available for analysis. The following criteria were used to select or reject counts, with the aim of obtaining the most accurate count from those available:

1. A count in the unit recommended by the instructions to observers in 1985–87 (Appendix III) was selected over those in other units.
2. A count made at the recommended time of year (Appendix III) was selected over those at other times of the year.
3. A census recorded over those given as "Accurate Count" was preferred to those given as "Minimum Estimate" and "Maximum Estimate" (Appendix III).

4. If two or more comparable counts were still available after these criteria had been applied, the most recent count was selected. Counts from 1988 were only used if no 1985–87 counts were available or if the latter were of poor quality (e.g. not in recommended units).

5. Counts made from land were used in preference to those made from a boat, unless land-based counts were known to have missed parts of the colony and no estimate was made for hidden sections.

Where the census count for a species was given in three parts on the Data Sheet (accurate count, minimum estimate, maximum estimate), a single "best estimate" was obtained by adding the accurate part of the count to the midpoint of the two estimates. Where only an accurate count and a minimum or maximum were given, the best estimate was obtained by adding the two counts together. The counts (or best estimates) were added to give totals for every species in each of the coastal counties in Ireland, England and Wales, in every coastal district in Scotland (Figure 2), and in the Isle of Man and Channel Islands. Unless otherwise stated, "Ireland" is used throughout to refer to Northern Ireland and the Republic of Ireland together, ignoring political boundaries; and the expression "England and Wales" includes, for convenience, the Isle of Man and the Channel Islands.

Some data in the Seabird Colony Register refer to inland colonies which, for the purpose of this analysis, were defined as those located in one kilometre Ordnance Survey squares which did not contain any coastline. Many of these were probably out of sight of the sea and therefore would have been excluded also from Operation Seafarer. Apart from those in Shetland and Orkney, where no seabird colony was considered to be truly inland, the counts from inland colonies were analysed separately and they are not included in county and district totals. Further survey is presently under way to census all inland seabird colonies. All counts have been retained on the Seabird Colony Register database whether or not they have been used in the current analysis.

The counting units used by the Seabird Colony Register require special explanation. In most species, counts were of apparently occupied nests (AON) or sites (AOS), or breeding territories (AOT) (for skuas), as defined in the instructions issued to observers (Appendix III). For convenience, each AOS was assumed to represent one pair of breeding birds. Birds in the breeding population which did not nest in that year and those pairs which failed in their nesting attempt and abandoned the colony before the census took place were unavoidably omitted by the counts. Most auk counts were of individual birds rather than nests as these species build no nest and usually either breed at high density (Guillemot) or lay their eggs out of sight under rocks or in burrows (Razorbill, Black Guillemot, Puffin). A count of birds in these species is *not* the same as the number of breeding pairs (see Part 2).

In some cases, observers were unable to make counts in the required units so that data were presented as birds instead of AOS or vice versa. Accurate conversion of counts from one unit to the other is impossible, but all the data collected were needed if complete population estimates were to be obtained. After consultation with the Censusing Committee of the Seabird Group, and with a sample of those who had contributed counts to the Seabird Colony

Register in 1985–87, it was decided to convert counts of birds to pairs (in all species except the auks, common and Arctic Terns) by assuming two birds in the colony represented one breeding pair and by dividing the number of birds by two. For the auks, common and Arctic Terns, different methods were used for converting counts of pairs to birds; these are described for each species in Part 2. It should be remembered that this use of conversion factors introduced considerable but unquantifiable error into the species totals. For this reason, the proportion of each total in converted units must be taken into account when using the data presented in the tables of Part 2.

Each species of seabird which breeds regularly in Britain and Ireland is covered separately in Part 2. An attempt to compare the breeding populations of Britain and Ireland with those in other parts of each species' range is shown in the first table. Estimated orders of magnitude for some breeding populations are given as Order 1 (1–10 pairs), or Order 2 (11–100 pairs), and so on. Europe is defined as excluding the USSR, Greenland, Svalbard, Jan Mayen and the Macronesian islands (Azores, Madeira, Salvage, Canary and Cape Verde). Another table compares breeding population estimates in 1985–87 and 1969–70 for the Isle of Man, the Channel Islands, and all the coastal counties or districts in Britain and Ireland. This gives an indication of how numbers have changed since Operation Seafarer. Totals for Scotland, England with the Channel Islands and the Isle of Man, Wales and Ireland are rounded (counts of < 100 to nearest 5, 100–1000 to nearest 10, > 1000 to nearest 100).

A distribution map for each species has been prepared from the counts made in 1985–87 to show the approximate size of colonies in different parts of Britain and Ireland. For clarity, adjacent colonies have often been combined by dividing the coastline into defined sections (about 600 in Great Britain and associated islands, and 220 in Ireland) and totalling seabird numbers within each section. The colony size symbol has been plotted centrally within each section. The county and district totals have been combined into regional totals (see Figure 2) in a second map for some species which summarises the approximate percentage change in numbers between Operation Seafarer and the 1985–87 surveys. The positions of the main seabird colonies in Britain and Ireland are shown on Figure 1, and Ordnance Survey references for all colonies mentioned in the text are given in the Gazetteer.

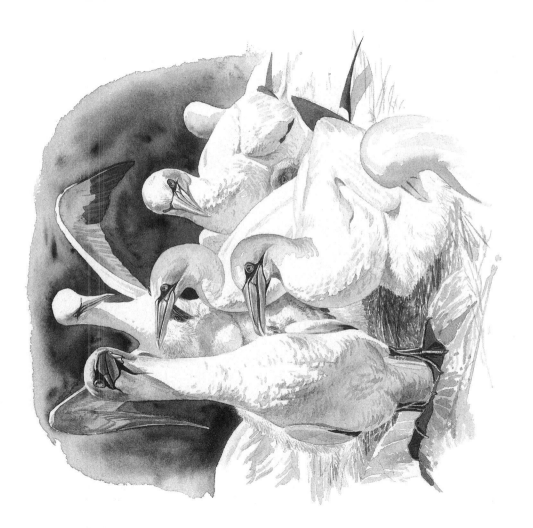

PART 2

The Species Accounts

Fulmar

Fulmarus glacialis

The Fulmar is the largest of the four species of petrel which breed in Britain and Ireland and has a wing-span of 102–112 cm. Colonies are found mostly on cliffs, but low banks and level ground also are used for nesting. A few birds nest on inland cliffs near the sea. Fulmars feed entirely at sea taking crustaceans, cephalopods and small fish. In the North Atlantic they also scavenge offal discarded from trawlers whilst planktonic crustaceans are common in the diet of birds breeding in the Arctic. The birds grab their food from the sea surface either in flight, or by alighting briefly on the water, or whilst swimming (Cramp and Simmons 1977). The Fulmar is also sometimes known as the Northern Fulmar to distinguish it from the Antarctic Fulmar *Fulmarus glacialoides*

INTERNATIONAL DISTRIBUTION AND STATUS

The Fulmar is one of the most numerous seabirds of the northern hemisphere. It breeds in the Canadian Arctic, Greenland and the islands of the Arctic Ocean as far east as Franz Josef Land and Novaya Zemlya. Fulmar colonies occur also in the North Pacific from southern Alaska to the Bering Sea and Aleutian

Islands and west to the Kuril archipelago, though these belong to a separate subspecies *F.g. rodgersii*.

The Fulmar is expanding its breeding range in the west Atlantic. It colonised east Newfoundland and southeast Labrador during the 1970s (Nettleship and Lock 1973) and has established new colonies in southwest Greenland in the last 40 years (Evans 1984). The heart of the Fulmar's distribution lies in the northwest Atlantic where the breeding populations in Iceland and the Faroe Islands each total many million pairs (Evans 1984). Britain and Ireland, by comparison, have just over half a million pairs; St Kilda is the largest single colony with 62,800 pairs of Fulmars. The world population probably lies between fifteen and twenty million pairs (Table 7).

Some Fulmar colonies reach gigantic size. The biggest ones in the Pacific, Hall and St Matthew islands in the Bering Sea, for example, hold almost half a million birds each (Sowls *et al.* 1978). In the Canadian Arctic, the biggest colonies are in the Hudson Straits area; two of the colonies on Devon Island each stretch for many kilometres and each has over 100,000 breeding pairs (Nettleship 1974).

Barely 350 years ago the Atlantic Fulmar population was apparently confined to only two or three breeding sites, one in Iceland and another (possibly two) in Scotland. Fulmars have probably bred in Iceland since the ninth century. Certainly they have nested on the island of Grimsay, off the north coast, since at least 1640. They may have bred on Kolbeinsey, an island even further north, earlier in the seventeenth century but by the mid-nineteenth century this island had become too eroded to provide nesting habitat (Fisher 1952a). In the middle of the eighteenth century Fulmars suddenly began to form new colonies off southwest Iceland, first on the Westmann Islands and later on Eldey. From here, during the nineteenth and early twentieth centuries, they spread steadily around the mainland of Iceland. They colonised the Faroe Islands in about 1839 and had reached all parts of the Faroes by 1900 (Fisher 1952a).

Excavation of early human settlements in Britain and Ireland has yielded clues to the former distribution of several species of seabirds because birds were caught and eaten by man and their bones discarded in middens. Fulmar remains have been discovered at the Viking settlement of Jarlshof on the Shetland Islands. There is no proof that the birds were breeding there in the sixth century but it seems possible since no Fulmar bones occur amongst the seabird remains in similar deposits elsewhere in Britain or Norway. But if Fulmars did breed in Shetland fourteen hundred years ago, there is no apparent reason why no further evidence of their colonies exists, or why they should have become extinct there. The oldest known British Fulmar colony is on St Kilda; like some Icelandic colonies, this may represent a relict population isolated by the advance of the last Ice Age (Salomonsen 1965). Fulmars may have been breeding on St Kilda when the Vikings arrived and were almost certainly nesting three hundred years later. Excavation of middens dating from the ninth century in the underground houses on Hirta led to the discovery of bones of Fulmars and many other seabirds (including the Great Auk), some of which still breed on the St Kilda group (Fisher 1966).

In 1878 the Fulmar spread, apparently not from St Kilda but from the Faroes, to Foula in the Shetland Islands. During the next century it colonised almost every part of the British and Irish coastline. Earlier this century it moved to Norway and recently reached France and West Germany (Cramp and Simmons 1977).

Recent studies in the North Sea and off northwest Scotland have shown Fulmars to be particularly widespread and abundant at sea throughout the year compared with other seabirds (Tasker *et al.* 1987, Benn *et al.* 1988). Densities around the North Sea breeding colonies, especially those on Orkney and Shetland, increased in March and April, but dropped during incubation. From May densities in the southern and eastern North Sea increased, probably as non-breeding birds moved there to moult. Fulmars were found frequently in association with ships and with oil installations in the North Sea.

Fulmars ringed in Britain are recovered up to at least their third year of life from large areas of the North Atlantic, Bay of Biscay, Norwegian Sea and European Arctic (Macdonald 1977a, S. Baillie *in litt.*). Older birds spend more of their time on land and consequently their range is more restricted. For example, ringing recoveries of breeding adults from the Orkney island of Eynhallow made during the birds' breeding season were all within 750 km of the colony (Dunnet and Ollason 1982). None of the nine birds actively breeding during the season of recovery were found further than 466 km away and six of them were within 100 km of Eynhallow.

On average, Fulmars breed for the first time at about nine years of age (males at eight, females at ten) and live a further 34–35 years (Dunnet and Ollason 1978). Those which survive to breeding age have a total life expectancy of about 44 years, longer than the duration of most research projects designed to study seabird survival. Fulmars breeding on Eynhallow, for example, have been studied since 1950. The first adult to be captured and marked there at the beginning of the project was still breeding on the roof of a ruined bothy twenty years later (Dunnet *et al.* 1979) and three birds ringed as breeders in 1951 bred successfully in 1988 (G. M. Dunnet *in litt.*).

CENSUS METHODS AND PROBLEMS

Fulmars occupy their colonies for more months of the year than any other British seabird. Breeding birds leave only to moult in late summer and again briefly just before egg laying in May (Dunnet *et al.* 1963, Macdonald 1977b). The numbers of pairs in a breeding colony can be censused most accurately in June when most are incubating. Paired Fulmars occupy a nest site for several years before starting to breed. The exact amount of time spent on land appears to depend on various factors such as the weather and food availability (Coulson and Horobin 1972, Dott 1975), or even how long the colony has been established (Slater 1987). Most occupied sites in a colony in June belong to breeding birds, but the ones belonging to non-breeders often cannot be distinguished from sites with eggs. Census counts inevitably include some non-breeding pairs and also include most failed breeders, which tend to remain in the colony until at least July (e.g. Hepburn 1973).

The census unit used to count Fulmars during Operation Seafarer, the recent surveys for the Seabird Colony Register, and for most counts in intervening years, was an apparently occupied site capable of holding an egg (AOS). This excluded obvious non-breeding birds on precarious ledges unsuitable for nesting, but included some pre-breeding birds. A small proportion of the Seafarer and 1985–87 counts were of individual birds on land in a colony. No satisfactory method exists for converting these to AOS but, as a very rough approximation, counts of birds have been divided by two and included in regional totals. No attempt has been made to estimate numbers of non-breeding site holders included in the totals.

THE FULMAR IN BRITAIN AND IRELAND

Numbers of Fulmars nesting in Britain and Ireland have increased for the last hundred years as the breeding range has edged its way around the coastline. Information on how most European seabird breeding populations have changed in the past is very sparse, but the pattern and rate of increase has been exceptionally well documented for the Fulmar. Virtually the whole British and Irish Fulmar population has been surveyed at regular intervals during the twentieth century (Harvie-Brown 1912, Fisher and Waterston 1941, Fisher 1952b, Fisher 1966), most recently during Operation Seafarer (Cramp et al. 1974) and again in 1985–87. These surveys showed increases of 13–19% per annum before 1939, excluding St Kilda for which there were no counts (Cramp et al. 1974). From 1939 to 1985–87 total numbers excluding St Kilda increased more gradually, slowing to 4% per annum. On St Kilda, Fulmar counts apparently changed little between 1949 and 1969, but then grew by about 3% a year from 1969 to 1986 (Table 8).

Long-term study of the Fulmar in Orkney has provided information on survival and age at first breeding which show that the spectacular increase in Fulmar numbers in Britain and Ireland earlier this century probably occurred with the help of immigration (details in Dunnet et al. 1979). Birds may have moved from St Kilda to other colonies in Britain and Ireland, or the immigrants may have arrived from elsewhere in Europe. On average only six breeding adults died each year from 100 breeding pairs in Dunnet's study. One hundred pairs of Fulmars produced between 16 and 52 chicks per year and these had an annual survival of 88% to 93% up to breeding age. Depending on how many chicks entered the year-class at fledging (and assuming a 50:50 sex ratio), on average between 1.5 and 27 birds would have survived long enough to join the breeding population. However, up to 44 birds per 100 pairs were needed to balance annual adult mortality and to provide the increase which is known to have occurred before 1939. The study in Orkney proved that Fulmars readily move between colonies in their pre-breeding years. Only 6–11% of those colour-ringed as chicks returned to their natal colony. The number of recruits required for the slower rate of increase since

Empty circles: coastline segments that held
more than 1% of Ireland's Fulmars in 1969/70
and were not surveyed in 1985 – 87.

Pairs

- ◂ 1 – 10
- · 11 – 100
- • 101 – 1000
- ● 1001 – 5000
- ⬤ 5001 – 10,000
- ⬤ 10,000 +

Figure 3. Distribution and size of Fulmar colonies (and grouped colonies), 1985 – 87.

(a)

(b)

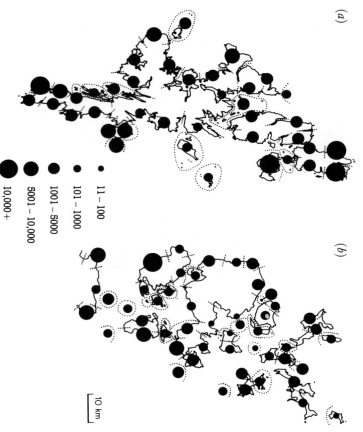

11 — 100
101 — 1000
1001 — 5000
5001 — 10,000
10,000+

10 km

Figure 3a. Detail of distribution and size of Fulmar colonies (and grouped colonies) in Shetland, 1985–87.
Figure 3b. Detail of distribution and size of Fulmar colonies (and grouped colonies) in Orkney, 1985–87.

1939 suggests that immigration need no longer be occurring on its previous scale.

A total of 309,100 pairs of Fulmars was recorded in Britain and Ireland by Operation Seafarer in 1969–70 and by 1985–87 this had increased to 570,000 pairs. Scotland held 93% of the breeding pairs in 1985–87 and most Scottish birds (98%) bred in either the northeast or northwest where all the very large colonies were situated. However, over half of the 1100 Fulmar colonies recorded in Scotland contained less than 100 pairs. Scottish Fulmars increased by 85% from 1969–70 to 1985–87, with the largest growth occurring in the north and northeast (Figure 4). Despite apparent low breeding success (B. Zonfrillo pers. comm.), Fulmars in the Firth of Clyde have followed the national trend, increasing by 8% a year from 1951 to 1969 and by 3% a year since. The rate with which new colonies have formed has accelerated in recent years (Monaghan and Zonfrillo 1986).

St Kilda was the site of the largest colony of Fulmars (62,800 pairs) in Britain or Ireland in 1985–87. Until the 1920s the resident islanders harvested up to half the Fulmar chicks each year. When the islands were evacuated in

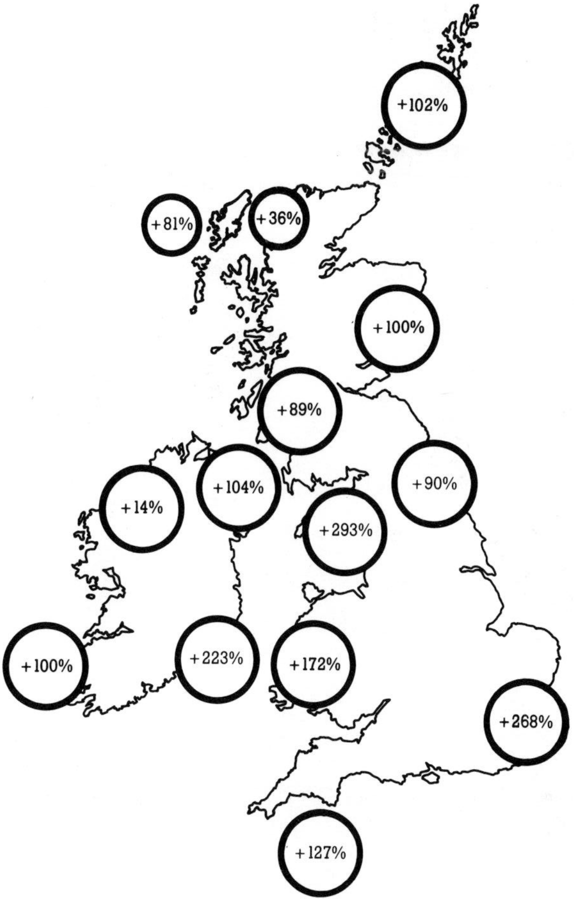

Figure 4.   Regional changes in numbers of breeding Fulmars, 1969–87. Percentages are calculated from counts at all colonies in Britain, and from those in Ireland covered in both national surveys. See Table 7 for counts and Figure 1 for regional divisions.

1930, Fulmar numbers may have fallen slightly (25,500 to 20,800 pairs 1929–39), but recovered within the next decade and remained approximately stable until 1969 (Table 8). On the more regularly surveyed islands of Hirta and Dun, at least, there is no evidence that a ceiling in numbers has been reached on St Kilda as was suggested by Cramp *et al.* (1974). A survey in 1987 found 47,367 pairs bred on the two islands compared with 21,624 pairs in 1969 (Tasker *et al.* 1988). Two other colonies in the Western Isles had over 5000 pairs of Fulmars. These were on Mingulay (9000 pairs) and Sula Sgeir (7800 pairs).

The other large Fulmar colonies were in Shetland where Fulmar nest sites

Plate 8. Hirta, St Kilda. Unstable cliffs provide nesting sites for the largest of Britain and Ireland's Fulmar colonies (Peter Moore)

were found on almost all the coastline apart from the sealochs or voes. The division of the cliffs into colonies was often arbitrary and was done mainly for convenience during censusing. For example, a total of over 16,000 pairs of Fulmars was counted from the sea in 1986 along 7 km of rampart-like cliffs on

Fitful Head near the southernmost tip of mainland Shetland. Two "colonies" or sections of this cliff each held over 6000 pairs. At the second biggest Shetland colony, on Fair Isle, numbers rose by 56% to 27,000 pairs between 1969 and 1987. Foula, with 46,800 pairs of breeding Fulmars, is the second largest and also the second oldest colony in Britain or Ireland. Numbers apparently increased fourfold from 10,000 pairs in 1969, a greater rate of increase than at most other Shetland colonies, possibly because the survey of the island during Operation Seafarer was incomplete (W.R.P. Bourne *in litt.*); an estimate in 1968 gave an island total of 20,000 pairs.

England and Wales had numerous small Fulmar colonies in 1985–87 and counts more than doubled overall since Operation Seafarer. There was a slower increase in eastern England where nesting habitat is limited by the low coastline, but a phenomenal 13-fold increase occurred since 1969–70 on the cliffs of Kent and East Sussex where many new colonies were established. Numbers of Fulmars breeding in most of Scotland may have grown more slowly than in the south of Britain because the northern colonies were reaching saturation point with few vacant areas for new colonies, though nesting habitat within existing colonies was not limited.

Many new Fulmar colonies were established in England and Wales between 1969–70 and 1985–87. Fulmars now breed on the south coast of Guernsey and in northwest Jersey; none was recorded in the Channel Islands during Operation Seafarer. The species has also colonised Somerset and Suffolk, and the number of colonies in Kent and East Sussex rose from 6 to 21 (from about 30 pairs to over 400). Forty-four pairs of breeding Fulmars were counted in the recent surveys on the Isle of Wight where only prospecting birds were found in 1969–70. The biggest Fulmar colonies in England and Wales were at Bempton on the Yorkshire coast (725 pairs) and Skomer off southwest Wales (472 pairs).

During the 1985–87 survey, 22,800 occupied Fulmar sites were counted in Ireland, compared with 19,300 sites in 1969–70. In addition, a number of known Fulmar colonies, especially in Donegal and Kerry, were not counted during the 1985–87 survey. Fulmars breed at scattered sites often without other species and these are particularly time-consuming to cover thoroughly. In order to estimate numbers on unsurveyed sections, a comparison of sections of coast counted in both 1969–70 and 1985–87 was made within each of the four defined regions (Figure 1) of Ireland. These comparisons were then used to estimate each county's 1985–87 total assuming that unsurveyed colonies had changed at the same rate as surveyed areas. On the basis of these estimates, the Fulmar population of Ireland was 31,300 pairs in 1985–87. This is probably a minimal estimate since new areas of coastline were still being colonised.

The fastest increases in the Irish colonies covered by both the national surveys were recorded on the east coast (Figure 4). Fulmars on the island of Lambay off Dublin, for example, increased from 75 to 560 pairs, although on the nearby mainland cliffs of Howth Head, lacking protection from disturbance and predators, numbers remained stable (40–50 pairs). By contrast, the increase in Fulmar numbers was apparently much smaller in Mayo and Donegal, though in part this may have been due to counting problems. The largest Irish Fulmar colonies were on the Blasket Islands off Kerry (2200 pairs) and at the Cliffs of Moher on the mainland of Clare (3100 pairs).

The long-term study of Fulmars on Eynhallow in Orkney showed that the amount by which numbers increase annually can be extremely variable (Dunnet *et al.* 1979). Several colonies where Fulmars were counted regularly between 1969–70 and 1985–87 also showed uneven growth although the overall trend in numbers was upwards (Figure 5). This year-to-year variation in numbers was probably determined mainly by the proportion of birds in the breeding population which did not attempt to nest in any one year (see first chapter Part 1).

Fulmar numbers have been monitored throughout the 1970s and 1980s, in greater detail than that provided by the two national censuses, by annual counts in sample plots of a selection of colonies in Britain and Ireland (see first

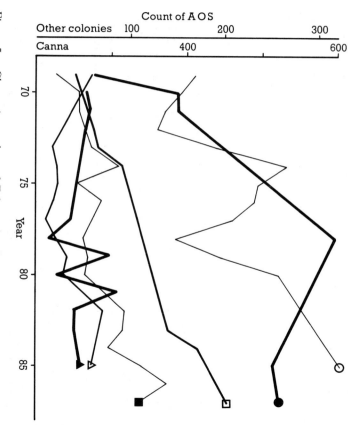

Figure 5. Change in numbers of Fulmars breeding in six colonies visited regularly between 1969 and 1987.

○ = *Great Saltee, Wexford.*
● = *Canna, Lochaber.*
■ = *Farne Islands, Northumberland.*
□ = *Craigleith, East Lothian.*
△ = *Weybourne—Sheringham, Norfolk.*
▲ = *Durlston—St Albans's, Dorset.*

chapter Part 1). Results varied regionally though numbers increased at most sites. In the west and southwest, there was no sign of a halt to the Fulmar's increase (e.g. Lundy, Davies and Price 1986; Skokholm, Rathlin, Stowe 1982), but in Scotland most Fulmar colonies were either stable (e.g. Berwickshire, Warman 1983; east Caithness, Mudge 1986) or declining slightly (e.g. Grampian, Lloyd and North 1987; Orkney, Benn *et al.* 1987); the study colonies in Shetland were still increasing (M. Heubeck pers. comm.).

Fulmars usually nest on cliff ledges although in parts of their range the cliff may be no more than a few metres high, as on the coast of East Anglia (Slater 1987). They can also breed on sand dunes, as on the Monach Isles off North Uist (Hepburn and Randall 1975) and at the Sands of Forvie, north of Aberdeen (Anderson 1982). In Orkney and Shetland, Fulmars nest widely both on the ground and in or on ruined buildings and stone walls. At several sites in east Scotland they breed on occupied buildings and in Youghal, Co. Cork, on a concrete roof. Fulmars on Foula and Eynhallow nest on boulder beaches and even deep under rocks in burrow-like sites. On the remote island of North Rona they nest on relatively flat ground. Elsewhere they select castle ramparts, as at Bamburgh, Dunstanburgh and Holy Island in Northumberland, Tantallon in East Lothian and Skelbo in east Sutherland. Fulmars sometimes breed in towns and cities; both Edinburgh and St Andrews in southeast Scotland have traditional Fulmar colonies (Brown 1983). They have been known to nest, albeit with little success, in trees (e.g. Warham 1975) and can also breed inland, many kilometres from open sea, especially in Iceland and on Svalbard. In Britain, this habit is commonest on the North Sea coast where inland colonies exist in east Sutherland, east Ross, Grampian, Fife and Northumberland. The present surveys also reported inland colonies in Derry and the Isle of Man, but none more than 10 km from open sea.

During their population spread and increase, Fulmars have been forced to compete with other seabirds for nest sites. Coulson and Horobin (1972) observed the gradual takeover of breeding ledges on Marsden Rock, Tyneside, by Kittiwakes following the Kittiwakes' arrival in the 1930s. Photographs of the cliff face showed that although Fulmars occupied the nest sites during winter, Kittiwakes returning in February easily evicted them. Elsewhere Fulmars have the upper hand in such contests. In northeast Scotland, Fulmars sometimes take over substantial Herring Gull nests. On the Isle of Man they have been seen using the nests of Herring Gulls, Kittiwakes, Shags, Hooded Crows and Ravens (Moore 1985); nests of the latter are also used by Fulmars on Wicklow Head on the east coast of Ireland (O.J. Merne *in litt.*) and in Kintyre, southwest Scotland (see Plate 9). There are many examples of birds, including Sea Eagles recently reintroduced to Scotland, being incapacitated by oil spat at them by nesting Fulmars (Broad 1974); this tactic presumably is used to repel both competitors for nesting space and would-be predators.

Fulmars have been of economic use to man for centuries and communities on remote islands such as the Faroes and St Kilda undoubtedly depended upon the annual harvest of eggs and seabirds. Steel (1965) recorded how, in the seventeenth century, the St Kildans ate mainly Gannets but by the mid 1700s had begun to rely on Fulmars for their staple diet. Unlike the Gannets,

Plate 9. Fulmars nesting in an old Raven's nest, Kintyre (B. Zonfrillo)

which nested on barely accessible offshore stacks, the Fulmars were numerous on the cliffs of the main island of Hirta. By 1897 it was estimated that about 9000 Fulmars, mostly chicks, were being caught annually. The community decided each year which part of the island would be harvested and the men descended the cliffs on ropes made first of straw and later of horsehair or manila and hemp.

The Fulmar bodies were plucked and the feathers were sold to the island's factor for export to the mainland or were kept to stuff mattresses. About a quarter of a litre of foul-smelling oil was collected from each bird by squeezing the carcass, and was either sold or used for lamp fuel or as an ointment for wounds. The Fulmar's body was then split and the guts removed to be used as a valuable source of compost. The flesh was eaten fresh or was salted, packed in barrels and stored for consumption during the winter months. As one of the men said in 1756 to Reverend Macaulay, a missionary to the island, "deprive us of the Fulmar and St Kilda is no more".

REASONS FOR CHANGE IN NUMBERS

The Fulmar in the Atlantic has shown one of the most remarkable range expansions and population explosions known in seabirds, yet the reasons for the increase are still unclear. Explanations include the provision of extra food for Fulmars, first in the form of offal from whaling fleets and later as discarded fish from trawlers (Fisher 1952b); the appearance in the population of a genotype favouring range-extension and colonisation (Wynne-Edwards 1962); and the gradual warming of the eastern Atlantic during the last century (Salomonsen 1965, Brown 1970). Possibly a combination of these factors has caused the Fulmar's population growth. With recent colonisation of Newfoundland and Labrador and apparent increases in Alaska (Lensink 1984), the change is not restricted to as small a part of the total population as thought by Salomonsen (1965).

Fulmars feeding chicks on St Kilda may differ distinctly in diet and feeding range from similar birds in Shetland (Furness and Todd 1984). Food samples were collected on St Kilda (in 1981) and Foula (between 1978 and 1982) when breeding birds regurgitated food while being ringed. A sample of birds on Foula was also marked with dye and later seen at sea. At both colonies Fulmar nets were watched to see how long adult birds were absent on feeding trips. During this study, the St Kilda birds fed their chicks largely on pelagic zooplankton (71% of food samples), especially euphausiids, which are accessible to the surface-feeding Fulmar only at night. The diet included some small fish (8% of samples), mostly Herring or Sprat. Birds on Foula, by contrast, fed mainly on sandeels (72% of food samples), but also took offal and some zooplankton. Elsewhere in Shetland, Fulmars feed extensively on offal discarded from fishing boats, usually excluding other species by their sheer numbers and agility in reaching patches of food (Hudson and Furness 1989).

Offal and fish, particularly sandeels, are higher quality foods than zooplankton and in Furness and Todd's study this factor affected the amount of foraging time the birds needed (although no effect upon breeding performance was reported). Feeding trips from St Kilda lasted on average 29 hours compared with under ten hours for Foula birds with the richer diet. The feeding habits of birds on St Kilda in this particular study were probably more similar to the traditional ancestral pattern. The flexible and opportunistic diet of the Shetland birds shows how it may have been possible for British and Irish Fulmar populations to expand so rapidly by exploiting new food sources.

Table 6. *Numbers of Fulmars breeding in Britain and Ireland 1969–87.*

	1985–87		1969–70	
	Pairs	Birds	Pairs	Birds
Shetland Islands	235,714	137	116,137	—
Orkney Islands	82,068	4769	42,430	27
Moray	201	—	261	—
Banff and Buchan	3192	—	2176	2
Gordon	974	—	810	—
Aberdeen	135	—	60	12
Kincardine and Deeside	4273	—	1173	—
Angus	805	580	522	—
Northeast Fife	1009	—	478	—
Kirkcaldy	—	—	3	—
Dunfermline	138	—	—	—
Edinburgh	85	—	37	—
East Lothian	902	—	364	—
Berwickshire	1301	—	764	—
Western Isles	118,052	—	65,328	—
Caithness	32,261	—	25,745	353
Sutherland	21,937	—	17,943	8
Ross and Cromarty	5268	44	3867	—
Skye and Lochalsh	6382	—	1421	—
Lochaber	2274	—	989	—
Argyll and Bute	7172	7	3804	—
Cunninghame	250	—	53	—
Kyle and Carrick	401	—	131	—
Wigtown	327	—	328	—
Stewartry	78	—	41	—
Scotland total	525,200	5537	284,900	400
Northumberland	482	—	248	—
Tyne and Wear	247	—	126	—
Durham	—	—	5	—
Cleveland	329	—	266	—
North Yorkshire	907	—	360	—
Humberside	985	—	546	—
Norfolk	181	—	146	—
Suffolk	21	—	—	—
Kent	293	—	27	—
East Sussex	116	—	5	—
Isle of Wight	44	—	—	—
Dorset	122	—	—	—
Devon	894	7	380	—
Cornwall	1692	—	869	—
Combined units[a]	528,000[a]		285,100[a]	
Birds converted to pairs		<1%		<1%

	1985–87		1969–70	
	Pairs	Birds	Pairs	Birds
Scilly Isles	108	—	17	—
Somerset	2	—	—	—
Channel Islands	156	—	—	—
Cumbria	112	—	23	—
Isle of Man	2283	—	586	—
England, Isle of Man and Channel Islands total	9000	—	3600	90
West Glamorgan	5	—	1	—
Dyfed	1505[b]	—	459	—
Gwynedd	945[b]	—	407	—
Clwyd	64	—	58	—
Wales total	2500	—	930	—
Derry	684	—	400	—
Antrim	2792[b]	—	1821	—
Down	64	—	18	—
Dublin	694	—	130	—
Wicklow	118	—	48	—
Wexford	614	—	230	—
Waterford	934	—	323	—
Cork	2046	—	540	—
Kerry	4211[b]	—	4214	—
Clare	3166[b]	—	1957	—
Galway	893	—	440	—
Mayo	4854[b]	—	5414	1
Sligo	367	—	271	—
Donegal	1589[b]	—	3512	—
Ireland total	23,000[b]	—	19,300	1
Estimated total	31,300[c]			
Percentage estimate	26%			
Britain and Ireland total	570,800[b]		309,100	
Percentage estimate	1%			

[a] Includes counts of birds divided by 2 to provide estimate of pairs; details in text.
[b] These are numbers counted. In these counties, at least 10% more pairs are estimated to occur at colonies not visited in 1985–87. An estimated 40% of Donegal's Fulmars were not counted.
[c] This total includes estimates for colonies not counted recently. It is based on the proportional change in numbers at colonies in each region where counts were conducted in both surveys.

All regional totals rounded, <100 to nearest 5, 100–1000 to nearest 10, >1000 to nearest 100.

Table 7. *Estimated world breeding population of the Fulmar.*

	No. of pairs	Comments
USSR—Kuril Islands	750,000	
USSR—Sea of Okhotsk	>200,000	
USSR—Kamchatka	600	
USSR—Novaya Zemlya	2,500	Total for Soviet Waters
USSR—Franz Josef Land	10,000	just over 2 million birds
USA—Alaska	1,500,000	
Canada	360,000	
Greenland	200,000–750,000	
Svalbard	0.5–1 million	
Jan Mayen	60,000–100,000	
Iceland	100,000–10 million	
Faroe Islands	0.5–1 million	
Norway	1000–1500	
Britain	539,500	
Ireland	31,300	
France	30	
West Germany	22	
Approximate total	15–20 million pairs	

Sources: Ilyichev and Flint (1982), Croxall *et al.* (1984), Vyatkin (1986), Hémery *et al.* (1988), Kondratiev in press, P. G. H. Evans (pers. comm.), Seabird Colony Register.

Table 8. *Increase in numbers of Fulmars (pairs) breeding in Britain and Ireland 1939–86.*

	1939	1949	1959[a]	1969–70	1985–87
Total minus St Kilda	35,200	70,500	97,000	272,500	508,000
Annual increase		1939–49 8%	1949–69 7%		1969–86 4%
St Kilda	20,800	38,200	37,500	36,600	62,800
Annual increase		1939–49 6%			1969–86 3%

[a] Incomplete count.

Sources: Cramp *et al.* (1974), Seabird Colony Register.

Manx Shearwater

Puffinus puffinus

The Manx Shearwater is a medium-sized petrel (wing-span 76–89 cm) which is seen near land mainly during stormy weather or, in evenings, near the breeding colonies. It feeds entirely at sea on fish, cephalopods and crustaceans caught on or near the water's surface, and on floating offal (Cramp and Simmons 1977).

INTERNATIONAL DISTRIBUTION AND STATUS

The Manx Shearwater found in Britain and Ireland is the nominate subspecies of *Puffinus puffinus*, a worldwide species that has many colloquial names. Other European subspecies are the Balearic (*P.p. mauretanicus*) and Levantine Shearwaters (*P.p. yelkouan*) of the Mediterranean. The breeding distribution of the Manx Shearwater is largely restricted to northwestern Europe, but it has recently colonised North America (Table 9). Worldwide, there are probably 300,000 breeding pairs of the nominate race, about 94% of which nest in Britain and Ireland.

Little is known about the status of the Manx Shearwater in Britain and Ireland or the rest of its range because the birds visit land only in darkness and nest underground in burrows. Added to this, almost all their breeding colonies

53

are on offshore islands where they are usually found on grassy slopes, often poised half-way down a steep cliff where the shearwaters are inaccessible to ground-predators and ornithologists alike.

Manx Shearwaters first nested in the west Atlantic in 1973 when a pair bred on an island off Massachusetts. Several small colonies became established on islands off Rhode Island during the mid 1970s, and a colony was discovered off Newfoundland in 1976 (Buckley and Buckley 1984). In France, where the species nests on the Atlantic coast, numbers are declining and the breeding range is contracting (Evans 1984).

Outside the breeding season Manx Shearwaters disperse away from the colonies into the open ocean. Recoveries of birds ringed in Britain, mostly in Wales, show that many migrate to the east coast of South America (Harris 1966a). Some return via the east coast of the USA, which may explain how the species has been able to colonise eastern North America.

CENSUS METHODS AND PROBLEMS

The combination of inaccessible colonies, burrow-nesting and nocturnal behaviour makes this species very difficult to census accurately. In the more accessible colonies, tape-recorded calls can be played in likely burrow entrances to elicit a response from birds underground (James and Robertson 1985). Although all Manx Shearwater breeding colonies known to have been occupied in 1969 were visited again during the 1985–87 survey, there were few confirmed breeding records and even fewer population estimates. In most cases observers were unable to remain in the shearwater breeding areas overnight, or had no time to search for occupied burrows during the day.

Checking sites where Manx Shearwaters have been reported in the past can be a worthwhile exercise. In April 1989, an overnight visit to Little Sark in the Channel Islands, where dead birds had been found 12 years previously, revealed 10–20 newly excavated burrows, some with calling shearwaters in residence. Later, a second probable colony was found on Jethou (M. Hill *in litt.*).

Almost all data collected by Operation Seafarer and during 1985–87 were provided only as estimated orders of colony size. Only very tentative population estimates are therefore possible for Britain and Ireland, and for other countries in the species' range. A few Manx Shearwater colonies are accessible or partly accessible, and better estimates of size have been made at these. Intensive ringing studies have provided relatively accurate censuses for Skokholm (Harris 1966b, Perrins 1968) and Skomer (Corkhill 1973, Alexander and Perrins 1980). Counts of occupied burrows (often difficult to distinguish from rabbit or Puffin burrows) made in sample areas of the colony have been used to estimate numbers on Rhum (Wormell 1976), Canna (Swann and Ramsay 1984), Lundy (Thomas 1981) and Skomer (Brooke 1990).

THE MANX SHEARWATER IN BRITAIN AND IRELAND

Manx Shearwaters breeding in Britain and Ireland are concentrated into three main areas: the island of Rhum off the west coast of Scotland, and groups of islands off southwest Wales and southwest Ireland. Together these islands hold a large proportion of the total (and world) population. There are very few Manx Shearwater colonies on the mainland of Britain or Ireland. In fact, the only sites at which mainland breeding has been proved or strongly suspected in the last 20 years are Carmel Head on Anglesey, Howth Head (Co. Dublin) and Bray Head (Co. Wicklow).

The island of Rhum off the west coast of Scotland has the largest Manx Shearwater colony in the world. The birds breed along ridges and on mountain tops at over 350 metres. Occupied burrows counted in sample plots and an estimate of the area covered by the shearwater colony from the distinctive vegetation produced by the birds' guano showed that between 96,900 and 135,300 pairs bred on Rhum in the late 1960s (Wormell 1976). When this survey was partly repeated in 1978, burrow density had increased but without a significant increase in numbers (Thompson and Thompson 1980).

Shearwater colonies elsewhere in Scotland are much smaller by comparison. Probably not more than a few hundred pairs bred in Shetland and maybe a few thousand pairs on St Kilda (M.P. Harris, M. Brooke pers. comms.). Canna had about 1000 pairs in the 1980s and other islands further south off the west coast of Scotland totalled less than 2000 pairs.

Colonies on the islands of Skokholm, Skomer and Midland off southwest Wales had at least 130,000 pairs in the early 1980s. The birds on Skokholm were studied intensively for 40 years from the 1930s onwards by R.M. Lockley and others, making it the longest studied Manx Shearwater colony (e.g. Lockley 1942, Harris 1966a, b, Brooke 1978a, b). Colonies elsewhere in Wales had about 4500 pairs in total.

Manx Shearwaters breed on four islands in the Isles of Scilly. The largest colony, on Annet, has declined since the mid 1970s (Table 10). This was attributed to the increase in breeding gulls on the island which may have resulted in heavy predation on adult and juvenile shearwaters (Harvey 1983).

At least three-quarters of the Manx Shearwaters in Ireland nest on islands off Kerry. A total of between 20,000 and 25,000 pairs were estimated to have bred on the islands of Deenish, Scariff, Puffin, Great Skellig and the Blaskets in the mid 1980s. Scariff, Puffin Island and Inishtooskert each had colonies of 1000 to 10,000 pairs, with Puffin Island closer to 10,000 pairs. Other Irish Manx Shearwater colonies had less than 1000 pairs each.

It is extremely difficult to judge how shearwater numbers may have changed recently, or during this century. If very major population change had occurred in any of the more regularly visited colonies (such as Skokholm, Skomer, Bardsey, Great Saltee, Calf of Man) during the last 30 years, at least an increase or reduction in the areas occupied by shearwater burrows would probably have been noticed. Changes on Annet in the Isles of Scilly, for example, were relatively well documented. At other colonies, where even proof of breeding is difficult to obtain and estimates of population size are impossible, extensive changes in burrow density and numbers could have occurred

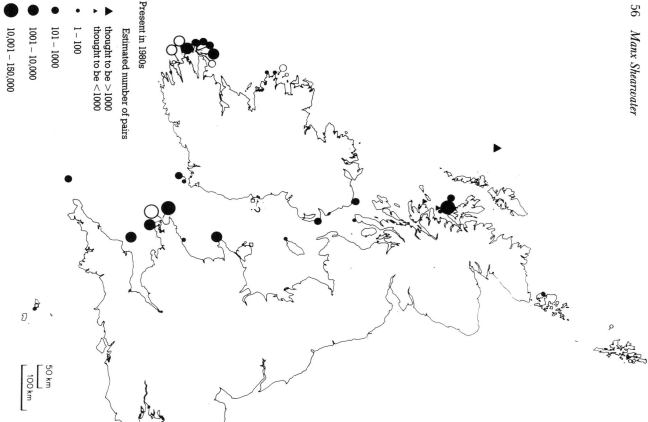

Present in 1980s

Estimated number of pairs

▶ thought to be >1000
▸ thought to be <1000

·   1 – 100

●   101 – 1000

●   1001 – 10,000

●   10,001 – 150,000

Empty circles: present, but no recent estimates,
estimate in past proportional to circle size.

□ = present, no proof of breeding

? = present in 1969/70, no recent evidence

50 km
100 km

Figure 6.   Distribution and approximate size of Manx Shearwater colonies in the 1980s.

undetected. Brooke (1990) considers that numbers are now stable in Britain and Ireland and may be increasing in colonies in southwest Wales.

Large numbers of shearwaters were caught by man for food on the Calf of Man and in Orkney in the last century, and many birds are still caught with baited hook and line off northern Spain (M. Brooke *in litt.*). A more important factor affecting colonies in Britain has been the presence of rats. Manx Shearwaters occupy their nesting burrows over a relatively long breeding season and this makes them especially vulnerable to ground-predators. The arrival of rats on islands such as the Calf of Man and Cardigan Island was followed by the extinction of Manx Shearwater colonies. (The Calf of Man was recolonised in the 1960s; and birds from Skomer introduced to Cardigan Island, following removal of the rats, seem likely to re-establish the colony.) Rats were known to be responsible for low breeding success among shearwaters on Lundy (Taylor 1985) and on Canna in 1982 (Swann and Ramsay 1984). Avian predators of breeding shearwaters, mainly raptors, crows and gulls, appear to have little overall effect on numbers (Brooke 1990).

Table 9. *Estimated world breeding population of the European subspecies of the Manx Shearwater.*

	No. of pairs
Canada—Newfoundland[a]	100
USA—New England[a]	<100
Faroe Islands[a]	10,000–15,000
Iceland[a]	1000–10,000
Britain[a]	220,000–250,000
Ireland[a]	30,000–50,000
France[a]	50
Azores[a]	<1000
Madeiran Islands[a]	50+
Canary Islands[a]	breeds
Spain	3000–5000
Italy	3500
Malta	250
Yugoslavia	500–5000
Greece	500–5000
Turkey	1–100
Tunisia	1–100
Approximate total	270,000–350,000
Total *Puffinus p. puffinus*	260,000–330,000 pairs

[a] = *Puffinus p. puffinus*.

Sources: Croxall *et al.* (1984), Hémery *et al.* (1988), Brooke (1990), P.G.H. Evans pers. comm., Seabird Colony Register.

Table 10. *Breeding sites of the Manx Shearwater in Britain and Ireland 1969–89.*

Colony name	Comments
Scotland	
Horse of Burravoe, Shetland	1983: chicks found; 1985: present
Lamb Hoga, Fetlar, Shetland	1969: c. 100 pairs; 1985: present
Foula, Shetland	1969: "a few pairs"; 1985: present
Enegars, Hoy, Orkney	1969: 2 colonies, of 1–9 pairs and 10–99 pairs respectively; 1986: 40–50 pairs
St Kilda, Western Isles	1969: present; 1987: present
Canna, Lochaber	1969: 1000+ pairs; 1985: c. 1000 pairs
Muck, Lochaber	1985: present
Rhum, Lochaber	1969: c. 70,000 pairs; 1975: 97,000–135,000 pairs (Wormwell 1976); 1978–79: c. 150,000 pairs (Thompson and Thompson 1980); 1986: present
Eigg, Lochaber	1969: 100 pairs (10–99 pairs in Cramp et al. 1974); 1986: 70–100 pairs
Treshnish Isles, Argyll and Bute	1969: present; 1986: present
Sanda Islands, Argyll and Bute	1977: present (Maguire 1978); 1987: 50–100 pairs
England, Isle of Man and Channel Islands	
Lundy, Devon	1969: c. 100 pairs; 1979: 2800–7700 pairs (Thomas 1981); 1985: c. 1200 pairs (Taylor 1985)
Isles of Scilly	
Annet	1969: c. 1000 pairs; 1974: 800–900 pairs (Allen 1977); 1977: 350–500 pairs (Harvey 1983); 1987: 50–300 birds (Birkin and Smith 1987)
Shipman Head, Bryher	1977: 25–30 pairs (Harvey 1983)
St Agnes	1974: 50 pairs (Scilly Isles Bird Report); 1977: 500 pairs (Allen 1977); 1983: present (Harvey 1983)
Round Island	1974: 50 pairs (Scilly Isles Bird Report); 1977: present (Harvey 1983); 1983: 24 occupied burrows (Harvey 1983); 1987: present (Birkin and Smith 1987)
Channel Islands	
Little Sark	1989: 10–20 burrows apparently occupied in April
Jethou	1989: 5–10 burrows apparently occupied in April
Calf of Man	1969: "very small numbers"; 1983: 32 occupied burrows; 1986: present
Wales	
Skokholm, Dyfed	1969: 30,000–40,000 pairs; 1986: present. Probably stable or increased slowly 1967–73 (Brooke 1990)
Skomer, Dyfed	1969: 60,000 pairs; 1971: 95,000 pairs (Corkhill 1973); 1978: 11% increase in sample of colony (Alexander and Perrins 1980); 1981: 100,000 pairs (Brooke 1990); 1986: present

Colony name	Comments
Midland/Middleholm, Dyfed	1969: 100 pairs; 1981: 3000 pairs; 1983: 2000+ pairs
Cardigan Island, Dyfed	1980–84: chicks from Skomer reintroduced; 1986: present, no proof of breeding
Bardsey, Gwynedd	1969: c. 2500 pairs; 1986: 4000–4500 pairs
Carmel Head, Anglesey	1969: present; 1972–82: birds calling over land in 5 years, late July–August
Ireland	
Rathlin, Antrim	1969: present (1000–9999 pairs in Cramp *et al.* 1974); 1976: c. 100 pairs (Chapman 1976); 1985: 320 birds
Copeland Islands, Down	1969: c. 300 pairs; 1985: c. 700 pairs
Lambay, Dublin	1970: 50–100 pairs
Howth Head, Dublin	1969: "several likely burrows seen from boat"; 1984: birds heard, less than 15 pairs
Great Saltee, Wexford	1969: c. 20 pairs; 1978: 100–150 pairs (Lloyd 1982a); 1985: present
Little Saltee, Wexford	1981: c. 30 pairs
Scariff Island, Kerry	1969: "thought to breed"; 1973: 1001–10,000 pairs (Davies 1980)
Deenish, Kerry	1978: 11–100 pairs (Davies 1980)
Puffin Island, Kerry	1973: 10,000–99,999 pairs; 1980: 1001–10,000 pairs (Brazier 1980); 1985: 1001–10,000 pairs
Great Skellig, Kerry	1969: 1000–9999 pairs; 1973: c. 5000 pairs (Evans and Lovegrove 1974); 1985: present
Inishvickillane, Kerry	1969: 100–999 pairs; 1980: 101–1000 pairs (Brazier 1980); 1988: 101–1000 pairs
Inishtearaght, Kerry	1969: 100–999 pairs; 1988: 800–1200 pairs
Inishnabro, Kerry	1969: 100–999 pairs; 1973: c. 3000 pairs (Evans and Lovegrove 1974); 1988: 101–1000 pairs
Inishtooskert, Kerry	1969: c. 100 pairs (100–999 pairs in Cramp *et al.* 1974); 1988: 1001–10,000 pairs
Great Blasket, Kerry	1969: c. 300 pairs ("thought to breed" in Cramp *et al.* 1974); 1988: present?
High Island, Galway	1969: 10–99 pairs; 1987: c. 100 pairs
Illaunamid, Slyne Hd, Galway	1969: 10–99 pairs (c. 15 in Cramp *et al.* 1974); 1980: c. 80 pairs
Davillaun, Inishbofin, Galway	1968: 100–500 pairs ("low order 3")
Inishturk, Mayo	1969: 4 occupied burrows
Clare Island, Mayo	1969: one heard calling
Approx. total Britain and Ireland	250,000–300,000 pairs

"present" = presumed breeding.

Storm Petrel

Hydrobates pelagicus

With a wing-span of only 36–39cm the Storm Petrel is the smallest species of seabird nesting in Britain and Ireland. The birds feed only at sea and usually far from land. Food is snatched from the water whilst the bird is still in flight and with its feet pattering along the surface. Some birds alight on the water to feed. The main foods are surface-living crustaceans, small fish, jellyfish and floating oily offal collected behind fishing boats (Cramp and Simmons 1977). The Storm Petrel is also sometimes called the British Storm Petrel to distinguish it from other storm petrels.

INTERNATIONAL DISTRIBUTION AND STATUS

About two-thirds to three-quarters of the world's Storm Petrels breed in Britain and Ireland. The species nests mainly in Europe, from Iceland and Norway to the Mediterranean; also on the Canary Islands and possibly on the Salvage Islands and in Turkey (Table 11). Storm Petrels are listed on Annex 1 of the EC Birds Directive 1979.

The world breeding population is probably between 135,000 and 380,000 pairs, but accurate censuses or even good estimates are impossible at most

60

Plate 10. Storm Petrel (B. Zonfrillo)

colonies. Indeed it is difficult to prove that breeding has occurred in some colonies because the birds visit land only at night and nest deep below boulders or in rock crevices or underground in burrows. Colonies are usually inaccessible and in remote areas, almost always on offshore islands close to oceanic water. No mainland colonies were found in Britain or Ireland during Operation Seafarer or in 1985–87.

Since the birds are so difficult to count, there is little indication of how numbers have changed recently in Britain and Ireland, or elsewhere. Massa and Catalisano (1986) reported that the species was declining in the Mediterranean and had disappeared from many former breeding sites. The tiny breeding population in northern Spain (possibly only 30 pairs Bárcena *et al.* 1984) appears to fluctuate, possibly in response to local feeding conditions. On average, 31% of the adults fail to breed in two successive years (Hémery *et al.* 1986).

Storm Petrels occupy their breeding colonies in Britain and Ireland from late April to October. Afterwards they disperse into the open ocean, and most birds migrate south to winter off the coasts of western and southern Africa (Cramp and Simmons 1977).

CENSUS METHODS AND PROBLEMS

There is no method of counting breeding Storm Petrels accurately and population totals for British and Irish colonies were presented only as estimated orders of abundance by Cramp *et al.* (1974). Proof of breeding is difficult to obtain. However, the presence of Storm Petrels can usually be detected, even by day, by their distinctive oily smell on the ground in likely nesting habitat or by birds calling from nest sites below ground in response to a tape-recording of Storm Petrel "song". In addition, corpses may be found in likely nesting habitat or burrow entrances. Eggs and chicks are usually out of reach, although birds flying about the colony can be trapped in mist nets after dark.

If a tape-recording of Storm Petrel song (or even calls of other birds, such as waders) is used to lure passing birds, mist nets set up on almost any island or headland can catch Storm Petrels successfully in late summer and autumn (e.g. Maguire 1980, Zonfrillo 1980). However, the majority of birds caught in this way are immature, non-breeding birds and even the presence of birds with brood patches does not necessarily indicate local breeding. Thousands of Storm Petrels were caught using a tape lure on Cape Clear Island off southwest Cork which is close to the large colonies on the Kerry islands. Breeding has never been proved, but was suspected in 1965 and a bird was found calling in a burrow in 1983 (Collins 1985); there are certainly no large numbers breeding. Hundreds of birds have been netted using the same method on the east coast of Scotland, near Aberdeen (Webb 1987), and on the Isle of May in the Firth of Forth (Zonfrillo 1980) where the nearest known breeding colonies are on the Pentland Skerries in Orkney.

THE STORM PETREL IN BRITAIN AND IRELAND

Breeding was confirmed or suspected in the late 1970s and 1980s on 34 islands or island groups in Scotland, 10 islands in the Isles of Scilly, two in the Channel Islands, the Calf of Man, four in Wales and at least 28 islands or island groups in Ireland. Breeding had been confirmed or suspected at 31 other sites between 1968 and 1972, but recent information is lacking for most of these. Many of these colonies may be still occupied, since observers did not always have time to search thoroughly for evidence of Storm Petrels.

There are few estimates of breeding numbers for Storm Petrel colonies in Britain and Ireland. The largest colonies in Britain, such as those on North Rona and Sule Skerry, could possibly hold a few tens of thousands of pairs each (e.g. Thom 1986), but probably less. Furness and Baillie (1981) compared "colony density" for different sites, as measured by the rate at which Storm Petrels were caught in mist nets, in similar weather conditions and without a tape lure. Colony density was higher on Priest Island in west Sutherland than on North Rona or Skokholm, and the lowest density they found was on Foula in the Shetland Islands.

The biggest Storm Petrel colonies in Britain and Ireland probably occur in southwest Ireland. In the 1980s, Great Skellig, Inishtearaght, Inishvickillane and Inishtooskert were estimated to have over 10,000 pairs each and four other islands had Order 4 colonies (1001–10,000 pairs). The island of Illaunmaster,

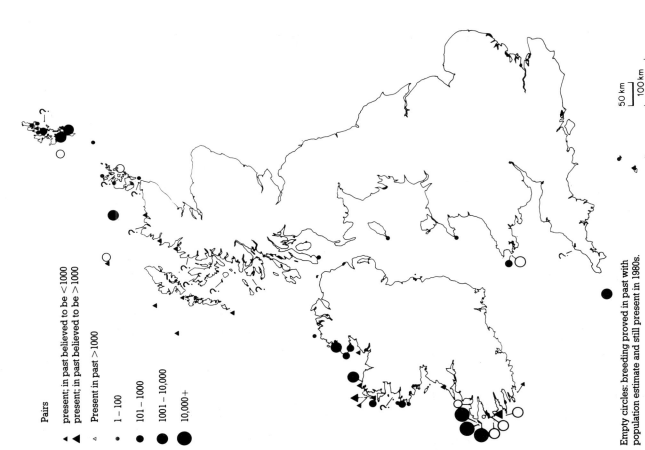

Pairs

▴ present; in past believed to be <1000
▲ present; in past believed to be >1000

◁ Present in past >1000

• 1 – 100

● 101 – 1000

⬤ 1001 – 10,000

⬤ 10,000 +

Empty circles: breeding proved in past with
population estimate and still present in 1980s.

? = breeding never proved, suspected in 1980s
or breeding proved in past, now suspected,
no population estimate or breeding proved
1968 – 79, but no recent information or past
population estimates.

50 km
100 km

Figure 7.   Distribution and approximate size of Storm Petrel colonies in late 1970s–1980s.

off the north coast of Mayo, had between 7500 and 10,000 pairs and Inishglora, further south, where up to 4000 birds have been ringed in a week, had at least 10,000 pairs.

The only Storm Petrel colony for which there is some evidence of recent population changes is in the Isles of Scilly. Estimated breeding numbers on Annet dropped from Order 4 (1000–9999 pairs) in 1969 to 1500 pairs in 1977 (Harvey 1983) and to about 500 pairs in 1987. Storm Petrels, like other burrow-nesting seabirds, are particularly vulnerable to ground-predators. All known Storm Petrel colonies are on islands thought to be free of rats. However, changes on Annet were attributed not to rats, but to the increase in numbers of gulls breeding on the island which may have caused heavy predation on the Storm Petrels (Harvey 1983). Manx Shearwater numbers on Annet also declined during the same period (see Table 10). The main Storm Petrel colony in the Channel Islands is on the island of Burhou off Alderney. Here numbers were estimated as Order 4 in 1969, but less than 100 pairs were estimated in 1987. The large gulls nesting on Burhou increased slightly during the same period, but this is considered more likely to have affected Puffin numbers than Storm Petrels (M. Hill *in litt.*).

Table 11.   *Estimated world breeding population of the Storm Petrel.*

	No. of pairs
Iceland	1000–10,000
Faroe Islands	50,000–100,000
Norway	< 100
Britain	20,000–150,000
Ireland	50,000–100,000
France	1000
Desertas, Madeira	breeds?
Salvage Islands	breeds?
Canary Islands	c. 1000
Spain	< 500
Balearic Islands	< 100
Italy	500–1000
Malta	10,000+
Yugoslavia	10–100
Greece	10–100
Turkey	10–100
Morocco	breeds?
Approximate total	135,000–380,000 pairs

Sources: Croxall *et al.* (1984), Massa and Catalisano (1986), Barrett and Stramm (1987), Paterson (1989), Nogales *in litt.*, P.G.H. Evans pers. comm.

Table 12. *Confirmed and possible breeding sites of the Storm Petrel in Britain and Ireland 1968–87. See Cramp et al. (1974) for additional historical information.*

Colony name	Comments
Scotland	
Brother Island, Shetland	1987: 5 pairs
Bigga, Shetland	1969: presence suspected; 1987: < 50 pairs
Samphrey, Shetland	1969: presence suspected; 1987: < 50 pairs
Linga, Shetland	1969: 2+ pairs; 1987: adult dead in burrow
Urie Lingey, Shetland	1970: 10–99 pairs; 1982–83: presence suspected
Sound Gruney, Shetland	1970: presence suspected; 1982–83: presence suspected
Daaey, Shetland	1970: 10–99 pairs; 1982–83: presence suspected
Haaf Gruney, Shetland	1970: 10–99 pairs; 1982–83: present
Hascosay, Shetland	1969: present; 1983: present
Copister Brough, Yell, Shetland	1987: 150–200 pairs
Lamb Hoga, Fetlar, Shetland	1969: 16+ pairs; 1987: present
Noss, Shetland	1970s: present; 1980s: regular finds of birds killed by cats
Mousa, Shetland	1969: present; 1983: > 1000 pairs ("possibly Order 4"); 1988: present
Foula, Shetland	1969: 101–999 pairs in 2 known colonies; 1988: present
Fair Isle, Shetland	1969: 10–99 pairs; 1986: > 5 pairs
Holm of Papa, Orkney	1983: present; 1986: 40 pairs
Rusk Holm, Orkney	1969: 30 pairs; 1985: present
Auskerry, Orkney	1969: 150 pairs; 1986: present
Eynhallow, Orkney	1986: 15 calling birds in one group
Switha, Orkney	1969: presence suspected; 1986: 4+ occupied burrows
Pentland Skerries, Orkney	1984: present; 1986: 2+ occupied burrows
Sule Skerry, Orkney	1969: present; 1986: 1000–10,000 pairs
North Rona, Western Isles	1969: present; 1972: 1000 pairs; 1986: present
Sula Sgeir, Western Isles	1969: present; 1986: present
St Kilda, Western Isles	1969: present; 1987: present
Flannan Isles, Western Isles	1988: present
Coppay, Harris, Western Isles	1988: present
Berneray, Western Isles	1985: present
Eilean nan Ron, Sutherland	1969: present; 1987: presence "likely"
Meall Mor, Sutherland	1986: present
Priest Island, W Ross	1969: present; 1986: present
Summer Isles, W Ross	1986: present Bottle Island and Eilean Dubh
Sanda, Argyll and Bute	1977: confirmed breeding; 1980: 100–500 pairs (Maguire 1978); 1987: 50–100 pairs
England, Isle of Man and Channel Islands	
Isles of Scilly	
Western Rocks	1969: 1–9 pairs on Gorregan; 1974: 1900+ pairs on Gorregan, Rosevean, Great Crebawethan (Allen 1974); 1977: present on Gorregan, Rosevean, Rosevear, Melledgan (Harvey 1983); 1983: present on same islands except Melledgan

Table 12. *Confirmed and possible breeding sites of the Storm Petrel in Britain and Ireland 1968-87. See Cramp et al. (1974) for additional historical information – cont.*

Colony name	Comments
Annet	1969: 1000–9999 pairs; 1974: 1800 pairs (Allen 1977); 1977: 1500 pairs (Harvey 1983); 1987: 500+ pairs
St Agnes and Gugh Northern Rocks	1974: c. 100 pairs (Scilly Isles Bird Report) 1977: present Mincarlo (Harvey 1983); 1987: present Round Island
Burhou, Channel Islands	1969: 1000–9999 pairs; 1987: < 100 pairs
L'Etac de Serk, Channel Islands	1987: several occupied holes
Calf of Man	1981: several calling from an inaccessible site; 1987: 1+ bird held territory June–August
Wales	
Skokholm, Dyfed	1969: 5000–7000 pairs; 1986: present
Skomer, Dyfed	1969: c. 100 pairs ("Order 2–3"); 1985: 500 pairs
Midland, Dyfed	1969: 1–9 pairs; 1985: present
Bardsey Island, Gwynedd	1984: proved breeding; declining since 1950s
Ireland	
Cape Clear Island, Cork	1965: reported ashore; 1983: bird calling from burrow (Collins 1985); (1937: chicks found, Lockley 1983)
Bull Rock, Cork	1969: 2000–5000 pairs (O.J. Merne *in litt.*), 1000–9999 pairs (Cramp *et al.* 1974); 1985: present
Scariff Island, Kerry	1969: 1000–9999 pairs; 1973: present
Puffin Island, Kerry	1969: 1000–9999 pairs; 1973: 1001–10,000 pairs; 1988: present
Great Skellig, Kerry	1969: 1000–9999 pairs; 1973: c. 10,000 pairs; 1987: present
Inishtearaght, Kerry	1968: c. 2000 pairs; 1969: 10,000–99,999 pairs; 1971: 25,000 pairs; 1988: 10,000–20,000 pairs
Inishvickillane, Kerry	1969: 10,000–99,999 pairs; 1988: 10,001–100,000 pairs
Inishnabro, Kerry	1969: 100–999 pairs; 1973: c. 1000 pairs; 1988: 1000–5000 pairs
Inishtooskert, Kerry	1969: 1000–9999 pairs; 1988: 5000–20,000 pairs
Beginish, Kerry	1969: 10–99 pairs (omitted by Cramp *et al.* 1974); 1988: present
Magharee Islands, Kerry	1969: 10–99 pairs in each of 2 colonies, breeding "suspected" at third; 1987: present on Illauntannig
Mattle Island, Clare	1984: present
Mutton Island, Clare	1960s: present; 1975: present; 1984: present
Illaunamid, Slyne Head, Galway	1980: c. 50 pairs
High Island, Galway	1987: c. 1000 pairs, also recorded 1940s
Inishbofin, Galway	1950s–60s: a few pairs thought to breed; 1983–87: present, probably < 100 pairs

Colony name	Comments
Blackrock, Mayo	1969: 1–9 pairs; 1987: present
Bills Rocks	1983: present; possibly 1000+ pairs
Duvillaun Islands, Mayo	1987: present; also recorded 1966
Inishglora, Mayo	1971: present; 1979: 10,000+ pairs
Inishkeeragh, Mayo	1987: present
Stags of Broadhaven, Mayo	1982: present, also recorded 1960s
Illaunmaster, Mayo	1976: 1001–10,000 pairs; 1980: 7500–10,000 pairs; 1985: present
Inishmurray, Sligo	1986: present
Inishduff, Donegal	1969: "breeds?"; 1980: c. 150 (Order 2 to low Order 3); 1985: 200–250 pairs
Rathlin O'Birne, Donegal	1970: 100–999 pairs; 1987: 500–1000 pairs
Roaninish, Donegal	1953–57: 250–300 pairs; 1975–76: 1001–10,000 pairs; 1986–87: unchanged
Tory Island, Donegal	1969: present; 1985–87: present, probably < 100 pairs
Approx. total Britain and Ireland	70,000–250,000 pairs

"present" = presumed breeding; see text for details.

Breeding proved at the following sites in 1968–72 but not more recently. (Details in Cramp *et al.*, 1974 or Sharrock, 1976): Junk, Hoy and Hoggs of Hoy (Shetland); Wart Holm, Skea Skerries (no longer exists), Muckle Skerry (Orkney); Stroma (Caithness); islands off N Skye (Skye and Lochalsh); Longa (W Ross); Canna (Lochaber); Lunga (Treshnish Isles, Argyll and Bute); Gulland Rock (Cornwall); Icho Tower Reef off Jersey (Channel Islands); Fastnet Rock (Cork); Great Blasket (Kerry); Caher (Mayo).

Breeding suspected at the following sites in 1968–72 but not more recently (details in Cramp *et al.* 1974 or Sharrock 1976): Papa Stour, Bruray, Sumburgh Head (Shetland, last 2 not mentioned by Cramp *et al.* 1974); Muckle Green Holm (Orkney); Shillay, Boreray (Sound of Harris), Monach Isles, Shiant Isles (Western Isles); Faraid Head (Sutherland); South Ascrib Islands (Skye and Lochalsh); Putrainez off Herm, Godin off Jersey (Channel Islands); Brannock Islands, Inishark, Inishark (Galway); Inishturk, Clare Island (Mayo); islands in Gweedore Bay, Inishkeeragh Inishbeg, (Donegal).

Leach's Petrel

Oceanodroma leucorhoa

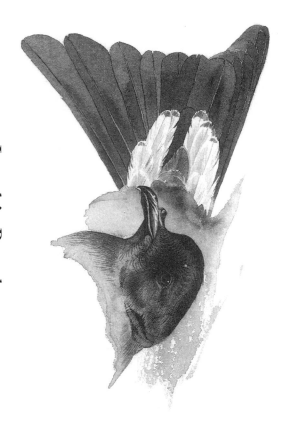

Leach's Petrel is a long-winged storm petrel (wing-span 45–48 cm) which spends most of its life at sea, far from land. It feeds on planktonic crustaceans, such as euphausiids and copepods, also on molluscs, small fish and offal (but rarely near fishing boats). The birds feed mostly whilst in flight. They patter along the surface or hang briefly above the water with wings raised and swoop down to pick up food items.

The Leach's Petrel found in Britain and Ireland is the nominate subspecies of *Oceanodroma leucorhoa* which breeds widely in the Pacific and Atlantic Oceans. The other three subspecies are rare by comparison and are confined to the west coast of North America. The centre of the Leach's Petrel breeding range is in Alaska, which holds a large majority of the estimated seven to nine million pairs in the world (Table 13). Britain and Ireland have probably less than 100,000 pairs (Evans 1984). The species is listed on Annex 1 of the EC Birds Directive 1979.

Leach's Petrels are most familiar to British and Irish birdwatchers during autumn, when birds may pass close to headlands, particularly on the western coasts. During extreme storms, large numbers may be blown inshore or inland and "wrecked". In 1952, total casualties were estimated to have been over

68

6700 (Boyd 1954). During surveys at sea to the west of Scotland, the majority of Leach's Petrels were found feeding over or beyond the edge of the continental shelf (Webb *et al.* 1990).

No accurate information exists on current breeding numbers or factors affecting Leach's Petrels in Britain and Ireland or in most other countries. In eastern North America, numbers of Leach's Petrels in New England colonies are known to have decreased during the present century due to predation by domestic dogs and cats, rats, disturbance by tourists, bombs and research workers, to destruction of nesting habitat by grazing sheep, and possibly to increased mortality caused by ingestion of plastic particles at sea (Buckley and Buckley 1984). The Leach's Petrel in California and Mexico is confined to only about 13 colonies, which are currently decreasing in size (Jehl 1984).

CENSUS METHODS AND PROBLEMS

Leach's Petrels cannot be censused accurately and few estimates of size have been made for the eight known colonies in Britain and Ireland. In fact, proving the species is actually breeding at a site may be very difficult because nests are hidden deep beneath rock or in burrows and the birds visit land only at night.

The presence of breeding storm petrels in accessible colonies can often be detected by the oily smell in burrows in suitable nesting habitat, but Leach's Petrels cannot be distinguished from Storm Petrels by smell. However, Leach's Petrels have characteristic calls and song, basically churring like the Storm Petrel, but with an additional "hiccoughing" call (also used in flight). Birds on their nests out of sight will often reply to a tape-recording of Leach's Petrel song played at the burrow entrance, but the presence of a singing bird in a burrow cannot be taken as proof of breeding. However, on colonies such as Boreray in the St Kilda group, where Leach's Petrels nest in close-cropped turf, it may be possible to estimate numbers of occupied burrows by using random quadrats and detecting the presence of birds by a combination of smell and call (Tasker *et al.* 1988).

Like Storm Petrels, Leach's Petrels can be caught in mist nets, especially during July and August. They have been trapped at several Storm Petrel colonies during the breeding season (e.g. Mousa, Shetland; Great Skellig, Inishtearaght and Inishvickillane, Kerry; Rathlin O'Birne, Donegal) but these cannot be regarded as breeding records.

THE LEACH'S PETREL IN BRITAIN AND IRELAND

There are seven confirmed Leach's Petrel colonies in Britain and one in Ireland. The former are in Shetland (2), Orkney (1) and the Western Isles (4); the species also breeds on the Stags of Broadhaven, off the north coast of Mayo. All colonies are on offshore islands close to deep oceanic water. Exact breeding

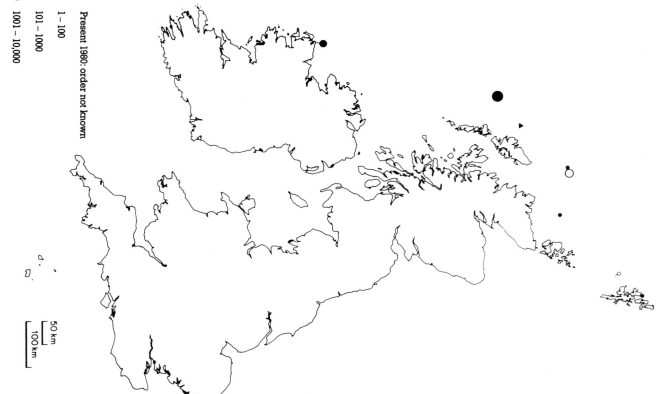

Present 1980: order not known

• 1 – 100

● 101 – 1000

● 1001 – 10,000

Empty circles: breeding proved in past with
population estimate and still present in 1980s.

50 km
100 km

Figure 8.   Distribution of Leach's Petrel colonies in the 1980s.

numbers are not known but probably only Eilean Mor on the Flannan Islands, and the St Kilda group have more than 1000 pairs.

Only four colonies were known in the early 1970s: St Kilda, the Flannan Islands, North Rona and Sula Sgeir (Cramp *et al.* 1974). Breeding has been proved since on Foula and Sule Skerry, both places where birds had been found nesting in the past and at which they had been seen, heard or caught in recent years. The seventh Leach's Petrel colony in Britain, on the island of Gruney in the Ramna Stacks off northwest Shetland, had never been suspected as a breeding colony and was discovered only in 1980 (Fowler 1982). Birds were seen and heard and an adult with a brood patch was caught in an empty burrow. Several nest sites were found containing eggs in the following year.

In Ireland, Leach's Petrels were seen on Chakbeg Stack in the Stags of Broadhaven in August 1946 and July 1947. On both occasions breeding was suspected but not proved (Ruttledge 1966). The Stags are precipitous stacks many kilometres from the nearest harbour and these were the first occasions that anyone had spent a night on them. The stacks were not revisited until July 1982 when Leach's Petrels were mist-netted on Chakbeg with the aid of a tape-lure and birds in possible nest sites responded to a tape-recording (Waring and Davis 1983). Three occupied Leach's Petrel burrows were discovered: these contained a pair of birds, a single bird and a Leach's Petrel egg. All three burrows also held nesting Puffins, and it seemed likely that competition was occurring for nest burrows in the island's steep and rocky soil. It is possible that this colony had been occupied by Leach's Petrels since at least the 1940s. Ruttledge (1966) made a special attempt to visit all likely Leach's Petrel sites off the coasts of Ireland during the 1950s and 1960s, but no more breeding colonies were found.

In the past Leach's Petrels have been found breeding on Inishnabro and Inishtearaght in the Blasket Islands, but the most recent records were in the 1930s (details in Brazier and Merne 1988). Four Leach's Petrels were trapped, using a tape-lure, on Inishtearaght and Inishvickillane in 1988. The three birds handled on Inishtearaght each had well-developed but unvascularised brood patches and breeding on the island was considered "possible to probable" (Brazier and Merne 1988). Birds tape-lured on Rathlin O'Birne, Donegal, in 1987 also had brood patches. Given the difficulties of proving breeding, especially if numbers were low, it seems likely that a few Leach's Petrels breed on these or other islands off the west coast of Ireland.

Table 13. *Estimated world breeding population of the Leach's Petrel.*

	No. of pairs
USSR—Sea of Okhotsk	? present
USSR—Kuril Islands	170,000
USSR—Bering Sea	?
USA—Alaska	5–7 million
Canada—British Columbia	1.1 million birds
USA—California	18,300 birds
Canada—Labrador and Newfoundland	750,000–1 million
USA—Maine and Massachusetts	19,000–20,000
Iceland	1000–10,000
Faroe Islands	100–500
Norway	<100
Britain and Ireland	10,000–100,000
New Zealand	? present
Approximate total	7–9 million pairs

Sources: Croxall *et al.* (1984), P.G.H. Evans pers. comm., Rodeway in press.

Table 14. *Breeding sites of the Leach's Petrel in Britain and Ireland 1969–87.*

Colony name	Comments
Scotland	
Gruney, Ramna Stacks, Shetland	1981: < 50 pairs (Fowler 1982)
Foula, Shetland	1969: "probably present"; probable breeding record in 1950s; 1974: present (Mainwood 1975); 1976: 50 pairs; 1987: present
Sule Skerry, Orkney	1986: 5+ pairs; first record since 1933
North Rona, Western Isles	1969: present; 1972: 500 pairs; 1986: present
Sula Sgeir, Western Isles	1969: present; 1980: 15 pairs; 1986: present
Flannan Islands, Western Isles	1969: present; 1988: present
St Kilda, Western Isles	1969: present; 1987: present; approx. 3200–6400 occupied burrows on Boreray (Tasker *et al.* 1988)
Ireland	
Stags of Broadhaven, Mayo	1982: 200+ pairs (Waring and Davis 1983), first record since 1940s
Approx. total Britain and Ireland	10,000–100,000 pairs

"present" = presumed breeding.

Gannet

Sula bassana

The Gannet is the largest of the seabirds breeding in Britain and Ireland (wing-span 165–180 cm). Its noisy, densely crowded colonies and habit of plunge-diving after fish make it one of the most spectacular seabirds. Breeding colonies are found on mainland cliffs and especially on islands, including some of the most remote islands off Scotland and Ireland. The Gannet feeds on shoaling fish, which it finds by foraging on the wing, and catches by a headlong dive from 10 to 40 metres above the water. The main fish species eaten by birds breeding in Britain and Ireland are Herring, Sprat, sandeels, Mackerel and various whitefish species; most are 2 to 30 cm in length (Cramp and Simmons 1977). Gannets are particularly successful at scavenging for fish discarded by fishing boats (Hudson and Furness 1989).

INTERNATIONAL DISTRIBUTION AND STATUS

Gannet colonies are found only in the North Atlantic, and the species is known internationally as the Northern or North Atlantic Gannet. The world's other two species of Gannet breed in South Africa (Cape Gannet *Sula capensis*), and in Australia and New Zealand (Australasian Gannet *Sula serrator*). In the east Atlantic, the Gannet breeds in Iceland (six colonies), the Faroes (one colony) Norway (five colonies with an additional unconfirmed site), France (one colony), Britain (17 colonies) and Ireland (four colonies with one addition in 1989). In the west Atlantic, there are three Gannet colonies in the Gulf of St Lawrence, Quebec and three on the east coast of Newfoundland. With a world population of at least 263,000 pairs (Table 15), it is a relatively rare seabird, but still more abundant than both other Gannet species (Nelson 1978). About 187,800 pairs of Gannets bred in Britain and Ireland in the mid 1980s. These represented about 84% of those in Europe and 71% of the world breeding population.

The world's largest Gannet colony, with over 50,000 breeding pairs, is on St Kilda off the west coast of Scotland. This was exceeded in size until earlier this century by the colony on Bird Rocks in the Gulf of St Lawrence. This held over 100,000 pairs in the 1830s before numbers were catastrophically reduced by man. The colony now has only 5300 pairs. The largest Canadian Gannet colony is on the island of Bonaventure, Quebec, and had 16,400 pairs in 1976 (Brown and Nettleship 1984a). This colony, too, was larger 20 years ago (21,215 pairs in 1966), but numbers have been declining (Nettleship 1975). The Newfoundland Gannet colonies have fared better than those in the Gulf of St Lawrence and were either increasing or stable in size in 1984 (Nettleship 1976, Montevecchi *et al.* 1980, Nettleship and Chapdelaine 1988).

In the east Atlantic, the Gannet population has increased at about 3% per year during this century (Nelson 1978). The rate of increase slowed to about 2% per year after 1969 although growth in the newest colonies exceeds this (Wanless 1987). Since 1920, three new colonies have been established in Iceland, seven (one since abandoned and one was a recolonisation) in Britain and three in Ireland. Birds from Britain have colonised Norway (five possibly six colonies), France (one colony) and the Channel Islands (two colonies).

Archaeological evidence suggests that Gannets may have once bred in Norway but the first modern gannetry was established there only in 1946. This was on the island of Runde off southern Norway. Later, colonies formed above the Arctic Circle, in the Lofoten Islands and at two mainland sites, including Syltefjordstauran, the world's most northerly gannetry, near the USSR border. Ringing has shown that Gannets from Bass Rock and Ailsa Craig were among those establishing new Norwegian colonies, and that movement of birds between colonies has speeded the growth of some younger ones (Barrett 1979).

Wanless (1987) reviewed the Gannet's status elsewhere in Europe. In Iceland, the oldest gannetries are on the Westmann Islands. These were established in the early 1700s and are still increasing in size, although large numbers of Gannet chicks are taken each year for human consumption. An even older colony, on Grimsey off the north coast of Iceland, became extinct in 1946 following earthquakes on the island. Overall the Icelandic Gannet population remains stable, with movement of birds from the west apparently accounting for continuing increases at east coast colonies (Gardarsson 1982,

1989); alternatively this growth may be caused by immigration from elsewhere, possibly from Britain and Ireland (Wanless 1987).

Gannet chicks are also harvested at the only Faroese colony, Mykineshólmur, which dates from at least the seventeenth century. The colony had about 2000 occupied sites in 1985 and appears to be increasing slowly. The only French Gannet colony, on Rouzic in the Sept-Isles nature reserve off Brittany, had 4500–4900 occupied sites in 1985 and is the most southerly gannetry. It was first occupied in 1937 and has increased steadily since.

The Gannets' distribution away from the colonies, both during and outside the breeding season, is relatively well known because the birds are large and conspicuous. Observations of birds at sea and recoveries of Gannets ringed in Britain and Ireland (Thomson 1974) show that non-breeders, mostly immatures, range as far south as West Africa and the Gulf of Mexico, and north to southeast Greenland and the seas around Jan Mayen and Bear Island. Breeding birds are partial migrants, remaining near the breeding colonies during winter or dispersing south to the Bay of Biscay, Iberia and the Mediterranean.

Many Gannets move out of the North Sea in winter, returning from February and March onwards as breeding colonies are re-occupied (Tasker *et al.* 1985a, 1987). Off north and west Scotland, many Gannets are seen over the continental shelf throughout the winter (Benn *et al.* 1988). Gannets breed for the first time at five or six years of age (Nelson 1978). Immature birds arrive in the vicinity of the colonies later in the year than adults. The main concentrations of adult Gannets during the breeding season are within 100 km of colonies and observations around Noss, Shetland, suggested that most birds forage within 150 km of the colony and many within only 37 km (Tasker *et al.* 1985a).

CENSUS METHODS AND PROBLEMS

The conspicuousness of adult Gannets allows accurate censuses from photographs of their breeding colonies. This method was used for most colonies during Operation Seafarer (Cramp *et al.* 1974) and many during the current survey. Gannet nests are arranged regularly within the colony. Nests belonging to breeding birds are substantial structures of seaweed and rubbish, including fishing net, picked from the sea. Immature birds and those nesting for the first time tend to gather at the edges of the colony. Some of these pairs build nests which are less permanent structures and from which material is constantly being stolen; or they may occupy a future breeding site without gathering any nest material. Thus a small proportion of occupied sites in the colony are either used only very briefly (where young birds lose their egg immediately after laying), or are not actually used for breeding.

In good quality photographs, occupied sites show up well enough to be counted by eye or using a low-powered microscope. During Operation Seafarer and more recent censuses, the photographs were taken from adjacent ground, from the sea or from the air during the late incubation or young chick stage of the breeding season (June–July). Occupied sites held by non-breeders

Plate 11. Gannet colony on north face of main rock, Les Etacs, Alderney. An excellent example of an aerial photograph of a Gannet colony from which census counts can be made (Mike G. Hill)

could not be distinguished in the photographs, and their proportion of the final census figure depended on factors such as the age and position of colonies or sub-colonies. A colony founded recently or a newly colonised stack at the edge of an old colony, for example, can be expected to have relatively large numbers of non-breeding Gannets occupying sites.

Most colonies with less than about 500 pairs of Gannets were counted in the field rather than from photographs. These counts generally excluded most non-breeding site holders which could be identified in the field. In the past, Gannet census figures have been expressed as occupied sites seen in photographs, or as occupied nests counted by visiting the colony. A survey of Gannet colonies in 1984–85 used both counting methods but recommended the occupied site as the best unit for wide-scale censuses (Wanless 1987). No conversion of one unit to the other is possible and counts in both units are combined here to give population totals.

THE GANNET IN BRITAIN AND IRELAND

The British and Irish Gannet breeding population was 187,900 pairs in 1985–87, compared with 137,700 pairs counted during Operation Seafarer in

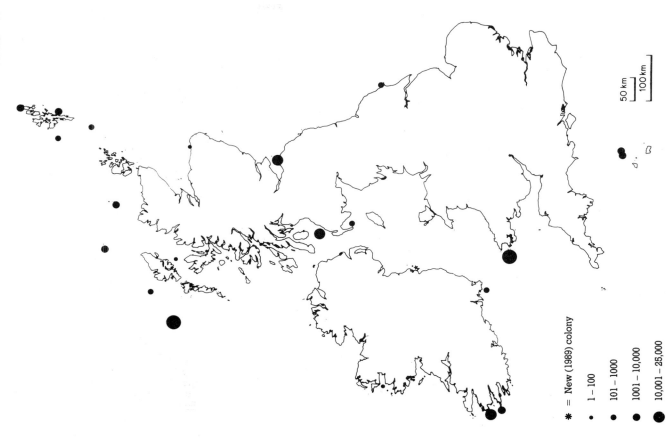

Figure 9.   Distribution and size of Gannet colonies in 1985–88.

= New (1989) colony

1 – 100

101 – 1000

1001 – 10,000

10,001 – 25,000

25,001+

1969–70. All the colonies in Britain and Ireland were visited in 1984 or 1985 during a survey organised by Sarah Wanless and partly funded by the NCC (Wanless 1987). Eleven of the colonies were surveyed again more recently.

Britain and Ireland's newest Gannet colony is on Ireland's Eye off Co. Dublin; this held 15–20 sites when first discovered in 1989 (O.J. Merne *in litt.*). Britain's newest colony is at Troup Head in northeast Scotland. It was first occupied by Gannets only in 1987 or 1988 (Matthews and North 1989). Other colonies formed since Operation Seafarer are on Foula (1980, Furness 1981a), Fair Isle (1975, Waterston 1976), Shiant Isles (1975, Buxton 1985 but reported abandoned in 1987, S. Angus *in litt.*) in Scotland, and Clare Island, Co. Mayo (1975, Preston 1979) in Ireland. Gannets almost certainly once bred at a number of colonies which are now extinct. These include Gulland Rock (north Cornwall), Lundy (Bristol Channel), Calf of Man (Isle of Man) and in Ireland on the Stags of Broadhaven (Mayo) (Nelson 1978).

In 1984–85, Britain and Ireland held 72% of the world's North Atlantic Gannets or 85% of those breeding in the east Atlantic (Wanless 1987). Including the most recent available counts, 68% of British and Irish Gannets breed in Scotland where the largest colonies are on St Kilda (50,050 sites), Bass Rock (21,600 sites) and Ailsa Craig (22,800 nests). Other large colonies are on Grassholm (30,000 sites) in Wales and Little Skellig (22,500 sites) in southwest Ireland.

Gannets and their colonies are conspicuous and easily found. Occupied nests are relatively simple to count so that Gannets have been censused more frequently than many other seabirds. Early in the life of a colony, single pairs of Gannets amidst crowds of Guillemots might be overlooked but, within a decade of becoming truly established, the gannetry spreads to whiten entire stacks or islands or cliffs. No one can (or should) miss the sight and sound and smell of an occupied Gannet colony. The increase in numbers early this century was noticed promptly, and regular surveys were undertaken to document changes in size of existing Gannet colonies and the formation of new ones. The first of these surveys, reported by Gurney (1913), also attempted to gather information for all 14 of the world's gannetries. Subsequent surveys in the early 1930s, 1939, 1949, 1955–66 and 1969–70 (Cramp *et al.* 1974, Nelson 1978) recorded the Gannet's steady increase and the formation of new colonies.

A new Gannet colony usually takes several years to become well established and then increases in size rapidly, attracting immigrants from other colonies until space or some other limiting factor causes growth to level off. A typical example is the colony of Great Saltee, Co. Wexford (details in Lloyd 1982a). Gannets first prospected the cliffs on the southwest tip of the island in the 1920s but, when one or two pairs finally bred, they produced only three fledged young in over 20 years. In the early 1950s, with enforced protection from disturbance, numbers began to increase quickly and reached 100 nests in 1965. The original cliff was fully occupied by the late 1970s and the Gannets began nesting on top of a stack off the south side of the island where they soon displaced the Guillemots. The colony has continued to grow and spread; it held 595 sites in 1986 and 710 in 1987. Other relatively young gannetries growing at a fast pace are Foula (62% per year 1976–84), Fair Isle (42% per year 1974–85) and the Flannan Isles (18% per year 1969–85) (Murray and Wanless 1986). Long-established Gannet colonies increase slowly by comparison (e.g. Bass Rock 5% per year 1969–85) or remain stable in size, for example, St Kilda (Wanless 1987).

In the St Kilda group, Gannets are spread over the precipitous island of Boreray on cliffs plunging "like a cascade of granite" (Fisher 1952a) over 400 metres to the sea, and on two adjacent stacks which are both more than 250 metres high. Counting Gannets on Boreray is not without problems, but numbers probably remained between 40,000 and 50,000 pairs from 1959 to 1985 (Wanless 1987). Counts earlier this century on St Kilda suggest that Gannets increased only very slightly, from about 14,500 to a maximum of 19,000 pairs, during nearly 50 years. There is no sign of a sudden increase when the human population was evacuated from St Kilda in 1930 and the killing of Gannet chicks ceased. The only likely explanation for the apparent spurt in growth between 1949 (17,035 pairs) and 1959 (44,526 pairs) is that counts in the 1930s and 1940s actually underestimated the size of the population. Otherwise the increase in breeding birds would be greater than could possibly be supplied by immigration from other known gannetries which were also growing fast (Wanless 1987).

Like the Fulmar, Gannets have been a valuable source of food for humans sharing their remote islands. Accounts of fowling on St Kilda suggest that, if the reported harvest is correct, Gannet numbers may once have been higher than they are today. In the late eighteenth century about 20,000 young Gannets were being taken annually from Stac Lee and Stac An Armin (25,350 pairs 1985) (Steel 1965). Fulmars were caught in preference to gannets from the mid eighteenth century onwards, possibly because their numbers had started to increase and they were nesting in more accessible parts of the islands. The Gannets on Boreray and the stacks had to be caught at night, a formidable task when one considers the climbing involved to reach the nests. The men scaled the cliffs in stockinged feet and lassoed sitting birds with a horsehair noose on the end of a rod. The young Gannets, known as gugas, were eaten fresh or dried and stored in stone-huts (cleits). Gannet feathers fetched a high price on the mainland and grease from the corpse was valued for its medicinal properties.

Sula Sgeir, 66 km north of the Western Isles, is the only gannetry in Britain at which chicks are still killed. Men from the parish of Ness on Lewis have traditional rights to the Gannets of Sula Sgeir and they visit the island once a year to take gugas for their own consumption. Before the Wildlife and Countryside Act of 1981, there was no need for licences to take Gannets. No reliable records of the size of the harvest exist, but probably 3000–4500 young birds were taken annually. The current licence is for 2000 chicks. The colony has remained apparently stable since at least 1965 (Murray and Wanless 1986).

REASONS FOR CHANGE IN NUMBERS

The increase in the Gannet breeding population this century has been made possible by the introduction of the bird protection laws about 100 years ago.

Gannets are large and are conspicuous on land and at sea. Despite their inaccessible breeding places, they were vulnerable to guns and egg collectors and to disturbance during the nesting season. Gannets grew in numbers and formed new colonies as the protection laws became effective. Between 1900 and 1940 eight new gannetries were established in Britain, Ireland and France, and only one (Lundy) was deserted (Cramp *et al.* 1974).

In Norway, the choice of sites for new Gannet colonies appeared to follow the distribution of the birds' main prey, Herring and Capelin (Brun 1972). One site in the Lofoten Islands was abandoned in 1978 following a period when local Herring stocks had failed, possibly through over-fishing, and the colony was disturbed. In Scotland, range extension and breeding population growth continued throughout the period (1970s) when the Gannets' main food stocks (Herring and Mackerel) were in decline, perhaps because alternative foods, for instance sandeels, were increasing (Wanless 1987).

Gannets also take advantage of food provided by man in the form of fish discarded by fishing boats. In a study carried out around the Shetland Islands in the mid 1980s, Gannets were found to compete vigorously with other birds for discarded whitefish. Only Great Black-backed Gulls succeeded in obtaining more of the fish than adult Gannets. Gannets were also able to swallow even the largest and most awkward discarded fish which other seabirds ignored (Hudson and Furness 1988, 1989).

Several factors affect Gannet numbers throughout the species' range but none constitutes a significant threat at present. In Norway disturbance and illegal egg collecting were partly responsible for desertion of the colony in the Lofoten Islands referred to above, and may have affected other Gannet colonies too (Brun 1972, Barrett and Vader 1984). In Canada earlier this century, human persecution, erosion of nesting habitat and disturbance during the construction of a lighthouse combined to reduce the gannetry on Bird Rocks in the Gulf of St Lawrence (Brown and Nettleship 1984a). Gannets will tolerate the presence of humans if they are not persecuted. Indeed the spectacular nature of gannetries makes them tourist attractions; many of those in Britain and Ireland are visited regularly by sightseeing boats. Although Gannets are still harvested on Sula Sgeir, and in the Westmann and Faroe colonies, the number of birds collected is limited by law or by tradition and over-exploitation is avoided.

Discarded fishing net, especially the indestructible, brightly coloured polyethylene type, is frequently collected by Gannets for building nests. Both young and adult birds can become entangled and starve to death although overall mortality is low. Toxic chemicals are present at relatively high levels in Gannets and their eggs on both sides of the Atlantic (e.g. Nettleship 1975, Parslow and Jefferies 1977), but numbers have increased despite this in most colonies in Europe. Eggshell thinning, low breeding success and declining numbers between 1966 and 1970 in Gannets on Bonaventure Island, Quebec have been attributed to a variety of causes including pollution of the birds' diet by toxic chemicals, particularly DDE (Nettleship 1975). A marked subsequent improvement in breeding performance coincided with a significant decline in DDT and dieldrin residues in eggs (Chapdelaine *et al.* 1987, Elliott *et al.* 1988).

Table 15.   *World breeding population of the Gannet.*

	No. of AOS	No. of colonies
Iceland	25,000	6
Faroe Islands	2000	1
Norway	2300 nests	5 (+ 1 possible)
Britain	163,000	16
Ireland	24,700	5
France	6000	1
East Atlantic total	223,500	
Newfoundland	11,900 pairs	4
Quebec	27,800 pairs	3
West Atlantic total	39,700 pairs	
World total	263,500 pairs	

One colony not counted in Iceland.

Sources: Wanless (1987), Gardarsson (1989), Seabird Colony Register.

Table 16.   *Numbers of Gannets breeding in Britain and Ireland with year of most recent count in brackets.*

Site name	1984–88		1968–70	
	AOS	Nests	AOS	Nests
Hermaness, Shetland	6900(84)		4300	
Noss, Shetland		9904(86)		5894
Foula, Shetland	124(87)		0	
Fair Isle, Shetland	258(86)		0	
Sule Stack, Orkney	5900(85)		4018	
Sula Sgeir, Western Isles	9143(85)		8964	
St Kilda, Western Isles	50,050(85)		52,099	
Flannans, Western Isles	414(88)		0	
Shiants, Western Isles	1(86),0(87)		0	
Troup Head, Grampian	2(88)		0	
Bass Rock, Lothian	21,591(85)		8077	
Ailsa Craig, Strathclyde	22,811(85)		13,058	
Scar Rocks, Dumfries and Galloway	770(84)		450	
Bempton, North Yorkshire	780(87)		18	
Ortac, Alderney	1985(87)		1000	
Les Etacs, Alderney	2536(87)		2000	
Grassholm, Dyfed		30,000(86)		16,128
Clare Island, Co. Mayo	2(86)		0	
Little Skellig, Co. Kerry	22,500(84)		20,000	
Bull Rock, Co. Cork	1511(85)		1500	
Great Saltee, Co. Wexford	710(87)		155	
Ireland's Eye, Co. Dublin	17(89)		0	
Total Britain and Ireland	187,908		137,661	
No. of colonies	22 (21)		16	

Source: Wanless (1987), Seabird Colony Register.

Cormorant

Phalacrocorax carbo

The Cormorant is a big, black seabird (wing-span 130–160 cm) which is found in coastal waters, estuaries or freshwater lakes and reservoirs. Most breeding colonies are on coastal cliffs, rocky stacks and inshore islands with some on islands in fresh water. Cormorants feed mainly on fish and at sea prefer flatfish, Wrasse, Saithe and Whiting. Estuarine and freshwater fish are also included in the diet (Cramp and Simmons 1977). The birds dive from the surface and swim underwater when fishing, and they collect most of their food on or near the bottom.

INTERNATIONAL DISTRIBUTION AND STATUS

The Cormorant has a worldwide distribution with breeding sites on all continents except South America. It is widely known as the Great Cormorant, or sometimes as the Common Cormorant. In New Zealand it is called the Black Shag, and in Africa the White-breasted Cormorant. There are five subspecies; the nominate *P.c. carbo* breeds in northern Europe with about 28% of its population in Britain and Ireland. *P.c. sinensis* has a huge inland range throughout central and southern Europe, the USSR, India and China and is probably the most numerous subspecies; *P.c. maroccanus*, endemic to northwest Africa, is the rarest (Table 17).

About 14% of the Cormorants in Europe breed in Britain and Ireland, but this proportion is likely to vary with persecution pressures on Cormorants in other countries. Some breeding populations have increased followed recolonisation (Sweden, Denmark) or reintroduction (Belgium), but most fluctuate in response to disturbance and nest destruction during the breeding season and to shooting during winter. The Cormorant is widely regarded as a competitor for fish stocks and thus a pest species. For example, 20,000 Cormorants and Shags were shot each winter from 1971 to 1979 in Norwegian waters. Cormorants have now received legal protection in the north of Norway, but about half the birds were shot in the southwest province of Møre and Romsdal (Barrett and Vader 1984). In Greenland, Cormorants, especially young birds, are hunted for food during winter.

After the breeding season, Cormorants disperse widely from their colonies. They are equally at home in freshwater, brackish water or saltwater habitat, and some birds travel long distances inland into central Asia and Europe. Cormorants very rarely fly over open sea and in the North Sea, for example, they are exclusively coastal (Tasker *et al.* 1987). Analysis of British and Irish ringing recoveries reported up to 1964 showed that birds from different breeding areas tended to show different patterns of dispersal (Coulson and Brazendale 1968). Combined coastal and inland breeding numbers were about 11,700 pairs in 1985–87 (Table 17), and the total population therefore roughly 31,000 to 35,000 birds. The majority of the Cormorants breeding in Britain and Ireland are residents or only move locally.

CENSUS METHODS AND PROBLEMS

Counting Cormorants does not present some of the problems encountered in other seabirds. Cormorant colonies are usually very conspicuous because the birds group their nests close together and a large area becomes covered in their droppings. Plants are killed off and the rocks are distinctively whitewashed. Most colonies are on top of stacks or flat islands and rarely, as at the Mull of Galloway in southwest Scotland and at several sites in Devon, on cliff ledges. Occupied nests are relatively easy to identify as they are usually substantial platforms of seaweed and vegetation cemented together with guano although immature non-breeders construct smaller, flimsy nests from which the material is often quickly stolen by neighbouring birds. Nests with young are obvious from a couple of weeks after hatching since the young are not continuously brooded by the adults; later in the nestling period they leave the nest and stand or hide nearby but, even at this stage, an occupied nest is hard to miss.

The breeding season varies in timing from one year to the next rather more in the Cormorant and Shag than in other seabirds. A census of nests in June one year may catch most birds still with eggs, but the next year may miss many whose young have fledged. Breeding synchrony is also low at many sites so

Plate 12. Cormorant colony on stacks at Braewick, Shetland (Dr M.P. Harris)

that a colony always contains nests at different stages of the breeding cycle. A single count of occupied nests can therefore underestimate numbers of pairs breeding in most colonies. The amount of year-to-year variation in nest counts at Cormorant colonies may also suggest that, like the Shag, a large but variable proportion of the breeding population does not attempt to breed in certain years. This can confuse interpretation of counts (see below).

During both national surveys in 1969–70 and 1985–87, most Cormorant colonies were visited only once, in June, and the birds censused at the same time as other seabirds present. Repeat visits and counts were confined to a handful of colonies where special studies were being made, or where a warden was permanently on hand. A study of the closely related Shag on the Isle of May in the Firth of Forth suggested that both the national surveys may have underestimated numbers by at least 10%. Harris and Forbes (1987) found that 290 sites were used by nesting Shags on the Isle of May during 1986, but only 240 of these were occupied at any one time, 90% of them in June. In addition, Shags which failed to breed successfully often moved to lay again in another nest site in the colony; this also occurs in Cormorants and may add to the error of a single annual census count.

A few counts during both Operation Seafarer and the latest survey were of birds in nesting habitat rather than of nests. Attendance at the breeding colony is more variable for the Cormorant (and Shag) than for almost any other seabird so that census counts of individual birds are of little use. In order to obtain complete regional and national totals, the counts of birds were divided by two, to provide an approximation estimate of pairs. No attempt has been made to "correct" the data for the temporal spread in breeding.

THE CORMORANT IN BRITAIN AND IRELAND

Cormorants breed on all coasts of Britain and Ireland, and have some inland colonies, mainly in the west of Scotland and west of Ireland. The latter were not completely covered by the recent survey (and are excluded from Table 18), but they can be assumed to represent a small proportion of the total population. A total of 10,400 pairs of Cormorants bred on the coasts of Britain and Ireland in 1985–87, compared with 8000 pairs in 1969–70.

Ireland had 50% of the coastal Cormorants in 1985–87, and also the two largest colonies. These were Sheep Island, of north Antrim (380 pairs) and Lambay north of Dublin (1027 pairs). Numbers of Cormorants breeding in Ireland more than doubled overall between 1969–70 and 1985–87, with the biggest increase in the northeast of the country (Figure 11). For example, only 112 pairs of Cormorants bred on Lambay in 1969 (Figure 12). All Irish Cormorant colonies were visited during 1985–86 in a survey organised by the Forest and Wildlife Service following growing concern at the effects of the increase in Cormorants (see below). A total of 4455 pairs were counted, and about 10% of these bred inland, with the main colonies on Lough Scannie (218 pairs) and Lough Cutra (166 pairs) (Macdonald 1987). Cormorants in many of the coastal colonies were counted again in 1986–87, for the Seabird Colony Register, updating the coastal total to over 4200 pairs.

Numbers of Cormorant breeding in England, the Channel Islands and the Isle of Man increased by about a third between Operation Seafarer and 1985–87, whilst those in Wales grew by a lesser amount. The largest colonies were on the Farne Islands (Northumberland) and Marsden Rock (Tyne and Wear) (239 and 153 pairs respectively), and on Little Orme Head and at Llanddeiniol in Wales (198 and 137 pairs). Counts of Cormorant nests at English and Welsh colonies which were visited more than four times between the 1969–70 and 1985–88 surveys showed that numbers mostly increased overall, but also varied widely from year to year (Figure 12).

Relatively few Cormorants breed in Scotland; 2900 pairs or just over a quarter of the Britain and Ireland total were counted there in 1985–87, and 85% of these were in north and west Scotland. A large majority (75%) of nearly 100 colonies found contained less than 50 pairs. The largest colonies were on the Calf of Eday in Orkney (223 pairs), and the North Sutor of Cromarty (203 pairs). The pattern of changes since Operation Seafarer differed between the east coast, and the north and west (Figure 11). Numbers increased by 165% in southeast Scotland, and grew from one to 18 pairs in the northeast. During the same period, there was a significant decline in Cormorant numbers in the rest of Scotland apart from the Orkney Islands and

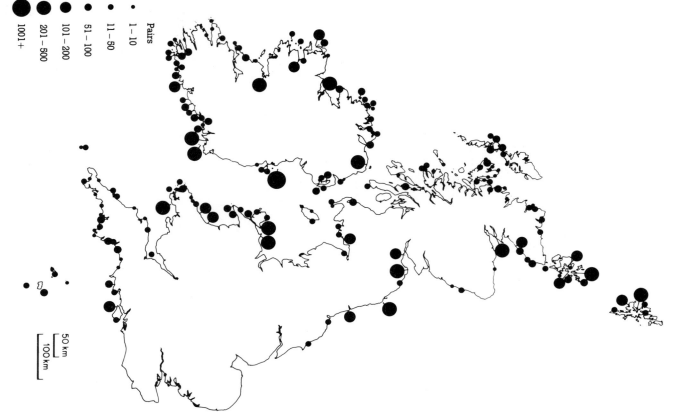

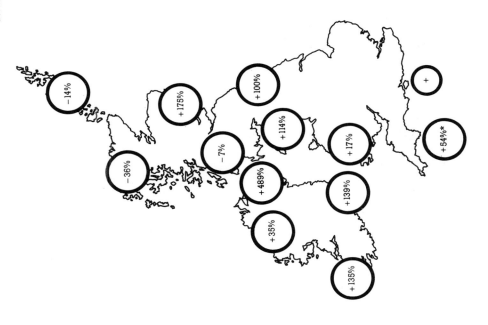

*Figure 11. Regional changes in numbers of coastal breeding Cormorants, 1969–87.
See Table 18 for counts and Figure 1 for regional divisions.
No figure is given if more than 10% of a county/regional total was derived from counts made
as individuals rather than pairs or where totals were less than 100 pairs.
* Cornwall not included.*

the southwest; here changes were so small that the breeding populations probably remained stable. For example, 570 pairs of Cormorants were counted during an aerial survey of Orkney during 1985 (Reynolds and Booth 1987), compared with 590 pairs found during Operation Seafarer.

The seven Cormorant colonies in Shetland had a total of 369 pairs in 1985. (In 1988, eight colonies were occupied and held 356 pairs (Okill 1989).) This was little changed from three years previously when 385 pairs nested, but fewer

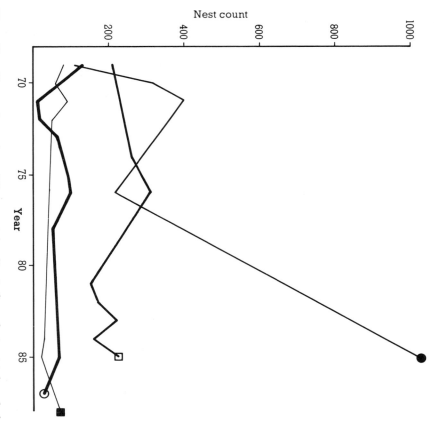

Figure 12.   Changes in numbers of Cormorants breeding in four colonies visited regularly between 1969 and 1987.

○ = *Main Bench Cliff, Isle of Wight.*
△ = *Lambay, Dublin.*
● = *Mattle Island, Clare.*
■ = *Calf of Eday, Orkney.*

than in 1975 (444 pairs) (Okill 1985), and only 78% of the 1969–70 total (500 pairs). Numbers also declined in the Western Isles where several Cormorant sites were abandoned between 1969–70 and 1985–87 (e.g. islands of Gasker and Scarp, off Lewis), and the large freshwater colony on Loch an Tomain in South Uist, which held 122 pairs in 1970, was deserted (Counsell 1983). Island colonies off the west coast of North Uist, on the Monach Isles and Causamul also declined.

During Operation Seafarer, over 825 pairs of Cormorants bred on the east coast of Caithness. By 1986 the colonies between Green Table and Ousdale

Burn had declined from 490 to 127 pairs, and the site between The Needle and Sron Mhor which held a further 162 pairs in 1969 had been deserted.

Sutherland and Wester Ross are the only parts of western Scotland where Cormorants seem to have increased in the last 18–20 years. In fact, an apparent new colony in Sutherland, on Eilean na Saile with 37 pairs in 1987, may have been missed during Operation Seafarer; and the recent figure for Wester Ross is high because of a count on Gruinard (68 pairs 1983) which was certainly not covered in 1969 or 1970 when the island was inaccessible due to anthrax contamination. Further south, the only Cormorant colony in Lochaber found during Operation Seafarer was on Eilean a'Chaolais (45 pairs 1970), and this had disappeared by 1986.

Cormorant colonies seem to fluctuate more widely in size from one year to the next than those of other seabirds. This confuses interpretation of census counts, especially those made on only one visit to a colony, and of breeding population trends. A typical example is the Cormorant colony on Mattle Island off the coast of Clare on the west coast of Ireland which held 82 pairs in 1969 and 70 pairs nineteen years later. During the intervening time numbers had risen to 90 pairs and dropped to 20 (Figure 12). Further confusion is added by the fact that changes in adjacent colonies are inversely related so that when breeding numbers are high in one, they are low in the other, and vice versa. This has been recorded at colonies throughout Britain from Orkney to the Isles of Scilly, and in southeast Ireland (e.g. Figure 13). Movement of breeding birds between colonies is the most likely explanation for this, and observations of ringed Cormorants confirmed that a few adults (probably less than 5%) breed at colonies other than their natal one (R.M. Sellers *in litt.*). However, during a twenty-year study of Cormorants in South Wales at two relatively

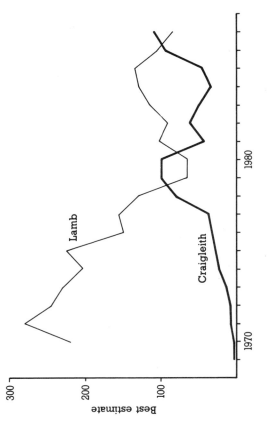

Figure 13. Counts of Cormorant nests at The Lamb and Craigleith in the Firth of Forth.

isolated colonies on St Margaret's Island and Sheep Island (Dyfed), (which has only recently included colour ringing), no birds were seen or recovered anywhere other than their natal colony (S.J. Sutcliffe *in litt.*).

In inland colonies, Cormorants often nest precariously in trees and bushes. After a few seasons, the trees are usually killed by the guano and soon break under the weight of birds and nests; the colony is then forced to move to another site. In parts of Poland where alternative habitat is limited, this destruction of trees has led to the desertion of some Cormorant sites (Przybysz *et al.* 1985). The largest inland Cormorant colonies found in Britain in 1985–87 were on Mochrum Loch in Dumfries and Galloway (415 pairs), and on Abberton Reservoir, Essex (151 pairs). Some inland colonies in central Europe are probably even larger; one in the Netherlands, for example, held 2000 pairs in the 1940s (Veldkamp 1986).

Cormorants sometimes select artificial nest sites. At Moricambe Bay in the Solway Firth and in Rigg Bay further west, Cormorants breed or have bred on platforms used by the army for target practice. Earlier this century, Cormorants nested in ruins on islands in many of the loughs in the west of Ireland (details in Lloyd 1982b). Cormorants are equally flexible elsewhere in the world. The Cape Cormorant *Phalacrocorax capensis*, for example, is encouraged to nest on artificial platforms so that its guano can be more conveniently harvested (e.g. Rand 1963), and the Double-crested Cormorant *Phalacrocorax auritus* in California nests on shipwrecks and abandoned wharves (Hatch 1984).

REASONS FOR CHANGE IN NUMBERS

Little is known about how the Cormorant's food supply may have altered during the last 15–20 years, or how this has influenced numbers. Cormorants in Shetland were apparently not affected by the reduced availability of sandeels in 1988 (Okill 1989) which caused widespread breeding failure in other seabirds (see Chapter 2).

Disturbance and persecution by man is an important factor in the control of breeding numbers and nesting success in most of the Cormorant's range. The species' recent increase and spread in France, for instance, has occurred since widespread protection was enforced in 1973 (Debout 1987). In Britain, although the Cormorant is protected under the 1981 Wildlife and Countryside Act, it may be killed under licence "for the purpose of preventing serious damage to . . . fisheries" (HMSO 1981); the exact definition of "serious damage" has yet to be established by a court. Licences have been issued to owners of riparian fisheries in Scotland, but at present no licences have been issued to fish farmers. However, a recent survey of over 2000 Cormorants and Shags a year shot illegally or tangled in nets, of which about 53% were Cormorants (Ross 1988). This must be considered as a minimum estimate of this type of mortality. The licensing situation in England and Wales is unclear, but much shooting occurs; for instance about 15% of the recoveries of Cormorants ringed at a colony in south Wales were reported as having been shot (R.M. Sellers *in litt.*).

In Ireland, the Cormorant receives complete protection under the 1976 Wildlife Act although some birds are killed illegally. Before the Act was passed, shooting Cormorants was encouraged by a bounty scheme organised by the Department of Fisheries and large numbers of birds were killed each year. Between 1973 and 1976, for example, 3527 Cormorants were shot under the scheme (Macdonald 1987). The contrast between the stable population in Britain (5% increase 1969–87) and the growing one in Ireland (142% increase 1969–87) reflects the difference in enforced legal protection the birds receive.

The Cormorants' habit of gathering into large fishing flocks and of feeding in sealochs, where fish farms are also usually situated, or inland on freshwater bodies favoured by fishermen, has made them widely regarded as pests. Several studies of diet, based on regurgitated pellets found besides nests, have sought to establish whether the birds take significant numbers of commercial fish (e.g. Mills 1969, West *et al.* 1975, Macdonald 1987). In these studies, Wrasse, sandeels and flatfish such as Dab were the most important foods at sea, and Roach and Perch in fresh water.

One of the most detailed studies of Cormorant damage to game fisheries was carried out by the Salmon Research Trust of Ireland (Macdonald 1987). Observations of feeding Cormorants, and of Sea Trout and Salmon smolts in rivers and lakes in the west of Ireland showed that the birds could take up to 9% of the migrating Salmon and Trout in some lakes. However, Brown Trout and many sea fish also acted as major predators of smolt. Most of the Salmon taken by Cormorants were smolt released from hatcheries and not wild ones; these were particularly vulnerable to predators. Macdonald concluded that over-exploitation of Salmon stocks by commercial fisheries, rather than increased predation by the growing Cormorant population, had been the prime cause of low recruitment rates recorded in salmon between 1970 and 1985. Up to 80% of Salmon trying to return and spawn in Irish lakes and rivers were netted at sea, and many of the survivors bore scars from nets when they reached freshwater.

In addition, the large-scale removal of Pike from loughs followed by their intensive stocking with Brown Trout in the 1970s and 1980s caused an increase in the Trout's natural predator, the Perch, which were previously removed by Pike. Perch formed an important part of the Cormorants' diet throughout the year but especially in midwinter, when they provided Cormorants with a buffer against winter mortality (Macdonald 1987).

Cormorant numbers can be controlled by destroying nests with eggs or young, by cutting down nesting trees, and by shooting adults. Persecuted birds become nervous and, as a result, breeding sites are readily deserted during the breeding season. Man has been the main cause of decline in Cormorants in Poland (Przybysz *et al.* 1985), the Netherlands (Veldkamp 1986) and many other parts of Europe (Table 17). In the USA, an official programme of control by spraying eggs took place in Maine from 1944 to 1953 in order to prevent the increase of Double-crested Cormorants. This was made even more effective than expected as it coincided with a natural halt in population growth; numbers did not recover until the 1970s (Hatch 1984).

Some other factors also affect Cormorant numbers. Relatively few Cormorants are caught in fishing nets, even in heavily netted areas such as off northwest Ireland (O.J. Merne pers. comm.). They seem able to avoid surface nets more successfully than other species. In the southeast Kattegat, where many other seabirds are netted, the few Cormorants caught were all found in herring nets rather than gill nets, and at depths of over 10 metres (Oldén et al. 1985).

Pesticide residues and polychlorinated biphenyls (PCB) found in Cormorant eggs in Ireland were not thought to have affected the birds' breeding performance (Wilson and Earley 1986). High levels of mercury and PCB were found in Cormorants and their eggs in the Netherlands, and this may have slowed the growth of some parts of the breeding population (Veldkamp 1986). In addition, concentrations of DDE in Cormorant eggs from the delta of the River Danube were considered high enough to have caused eggshell thinning (Fossi et al. 1984). Pesticide residues have been similarly implicated in the decline of Double-crested Cormorants in New England and on the Great Lakes (Hatch 1984).

Table 17. *Estimated world breeding population of the Cormorant.*

	No. of pairs	Comments
USSR—southeast	<100	
Eastern Canada	100–500	
USA	2030	First nested 1979
West Greenland	750–1500	Recolonised Maine 1983 and Massachusetts 1984
		Hunting pressure despite closed season
Iceland	3500	
Faroe Islands	1–10	Once commmon, now almost extinct
Norway	21,000	Increasing, protected in north
Sweden	3400	Persecuted to extinction 19th century, recolonised late 1940s and increasing
Denmark	14,100	Persecuted to extinction c. 1876, recolonised 1938 and increasing
Netherlands	13,600	Threatened by persecution, land claim and pollution
Britain	7000	Decreasing despite some protection. Includes c. 800 pairs inland
Ireland	4700	Increasing with protection. Includes c. 500 pairs inland
Belgium	<100	Persecuted to extinction 1965, reintroduced 1970
France	1600	Increasing with protection
USSR—Baltic	c. 100	Some new colonies
Poland	5130	Threatened by industrialisation and loss of nesting habitat

	No. of pairs	Comments
East Germany	4100	
West Germany	960	
Austria	<50	
Czechoslovakia	520	
Hungary	600	
Turkey	900	
Spain	1–10	4 known colonies Colonised Medas Islands, near Barcelona 1973
Italy	200	40 on Sardinia and breeding attempt in NE Italy reported 1982, increasing
Tunisia	?	
Yugoslavia	100–1000	Persecuted, various estimates of numbers
Romania	4000	
Bulgaria	600	
Greece	180	Two known colonies
Southern USSR	?	Volga Delta 18,000 pairs, largest Crimean colony 356 pairs
China	?	Domesticated for fishing, wet-land nesting habitat threat-ened by reclamation
India	?	
Mauritania and Senegambia	<1000	Mainly Banc d'Arguin
Namibia	1400	Nesting habitat destroyed by guano harvesting
South Africa	1100	
East Africa	?	Inland
New Zealand	5000–10,000	
Australia	?	"Huge numbers" breed inland especially in SE
Approximate total	110,000–120,000 pairs	

Sources: Cramp and Simmons (1977), Brooke *et al.* (1982), Croxall *et al.* (1984), Røv and Strann (1986), Debout (1987), Van Eerden and Zijlstra (1990), Litvinenko and Shibaev in press, P.G.H. Evans pers. comm., Seabird Colony Register.
? = Breeds, numbers unknown.

Table 18. *Numbers of Cormorants breeding on coasts of Britain and Ireland 1969–87.*

	1985–87		1969–70	
	Pairs	Birds	Pairs	Birds
Shetland Islands	369	—	500	4
Orkney Islands	570	—	587	5
Moray	5	—	1	—
Aberdeen	12	—	—	—
Kincardine and Deeside	1	—	—	—
Dunfermline	137	—	—	—
East Lothian	228	—	152	—
Berwickshire	41	—	1	—
Western Isles	257	—	383	18
Caithness	268	—	825	5
Sutherland	88	1	56	—
Ross and Cromarty	329	—	276	—
Skye and Lochalsh	149	50	144	14
Lochaber	—	2	45	—
Stewartry	130	—	124	—
Wigtown	17	—	148	—
Kyle and Carrick	96	—	97	—
Cunninghame	—	—	14	—
Argyll and Bute	164	10	61	—
Scotland total	2900	63	3400	46
Humberside	—	—	20	—
North Yorkshire	25	—	—	118
Cleveland	36	—	18	—
Tyne and Wear	153	—	25	—
Northumberland	239	—	214	—
Isle of Wight	—	360	184	—
Avon	38	—	39	—
Scilly Isles	51	—	50	—
Cornwall	136	8	147	—
Devon	292	20	178	—
Dorset	197	—	122	—
Channel Islands	105	—	62	—
Cumbria	28	—	1	—
Isle of Man	49	—	35	—
England, Isle of Man and Channel Islands total	1400	390	1100	120
Combined units[a]	1600[a]	—	1200[a]	—
Birds converted to pairs	12%	—	5%	—
West Glamorgan	—	—	10	—
Dyfed	650	—	550	—
Gwynedd	1063	—	908	—
Wales total	1700	—	1500	—

	1985–87		1969–70	
	Pairs	Birds	Pairs	Birds
Antrim	426	—	108	—
Down	210	—	—	—
Dublin	1046	24	317	—
Wicklow	2	—	—	—
Wexford	473	—	388	—
Waterford	342	—	79	—
Cork	446	—	38	—
Kerry	51	—	117	—
Clare	245	—	150	23
Galway	14	—	150	5
Mayo	408	17	159	—
Sligo	205	—	118	—
Donegal	361	—	311	—
Ireland total	4200	40	1900	30
Britain and Ireland total	10,400		8000	

Totals rounded, <100 to nearest 5, 100–1000 to nearest 10, >1000 to nearest 100.

[a] Includes counts of birds divided by 2 to provide estimate of pairs, details in text.

Shag

Phalacrocorax aristotelis

The Shag (wing-span 90–105 cm) is found in coastal waters and, sometimes, in estuaries. Unlike its larger relative the Cormorant, it rarely enters fresh water. Shag colonies are situated on coastal cliffs of the mainland and on offshore islands. The birds dive from the surface to swim and forage underwater for fish. The diet depends upon where the birds are feeding, but those in Britain and Ireland feed mainly on sandeels, Herring and Saithe (Cramp and Simmons 1977).

DISTRIBUTION AND INTERNATIONAL STATUS

The Shag is confined to the northeastern Atlantic and Mediterranean. It has a relatively restricted breeding distribution which stretches from northwest Iceland to Murmansk, south to the Chafarinas Islands off the north coast of Morocco, and east to the coasts of the Black Sea. There are three subspecies; the nominate subspecies breeds in Britain and Ireland and throughout the northwest USSR and northern Europe, south to west Spain and Portugal.

Plate 13. Shag on nest, Farne Islands (Peter Hawkey)

Numbers in the USSR and east Europe are not known, but *P.a. aristotelis* is far more common than the southern subspecies (*P.a. desmarestii*) which nests around the Mediterranean and Black Sea. The third subspecies (*P.a. rigenbachi*) is very rare and is now found only in the Chafarinas Islands where one or two pairs nest (de Juana *et al.* 1984). The world breeding population of the Shag is probably between 70,000 and 180,000 pairs of which Britain and Ireland have over 47,000 pairs (Table 19). These represent about 38% of the European breeding population.

Between 1969–70 and 1985–87 numbers of Shags increased by about a quarter in Britain and may have more than doubled in Ireland. Numbers have also grown in France; the small Brittany breeding population expanded by 5% per annum from 1960 to 1975 (Debout 1987). In northwest Norway (Troms), numbers halved between the 1930s and 1980s, and in the southwest region of Møre and Romsdal numbers halved during the 1970s and 1980s (Barrett and Vader 1984). Elsewhere in Norway the population appeared to be stable or increasing (Røv 1985). Shag numbers were also about stable on the Atlantic coast of Spain in the 1980s (Bárcena *et al.* 1984), although the species was only a rare breeder on the Mediterranean mainland coast. At the same time, colonies in the Balearic Islands were declining, as were those on the north coast of Africa (de Juana 1984). Numbers in the rest of the Mediterranean declined in the 1960s and 1970s, but remained nearly stable in the 1980s (James 1984). Shags declined in probably the largest group of colonies in the Black Sea, situated on the Takhankut peninsula in the Crimea (Golovkin 1984).

Ringing recoveries show that outside the breeding season in northern Europe, most Shags disperse along the coastline away from their colonies (Galbraith *et al.* 1986). A majority of birds remain in coastal waters, sometimes gathering into large wintering flocks; some British birds cross the North Sea to the Norwegian coast. Shags from different areas of Britain show different degrees of consistency in their winter movements. This appears to be related to the availability of sheltered feeding grounds and may be influenced by annual fluctuations in food supply. Almost all (95%) recoveries of Shags ringed at Irish colonies have been reported from Irish coasts, but some birds cross to the west and south coasts of Britain (O.J. Merne *in litt.*).

Shags do not breed inland, or in brackish or freshwater habitats, but throughout the year they roost on land at night. This is usually in the colonies, on other cliffs or on convenient structures such as harbour piers. Shags have even been seen roosting on oil platforms in the North Sea (Tasker *et al.* 1987). Birds wintering on coasts without good roost sites, such as east and southeast England, are often blown inland; some survive but many are grounded and killed or captured alive (Coulson 1961, Galbraith *et al.* 1986).

CENSUS METHODS AND PROBLEMS

Shags nest in a variety of sites from large and conspicuous open cliff colonies to isolated nests under boulders or in caves. At a Normandy colony they even nested under dense thorn bushes (Debout 1987). Although most occupied nests are substantial and obvious, they are often hidden away in deep gullies, in caves or under overhanging rock. Many are missed during a census unless a coastline can be searched thoroughly. The only effective way of surveying inaccessible or indented coastline for this species is by boat. Most of the coast of Shetland and parts of the west of Scotland and its islands was covered in this way in 1985–87. However, since time was limited during both Operation Seafarer and the surveys in 1985–87, deliberate searches for Shag nests were usually not possible. In Shetland, this was known to have reduced the total numbers counted in 1986 (M. Heubeck pers. comm.); the same was probably true in other parts of the country and during Operation Seafarer. Thus the two national surveys are considered to have provided only minimum totals for the Shag.

Unfortunately two features of the Shag's breeding biology make it difficult to obtain an accurate measure of population size at a colony from a single annual count of nests. First, Shags have variable breeding seasons; both the timing of laying and the numbers of weeks over which it is spread vary widely from year to year. On the Isle of May off Fife, for example, first egg dates for 20 of the years between 1962 and 1986 varied from March 23 to May 20, with a mean of April 21 (Harris and Forbes 1987). The degree of synchrony in breeding also varies and this influences the number of occupied nests that can be counted in June. Eggs can be laid any time from March to July although, on the Isle of May, years in which most Shags bred late tended to have the most

Plate 14.   Shag colony at Ladies Bed, Isle of May (Dr M.P. Harris)

synchronised breeding seasons. During a single census count in June, such as those for Operation Seafarer and the Seabird Colony Register, some breeding pairs will be missed because they have already failed in their nesting attempt and abandoned the colony, whilst others will be missed because they have laid early and left the colony with their young. In Harris and Forbes' study, a maximum of 240 (83%) of the total of 290 nests started in the study area were occupied at any one time; over 90% of sites had at least a trace of a nest by mid June and might have been included in a conventional census. In conclusion, counts of Shag nests in June usually underestimate the number of pairs breeding in a colony, but the size of this error varies both from year to year and between colonies.

The other feature of Shag breeding behaviour which biases census results is the fact that large numbers of adults sometimes fail to breed. This appears to be a response to poor feeding conditions, especially a cold spring (Aebischer 1986, Harris *et al.* 1987). Typically a colony shows a sudden drop in numbers of occupied nests compared with the previous year, followed by a swift recovery to more or less its previous size, usually within a few years (Figure 14). However, the scale of the decline and the rate and extent of recovery varies from one colony to the next. Similar annual variation in numbers of breeding birds have been recorded at colonies elsewhere in the Shag's range (e.g. Chapdelaine 1980). In those colonies where nests are counted regularly, these temporary crashes in numbers of nesting Shags can be detected. But most

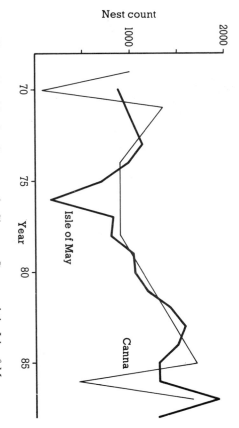

Figure 14. Non-breeding years for Shags on Canna and the Isle of May.

Shag colonies in Britain and Ireland have been censused very rarely, possibly only during Operation Seafarer and the 1985–87 counts, for example. If one of these surveys coincided with a non-breeding year or recovery from such an event, counts would not have reflected the size of the breeding population at that colony.

During both Operation Seafarer and the Seabird Colony Register Surveys, Shags were counted as apparently occupied nest sites (AOS). At some colonies where precise counts of Shag nests were found to be impossible, such as at colonies with extensive boulder scree, birds on land near apparent nest sites were counted instead. In order to obtain complete population estimates, counts of birds were divided by two and added to counts of nests. This will probably have added considerable and unquantifiable error to some of the totals for Scotland, Wales and Ireland in Table 20.

THE SHAG IN BRITAIN AND IRELAND

About three-quarters of the Shags in Britain and Ireland (72%) nested in Scotland and Northumberland in 1985–87. The rest were mostly in small colonies scattered around the remaining coastline. Apart from colonies on the Isle of Wight, no Shags bred between Flamborough Head, Humberside and Durlston Head, Dorset. There were colonies of over a thousand pairs on Foula (2400 pairs), Shiants (1776), Lambay (1597), Isle of May (1524) and the Farne Islands (1248). Numbers had increased by almost 40% since 1969–70, from 33,800 pairs to 47,300 pairs in 1985–87.

The biggest increase in numbers of breeding Shags appeared to have taken place in the northeast of England where counts were almost six times higher in

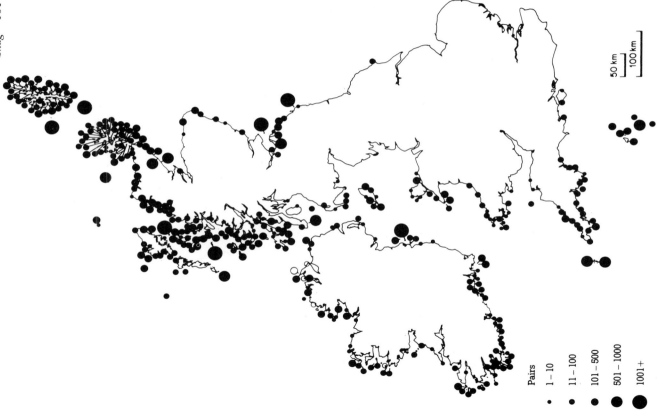

50 km
100 km

Pairs

• 1 – 10

• 11 – 100

● 101 – 500

● 501 – 1000

● 1001+

Empty circles: coastline segments that held
more than 1% of Ireland's Shags in 1969 – 70
and were not surveyed 1985 – 87.

Figure 15. Distribution and size of Shag colonies (and grouped colonies), 1985–87.

1985–87 than they had been in 1969–70 (Figure 16). However, the main colony in the area, on the Farnes Islands, held only 161 nests in 1969 following the death of 80% of the breeding Shags in a "red tide" incident during the previous year (Coulson *et al.* 1968). Five years later, 368 nests were present and numbers had returned to their pre-crash levels. By 1987, the population had increased to 1248 pairs.

The only exceptions to the overall increase in Shags since 1969 were on

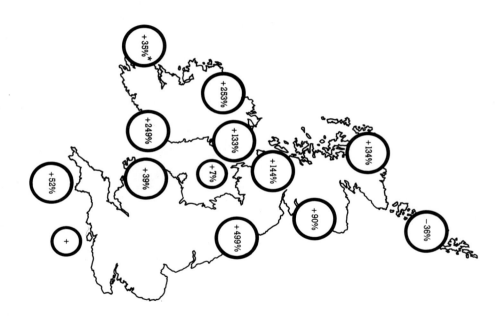

Figure 16. Regional changes in numbers of breeding Shags, 1969–87. See Table 20 for counts and Figure 1 for regional divisions.

No figure is given if more than 10% of a county/regional total was derived from counts made as individuals rather than pairs or where totals were less than 400 pairs.

* Excludes Cork and Clare.

Shetland and Orkney, where numbers have declined by 38% and 30% respectively; and on the Isle of Man where the breeding population remained about stable. Annual counts at study colonies in Shetland indicated that the main decline in Shag numbers since 1969–70 occurred in the 1980s (M. Heubeck per. comm.).

REASONS FOR CHANGE IN NUMBERS

Short-term variations in food availability appear to influence how many of the Shags in the breeding population attempt to nest each year. This seems to occur to a greater degree in the Shag than in other seabirds so that annual changes in total numbers of breeding birds do not give a clear indication of long-term population trends. British and Irish birds are non-migratory, inshore feeders, which gives them little latitude for flexibility in diet or foraging range when faced with declining food supplies. In Norway, by contrast, where Shags are migratory, wintering grounds shifted in the 1970s as Herring stocks declined (Johansen 1975). Some local breeding failures during the 1980s coincided with the collapse of Norwegian Saithe stocks which formed an important food source for Shags (Barrett and Vader 1984).

Shags are rigid rather than opportunistic in their choice of where to nest, compared, for example, with many species of terns, some gulls and even the closely related Cormorant, whose colonies move around from year to year. Most Shags are also faithful to their natal colony both before and after they start to breed. Potts (1969) estimated that emigration of Shags from the Farne Islands before their first breeding attempt at the age of two years was only 8%; fewer than 1% of breeding adults from the Farnes moved to another colony. However, Shags were known to have moved between adjacent colonies in the Isles of Scilly during the early 1980s, apparently in order to avoid disturbance (Birkin and Smith 1987).

Generally, Shags respond to deteriorating feeding conditions, especially in spring, by not breeding. Between 1973 and 1976, the number of Shags nesting on the Isle of May halved from over a thousand pairs. A similar drop in breeding numbers occurred at the colony in 1985–86. The decline was not accompanied by increased adult mortality or by more emigration from the colony; numbers of occupied nests on the island simply fell and recovered soon afterwards. Harris *et al.* (1987) suggested that between 10% and 35% of the breeding adults on the Isle of May failed to nest in 1985 or 1986 or both years. Similar non-breeding years may have caused the dips in annual counts of Shags breeding at other colonies (e.g. Figure 14).

Studies at two Shag colonies on the east coast of Britain, at the Farne Islands and the Isle of May, have linked feeding conditions to breeding ecology, non-breeding years and survival (Potts 1969, Aebischer 1986). Prolonged periods of onshore winds, rough seas and heavy rainfall may have caused one of the main dietary components, sandeels, to become scarce or unavailable to Shags. This kind of weather preceded many of the eruptions of Shags from the Farne Islands, during which birds moved unusually long distances from the colony.

A combined failure of both Herring and sandeel stocks during the breeding season was considered to be the main reason for the non-breeding years on the Isle of May in 1974–76 and 1985–86. The pairs which did manage to nest laid later and bred with less success than usual. Aebischer (1986) found that the timing of laying in the Shags was closely related to the abundance of young Herring in the waters off the Isle of May in February, although it was not clear from his study whether the lack of Herring, or some other factor related to Herring abundance, caused the Shags to delay or refrain from laying. Additional evidence from a study of Puffins on the island suggested that sandeels may have been scarce or unavailable to seabirds in 1974–76 and 1985–86. Production of Shag chicks was reduced and juvenile mortality occurred earlier than usual in these years.

The introduction of bird protection laws in Britain and several other European countries around the turn of the century led to a gradual reduction in the amount of persecution of Shags. During the last few decades, for which data on breeding numbers are available, Shags have increased in most of Europe. However, in many countries Shags are still regarded by fishermen, and recently by fish farmers, as pests. In addition, many hundreds of Shags were shot each year in Norway in the 1970s, mainly for sport (Barrett and Vader 1984).

Both Shags and Cormorants receive legal protection in Britain, but Shags are easily confused with Cormorants which can still be shot under licence. Before the Wildlife Act was passed in Ireland in 1976, bounty schemes operated for the Cormorants in many parts of the country and large numbers of Shags were also shot in cases of mistaken identity (occasionally deliberate). Cormorants and Shags are now legally protected in Ireland and since 1969 both species have increased there by more than in Britain (for Shag by perhaps as much as 190% in Ireland, versus 24% in Britain).

Several other factors may affect numbers of Shags breeding in Britain and Ireland and the rest of Europe. On the Farne Islands, the number of suitable nest sites for Shags was limited during the 1970s and this was expected to restrict the breeding population (Potts *et al.* 1980). A similar situation may exist in crowded colonies elsewhere. Relatively few British Shags die by becoming entangled in fishing gear such as nets or lobster pots; for example, only 16.5% of ringing recoveries of Isle of May birds resulted from drowning in fishing gear (Galbraith *et al.* 1981). However, nearly 40% of recoveries of Shags ringed in Ireland during the 1980s were caused by fishing nets, mostly on the Irish coast (O.J. Merne *in litt.*). In Norway, thousands of Shags are caught every year in fishing nets (Barrett and Vader 1984). Netting of Shags also occurs on the Atlantic coast of Spain (Bárcena *et al.* 1984) and around Corsica (Guyot 1988). In addition, Spanish Shag chicks in both Atlantic and Mediterranean colonies are harvested for human consumption; and in the Balearic Islands the adult birds are persecuted by fishermen (de Juana 1984).

Many Shags die after becoming oiled, probably far more than are reported by Beach Bird Surveys because the naturally dark plumage often leads to oiling being overlooked. Pesticide derivatives, organochlorines and other toxic chemicals, especially mercury, have been found at high levels in Shags' eggs in Britain (Potts 1968, Coulson *et al.* 1972), Ireland (Wilson and Earley 1986) and Norway (Barrett *et al.* 1985), but without any obvious effect upon breeding performance. Finally, Shags seem to be particularly susceptible to the toxins produced by planktonic dinoflagellates during "red tide" incidents. For example, 80% of the breeding birds on the Farne Islands were killed in 1968 and 60% in 1975 by red tides (Coulson *et al.* 1968, Armstrong *et al.* 1978).

Table 19. *Estimated world breeding population of the Shag.*

	No. of pairs	Comment
USSR—Murmansk	1000–10,000	Unknown, Order 4
USSR—Baltic Sea	<500	Unknown
Iceland	6600	
Faroe Islands	5000–10,000	Unknown, Order 4
Norway	10,000–100,000	Unknown, Order 5, local declines but stable overall
Britain	38,500	Increased since 1969
Ireland	8800	Increased since 1969
North France	2900	Mainly in Brittany, increasing
Portugal	100–150	Approximately stable
Spain	2100–2200[a]	Most on Balearics, rare on mainland, declining
France—South	1000[a]	
Italy	1190[a]	
Yugoslavia	1000[a]	
Greece	<500[a]	Declined in past, now stable
Turkey		
Cyprus	50[a]	
Libya and Tunisia	<100[a]	
Algeria	20–40[a]	
USSR—Black Sea	<1000	Unknown, probably declining
Approximate total	c. 70,000–180,000 pairs	

Sources: Cramp and Simmons (1977), Croxall *et al.* (1984), (note figure in Barrett and Vader 1984 is incomplete), Hémery *et al.* (1988), E. Benussi (MEDMARAVIS) pers. comm., P.G.H. Evans pers. comm., Seabird Colony Register.

[a] 10,000 pairs reported recently in Mediterranean (Paterson 1989).

Table 20. *Numbers of Shags breeding in Britain and Ireland 1969-88.*

	1985-87		1969-70	
	Pairs	Birds	Pairs	Birds
Shetland Islands	6003	962	10,536	—
Orkney Islands	2433	356	3709	30
Banff and Buchan	552	—	243	—
Gordon	23	—	10	—
Aberdeen	4	—	3	—
Kincardine and Deeside	54	—	37	—
Angus	25	—	28	—
Northeast Fife	1536	880	880	—
Dunfermline	28	—	—	—
East Lothian	507	—	438	—
Berwickshire	666	—	149	—
Western Isles	4719	21	2749	28
Caithness	2655	5	1557	75
Sutherland	1819	60	2076	40
Ross and Cromarty	421	—	594	—
Skye and Lochalsh	2522	31	660	—
Lochaber	2022	234	1153	40
Argyll and Bute	4883	254	1774	—
Cunninghame	11	—	22	—
Kyle and Carrick	47	—	211	—
Wigtown	178	—	129	—
Stewartry	3	—	12	—
Scotland total	31,100	1900	27,000	215
Combined units[a]	32,100[a]		27,100[a]	
Birds converted to pairs	3%			
Northumberland	1251	—	164	—
North Yorkshire	—	—	45	—
Humberside	15	47	13	—
Isle of Wight	—	37	10	—
Dorset	79	—	51	8
Devon	290	1	138	—
Cornwall	675	—	684	3
Scilly Isles	1156	—	1000	—
Channel Islands	1453	11	570	—
Isle of Man	608	—	567	—
England, Isle of Man and Channel Islands total	5500	96	3200[a]	10
Combined units	5600[a]			

	1985–87		1969–70	
	Pairs	Birds	Pairs	Birds
West Glamorgan	1	—	2	—
Dyfed	150	5	198	—
Gwynedd	605	10	317	65
Wales total	760	15	520	65
Combined units[a]	770[a]		550[a]	
Birds converted to pairs			6%	
Antrim	212[b]	1	195	—
Down	62	—	23	—
Dublin	1734	—	271	—
Wicklow	7	—	5	—
Wexford	571	—	327	—
Waterford	160	—	105	—
Cork	437	—	178	74
Kerry	393[b]	120[b]	392	114
Clare	71	—	34	194
Galway	122[b]	22[b]	152	—
Mayo	264[b]	33[b]	214	—
Sligo	241[b]	—	34	—
Donegal	647[b]	214[b]	879	2
Ireland total	4900	400	2800	400
Combined units + estimate	8800[c]		3000[a]	
Birds converted to pairs or estimated	45%		6%	
Britain and Ireland total	47,300[c]		33,800[a]	

Totals rounded, <100 to nearest 5, 100–1000 to nearest 10, >1000 to nearest 100.

[a] Includes counts of birds divided by 2 to provide an estimate of pairs, details in text.
[b] These are numbers counted. In these counties, at least 10% more pairs are estimated to occur at colonies not visited in 1985–87. At least an estimated 75% of Donegal's Shags were not counted.
[c] This total includes estimates for colonies not counted recently. It is based on the proportional change in numbers at colonies in each region where counts were conducted in both surveys.

Arctic Skua

Stercorarius parasiticus

Two species of skuas breed in Britain, both of them only in Scotland; the Arctic Skua is the smaller of the two (wing-span 96–114 cm). Colonies are often no more than a loose group of scattered breeding territories, and most are found on coastal moorland near other seabird colonies. Skuas obtain most of their food by piracy (also called kleptoparasitism), chasing other seabirds and forcing them to regurgitate or drop the food they are carrying. Arctic Skuas are incredibly agile in the pursuit and harrying of their "host" species and in swooping to catch any food the host drops before it reaches the ground or sea. Arctic Skuas in Scotland chase mainly smaller seabirds such as auks, terns and Kittiwakes and steal sandeels and other small fish from them. They can also fish for themselves from surface waters, and sometimes scavenge behind fishing boats but are rather unsuccessful in competition with larger scavengers. Some Arctic Skuas also prey on seabird eggs and chicks on the breeding grounds (Cramp and Simmons 1983, Furness 1987).

INTERNATIONAL DISTRIBUTION AND STATUS

The Arctic Skua is one of only two seabirds breeding in Britain with a truly circumpolar distribution; the other is the Arctic Tern. Its breeding distribution extends as far south as the Kamchatka peninsula and the Aleutian Islands in the Pacific, and northern Scotland in the Atlantic. A consequence of this broad range is that Arctic Skuas are relatively numerous and may actually be the most abundant skua in the world (Furness 1987). The huge breeding populations in Canada, Alaska and the USSR have never been censused so that the world population is unknown, but it is likely to lie between 100,000 and 300,000 pairs (Table 21). The closely related Long-tailed and Pomarine Skuas (*Stercorarius longicaudus* and *S. pomarinus*), by comparison, have breeding populations each estimated to be about 100,000 pairs (Furness 1987).

The Arctic Skua has two distinct plumage phases and is one of the few polymorphic European seabirds. Light-coloured birds predominate in the far north of the breeding range and on the tundra of northern Canada. In Iceland, Norway and Scotland, dark birds are in the majority and the percentage of light birds has decreased in the last 50 years (Furness 1987).

Within Britain, Arctic Skuas breed only in north and west Scotland. They nest both further inland and further south than the Great Skua. Neither species has ever been recorded breeding in Ireland. An estimated 3350 pairs of Arctic Skuas nested in Scotland in 1985–87 and these represented roughly 20% of the European population. The skua's numbers appeared to have increased substantially in Scotland since Operation Seafarer (Table 22). Colonies where the skuas have been counted regularly (e.g. Foula) have increased for much of the last 100 years. The only other breeding population whose status is known is on the Faroe Islands where numbers have declined during the last 25 years (Furness 1987).

The Arctic Skua has an enormous range outside the breeding season, described by Furness (1987) from ringing recoveries off Shetland breeding birds and from recorded sightings. From across their circumpolar range, birds migrate south from their nesting grounds into the Pacific, Indian and Atlantic Oceans. They move long distances over land through central Asia, northern Africa and North America, but most follow the oceanic coastlines southwards. Wintering areas are mainly in the temperate zones of South America, southwest and southern Africa, southern Australia and New Zealand.

Few birds remain in the northern hemisphere during the winter; none were seen between January and March during a seven year study of birds in the North Sea (Tasker *et al.* 1987). Arctic Skuas breed for the first time at about four years of age and most immature birds remain in the wintering areas during the northern summer; some follow the adults slowly northwards to the breeding grounds or wander widely in northern waters.

CENSUS METHODS AND PROBLEMS

Counting Arctic Skuas can be difficult due to the birds' habit of nesting at low density over wide areas of suitable moorland habitat. The species' breeding biology and behaviour has been studied at length in the last 40 years, partly because of interest in the causes of variations of plumage colour. These studies have aided the development of census techniques and interpretation of results. Most is known about the Arctic Skua populations on the islands of Fair Isle (e.g. Berry and Davis 1970, O'Donald and Davis 1975) and Foula (Furness 1980). The recommended census technique (details in chapter on Great Skua pages 118–119), uses an "apparently occupied territory" (AOT), as defined by Ewins *et al.* (1988), as the counting unit. This unit can be counted relatively easily with reasonable consistency and provides more accurate results than other units used in the past. Counts of AOT may underestimate actual breeding numbers by about 4% (Furness 1982, Ewins et al. 1988).

The census method recommended for skuas during the Operation Seafarer survey was to walk through a known nesting area several times and to estimate the number of territories. This is even more difficult to do for the Arctic Skua than the Great Skua, especially when censusing other seabirds at the same time. Operation Seafarer covered only coastal colonies and, though some inland skua areas were visited, many Arctic Skua territories were not counted. A survey of both inland and coastal nesting areas in 1974 and 1975 used "pairs holding territories" as the counting unit (Everett 1982). AOTs were used by surveys of skuas in Orkney in 1982 (Meek et al. 1985) and in Shetland in 1985 and 1986 by the RSPB, NCC and others (Ewins et al. 1988). Elsewhere in Scotland, Arctic Skuas in Caithness were counted during an Upland Bird Survey by the NCC (Reed et al. 1983) and all coastal breeding sites were visited between 1986 and 1987 during the surveys for the Seabird Colony Register. A combination of these data provided the 1985-87 census with complete coverage for the Arctic Skua in Scotland.

Some counts made for Operation Seafarer and for the Seabird Colony Register were recorded as individual birds on territories rather than AOT. There is no reliable way of converting counts of birds to occupied territories but fortunately the proportion of the counts in the wrong unit is small. The total count of AOT in each case has been rounded up (as indicated in Table 22) to allow for these few extra territories.

THE ARCTIC SKUA IN SCOTLAND

Scottish Arctic Skuas increased from a minimum of 1050 pairs in 1969–70 to about 3350 pairs in 1985–87, when about 57% of the birds nested in Shetland and a further 36% in Orkney. Arctic Skuas were spread more evenly throughout Shetland than Great Skuas, but large concentrations of territories occurred on Foula (168 in 1987), Fair Isle (95 in 1987) and in the northern islands (Unst 267, Yell 192, Fetlar 180). Operation Seafarer instructions did not define "coastal" and "inland" seabird colonies, but it has been assumed that most of the skua colonies more than 1 km from the sea would have been out of sight of the coast and would have been excluded from the 1969–70 survey. Ewins et al. (1988) found that 40% of Arctic Skuas in Shetland bred more than 1 km from the nearest sea. If this were so in 1969–70, the total population would have been about 1000 pairs compared with the 709 pairs recorded on the Seafarer cards. Everett (1982) recorded a minimum of 1631 pairs of Arctic Skuas in Shetland in 1974–75; an apparent increase of 64% in five years. However, when Ewins et al. (1988) re-analysed the 1974–75 counts and compared them, where possible, with the results of the 1985–86 survey, they found that Arctic Skuas had increased by less than 1% a year overall, with a slight decline in numbers on the islands but increases on the mainland.

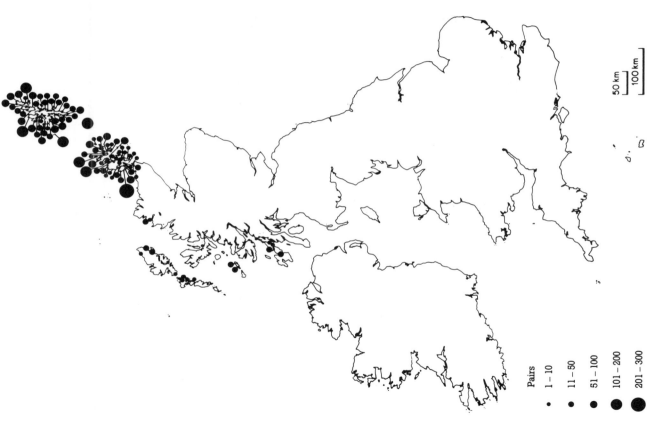

Pairs

· 1–10

• 11–50

● 51–100

⬤ 101–200

⬤ 201–300

50 km

100 km

Figure 17.   *Distribution and size of coastal Arctic Skua colonies (and grouped colonies), 1985–87. Detailed mapping of Shetland colonies in Ewins et al. (1988), and Orkney in Meek et al. (1985).*

In Orkney, the largest concentration of Arctic Skuas was on Hoy where 407 territories were counted in 1982 (Meek *et al.* 1985). If 40% of the Orkney skuas also nested out of sight of the sea in 1969–70, the total breeding population at the time of Operation Seafarer would have been about 360 pairs. Even allowing for this, numbers nearly doubled, to 716 pairs, by 1974–75 (Everett 1982) and increased to 1034 pairs by 1982 (Meek *et al.* 1985). Arctic Skua territories were counted in a few parts of Orkney during the Seabird Colony Register survey 1986–87. The areas for which recent counts are available held 248 territories in 1982 (24% of the total); these areas had 209 AOT and 182 birds on territories in 1986–87. Where AOT had been counted in both 1982 and 1986–87, numbers had increased by 15% overall. Assuming that a similar increase took place in the whole of Orkney, the 1985–87 Arctic Skua total was estimated at 1190 pairs. As in Shetland, the breeding population was growing, but more slowly than during the 1970s.

On the mainland of Scotland, Reed *et al.* (1983) recorded 41–43 occupied Arctic Skua territories in Caithness during 1979–80, with several new sites and an overall increase in numbers since 1974–75. Nine of the sites visited in 1979–80 were resurveyed in 1987 (NCC Moorland Bird Study, unpublished). Despite some afforestation at four of the sites, Arctic Skua numbers had remained stable or increased in all but two of the nine partly-afforested sites. Two new sites were found during surveys for the Seabird Colony Register in Caithness; six Arctic Skuas were recorded on territories at Holborn Head and two occupied territories were found on the island of Stroma in the Pentland Firth. The Caithness breeding population was estimated to be over 60 pairs and was considered to have been increasing since at least 1969–70.

The main Sutherland colony in 1985–87 was on Handa where Arctic Skuas had increased from one pair in 1970 to 30 territories in 1986. A new breeding site was recorded on the mainland nearby, at Rubha Shois in 1987. Arctic Skuas also increased in the Western Isles between 1969–70 and 1985–87; there were nine known breeding areas compared with only three in Operation Seafarer. Further south, the skuas nested on Coll (49 AOT in 1987) and Jura (42 AOT + 27 birds in 1987), but were not proved breeding on Colonsay where they nested in 1975 (Everett 1982).

The two most important factors allegedly affecting Arctic Skua numbers in Scotland during the 1980s were loss of nesting habitat and increasing Great Skua numbers (see below for details). For various reasons, these are both likely to become significant threats in future. The Shetland skua survey showed that Arctic Skuas preferred to nest in short heather moorland or maritime heath or the distinctive heathland covering serpentine bedrock (Ewins *et al.* 1988). In general, Great Skuas differed in their choice of habitat, selecting moors with long vegetation for nesting. Very few skuas of either species attempted to nest on agricultural grassland.

In the 1980s huge amounts of moorland in both Shetland and Orkney were modified for grazing or reclaimed for agriculture. One application of lime in spring is sufficient to kill most heather plants and allow grass to grow within a few months. Such areas are usually fenced in and surface seeded, and stocking levels are then increased to take advantage of the improved grazing with the result that moorland can be swiftly transformed into a close-cropped green sward. Some moorland is ploughed and then re-seeded for grazing or used to grow arable crops or trees. Much of the natural habitat "improved" in this manner is the short vegetation on moors and heaths preferred by nesting Arctic Skuas. On Sanday in Orkney, where extensive heathland destruction occurred in the late 1970s, numbers of Arctic Skuas fell from 45 to 25 territories between the 1974 and 1982 surveys (Meek et al. 1985). However, large areas of moorland were also ploughed on the nearby islands of Stronsay and Eday, but there skua numbers increased. Alternative habitat is usually available to the skuas but the continual shrinkage of suitable nesting areas brings them into potential conflict with man and with Great Skuas.

Great Skuas have been blamed for alleged declines of Arctic Skuas in Shetland earlier this century. Furness (1987) concluded that the claims were based on circumstantial evidence and that, for colonies where counts are available, Arctic Skua numbers had been growing at the same time as those of the Great Skua. Arctic Skuas were most under pressure near the very large Great Skua colonies on Foula, Hermaness, Noss and Fair Isle. Here the smaller skuas were forced into the poorest nesting habitats, causing their breeding density to increase (although the rise in density was especially marked on Foula and Noss where Arctic Skuas were unable to move into new areas). This competition for space tended to lead to smaller Arctic Skua nesting territories and to encourage predation by Great Skuas on Arctic Skuas and their young. At present the Arctic Skuas seem able to withstand the conflict with Great Skuas, with no significant effect on Arctic Skua numbers. Although Great Skuas killed over 3% of adult Arctic Skuas on Foula in 1975 and nearly 15% of their fledglings, there was no sign that the amount of predation had changed in the previous six years during which time Arctic Skua numbers on the island had risen from 100 to 250 pairs (Furness 1977, 1987).

Arctic Skuas in Scotland feed themselves and their young during the breeding season by stealing fish from other seabirds. This habit makes it necessary for the skuas to nest as close as possible to colonies of seabirds such as Arctic Terns, Kittiwakes and auks from which they can obtain a constant food supply. Where Arctic Skuas nest far from the sea and away from other seabirds, such as on the arctic tundra, the diet is mainly berries, insects and small mammals. Kleptoparasitism occurs in the Arctic Skua populations of Iceland, the Faroe Islands and Scotland; the habit has been studied on Foula and elsewhere in Shetland by Furness (1981b). The skuas' preferred target species were Puffins and Arctic Terns, depending on the breeding numbers of these host species in any one year and the size of the fish, mainly sandeels, which the Puffins and terns brought to their chicks. Sometimes both Great and Arctic Skuas chased the same group of birds. This usually resulted in lower success for the skuas in obtaining fish because of interference in chases and increased caution on the part of the host species.

Until the early 1980s, Scottish Arctic Skuas seemed to be able to find enough food for themselves and their chicks without much difficulty, and they spent as little as one-third of their time foraging (Furness 1980). The recent decline in sandeel availability around Shetland (see second chapter Part 1) influenced Arctic Skuas in several ways. The consequent large-scale breeding failures in Arctic Terns and **Kittiwakes** meant that colonies were deserted early in the season, leaving few, if any, birds carrying fish for the skuas to rob. In the long-term, repeated breeding failure is likely to lead to a decline in these host species, with corresponding adverse effects on the Arctic Skua. Even by 1987 the skuas on Foula were having to work harder for their food during the breeding season (Hamer *et al.* in press).

Great Skuas also feed directly on sandeels and, if the latter continue to be scarce, it seems likely that Great Skuas will turn increasingly to robbing or killing Arctic Skuas and other seabirds. Great Skuas scavenge for discarded fish behind whitefish trawlers around Shetland. Recent changes in legal mesh size for fishing nets (see chapter on Great Skua) means that fewer suitable fish will be available to Great Skuas from this source in future (Furness 1988). This too may force the Great Skuas to compensate by using other feeding methods which may adversely affect Arctic Skuas. In 1988 on Foula, for example, when adult Arctic Skuas spent less time than usual on their breeding territories, almost every one of their chicks was killed by Great Skuas (R.W. Furness *in litt.*).

Other threats to Arctic Skuas include loss of habitat through peat-digging or heather-burning, and disturbance from tourists and egg collectors, but none of these were considered serious by Everett (1982) or Ewins *et al.* (1988). The birds' aggressive defence of nesting territories by dive-bombing and harassing intruders makes them a prime target for human persecution. The recent decline of Arctic Skuas in the Faroe Islands was attributed partly to human interference (Furness 1987). Arctic Skuas are more skilful and more persistent than Great Skuas in venting their aggression and are widely regarded as annoying, or even threatening, to humans (Meek *et al.* 1985, Ewins *et al.* 1988). Arctic Skuas in Shetland have been blamed for disturbing livestock, particularly sheep, preventing them grazing, causing stampedes and occasionally disrupting the mustering of flocks by attacking and distracting sheep dogs. This interference is usually tolerated, with little or no persecution except on Fair Isle. Here the exceptionally high density of Arctic Skuas has brought them into conflict with the local community and birds have been shot and nests destroyed.

Table 21. *Estimated world breeding population of the Arctic Skua.*

	Apparently occupied territories/pairs	Comments
USSR	50,000–100,000	100,000–200,000 birds (Ilyichev and Zubakin 1988)
Alaska	10,000–100,000	
Canada	10,000–100,000	
Greenland	1000–10,000	
Svalbard	1000–10,000	
Jan Mayen	30[a]	
Iceland	4000	
Faroes	1300	
Norway	8000	
Sweden	400	
Finland	400	
Scotland	3350	
Approximate total	90,000–340,000 pairs	

[a] No survey since 1940.

Sources: Furness (1987), Ilyichev and Zubakin (1988), Hildén (1988), Seabird Colony Register.

Table 22. *Numbers of Arctic Skuas breeding in Scotland 1969–87 (AOT = apparently occupied territories).*

	1985–87		1969–70[a]	
	AOT	Birds	AOT	Birds
Shetland Islands	1899	—	709	1
Orkney Islands	1190[b]	—	253	7
Western Isles	65	19	36	—
Caithness	60[c]	—	—	21
Sutherland	31	—	1	—
Argyll and Bute	91	27	21	12
Scotland total	3336	46	1041	20
Combined units	c. 3350		c. 1050	

[a] Operation Seafarer excluded many inland colonies.

[b] Estimate allowing for 15% increase since 1982; see text for details

[c] Estimate, from last complete survey in 1979–80 and partial update in 1987; see text for details.

Great Skua

Catharacta skua

The Great Skua, or Bonxie as it is known in Orkney and Shetland, is the most aggressive of all European seabirds. With a wing-span of 145–155 cm, it is also one of the largest. Some Great Skua breeding colonies are very big, but most are loose groups of scattered nests, usually on moorland near the sea. Great Skuas in Scotland collect most of their food during the breeding season by scavenging behind trawlers or fishing for sandeels. They also feed by aerial piracy, chasing seabirds such as auks, terns, Kittiwakes and even Gannets until they are forced to regurgitate or drop their own food; and by predation of other seabirds, their eggs and chicks (Furness 1987).

INTERNATIONAL DISTRIBUTION AND STATUS

The Great Skua is the nominate subspecies of *Catharacta skua*; the other subspecies (Tristan Skua *C.s. hamiltoni*, Falkland Skua *C.s. antarctica* and Brown Skua *S.c. lonnbergi*) are confined to the southern hemisphere. This makes the Great Skua the only vertebrate species to breed naturally in both the north and south sub-polar regions (Furness 1987). (The Leach's Petrel is the only other seabird in Britain and Ireland which may also breed in the southern hemisphere.) The Great Skua has a current world breeding population of

116

Plate 15.   Great Skuas (Peter Moore)

about 13,600 pairs (Table 23), compared with about 2500 pairs of Tristan Skuas, 4000 pairs of Falkland Skuas and 7000 pairs of Brown Skuas (Furness 1987). The Scottish breeding population of the Great Skua is about 7900 pairs and represents 58% of the subspecies' estimated world total.

Very little is known about the history of most British and Irish seabird breeding populations before the eighteenth century. Clues to the distribution of some species can be found among the bones retrieved during the excavation of middens in ancient human settlements. Great Skua remains are absent from these deposits suggesting that, unlike other species, it is a relative newcomer to Europe and indeed to the North Atlantic. In Britain, Great Skuas breed only in north and west Scotland; despite recent increases in range, none have been known to nest in Ireland.

The age of the Icelandic population is unknown, but Great Skuas almost certainly colonised Iceland within historical times, probably just before the sixteenth century, and spread from there to the Faroes and Scotland (Furness 1987). The earliest records of Great Skuas nesting in these two countries are in the eighteenth century and refer to only small numbers of pairs. Furness concludes that the record of thousands of skuas being harvested on one of the Faroe Islands around 1700 is erroneous, particularly since only ten pairs were found on the island in 1782. The first full census of the Faroese Great Skuas almost 100 years later revealed only 36 pairs. The naturalist Reverend George Low, who toured Shetland and Orkney in 1774, has provided many of the earliest wildlife records for the islands. He found Great Skuas breeding in only two places, both in Shetland. Three pairs nested at Saxavord on the northernmost island of Unst, and six or seven pairs bred on Foula, 40 km west of the Shetland mainland.

The initial colonisation of the North Atlantic almost ended prematurely in the nineteenth century. Throughout the late 1800s, as Great Skuas became prized exhibits, egg collectors and skin collectors invaded first Shetland and then the Faroes, shooting birds and destroying nests. Numbers declined in Shetland despite the formation of new colonies. By 1897 only four pairs of Great Skuas remained in the Faroes, each nesting on different islands. Only the Icelandic Great Skuas remained relatively unscathed. The implementation of new bird protection laws in both Britain and the Faroes allowed skua numbers to recover during the early twentieth century, although eggs continued to be harvested as food on Foula. Numbers have continued to increase and the species has also been able to expand its breeding range, first to the mainland and Western Isles of Scotland and, most recently, northwards to Norway, Bear Island, Svalbard and possibly Jan Mayen.

Information on the distribution of Great Skuas away from the breeding colonies and outside the breeding season has been obtained from analysis of ringing recoveries of Scottish and Icelandic birds (few have been ringed elsewhere), and from observation of the birds at sea. Recoveries of birds ringed in Shetland showed that after fledging, juvenile Great Skuas move south to winter anywhere from the Bay of Biscay and west Mediterranean to the Azores, Canaries and Cape Verde Islands and the adjacent coast of West Africa (Furness 1978, 1987). During the next 18 months they disperse further into the Mediterranean, or move south to catch the northeast trade winds of the sub-tropics which take them to the coast of South America and the West Indies. Icelandic birds of the same age disperse northwards to Svalbard and Murmansk or westwards reaching Greenland, Quebec and Newfoundland by their second summer of life. The main wintering grounds of adult Great Skuas from Icelandic colonies are on the Grand Banks southeast of Newfoundland although some birds join adults from Scottish colonies and move south to the coasts of the Iberian peninsula. Great Skuas were seen throughout the North Sea from July to September, especially around the breeding colonies. There were fewer records for March to June or in October and November and the birds moved out of the area in winter (Tasker et al. 1987). Small numbers occur off British and Irish coasts between December and February (Jones and Tasker 1982) especially during onshore gales, but the main return to these waters is not until March.

CENSUS METHODS AND PROBLEMS

Great Skuas on Foula and elsewhere in Shetland have been studied in detail for nearly twenty years. As a result, Furness (1987) was able to provide a valuable review of the species' breeding biology and behaviour. This information has permitted an effective census technique to be developed and recommended for use elsewhere in Scotland (Furness 1982).

The unit used by recent Great Skua surveys, including those made for the Seabird Colony Register was, as for Arctic Skua, an "apparently occupied territory" (AOT). Skua breeding territories are less time-consuming to find than actual occupied nests and are more accurate to count than aggressive encounters with breeding birds. AOTs were defined, in descending order of certainty that breeding had occurred, by positive proof of breeding (nest, eggs or young), by the presence of an incubating or brooding adult, by the presence of a distracting or alarm-calling adult, or by one or two birds in potential breeding habitat and apparently attached to a certain area (Ewins *et al.* 1988). Counts of apparently occupied Great Skua territories in 1980 were thought to have underestimated actual breeding numbers by about 7% (Furness 1982), but errors can be expected to vary from year to year depending on the effect of current food availability upon territory attendance by adults.

Many Great Skuas' nests and territories were not counted during the 1969–70 Operation Seafarer survey, which was confined to coastal seabird colonies. No attempt was made in that survey to cover moorland away from the coast, where many of the Orkney and Shetland skuas nested. Coverage of coastal skua colonies was limited by time available to search for nests or territories during a survey which included all other breeding seabirds. A subsequent survey, arranged by the RSPB in 1974 and 1975, aimed to improve coverage for Great Skua colonies, but unfortunately the counting unit used was poorly defined ("pairs holding territories") (Everett 1982).

Meek *et al.* (1985) used the currently recommended techniques and counting unit for a complete survey of Great Skuas in Orkney during 1982 and this was updated by a rough estimate made in 1984 (Furness 1986). Most moorland colonies in Shetland were surveyed in 1985 by the RSPB and NCC (Peacock *et al.* 1985, Wynde and Richardson 1986), and the census of Shetland Great Skuas was completed in 1986 during the Seabird Colony Register survey (Ewins *et al.* 1988). Few Great Skuas breed elsewhere in Scotland but their low nesting density makes coverage difficult. Rennie (1988) reviewed some Great Skua breeding records for the Western Isles and the 1985–87 survey collected further information for these islands, Caithness, Sutherland, and Ross and Cromarty between 1985 and 1987.

Combining data from all these sources gives complete coverage of Great Skuas breeding in Scotland. Counts reported as pairs have been added to those of apparently occupied territories without conversion.

THE GREAT SKUA IN SCOTLAND

Shetland had 5647 occupied Great Skua territories in 1985–87 and held 72% of the British population. The largest Great Skua colony in the world is on Foula where 2500 territories were found in 1987 and where numbers were known to have been even higher earlier in the 1980s. The next biggest in Shetland is at Hermaness (676 territories in 1986) on Unst. Ewins *et al.* (1988)

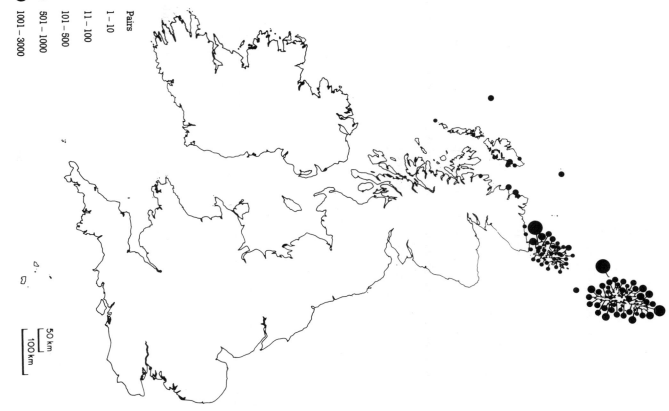

Pairs

• 1 – 10

• 11 – 100

● 101 – 500

⬤ 501 – 1000

⬤ 1001 – 3000

50 km
100 km

Figure 18. Distribution and size of Great Skua colonies (and grouped colonies), 1985–87. Detailed mapping of Shetland colonies in Ewins et al. (1988), and Orkney in Meek et al. (1985).

found that the main concentrations of skuas were in the northern islands of Shetland, with a total of 1257 territories on Unst, 313 on Yell and 248 on Fetlar. Comparison with previous surveys is hampered by different census techniques and poorly defined units.

Because the Operation Seafarer survey did not cover inland seabird colonies, most of the skuas breeding out of sight of the sea in 1969–70 would have been excluded from the Seafarer total. In 1985–86, 21% of Great Skuas in Shetland nested more than 1 km from the sea (Ewins *et al.* 1988). If this were so in Shetland in 1969–70, the total Great Skua population would have been just over 3600 pairs rather than the 2968 pairs recorded on the Seafarer cards. The census of inland and coastal colonies in 1974–75 found a minimum of 5451 pairs on territories in Shetland (Everett 1982). Numbers continued to grow between 1974–75 and 1985–87 at 9% per year on the Shetland mainland but, because of slower growth on Foula, at only 1.3% per year overall (Ewins *et al.* 1988).

The increase in Great Skuas in Orkney since 1969–70 began at an even faster rate than in Shetland and then slowed to a similar rate in the 1980s. Assuming that, as in Shetland, 21% of territories were too far from the coast to be included in Operation Seafarer, the Orkney population in 1969–70 would have been about 106 pairs. These had increased to 485 by 1974–75 (an apparent 72% per year), to 1652 by 1982 (30% per year), and probably to about 2000 by 1984 (10.5% per year) (Everett 1982, Meek *et al.* 1985, Furness 1986). The biggest concentration of birds was on Hoy where 1573 occupied territories were counted in 1982.

After Shetland and Orkney, the next largest concentration of Great Skuas was in the Western Isles where many new breeding sites have been established since Operation Seafarer. The biggest colony was on Hirta (St Kilda) which had 44 pairs in 1987 (Tasker *et al.* 1988). Another important colony was on Handa, off the northwest corner of Sutherland. Only three pairs of Great Skuas bred on the island in 1970 and eight pairs were counted in 1975, but these had increased to 66 by 1986. Skuas colonised Point of Stoer and nearby Eilean an Roin between 1969–70 and 1985–87 and their continued spread on the mainland seems inevitable.

Individuals and paired birds were encountered at 12 sites inland in Caithness by the NCC's Moorland Bird Study teams in 1987 and one pair was considered to be occupying a breeding territory. Another new breeding site was on the island of Longa in Loch Gairloch (Ross and Cromarty) where Great Skuas nested for the first time in 1985. A couple of pairs bred in the Summer Isles (Bottle Island and Eilean Dubh) in 1982, but though Great Skuas were present in 1986, breeding was not proved.

REASONS FOR CHANGE IN NUMBERS

Disturbance and persecution by man was probably the main factor affecting Great Skua numbers in the nineteenth and early twentieth centuries. Large-scale egg collecting and shooting ceased early in the 1900s, and numbers in

Scotland and elsewhere have grown ever since. However, Great Skuas are conspicuous, because of their large size and aggressive defence of breeding territories, and can easily antagonise humans. They are actually less vocal and less agile than Arctic Skuas when dive-bombing farm animals, ground-predators or humans near their nests, but the sudden and often unexpected rush of wings past one's ear or hard knock from a Great Skua's feet as it flashes by in a blur of brown wings delivers a powerful message to intruders.

In Shetland Great Skuas were initially thought by the crofters to be beneficial because they protected sheep from attack by eagles and other predators. Soon the skuas themselves were regarded as predators of lambs and sheep. Furness (1987) concluded that though Great Skuas occasionally killed a lamb or ewe, the birds more often fed by scavenging at lambing time or from sheep carcasses. Losses from other causes far exceeded those attributed to Great Skuas. Despite this, illegal killing of skuas, removal of eggs and nest destruction occurred in the 1980s on both Orkney (Meek *et al.* 1985) and Shetland (Ewins *et al.* 1988). Persecution has also caused a drop in numbers during the last 20 years on the Faroe Islands (Evans 1984) where, in the absence of sandeel shoals, the birds have to be even more predatory than they are in Shetland and Orkney (Furness 1989). Scottish Great Skuas are considered to be one of the world's vulnerable skua populations solely because of persecution by man (Furness 1987).

Other threats to Great Skuas include the loss of nesting habitat through peat digging or heather burning, and pollution by toxic chemicals such as organochlorines and heavy metals, but these are probably relatively unimportant (Meek *et al.* 1985, Furness 1987, Ewins *et al.* 1988). In Shetland, Great Skuas prefer to nest in vegetation up to 12 cm high including heather, crowberry and clumps of rushes and rough grass (Ewins *et al.* 1988). As a result, they are less affected than Arctic Skuas by the agricultural reclamation schemes which threaten much of the unimproved moorland and serpentine heath in Shetland and Orkney.

The other major factor currently influencing skua numbers is the availability of their food. Outside the breeding season Great Skuas feed by scavenging, especially behind fishing boats, and by stealing fish from other seabirds. This behaviour continues through the breeding season in the north of the Great Skua's range, but observations of skuas at sea and in the colonies on Shetland and Orkney show that breeding birds switch to sandeels which they catch for themselves (Tasker *et al.* 1985b, Furness 1987). These fish are of higher calorific value than those collected by scavenging and are easily caught in quantity when shoals rise to the sea surface in characteristic "sandeel balls". The length of the period in early summer for which sandeels are available in this way varies from year to year, but they form an important proportion of the diet of chicks and breeding birds (Furness 1987).

Recent developments in the waters around Shetland have drastically affected Great Skuas and may cause their population to change in future. The marked reduction in the availability of sandeels, especially in 1987 and 1988, caused a marked decline in breeding success amongst Great Skuas on Foula (see Second Chapter, Part 1). Non-breeding birds relied on scavenging instead of sandeels, but breeding birds needed sandeels as a high quality food for their chicks (Furness and Hislop 1981). As sandeels became scarce, the skuas attempted to supplement their catches by predation and piracy. However, food from these sources was also in short supply because so many seabirds had experienced the same fish shortage and failed in their breeding attempts; there were few chicks and birds left for the Great Skuas to kill and few birds carrying food which they could rob. As a result, the only skuas to breed successfully were those in colonies close to the gannetries on Noss and Hermaness. Gannets were apparently unaffected by the scarcity of sandeels in surface waters, and the skuas were able to steal food from them.

In addition to fishing, Great Skuas in Shetland collect some of their food by scavenging behind trawlers where they grab discarded fish and attempt to steal from other scavenging birds. In fact, a study by Hudson and Furness (1988) in the mid 1980s showed that Great Skuas were surprisingly inefficient at this feeding method. The skuas found most fish too big to swallow and lost more to other kleptoparasites than they stole for themselves. In 1987 the legal minimum mesh size for fishing nets in the North Sea was increased from 80 to 85 mm, in an attempt to preserve fish stocks by allowing more small fish to escape. As a result the amount of discarded fish available to seabirds decreased and the average length of discards increased. Being large and aggressive, Great Skuas probably continued to compete successfully with other seabirds for access to discarded fish, even when supplies diminished; but the predo-minance of bigger fish will have been to their disadvantage. The change in net mesh size is likely to have significantly reduced the amount of food available to Great Skuas scavenging at trawlers (Furness 1988). In future, especially if sandeels remain difficult to catch, Great Skuas may be forced increasingly to turn to robbing and killing other seabirds for food, and to scavenging more generally at sea and on land (Furness 1987). At present, non-breeding Great Skuas depend mainly on discarded fish in the summer months; if in future the entire skua population has to obtain more food by predation on each other, on Arctic Skuas or on other seabirds, the effects on local breeding populations could be serious.

Table 23. *Estimated world breeding population of the Great Skua.*

	Apparently occupied territories/pairs
Svalbard	62
Jan Mayen	1
Iceland	5378
Faroe Islands	250
Norway	4
Scotland	7900
Approximate total	13,600 pairs

Sources: Furness (1987), C.J. Camphuysen pers. comm., Seabird Colony Register.

Table 24.   *Numbers of Great Skuas breeding in Scotland 1969–87*

	1985–87 AOT/pairs	1969–70[b] AOT/pairs
Shetland Islands	5647	2968
Orkney Islands	2000	88
Western Isles	128[a]	19
Caithness	1	0
Sutherland	82	4
Ross and Cromarty	2	0
Scotland total	7900	3100

Sources: Furness (1987), Ewins *et al.* (1988), Seabird Colony Register.

Totals rounded to nearest 100 pairs.

AOT = apparent occupied territory.

[a] 11 birds in breeding habitat (Harris) included as 5 AOT.

[b] From Operation Seafarer cards; excludes many inland colonies.

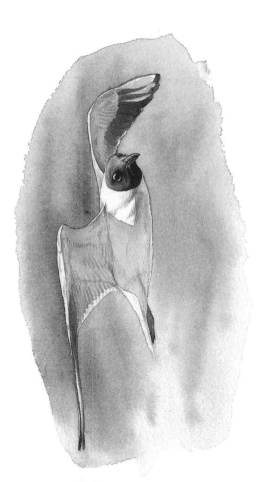

Black-headed Gull

Larus ridibundus

The Black-headed Gull is the smallest gull breeding regularly in Britain and Ireland (wing-span 91–94 cm). It nests, mostly inland, in colonies situated on low-lying islands or spits in marshes, lakes and estuaries. Most birds nest on the ground, but low trees and bushes are also sometimes used. Throughout the year, Black-headed Gulls can be seen feeding behind ploughs and in wet pastures. Their main diet is insect larvae and earthworms but they also forage for other invertebrates on rocky shores, tidal mud-flats and saltmarshes, hawk for insects in aerial swarms and scavenge at rubbish dumps and sewage farms. They are accomplished pirates, but obtain relatively little of their food by this method (Cramp and Simmons 1983).

DISTRIBUTION AND INTERNATIONAL STATUS

Since a large majority of Black-headed Gulls breed inland rather than on the coast, neither the breeding distribution nor the numbers in most countries are known precisely. The Black-headed Gull has a world breeding population of at least one and a half million pairs confined to the Palearctic region until recently (Table 25). However, a pair of birds with newly fledged young was seen in west Newfoundland in 1977 and this, together with the increasing frequency with which Black-headed Gulls are recorded during the breeding season elsewhere in eastern Canada, suggests that the species may soon colonise North America (Brown and Nettleship 1984a).

125

Plate 16. Black-headed Gulls feeding behind tractor with disc harrow (Richard T. Mills)

Black-headed Gull colonies occur around the coasts of much of north-western Europe and in a few places in the Mediterranean. The largest coastal breeding populations are in northwest USSR, Sweden, Denmark, Holland and Britain. Coastal and inland colonies in Britain and Ireland held at least 233,000 pairs in 1985–87, or about 18% of the European total. Black-headed Gulls breed widely inland throughout Europe although the countries without coastal colonies contribute relatively little to the total population. They also breed across central Asia from the Baltic to the Sea of Okhotsk and through much of northern China. Numbers in these latter areas are unknown.

The Black-headed Gull extended its breeding range in Europe (and possibly in Asia) during the late nineteenth and early twentieth centuries and increased in numbers. Colonies were established in Norway, the Faroes and Finland in the 1800s, and in Iceland, Greenland, West Germany, Spain and Italy between 1900 and 1960. Black-headed Gulls are currently increasing almost everywhere apart from a few local declines. For example, in Denmark numbers breeding in coastal colonies halved between the 1940s and 1974, whilst numbers inland increased (Møller 1978).

Analysis of ringing recoveries has shown that Black-headed Gulls from Britain and Ireland migrate to southern Europe, and that wintering birds in Britain come mostly from parts of Europe to the east and north, especially

Scandinavia (Horton *et al.* 1984). Birds from the more northerly breeding locations, such as Iceland, tend to winter in northern Britain, whilst those from countries to the east gather in south and east Britain. Black-headed Gulls occur inland, on estuaries or in inshore waters throughout the year. Over half a million wintering birds were counted in England and Wales in 1973, excluding the large roosts on the main north London reservoirs (Hickling 1977). This represented an increase of 107% since the previous winter survey in 1963, which matches the expansion in the breeding populations of most northwest European countries.

CENSUS METHODS AND PROBLEMS

Almost all counts of Black-headed Gulls during Operation Seafarer were recorded as apparently occupied sites (AOS) or pairs. In 1985–87, a large portion of the birds counted in Scotland and some of those in England were recorded as birds rather than AOS. In order to allow use of all the data collected by both surveys, counts of birds were divided by two to give an estimate of the numbers of pairs, although this introduced additional error into the totals.

Plate 17.   Black-headed Gull colony, on an inland lake in Ireland (Richard T. Mills)

In general, few problems were reported for Black-headed Gull counts, except where the birds nested amongst or close to terns which could not be disturbed. However, some colonies are so large and extensive that they cannot be counted easily and also the spread of laying, and repeat layings after loss of first clutches, made more than one visit to a colony essential for an accurate census. Fortunately, most of the larger coastal Black-headed Gull colonies were on nature reserves or in areas well covered by local ornithologists so that a reasonably continuous assessment of breeding numbers could be made through the season.

THE BLACK-HEADED GULL IN BRITAIN AND IRELAND

Numbers of Black-headed Gulls breeding in coastal colonies have increased slightly between 1969–70 (74,600 pairs) and 1985–87 (88,200 pairs). However, previous surveys (Gribble 1976) have found that over 60% of the breeding population is in inland colonies; these were not covered thoroughly either by Operation Seafarer or by the most recent surveys. On the coasts of England and Wales, Black-headed Gull numbers appear to have increased since 1969–70, but may have actually declined slightly since 1973, when another survey was carried out (Table 27). On Irish coasts, numbers increased sharply, almost entirely due to an increase in Co. Down. There appears to have been a sharp decline in numbers in coastal Scotland and Wales between 1969–70 and 1985–87. Inland numbers in England and Wales may have increased since the most recent survey in 1973, following a doubling in this population between 1958 and 1973 (Table 27). Unfortunately, there are so few recent censuses of colonies counted in 1973 that it is impossible to be sure of any trend.

Over 80% of Britain and Ireland's coastal Black-headed Gulls in 1985–87 were in England. The largest colony was on Bank's Marsh in the Ribble estuary in Lancashire (20,000 pairs). The next largest colonies were in the Solent on the Pennington–Keyhaven marshes (8000 pairs) and at Needs Ore Point (7000 pairs). Total numbers at the latter site exceeded 15,000 pairs in the 1970s. Three other big colonies, at Holkham (Norfolk), on Garnham's Island (Essex) and on Round and Spartina Islands (Poole Harbour), each had 2000 or more pairs. Scotland had 10% of the coastal Black-headed Gulls, with only one colony (Loch of Strathbeg, Grampian) of over 1000 pairs. The biggest colony on the Irish coast was on Jackdaw Island, in the tidal waters of Strangford Lough (2500 pairs).

The Black-headed Gulls in a few coastal colonies had been counted regularly between Operation Seafarer and the most recent surveys. Some of these colonies increased steadily in size over the years (e.g. Coquet Island, Northumberland), whilst others declined (e.g. Foulness Point, Essex) and in some places birds appeared to have moved from a declining colony (e.g. Scolt Head, Norfolk) to an increasing one nearby (e.g. Blakeney Point, Norfolk). However, the coastal birds cannot be considered in isolation from those breeding inland.

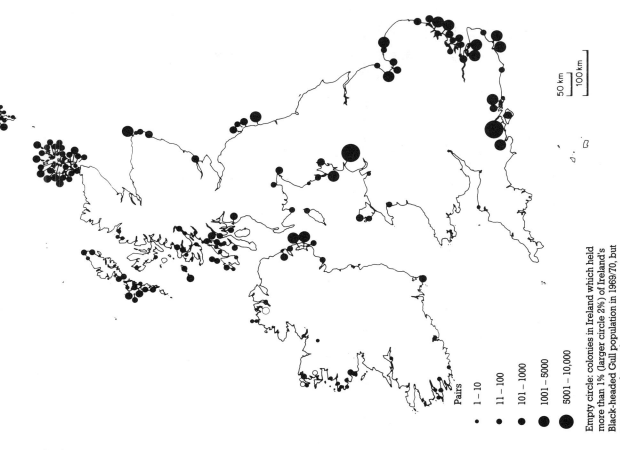

Pairs

1 – 10

11 – 100

101 – 1000

1001 – 5000

5001 – 10,000

Empty circle: colonies in Ireland which held more than 1% (larger circle 2%) of Ireland's Black-headed Gull population in 1969/70, but not surveyed recently.

50 km

100 km

Figure 19. Distribution and size of coastal Black-headed Gull colonies (and grouped colonies), 1985–87.

Black-headed Gulls breeding in both coastal and inland colonies in England and Wales have been censused thoroughly on three occasions in the past, in 1938, 1958 and 1973 (Gribble 1976). The increase in these colonies between 1958 and 1973 was about 5% per year. If this rate had continued, then an estimated 59,800 pairs would have nested inland in England and Wales by 1986. On the other hand, if the coastal breeding population remained at about 71% of the total (as in 1958 and 1973), the estimate would have been 28,200 pairs (Table 27). This latter figure is likely to be an absolute minimum as the Black-headed Gull colony at Sunbiggin Tarn in Cumbria alone holds about 25,000 pairs (J.C. Coulson, *pers. comm.*). However, there is no evidence to support either supposition, and precise numbers nesting inland in England will remain obscure until the next comprehensive survey. Black-headed Gulls at Hanningfield Reservoir in Essex have been counted almost annually from 1970 to 1987, but during this time numbers fluctuated between 15 and 200 pairs.

In Scotland, coverage of inland gull colonies inland for the Seabird Colony Register was incomplete. Just under 30,000 pairs were found, with the largest recorded colony at Bemersyde in the Borders (11,600 pairs, 1987). Hamilton (1962) reported on an earlier incomplete survey, and Gibson (1986) listed several large colonies both inland and on the Firth of Clyde which declined or disappeared between the mid 1970s and early 1980s. Since there has never been a complete survey of inland gull colonies in Scotland, nothing is known about how numbers of inland breeding Black-headed Gulls may have changed.

In Ireland, a complete survey of inland gull colonies in the counties of Galway, Mayo, Sligo and Donegal took place in 1977 and 1978 (Whilde 1978), when a total of 16,414 nests were located. A repeat count was made in 1983 at the five main loughs which had held 69% of the Black-headed Gulls in 1977–78 (Whilde 1983). Numbers of birds at these colonies had increased by 4% in the intervening period. Davidson (1987) surveyed Lough Neagh in Northern Ireland and found a total of 33,000 nests, with an extraordinary concentration of 20,000 nests on one small island. Incomplete surveys during 1985–87 found 3500 pairs in Co. Fermanagh and 1200 in Co. Tipperary. A further 800 pairs were found associated with inland tern colonies during the All Ireland Tern Survey (Whilde 1985). At least another 4000 could be nesting on the bogs of midland Ireland away from Tipperary (c.f. Sharrock 1976), giving an overall minimum estimate for inland colonies in Ireland of 59,000 pairs.

The total Black-headed population estimate for Britain and Ireland of 233,000 pairs (Table 25) compares well with an estimate of 150,000 to 300,000 pairs in 1968–72 (Sharrock 1976).

There have been dramatic changes in numbers at some coastal colonies, and it is tempting to speculate that some birds have moved from coastal to inland sites. Colonies on the west side of the Wash, for example, were once very large. There was disagreement in estimates made during Operation Seafarer, but at least 4050 pairs bred on the saltings and adjacent marshes. Gribble (1976) listed the colony on the saltings between Kirton and Frampton (7800 pairs in 1973, but possibly up to twice this size), as one of the 21 largest colonies in

England and Wales. By 1986 this colony had declined to 1362 pairs and the west side of the Wash held only 2625 pairs in total. The largest colony of Black-headed Gulls on the Wash (900 pairs, 1987) is now on the offshore bund (a trial intertidal reservoir bank) at Terrington. On the other side of England, the enormous colony in the dunes at Ravenglass in Cumbria, which held 10,000 pairs of Black-headed Gulls in 1969, had disappeared completely by the early 1980s, possibly because of fox predation. A few birds colonised nearby Foulney Island and this colony had 675 pairs in 1986. Also in northwest England, the colony at Bank's Marsh on the Ribble grew from around 7100 to 20,000 pairs between 1973 and 1989. In England and Wales, birds readily move between inland sites, depending on factors such as disturbance and water levels and this may be responsible for the fluctuations in numbers at many colonies (Gribble 1976).

REASONS FOR CHANGE IN NUMBERS

In 1884, following a period of extensive egg collecting and persecution, Black-headed Gulls were considered to be in danger of extinction in Britain (Gurney 1919). During the present century, the growth of the human population in Britain may have increased the amount of nesting and wintering habitat available to Black-headed Gulls. During Gribble's (1976) survey, 44% of colonies were found on moorland pools or disused mining reservoirs, 30% in artificial habitat such as sewage farms and flooded gravel and clay pits, and the rest (26%) on coastal saltmarsh and dunes. The provision of safe roosting areas in the form of gravel pits and reservoirs was thought to have aided overwinter survival. This, coupled with legal protection from persecution, appears to be the main cause of the increase in breeding numbers during the present century (Cramp et al. 1974, Evans 1984).

In the Camargue in the south of France, the use of new food sources during winter has been accompanied by an increase in breeding numbers (Lebreton and Isenmann 1976). For example, Black-headed Gulls have been recorded feeding behind trawlers in the Mediterranean (Isenmann and Czajkowski 1978); this also occasionally occurs in the Irish Sea (Watson 1980). Change in feeding ecology is also thought to have contributed to colonisation of coastal habitat by nesting Black-headed Gulls in West Germany (Gorke et al. 1988), but there is no clear evidence that food or feeding habits have changed in the last 15–20 years for those nesting in Britain and Ireland.

Gribble (1976) considered that protection on reserves was the main factor behind the increase in Black-headed Gull numbers in England and Wales between 1958 and 1973, despite measures taken in some areas to control Black-headed Gull numbers. Egg collecting and deliberate destruction of colonies together with casual disturbance by birdwatchers and tourists, flooding by high tides and predation of eggs and chicks by foxes, mink and other birds were reported as causing nesting failure or colony desertion, especially in colonies of less than 50 pairs. Similar factors affected Black-headed Gulls breeding in the declining coastal colonies in Denmark during the 1970s (Møller 1978). Botulism has been recorded in wintering Black-headed Gulls in Co. Cork (Buckley and O'Halloran 1986).

The reason for the decline of Black-headed Gull colonies in some coastal areas of Britain (especially Scotland) since 1969 is unclear. There has been no apparent increase in the amount of predation, flooding or other factors adversely affecting coastal birds, but some of the large saltmarsh and sand dune colonies have disappeared during the last 10–15 years. Commercial egg collecting occurs under licence, and on a large scale, in parts of Scotland and the south of England, For example, the egg quota for Needs Ore Point was 153,000 in the 1987 season and 38,000 eggs were known to have been collected from the colony and sold. Large-scale, unlicensed collecting of eggs certainly affects Black-headed Gull numbers in colonies elsewhere in Britain.

Table 25. *Estimated world population of the Black-headed Gull.*

	No. of pairs	Comments
USSR—Moscow region	30,000–32,000	Increasing
USSR—Caspian Sea	5,000	Unknown
USSR—Baltic coast	300,000	
USSR—Sea of Okhotsk	?	Breeds W Xinjiang, Jilin and
China	?	Heilongjiang provinces
Canada	1–2	Possibly bred 1977, west New-foundland
Greenland	<100	First bred 1969, increasing
Iceland	10,000	First bred 1911
Faroe Islands	170–200	First bred 1848, increased 1930 onwards but now declining
Norway	16,000–17,000	First bred 1867, most colonies in SE but spreading north
Sweden	200,000	Increased and spread since last century
Finland	150,000	First bred early 1800s, increased and spread, now declining in south but expanding in north
Poland	30,000	Decreasing Silesia, increasing elsewhere
East Germany	99,900	Increase in recent years
Denmark	200,000	Coastal population declined from 250,000 to 110,000 pairs 1940s–74, now increasing inland
West Germany	40,400	First bred on coast 1931, increased 1960–75
Britain	167,000	Includes estimated 90,000 pairs inland
Ireland	66,000	Increasing, includes estimated 59,000 pairs inland
Netherlands	200,000	Increasing
Belgium	10,000–15,000	Increasing
France	20,000–25,000	Increasing
Spain	700–1000	First bred 1960, slow increase and spread since
Italy	780	First bred 1960, increasing

Table 25. *Estimated world population of the Black-headed Gull – cont.*

	No. of pairs	Comments
Yugoslavia	>1500	Increasing
Turkey	<1000	
Hungary	18,000–20,000	
Czechoslovakia	75,000	
Bulgaria and Romania	<1000	Fluctuating
Austria	8300–8700	Increased up to 1960s, now stable or declining
Switzerland	3000	
Approximate total	c. 1.7 million pairs	

Sources: Cramp and Simmons (1983), Croxall *et al.* (1984), Fasola (1986), Ilychev and Zubakin (1988), **P.G.H. Evans** pers. comm., Seabird Colony Register.
? = Breeds, numbers unknown.

Table 26. *Numbers of Black-headed Gulls in coastal colonies in Britain and Ireland 1969–87.*

	1985–87		1969–70	
	Pairs	Birds	Pairs	Birds
Shetland Islands	258	158	502	—
Orkney Islands	1535	2332	4656	—
Banff and Buchan	1610	88	33	—
Gordon	572	—	2220	—
Angus	400	—	—	—
Northeast Fife	—	—	8000	—
Western Isles	490	622	800	30
Caithness	65	—	86	—
Sutherland	—	—	27	—
Ross and Cromarty	7	—	55	—
Skye and Lochalsh	4	—	84	25
Lochaber	57	—	1	—
Argyll and Bute	1171	172	425	6
Cunninghame	—	—	73	—
Kyle and Carrick	—	—	882	—
Wigtown	45	—	260	—
Stewartry	—	—	92	—
Nithsdale	20	—	—	—
Scotland total	6200	3400	18,200	60
Combined units[a]	7900[a]			
Birds converted to pairs	21%			
Northumberland	4753	—	3313	—
Lincolnshire	2625	—	4050	—
Norfolk	4717	—	1313	—

Table 26. Numbers of Black-headed Gulls in coastal colonies in Britain and Ireland 1969-87 – cont.

	1985-87		1969-70	
	Pairs	Birds	Pairs	Birds
Suffolk	2096	1000	2153	—
Essex	3677	—	3822	5
Kent	7253	—	3778	—
East Sussex	1377	—	260	—
West Sussex	1521	—	—	2
Hampshire	15,183	—	22,058	—
Isle of Wight	250	—	283	—
Dorset	2800	—	21	—
Lancashire	21,761	—	1708	—
Cumbria	730	—	10,380	—
Isle of Man	93	—	—	—
England and Isle of Man total	68,900	1000	53,100	10
Combined units[a]	69,300[a]			
Birds converted to pairs	1%			
Gwynedd	197	—	700	—
Clwyd	10	—	100	—
Wales total	200	—	800	—
Antrim	109	—	33	—
Down	4359	—	1361	—
Wexford	200	—	500	—
Cork	7	—	—	—
Kerry	—[b]	—	4	—
Limerick	6	—	—	—
Galway	18[b]	—	286	1
Mayo	32[b]	—	45	—
Sligo	2[b]	—	4	—
Donegal	2	—	526	—
Ireland total	4700	2	2500	1
Britain and Ireland total	84,200		74,600	
Estimated total	6800[c]			
Proportion estimated	31%			

Totals rounded, < 100 to nearest 10, 100–1000 to nearest 50, > 1000 to nearest 100.
[a] Includes counts of birds divided by 2 to provide an estimate of pairs; details in text.
[b] In these counties, at least 40% more pairs are estimated to occur at colonies not visited in 1985-87.
[c] This total includes estimates for colonies not counted recently. It is based on the proportional change in numbers in each region at colonies counted in both surveys.

Table 27. *Pairs of Black-headed Gulls breeding in coastal and inland colonies in England and Wales 1938–88. Figures for 1938, 1958 and 1973 are midpoints of maxima and minima given by Gribble (1976), and 1985–87 from Seabird Colony Register.*

	1938	1958	1969/70	1973	1985–87
Coast	15,900	35,500	53,900	74,600	69,500
Inland	22,000	14,300	?	30,200	28,200[a]–60,000[b]
All	37,900	49,800	?	105,200	97,700[a]–126,000[b]
On coast	42%	71%		71%	71–52%

[a] Calculated assuming that population on coast remained at 71%.
[b] Calculated on assumption that the 5% per year increase from 1958 to 1973 continued to 1986.

See text and Table 26 for further details.

Common Gull

Larus canus

The Common Gull is a medium-sized gull (wing-span 119–122 cm) which spends most of its time, not on the coast or at sea, but inland where it breeds in colonies on moorland and on islands in lochs. The birds forage mostly on the ground by walking through damp pasture or moorland and by following ploughs. Common Gulls also sometimes feed by scavenging and piracy.

DISTRIBUTION AND INTERNATIONAL STATUS

The Common Gull breeds in northwest Europe and across the USSR to Alaska and northwest Canada. Its largest breeding populations are in Norway and Sweden where most colonies are on or near the coast. In other countries, including Britain and Ireland, the majority of birds nest inland. The world population is just over half a million pairs of which about 12% breed in Britain and Ireland (Table 28). However, most census data available were collected more than ten years ago and there is no information on the current status of the species in many countries. The Common Gull has four subspecies of which the

136

nominate, *L.c. canus*, breeding through northwest Europe and east to the White Sea, is by far the most abundant.

Britain is a wintering area for Common Gulls breeding in Norway and Denmark. Those from Britain and Irish colonies mainly disperse south and west after breeding; many birds from Scotland winter in Ireland and around the Irish Sea (Cramp and Simmons 1983).

CENSUS METHODS AND PROBLEMS

Fewer problems were encountered in censusing Common Gulls on the coast than with the other gull species because colony size was usually considerably smaller. Identification of breeding pairs or occupied nests was sometimes confused in mixed-species colonies by the presence of more numerous large gulls. Sampling methods were used to estimate the size of the very large inland colonies in northeast Scotland (Tasker *et al.* in prep.).

THE COMMON GULL IN BRITAIN AND IRELAND

About 15,700 pairs of Common Gulls nested on the coasts of Britain and Ireland in 1985–87. Scotland had 94% of the birds and over 70% of these (approximately 10,800 pairs) were in Shetland and Orkney. However, a large proportion of the Orkney population was counted using birds as units, so there is a large and unquantifiable error on these figures. Argyll and Bute had over 2000 pairs in a string of small colonies scattered down the coast and on islands. Numbers increased by about a quarter in Britain between 1969–70 and 1985–87. Less than 300 pairs were counted in coastal colonies in Ireland in 1985–87, compared with over 700 pairs in 1969–70, but many colonies were not visited. The estimated increase in coastal population, based on those colonies counted in both surveys, was similar to that in Britain.

Common Gulls breed extensively inland throughout Scotland, especially north of a line joining Glasgow and Edinburgh, at many sites in northwest Ireland, and at a few sites in the north of England (Sharrock 1976). The numbers of birds breeding inland in Scotland and Ireland clearly exceed those breeding on the coast, but there has been no complete census of gulls nesting inland in recent years. Probably the largest inland colonies occur in northeast Scotland. Here Common Gulls also nest in small but increasing numbers on rooftops in cities (Sullivan 1985, Stewart 1986). Colonies at which counts or estimates are available for past years appear to have increased in size since the mid 1970s. The one on the Correen Hills, for example, was thought to have 4000–5000 pairs of Common Gulls in 1976 (Bourne *et al.* 1978), whilst a more detailed survey in 1987 gave an estimate of 13,500–24,000 pairs (Tasker *et al.* in prep.). Another large colony is situated in the Mortlach Hills where 1300 pairs were found at Corsemaul and Craigwatch in 1978 (A.F.G. Dowse in Knox and Bell 1979). These areas held between 5000 and 6700 pairs in 1988,

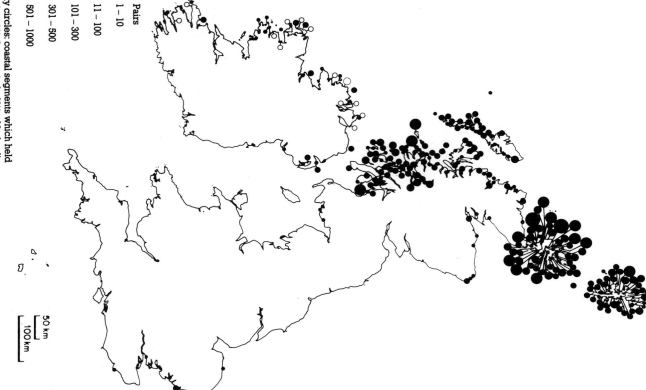

Pairs

- · 1–10
- • 11–100
- ● 101–300
- ● 301–500
- ● 501–1000

Empty circles: coastal segments which held more than 1% (larger circle 2%) of Ireland's coastal Common Gulls in 1969/70 and not surveyed recently.

50 km
100 km

Figure 20. Distribution and size of coastal Common Gull colonies (and grouped colonies), 1985–87.

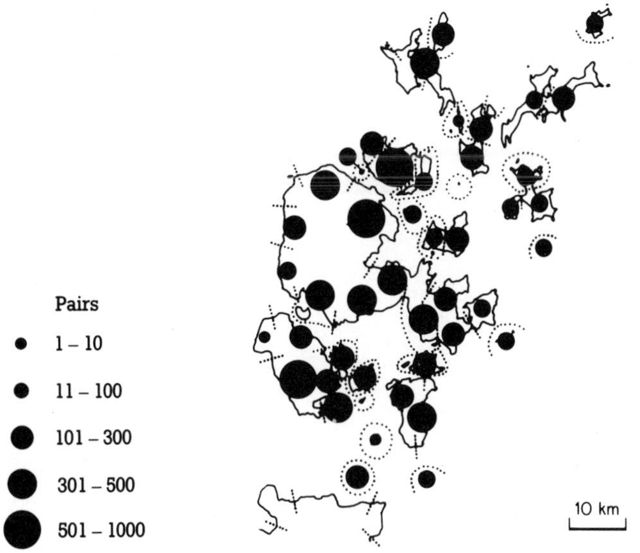

Pairs

· 1–10

· 11–100

● 101–300

● 301–500

● 501–1000

10 km

Figure 20a. Detail of distribution and size of coastal Common Gull colonies (and grouped colonies) in Orkney, 1985–87.

while the remainder of the Mortlach Hills held between 6100 and 9500 in 1988–89 (Tasker *et al.* in prep.).

Inland Common Gull colonies in the west of Ireland were covered by a special survey in 1977–78 which was partially repeated in 1983 (Whilde 1978, 1983). Allowing for colonies on Lough Conn missed during the first survey, about 5000 Common Gulls (birds) were nesting inland in 1977–78. No change in numbers was detected at loughs in Mayo and Galway which were resurveyed in 1983.

Sharrock (1976) estimated the total breeding population of Common Gulls in Britain and Ireland to be about 50,000 pairs based on an average density (50 pairs/10 km square) recorded during the BTO/IWC Atlas surveys in 1968–72. In the 1980s, probably about 3600 pairs nested inland and on the coast in Ireland, and another 14,800 pairs on the coasts of Britain. Approximately 33,000 pairs nested inland in the Grampian region of Scotland. Although no further large inland colonies are known in Scotland, Common Gulls are found breeding on many hill and mires. At least another 20,000 pairs are estimated to have bred inland in Scotland, giving a total of over 70,000 pairs of Common Gulls in the whole of Britain and Ireland.

In Scotland, the largest coastal Common Gull colonies are found in Orkney (Figure 20a). Many colonies of 200–300 pairs were recorded there in 1985–87, especially on Hoy. Other areas with colonies of more than 200 pairs were on Harris, Tiree and islands off the mainland of Argyll and Bute. Most of the districts on the Scottish mainland held fewer Common Gulls in 1985–87 than

Plate 18.   Common Gull colony on islet in Lough Corrib, Co. Galway (Richard T. Mills)

in 1969–70, but apparent increases in the size of coastal colonies in the Western Isles, Orkney and Shetland more than compensated for these. Some colonies on moorland and sealochs in Lewis which were included in the 1985–87 surveys were not surveyed during Operation Seafarer although several of these were examined from the air in 1977 (Bourne and Currie 1983).

Changes in Common Gull colonies on the coast of Ireland since 1969 are unclear in view of limited recent coverage, but the available counts suggest approximately stable numbers. However, numbers increased in the northeast, on Rathlin Island and the Copeland Islands (6 and 30 pairs in 1969, to 64 and 71 pairs in 1985 respectively), and also on islets in Strangford Lough (9 to 40 pairs). Many of the colonies found during Operation Seafarer between Kerry to Donegal were not surveyed in 1985–87, but there seems to have been little or no change overall at colonies which were revisited.

REASONS FOR CHANGE IN NUMBERS

The Common Gull is a little-studied species and the true size of its breeding population in Britain and Ireland has never been established. Past data for individual colonies are scarce so that it is difficult to evaluate any changes in numbers that may have occurred either during the past 15–20 years or previously. Cramp *et al.* (1974) documented the increase and spread of Common Gulls in Britain and Ireland since 1900 and concluded that the species was extending its breeding range southwards. Breeding has since started at Scolt Head (Norfolk) and Orfordness (Suffolk), and numbers have doubled, to eight pairs, at Dungeness (Kent).

Table 28. *Estimated world breeding population of the Common Gull.*

	No. of pairs	Comments
USSR—Baltic to White Sea	42,000 + (1976)	Increasing and spreading inland, majority in Estonia
USSR—Kurils and Sea of Okhotsk	?	
USA—Alaska	50,000 +	Increasing Gulf of Alaska
Canada—northwest	?	
Iceland	<100	First bred probably 1936
Faroe Islands	700–1000	Increased earlier this century, now stable
Norway	150,000 (1970)	Moving inland
Sweden	144,000 (1976)	
Finland	60,000 (1958)	Increased 1940s, stable 1950s
Poland	5000–10,000	
East Germany	4500	Controlled since 1972, <50 inland
Denmark	40,000 (1974)	Marked spread this century, decreased 1950s–60s
West Germany	2500	Spread inland in 1960s
Britain	67,800	Includes estimated 53,000 inland. Increased on coast (and probably inland) since 1969
Ireland	3600	Includes 2700 inland. Stable or increased on coast since 1969
Netherlands	7000 (1978)	Recolonised 1908, increased 1960s–70s
Belgium	<10	First bred 1924, regularly since 1970
France	<10	Bred regularly since 1976
Austria	<50	
Switzerland	<10 (1979)	First bred 1966
Approximate total	578,000–585,000 pairs	

Sources: Cramp and Simmons (1983), Croxall *et al.* (1984), P.G.H. Evans pers. com., Seabird Colony Register.
Year of most recent estimate (if pre-1980) given in brackets.

Table 29. *Numbers of Common Gulls breeding in coastal colonies in Britain and Ireland 1969–87.*

	1985–87		1969–70	
	Pairs	Birds	Pairs	Birds
Shetland Islands	2382	254	1336	—
Orkney Islands	3781	8183	4895	—
Nairn	—	—	12	—
Moray	13	15	60	15
Banff and Buchan	3	20	16	—
Kincardine and Deeside	—	—	43	—
Western Isles	483	521	648	23
Caithness	136	—	36	—
Sutherland	86	—	380	—
Ross and Cromarty	138	—	403	—
Inverness	38	—	10	—
Skye and Lochalsh	304	60	405	250
Lochaber	363	4	533	16
Argyll and Bute	2038	462	2562	198
Cunninghame	185	—	495	—
Kyle and Carrick	1	—	48	—
Stewartry	1	—	96	—
Nithsdale	—	—	1	—
Scotland total	9997	9519	11,979	502
Combined units^a	14,800^a		12,200^a	
Birds converted to pairs	32%		2%	
Norfolk	3	—	2	—
Suffolk	23	—	—	—
Kent	8	—	4	—
East Sussex	—	—	1	—
Cumbria	—	—	1	—
England total	35	—	8	—
Gwynedd	—	—	2	—
Wales total	—	—	2	—

	1985–87		1969–70	
	Pairs	Birds	Pairs	Birds
Antrim	64	—	12	—
Down	111	—	44	—
Cork	4	—	4	—
Kerry	30[b]	—	64	—
Galway	—[b]	—	51	11
Mayo	47[b]	12	178	—
Sligo	12	—	3	—
Donegal	1[b]	30	330	104
Ireland total	270[b]	42	690	110
Estimated total	900[c]		740	
Proportion estimated/converted	46%		3%	
Britain and Ireland total	15,700[a]		13,000[a]	

Totals rounded, <100 to nearest 5, 100–1000 to nearest 10, >1000 to nearest 100.

[a] Includes counts of birds divided by 2 to provide an estimate of pairs; details in text.

[b] In these counties, at least 40% more pairs are estimated to occur at colonies not visited in 1985–87.

[c] This total includes estimates for colonies not counted recently. It is based on the proportional change in numbers at colonies in each region where counts were conducted in both surveys.

Lesser Black-backed Gull

Larus fuscus

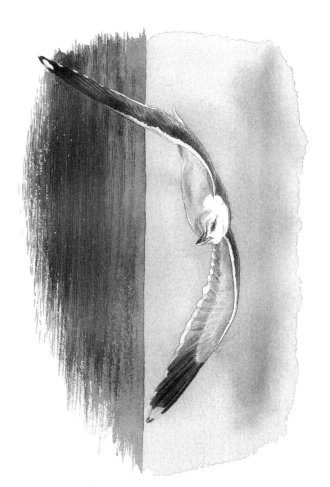

The Lesser Black-backed Gull, with a wing-span of 124–127 cm, is the smallest of the three species of large gulls which nest in Britain and Ireland. Its breeding colonies are found on offshore islands, in coastal sand dunes and on islets in brackish or tidal lagoons. Some birds breed inland on lakes or moorland. Lesser Black-backed Gulls are omnivorous. They feed by scavenging and predation, and they will eat almost any vertebrate or invertebrate foods of suitable size, collected at sea or on land. At the two largest British colonies, fish predominates in the diet during the breeding season (Cramp and Simmons 1983).

DISTRIBUTION AND INTERNATIONAL STATUS

The Lesser Black-backed Gull breeds in north and west Europe and northern USSR, from Iceland to the Taymyr peninsula and south to Portugal. Within this comparatively small range there are five subspecies; all birds breeding in Britain and Ireland are *L.f. graellsii* (Cramp and Simmons 1983). The world population of the three sub-species breeding in Europe is approximately 205,000 pairs and about a third of these (or three-quarters of the world's *L.f. graellsii*) nest in Britain and Ireland (Table 30). The two other

Plate 19. Lesser Black-backed Gull and chick (Richard T. Mills)

subspecies nest east of the White Sea in the USSR, but nothing is known of their population size.

Like the closely related Herring Gull, which is both more numerous and more widespread, the Lesser Black-backed Gull has increased its numbers and its range this century. Lesser Black-backed Gulls bred for the first time in Iceland, the Netherlands and West Germany during 1920–30 and re-colonised northern France. During the 1970s, the species spread south to Spain and Portugal (details in Cramp and Simmons 1983). Some breeding populations are declining (Finland, Sweden, Denmark), but numbers breeding in Britain and Ireland increased by about a quarter between 1969–70 and 1985–87.

Most Lesser Black-backed Gulls migrate south after breeding, although during the last 30 years increasing numbers have overwintered in southern Britain (Baker 1980). Birds from the breeding populations between Iceland, Scandinavia and France, including Britain and Ireland, travel south to winter off Portugal, southwest Spain and northwest Africa with fewer birds travelling as far south as Mauritania, Senegal and the Gulf of Guinea (Harris 1962a, Baker 1980, E.K. Dunn pers. comm.). Vagrants, perhaps from Iceland, are recorded regularly on the east coast of North America, south to Florida. Birds from the eastern part of the species' breeding range move south by a more easterly migration route to winter in the Mediterranean and Black Sea, the

Red Sea, Arabian Gulf, north and east coasts of the Indian Ocean and inland into East Africa (Cramp and Simmons 1983).

CENSUS METHODS AND PROBLEMS

Many of the problems encountered when censusing Lesser Black-backed Gulls are similar to those for Herring Gulls especially since the two species often form mixed colonies (see chapter on Herring Gull). Small numbers of Lesser Black-backed Gulls sometimes nest scattered amongst Herring Gulls where their presence may go undetected.

During the surveys in 1985–87, a large proportion of the counts of Lesser Black-backed Gulls in Orkney, the Western Isles and Argyll and Bute were recorded as birds rather than pairs. In order to use all data collected and to obtain complete estimates of the breeding population, all counts of birds were divided by two and combined with the counts of nests despite the considerable but unquantifiable error this introduced. The proportion of each count which consists of birds "converted" to pairs must be considered when comparing totals in Table 31.

THE LESSER BLACK-BACKED GULL IN BRITAIN AND IRELAND

During Operation Seafarer in 1969–70, there were 50,100 pairs of Lesser Black-backed Gulls on the coasts of Britain and Ireland. Increases in both Britain and Ireland brought the total to an estimated 64,500 by 1985–87.

In 1985–87 more than half (58%) the Lesser Black-backed Gulls in coastal colonies in Britain and Ireland were found in the west of England and Wales, between the Isles of Scilly and Cumbria. Almost four-fifths (79%) of the birds bred in the 17 largest colonies, each with over 500 pairs. The two biggest coastal ones were on Skomer off southwest Wales (13,205 pairs) and at South Walney in Cumbria (10,000 pairs). Other coastal colonies of more than 2000 pairs were on Little Cumbrae in the Firth of Clyde (3000 pairs) and at Orfordness in Suffolk (5000 pairs).

Numbers of Lesser Black-backed Gull in coastal colonies remained approximately stable in England between 1969–70 and 1985–87, and increased in Scotland by 55%, in Wales by 65% and in Ireland by 29%. Large changes appear to have occurred during this time in several different areas (Figure 22), but the figures are biased by the exclusion of counts of birds expressed as pairs (Orkney, Western Isles, Argyll and Bute), or because the total breeding numbers are small (less than 5000 pairs in Shetland, southeast England excluding Orfordness, and all of Ireland except the southwest). Apart from these areas, there was a general upward trend in breeding numbers between 1969 and 1987.

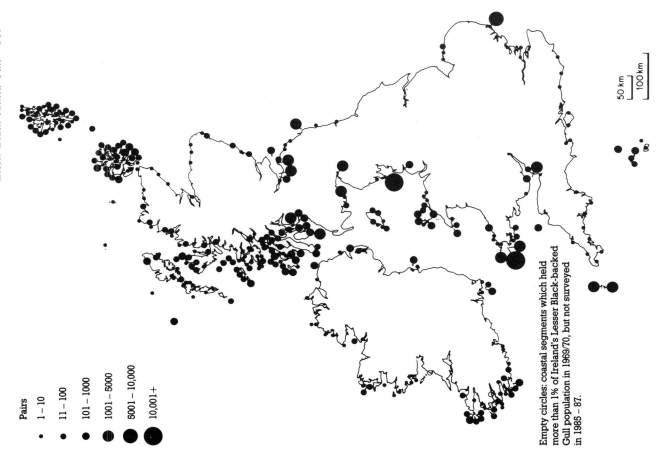

Pairs

• 1 – 10

• 11 – 100

● 101 – 1000

● 1001 – 5000

● 5001 – 10,000

● 10,001+

Empty circles: coastal segments which held more than 1% of Ireland's Lesser Black-backed Gull population in 1969/70, but not surveyed in 1985 – 87.

50 km

100 km

Figure 21. Distribution and size of coastal Lesser Black-backed Gull colonies (and grouped colonies), 1985–87.

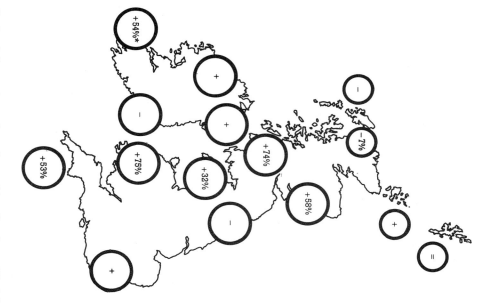

Figure 22.   Regional changes in numbers of coastal breeding Lesser Black-backed Gulls, 1969–87.
See Table 31 for counts and Figure 1 for regional divisions.
No figure is given if more than 10% of a county/regional total was derived from counts made as individuals rather than pairs or where totals were less than 400 pairs. Orfordness excluded from SE England total.
* Cork and Kerry only

Lesser Black-backed Gulls breeding on the Farne Islands in Northumberland apparently decreased during this period although counts in 1986 did not distinguish Lesser Black-backed and Herring Gulls. Both species were culled annually from islands managed for breeding terns. The gulls also declined on South Walney in Cumbria; this colony had 17,500 pairs of Lesser Black-backed Gulls in 1969, but only 10,000 pairs in 1985. There is no obvious reason for this although some birds from South Walney were known to have moved to the large inland colony at Abbeystead in the 1960s–70s (Duncan 1981a).

There was an enormous increase in numbers of gulls breeding on the shingle spit at Orfordness. The colony became established on Ministry of Defence land in the mid 1960s, and 300 pairs of Herring and Lesser Black-backed Gulls were nesting there in 1969. The size of the colony was monitored during the 1970s and early 1980s because of its proximity to the RSPB reserve at Haver-gate Island with its large breeding colony of Avocets, and to the Little Tern colony on Orfordness beach (Thomas *et al.* 1982). The number of nests was estimated from a convenient observation tower, and the gulls' diet analysed from regurgitated pellets and food remains collected at the nests. The RSPB study revealed that numbers of Lesser Black-backed Gulls increased each year from 1973 to 1981, apart from 1977–79. By 1986, the colony had grown to over 5000 pairs. Herring Gulls increased to more than 3000 pairs in the same period, with two spurts of growth, between 1969 and 1973, and from 1980 onwards. The increase in gull numbers, it was concluded, could only have occurred with considerable immigration of birds into the colony.

Inland and most urban Lesser Black-backed Gulls were not included in the recent surveys for the Seabird Colony Register. By far the biggest inland colony in England and Wales is on west Pennine moorland at Abbeystead (Duncan 1981a, Wanless and Langslow 1983). In 1978, 24,740 pairs of gulls (about 86% Lesser Black-backed, the rest Herring) bred between Abbeystead and Mallow-dale and an annual cull of breeding birds was started by the North-West Water Authority with the aim of lessening pollution of local domestic water supplies. The gulls had been reduced to 9480 pairs in 1982 (95% Lesser Black-backed) and have since fallen to about 9000 pairs (Thomas and Tasker 1988).

The only other large inland colonies of Lesser Black-backed Gulls are west of Stirling in Scotland. The gullery at Flanders Moss was considered to be the largest Scottish colony of Black-headed Gulls in the 1880s, but persecution by local gamekeepers and egg collectors forced it into extinction by 1920. Lesser Black-backed Gulls began breeding on Flanders Moss some time between 1928 and 1935, and by 1980 they had increased to about 8000 pairs (Whitelaw 1987). Very few pairs now breed on the moss though a new colony has become established nearby on Meall a' Choire Odhair (about 1200 nests, 1988). The decline of the Flanders Moss colony coincided with intense egg collecting, probably for commercial purposes (H. Galbraith pers. comm.), and the infringement of the nesting grounds by a thick growth of birch scrub (B. Zonfrillo pers. comm.); heavy predation of eggs and chicks by dogs and cats has also been recorded (Whitelaw 1987). The total inland breeding population of Lesser Black-backed Gulls in Britain during the 1980s is likely to have been about 20,000 pairs.

In Ireland, far more Lesser Black-backed Gulls breed inland than on the coasts, especially in the west of the country. Over 200 pairs nested on the islands of Upper and Lower Lough Erne in 1986. A further 2500 pairs were found in 1978 in the west of Ireland, mainly on Lough Corrib in Galway (Whilde 1978). A repeat survey of Lough Corrib and the other main breeding loughs in 1983 suggested little change in numbers had occurred (Whilde 1983).

Lesser Black-backed Gulls were reported nesting on buildings in 12 locali-ties during 1976; these were mostly in the Bristol Channel area and none were in Ireland (Monaghan and Coulson 1977). Numbers had increased by 28% per annum since 1969 to over 300 pairs. Few more recent data are available for roof-nesting gulls in Britain but the growth in numbers appears to have continued. An increase of 5% per annum was reported for urban colonies in Glamorgan between 1975 and 1980 (Hurford 1985). At Cardiff and Barry, Lesser Black-backed Gulls on roofs increased from 23 breeding pairs in 1970, to 156 pairs in 1976 and 240 pairs in 1986. Five other pairs also bred on waste ground in Cardiff. In Scotland, a colony estimated to hold over a hundred pairs of Lesser Black-backed Gulls was found recently on buildings in the Royal Naval Dockyard in Rosyth (Bourne 1988).

REASONS FOR CHANGE IN NUMBERS

Two main sources of food for gulls in Britain and Ireland are the fishing industry and rubbish tips. Both of these have expanded in the last 40 years, but perhaps with less advantage for Lesser Black-backed Gulls than for other species. The fishing industry has grown throughout Britain and Ireland since 1950, both at sea and on land where the catches are processed. Offal and discarded fish provide plentiful food for Lesser Black-backed Gull in southwest Scotland and the Irish Sea where the majority of the breeding colonies are found. In Shetland, where breeding numbers are small, the gulls have to compete with Gannets, Great Skuas and Great Black-backed Gulls for discards from whitefish trawlers (Hudson and Furness 1988). Over 60% of the fish picked up by the Lesser Black-backed Gulls in Hudson's study during the mid 1980s was either dropped, or stolen from them by larger gulls and skuas.

Rubbish tips also provide food for gulls in certain parts of the country, such as south Wales (Ferns and Mudge 1982). Lesser Black-backed Gulls feed on them in large numbers especially in winter. Although this food source has increased since the 1940s as the human population has grown, particularly in urban areas, Lesser Black-backed Gulls have not assumed the habit of feeding on rubbish as widely as Herring Gulls (Greig et al. 1986). Possibly as a result, Lesser Black-backed Gulls are rarely affected by botulism which Herring Gulls seem to contract when feeding on rubbish tips.

Little is known about how the birds' diet may have changed. Most of their diet is obtained by scavenging at sea or feeding on land and not by fishing for themselves although poor breeding success and decline of Lesser Black-backed Gulls (*L.f. fuscus*) in northern Norway was attributed to shortage of food at sea (Røv 1986). The same subspecies of Lesser Black-backed Gull has a different diet in Finland, feeding almost exclusively in brackish and freshwater habitats both during breeding and on migration, yet breeding success is also very low (Kilpi and Saurola 1984).

The reasons for the dramatic expansion of gulls at Orfordness are unclear but it remains one of the few large gull colonies at which no culling takes place. In the 1970s and early 1980s the birds fed their chicks largely on cereal grains and fish including Whiting and Poor Cod which could have been caught near the surface (Thomas *et al.* 1982) or scavenged from fishing boats. Foxes are absent from the spit and, since the public are excluded by the Ministry of Defence, disturbance to the gull colony is exceptionally low. However, following bomb clearance between 1976 and 1986, the area is likely to become gradually more accessible in future (J. Shackles pers. comm.). At least some of the immigrants to Orfordness have come from the west coast. Two of the four recoveries of ringed Lesser Black-backed Gulls found in and near the colony were of birds originally from South Walney; the others were from Sussex and Anglesey (M. Wright *in litt.*).

Lesser Black-backed Gulls are culled, along with other large gulls, on many nature reserves in Britain and Ireland (see chapter on Herring Gull). For example, over 4000 Lesser Black-backed Gulls were removed from the Isle of May between 1972 and 1979, but the colony was considered to be still thriving in the 1980s, apparently because many of the birds were able to breed successfully despite the annual cull (Duncan 1981b). Numbers also increased between 1969–70 and 1985–87 at other colonies in the Firth of Forth (Table 32). By contrast, five seasons of culling at the Abbeystead colony reduced the breeding pairs by more than half, and numbers also declined at adjacent coastal colonies which acted as a source of immigrants (Duncan 1981b).

The cause of the increase in the breeding population of the Lesser Black-backed Gull in Britain can only be speculated upon, but it contrasts strongly with the decline in the closely related Herring Gull in both Britain and Ireland. Increased supplies of food from artificial sources, and numerous reservoirs and flooded gravel pits for safe roosting have proved attractive to Lesser Black-backed Gulls. Since the 1960s, more and more of them have overwintered in Britain instead of migrating south (Baker 1980). Avoidance of the risks and rigours of migration coupled with generally beneficial winter conditions in Britain may have reduced annual mortality. Proof of this should be available from ringed recoveries but unfortunately these are relatively scarce before the 1960s. Fewer birds were ringed then and the rings used on gulls and other seabirds tended to wear through and fall off before the bird was retrapped or recovered dead so that there are no good estimates of survival rate.

Table 30.   *Estimated European breeding population of the Lesser Black-backed Gull.*

	No. of pairs	Comments
USSR—White Sea	350	"Occasional pairs" breed
USSR—Baltic Sea	>10,000	Unknown, Order 5 (10,001–100,000 pairs) but only "small breeding colonies" in Gulf of Finland and "several hundred of these birds" in colonies elsewhere
Iceland	10,000 (1970)	First bred 1920–30, still spreading north and west
Faroe Islands	9000	
Norway	16,000–20,000	
Sweden	29,000	Increasing in south, decreasing in north

Table 30. *Estimated European breeding population of the Lesser Black-backed Gull – cont.*

	No. of pairs	Comments
Finland	10,000–15,000	Increased up to 1960s, then accelerating decline
Denmark	1100	Increased up to 1930s, then declined
West Germany	1800	First bred 1927, increasing
Britain	83,500	Increasing; includes 20,000 pairs inland
Ireland	5200	Stable on coast, increasing inland; includes 3000 pairs inland and urban
Netherlands	8700–9700 (1978)	First bred 1926, increasing especially since 1974
France	16,000–17,000	Became extinct in Normandy but recolonised Brittany in 1925, increased at 8.5–11.4% per annum and spread
Spain	200–300	First bred 1971, increasing
Portugal	5–10	First bred 1978
Approximate total	c. 205,000 pairs	

Sources: Cramp and Simmons (1983), Croxall *et al.* (1984), Røv (1986), P.G.H. Evans pers. comm., Seabird Colony Register.
Year in brackets indicates date of latest census if pre-1980. The size of the populations of the two eastern sub-species *heuglini* and *taimyrensis* are not known.

Table 31. *Numbers of Lesser Black-backed Gulls breeding on coasts of Britain and Ireland 1969–87.*

	1985–87		1969–70	
	Pairs	Birds	Pairs	Birds
Shetland Islands	464[b]	59	541	—
Orkney Islands	1038	1215	910	—
Nairn	—	—	6	—
Moray	—	—	42	—
Banff and Buchan	23	—	15	—
Gordon	45	—	1	—
Kincardine and Deeside	27	—	3	—
Angus	16	—	—	—
Northeast Fife	2273	—	2300	—
Dunfermline	730	—	10	—
Edinburgh	10	—	2	—
East Lothian	1170	—	335	—
Berwickshire	5	—	7	—
Western Isles	322	562	684	17
Caithness	16	—	11	10
Sutherland	72	2	371	—
Ross and Cromarty	132	11	258	4
Skye and Lochalsh	344	92	47	1
Lochaber	171	4	149	6

	1985–87		1969–70	
	Pairs	Birds	Pairs	Birds
Argyll and Bute	3412	890[b]	3979	425
Cunninghame	3750	—	1045	—
Kyle and Carrick	2070	—	429	10
Wigtown	—	—	6	—
Stewartry	1339	—	645	—
Scotland total	17,400	2800	11,800	500
Combined units[a]	18,800[a]		12,100[a]	
Birds converted to pairs	7%		2%	
Northumberland	1050[c]	—	1583	—
Tyne and Wear	1	—	—	—
Norfolk	37	—	—	—
Suffolk	5043	—	150	—
Essex	3	—	—	—
East Sussex	4	—	2	—
West Sussex	2	—	—	—
Isle of Wight	—	4	1	—
Dorset	2	2	—	2
Devon	180	2	101	—
Cornwall	13	—	13	1
Isles of Scilly	3981	—	2500	—
Somerset	—	—	171	—
Avon	2080	—	1730	—
Channel Islands	1103	30	304	—
Lancashire	340	—	7	—
Cumbria	12,000	10	18,175	—
Isle of Man	100	1	54	—
England, Isle of Man and Channel Islands total	25,700	50	24,800	5
Gwent	48	—	10	—
South Glamorgan	280	4	—	—
Mid Glamorgan	3	—	—	—
West Glamorgan	—	—	1	—
Dyfed	16,551	—	7782	—
Gwynedd	2101	—	3727	—
Clwyd	8	—	9	—
Wales total	19,000	5	11,500	—
Antrim	160	—	64	—
Down	284	—	159	—
Dublin	158	—	45	—
Wexford	127	1	468	—
Waterford	—	—	25	—

Table 31. *Numbers of Lesser Black-backed Gulls breeding on coasts of Britain and Ireland 1969–87 – cont.*

	1985–87		1969–70	
	Pairs	Birds	Pairs	Birds
Cork	346[d]	—	132	—
Kerry	558[d]	—	587	—
Clare	—[d]	—	—	48
Galway	5	—	68	—
Mayo	40	—	58	4
Sligo	—	46	16	—
Donegal	8	6	35	1
Ireland total	1700[d]	50[d]	1700	50
Estimated total	2200[e]		1700	
Proportion estimated/converted	25%		1%	
Britain and Ireland total	64,400		50,100	

Totals rounded, <100 to nearest 5, 100–1000 to nearest 10, >1000 to nearest 100.
[a] Includes counts of birds divided by 2 to provide an estimate of pairs; details in text.
[b] Excludes Lesser Black-backed/Herring Gulls: 61 pairs Hascosay, 510 birds Gunna.
[c] Includes estimated 1040 pairs for Farne Islands; 1283 pairs Lesser Black-backed/Herring Gulls counted. Estimate assumes ratio 4:1, as in 1969.
[d] In these counties, at least 10% more pairs are estimated to occur at colonies not visited in 1985–87.
[e] This total includes estimates for colonies not counted recently. It is based on the proportional change in numbers at colonies in each region where counts were conducted in both surveys.

Table 32. *Changes in pairs of Lesser Black-backed Gulls breeding in the Firth of Forth.*

	1985–87	1969–70
Inchkeith	1750	300
Isle of May[a]	520	2000
Car Craig and Haystack	0	10
Incholm	730	0
Inchgarvie	10	2
Inchmickery[a]	60	5
Fidra[a]	140	0
Lamb	10	5
Craigleith	930	275
Bass Rock	30	50
Siccar Point—Broadhaven	1	4
St Abb's Head	2	3
Approximate total	4190	2650

See also Table 35 for Herring Gulls.
[a] Colonies where adults are or were culled.

Herring Gull

Larus argentatus

The Herring Gull (wing-span 137–142 cm) is the commonest of the three species of large gull breeding in Britain and Ireland. It feeds and breeds mostly on the coasts but is often seen far inland. Like the other large gulls, it is an omnivorous scavenger, predator and pirate. It obtains most of its food by foraging in the intertidal zone or by scavenging behind fishing boats and on rubbish tips. Breeding colonies occur in a wide range of habitats including coastal cliffs and islands, sand dunes, low-lying spits and islets, inland lakes and moorland and on urban buildings.

DISTRIBUTION AND INTERNATIONAL STATUS

The Herring Gull has a circumpolar breeding distribution in the temperate zone of the northern hemisphere. There are several subspecies within the breeding range which stretches from the coast of northwest Europe through northern and central Asia to Canada (Barth 1975, Cramp and Simmons 1983). Birds breeding in Britain and Ireland belong to the nominate subspecies. Six subspecies occurring to the south and east of Britain and Ireland are sometimes grouped together and regarded as a separate species, the Yellow-legged Herring Gull *Larus cachinnans* (e.g. Croxall *et al.* 1984).

155

The greatest concentration of breeding Herring Gulls occurs in the extreme northwest of Europe (Table 33). Numbers on the coasts and in inland areas of the Baltic, White and Barents Seas are not known but probably lie between 100,000 and 200,000 pairs (Golovkin 1984). Norway has more than a quarter of a million pairs and, despite recent declines, Britain and Ireland have about 200,000 pairs, or about 20% of the birds breeding in Europe and the Mediterranean. The world population of the Herring Gull is probably almost two million pairs and it is the most numerous of the larger gulls breeding in Europe.

The limit of the Herring Gull's breeding range moved further north earlier this century when new colonies were established in Iceland, on Bear Island and probably Spitsbergen between 1930 and 1950 (Cramp and Simmons 1983). Similar northward expansion may have occurred on the Canadian tundra (Brown and Nettleship 1984a) and in the USSR (Golovkin 1984), but in both these areas the species' distribution is not accurately known. Since 1960, Herring Gulls have started breeding inland in Yugoslavia and have colonised both Switzerland and Poland. Other inland populations such as those in France and West Germany have also expanded. Herring Gull numbers have increased throughout their range during the present century; for example, by 13% per annum in Britain up to the mid 1970s (Chabrzyk and Coulson 1976). However, this increase appears recently to have halted or to have reversed in places (e.g. Scandinavia, Evans 1984, Barrett and Vader 1984). Herring Gulls breeding on the coast in Britain and Ireland almost halved in numbers between 1969 and 1987 (Table 34).

Widespread collection of gulls' eggs and shooting of birds probably kept both North American and European populations low during the nineteenth century. Bird protection laws enforced around the turn of the century, coupled with increasing supplies of food from artificial sources such as rubbish tips and fishing boats enabled numbers to build up rapidly. Control measures were introduced in several areas where the birds were regarded as pests including the eastern USA, Denmark, Netherlands and Germany (Drury and Kadlec 1974, Møller 1981a,b, Cramp and Simmons 1983). Herring Gulls were one of the few seabirds in the 1980s not fully protected by law in Britain or Ireland.

Information from the numerous ringing recoveries available has provided a detailed picture of the Herring Gull's movements in northwest Europe outside the breeding season (Harris 1964, Stanley et al. 1981, Coulson and Butterfield 1985). Birds in the north of the species' range migrate southwards for the winter. Many Herring Gulls wintering in eastern England, for example, come from northern Norway and USSR (Stanley et al. 1981, Coulson et al. 1984a). Gulls breeding in Britain and Ireland disperse from the colonies to winter near local feeding grounds, often in urban areas. Breeding colonies may be used for roosting throughout the year. In a study of Herring Gull recoveries from birds ringed on the Isle of May, young birds tended to move further south than the adults (Parsons and Duncan 1978). Most wintering birds remain on coasts and estuaries in Britain but numbers feeding and roosting inland increase during winter (Hickling 1986). Observations of birds at sea in the 1980s showed that few Herring Gulls occurred far offshore either in the North Sea or over the continental shelf northwest of Scotland unless following fishing boats (Tasker et al. 1987, Benn et al. 1988).

CENSUS METHODS AND PROBLEMS IN COUNTING LARGE GULLS

The problems encountered when censusing Herring Gulls are similar to those for Great and Lesser Black-backed Gulls so that all three species are dealt with together here. Most of the larger gulls nest in conspicuous colonies which are not easily overlooked. However, almost all of the largest Herring Gull colonies declined in size after 1969; in 1985–87 small groups of a few pairs dispersed at low density along stretches of suitable coast were common. In Scotland, for example, over 90% of the birds bred in colonies of less than 100 pairs in 1985–87, compared with 72% in 1969–70. This made census work difficult as small colonies and isolated pairs may have been more easily missed.

There are several major problems in censusing gulls in all but very small gull colonies. First, there is usually no one time during the breeding season when all the pairs using the colony are present with identifiable nests. A single visit to the colony in late May or early June was recommended for the national censuses in 1969–70 and 1985–87, partly because other seabirds could also be counted at this time of year, but also because this coincides approximately with the peak of incubation (Wanless and Harris 1984) when maximum numbers of birds will be sitting on eggs. However, laying and hatching overlap to a considerable extent at most colonies so that there is no optimum time for a single representative count of nests. This is because some pairs which lose their eggs early in the season re-nest. On the Isle of May, Wanless and Harris (1984) found that at least 15% of Herring and Lesser Black-backed Gull clutches were laid after hatching had started in the colony. Other estimates suggest that the error from nest failure and spread of laying may be even higher than this (Green and Hirons 1988).

Secondly, it can be very difficult to count gull nests accurately. A colony may cover a large area of ground, or be situated in deep vegetation such as bracken or among boulders, so that finding all nests is impossible. In such colonies, several observers are needed to walk parallel transects counting nests either side of their path. Even then many nests are missed. Ferns and Mudge (1981) showed that about 17% of nests were omitted by a single count at their mixed-species study colony. They used a team of ten experienced observers to count and mark Herring and Lesser Black-backed Gull nests in different areas of the island of Flat Holm in the Bristol Channel. A second survey carried out immediately afterwards revealed that from 5% to 49% of the occupied gull nests in different areas of the colony had been missed by the first survey. In similar studies on the Isle of May, Wanless and Harris (1984) found that 9% of nests were missed during a single count, although Coulson *et al.* (1982) estimated the error to be as low as 4% (see also Coulson 1985, Wanless and Harris 1985).

Thirdly, gulls in inaccessible colonies are usually censused from a boat, and in remote sites, such as islands far offshore which may be visited only once a year, observers are often involved simultaneously in censusing other species. These gull counts cannot be made as thoroughly as those in accessible or regularly visited colonies, such as those on nature reserves.

Another source of error concerns the counting unit used. When censusing gulls from a distance or from a boat, apparently occupied sites in a colony are not easy to identify. Birds which can be seen actually incubating or standing near their nests can be counted, but those which are visible are an unknown proportion of all those with nests. One possibility is to count the birds present in the colony instead of nests. However, some birds may still be hidden and observations at several Herring Gull colonies have shown that the ratio of birds present to occupied nests varies widely in different parts of a colony (Wanless and Harris 1984). Variation in this ratio occurs also through the day, through the season, and between years. Kilpi (1987) found that a single count of adults can underestimate the number of birds actually occupying the colony by anything from 12% to 44%. Estimating numbers of breeding pairs from counts of birds is at best unreliable and may be extremely inaccurate. However, in the present survey it was sometimes necessary to convert counts of birds to pairs (see below).

Finally, in colonies with both Herring and Lesser Black-backed Gulls it is impossible to distinguish nests of each species. The census method commonly used in these situations is to make a complete nest count and also to count the ratio of the two species present in the colony. This ratio is then used to estimate the proportion of nests belonging to each species. This introduces further error, of unknown but possibly high magnitude, to the estimates of breeding numbers.

During the 1985-87 surveys, roughly 10% of the population of Herring Gulls in Scotland was counted as birds rather than apparently occupied sites. The main areas affected were the Shetland and Orkney Islands, the Western Isles and Angus (Table 34). To include these data in the population totals, counts of birds were divided by two to give an approximate estimate of the number of occupied sites they represented. When regional or local population totals from Table 34 are compared, the proportion of each count which has been converted from birds to pairs must be considered. It must be emphasised that these "converted" figures are of unknown and possibly very low accuracy.

THE HERRING GULL IN BRITAIN AND IRELAND

About 181,000 pairs of Herring Gulls were estimated to have bred in coastal colonies in Britain and Ireland in the period 1985 to 1987, compared with over 335,000 pairs found during Operation Seafarer. In 1985-87, more than half (53%) the birds bred in Scotland and 22% in England. The main centres of the breeding population were in northeast Caithness and, in the west, in Argyll and Bute (Figure 23a), Cumbria and in Northern Ireland, Down. Colonies of over 4000 pairs were found on Inchkeith in the Firth of Forth (4100 pairs) and, on the east coast of Ireland, on Rathlin Island (4000 pairs), the Copeland Islands (7000 pairs) and Lambay (5500 pairs).

Most Herring Gull colonies were on level ground, sloping rock, low cliffs or on buildings. Some Herring Gulls nested inland on islands in lakes, on moorland, or in abandoned quarries. In almost all coastal towns in Britain (and some in Ireland), especially on the east coast, Herring Gulls also nested on

Pairs

• 1 – 10

• 11 – 100

● 101 – 1000

● 1001 – 5000

● 5001 +

50 km
100 km

*Figure 23.   Distribution and size of coastal Herring Gull colonies (and grouped colonies),
1985–87.*

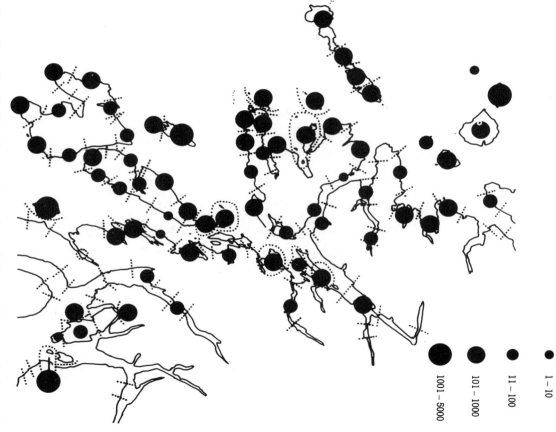

Figure 23a.　*Detail of distribution and size of coastal Herring Gull colonies (and grouped colonies) in western Scotland, 1985–87.*

occupied and unoccupied buildings and similar artificial structures (Cramp 1971, O'Meara 1975, Monaghan and Coulson 1977, Hutchinson 1989). Herring Gull numbers declined in almost all parts of Britain and Ireland between the two complete population censuses in 1969–70 and 1985–87 (Figure 24). The largest proportional decreases appeared to have taken place

1–10

11–100

101–1000

1001–5000

in colonies in the west, and numbers were estimated to have more than halved in north and west Scotland, southeast and southwest Ireland, Wales and southwest England. The main exception to the downward trend in numbers during the 1970s and 1980s was at Orfordness in Suffolk. Here numbers grew from 150 pairs in 1969 to nearly 1400 pairs in 1973. The colony remained approximately stable at this level until 1981 and increased again to 3390 pairs in 1986. The source of immigrants which are assumed to

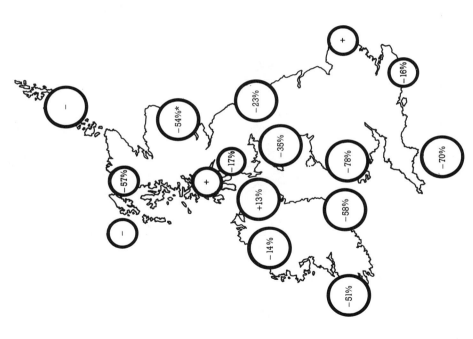

Figure 24.   Regional changes in numbers of coastal breeding Herring Gulls, 1969–87. See Table 34 for counts and Figure 1 for regional boundaries.
No figure is given if more than 10% of the regional total was derived from counts made as individuals rather than pairs or where totals were less than 400 pairs. Orfordness excluded from SE England total.
* Excludes Angus.

have fuelled this expansion was unknown (Thomas *et al.* 1982) although one bird ringed as a chick in Holland was recovered at Orfordness (M.T. Wright *in litt.*).

The only other places where Herring Gulls increased between 1969–70 and 1985–87 were in southwest Scotland (Isle of Skye to Kyle and Carrick), on the adjacent coast of Northern Ireland and, based on incomplete surveys, northwest Ireland. In Northern Ireland this was due to the growth of large colonies on islands off the coast of Down. The Copeland Islands were estimated to have had 3250 pairs of Herring Gulls in 1969; these had more than doubled to 7000 pairs by 1985, making this the largest colony in Ireland. Further south in Down, the Herring Gull colony on Gun's Island also grew from about 1350 pairs in 1969 to 1900 pairs in 1985 (1770 in 1987), and the one nearby on Burial Island expanded from about 100 to 1250 pairs during the same period. These increases occurred at a time when an estimated overall decline of 26% took place in the Irish breeding population.

In the west of Scotland the situation is less clear. Some colonies increased in size after 1969 whilst others decreased, but by 1985–87 there had been an overall decrease of between a fifth and a quarter in the number of pairs breeding. Counts of Herring Gulls nesting in the Firth of Clyde suggested that, although these colonies never grew as much as those in the rest of Britain or Ireland during the 1960s, the breeding population increased right up to the mid 1980s (Gibson 1985, 1986, Monaghan and Zonfrillo 1986).

However, all the colonies in southwest Scotland which held over 500 pairs in 1969–70 either remained stable (e.g. Canna), or had declined in size (e.g. Treshnish Islands, west Jura, Inchmarnock Island) by 1985–87. The island of Little Cumbrae in the Firth of Clyde held the only large colony in 1969–70 (700 pairs) which had grown even larger by 1985–87 (3500 pairs). A few colonies increased to over 500 pairs during the same period (e.g. Ceann a'Mhara and the rest of Tiree, Holy Isle off Arran, northwest Colonsay, Sanda, Ailsa Craig). The last three of these with Little Cumbrae are now the only sites in the west of Scotland with over 1000 pairs of Herring Gulls each.

A survey of gulls nesting in urban areas in 1976 found about 3000 pairs of Herring Gulls on buildings in Britain and two colonies in Ireland (Monaghan and Coulson 1977). Numbers had increased by 17% per annum since 1969. Because many urban-nesting gulls were classed as inland by the 1985–87 surveys, no attempt was made to cover all town rooftops. From the scattering of records submitted to the Seabird Colony Register, it seems that the increase in roof-nesting may have continued through to the mid 1980s, but probably not as fast as during the early 1970s. For example, the surveys in 1985–87 showed 380 pairs on roofs in Dover, 450 pairs in Folkestone and 130 pairs in Cardiff. Numbers of Herring Gulls nesting on buildings in the east of Scotland increased during the 1970s, though no colonies were larger than a few pairs (Bourne 1979). In 1987 an estimated 100 pairs or more of Herring Gulls (with a similar number of Lesser Black-backed Gulls) were reported nesting on buildings in the Royal Naval Dockyard at Rosyth (Bourne 1988). In south Wales, Herring Gulls nesting in towns in Glamorgan apparently declined after the mid 1970s; their numbers nearly halved between 1974 and 1980 (Hurford

Plate 20.   Herring Gulls at roof nest site, St Ives, Cornwall (J.B. and S. Bottomley)

1985). During the 1970s and 1980s, Herring Gulls were reported nesting in towns at eight locations in Ireland, including a first record for the west coast (one pair on a chimney in Galway, 1982) (Hutchinson 1989).

Herring Gulls breeding at other colonies inland were also excluded from the 1985–87 surveys in Scotland and England; 150 pairs were found on islands in reservoirs and lakes during a complete survey of inland colonies in Wales. There has been no survey of the other inland breeding populations in Britain, or of how these may have changed in the last 20 years. Numbers of Herring Gulls in the mid-Glamorgan quarries are known to have declined from 133 pairs in 1974 to 48 pairs in 1980 (Hurford 1985). At least 3400 pairs of Herring Gulls bred in the large west Pennine gull colony at Abbeystead in 1978 but, after five seasons of culling adults, this colony had declined to under 500 pairs (Wanless and Langslow 1983) and has since been reduced to below 200 pairs (Thomas and Tasker 1988).

A survey of the main inland gull colonies in the west of Ireland, from Donegal to Galway, during 1977 and 1978 found 827 (individual) Herring Gulls; the species was thought to have colonised freshwater loughs in large numbers only recently (Whilde 1978). A repeat survey of the main loughs in 1983 indicated little real change in numbers (Whilde 1983).

REASONS FOR CHANGE IN NUMBERS

The number of Herring Gulls breeding in Britain increased at an estimated 10–13% a year from at least the 1940s up to the mid 1970s (Chabrzyk and Coulson 1976). Existing colonies grew in size, new ones were established, and the species colonised many inland and urban sites during this period (Cramp *et al.* 1974). The Herring Gull's success since the turn of the century has been attributed to the cessation of human persecution and to the abundance of food provided throughout the year from new sources such as fishing boats, rubbish tips, sewage outlets and fish factories.

From the 1940s up to about the late 1970s, gulls were supplied with more and more food from these artificial sources on land and at sea. Growth in the human population during this period led to a vast increase in the quantity of rubbish discarded and sewage discharged; and modern fishing practices, such as stern trawling and freezing of catches, have increased the amounts of fish caught and of offal produced after processing catches at sea and in fishing ports. Overwinter survival may have been enhanced by this extra food available to Herring Gulls (Harris 1970). In Britain, at least some of the birds which fed at rubbish tips and fish docks may have bred more successfully than those at neighbouring nests which did not feed on artificial foods (Davis 1974). Herring Gulls nesting in cities also appear to be highly productive compared with those elsewhere. Monaghan (1979) reported that gulls on rooftops in South Shields (northeast England) reared 1.2 to 1.6 chicks per pair in the 1970s, compared with 0.6 to 1.2 chicks per pair recorded by various studies in natural coastal colonies elsewhere. This was due mainly to low levels of cannibalism and intra-specific disturbance in the town-nesting gulls.

Feeding on rubbish tips also has disadvantages for the gulls. About 10% of over 8000 Herring Gulls caught at tips in the Firth of Clyde area between 1978 and 1984 were found to be carrying *Salmonella* bacteria in their guts (Monaghan *et al.* 1985). Particularly in the warm summer months, decaying rubbish and stagnant water provide ideal conditions for the build-up of the bacterium *Clostridium botulinum*. Gulls feeding at tips or loafing around evaporating puddles at feeding grounds and breeding colonies are poisoned by toxins produced by the bacteria, producing a condition known as botulism. Until the mid 1970s, known incidents of botulism in wild birds in Britain were rare. In the summer of 1975 nearly 6000 birds, mostly Herring Gulls, died in a series of outbreaks of the disease in Britain and Northern Ireland (Lloyd *et al.* 1976). Since 1975 botulism has been proved or strongly suspected to have caused a number of different mortality incidents among gulls both on and off the breeding colonies throughout Britain and Ireland. The numerous examples include northeast Scotland (Bell 1985, E. Cameron pers. comm.), the Firth of Forth (MacDonald and Standring 1978), Orfordness (J. Shackles pers. comm.), south Wales (Sutcliffe 1986), many parts of Ireland (including Co. Cork, where Black-headed Gulls were the main species affected in one incident (Buckley and O'Halloran 1986)), and Guernsey in the Channel Islands (M. Hill *in litt.*).

As well as feeding in the intertidal zone and inland, some Herring Gulls collect food by scavenging behind fishing boats. The way in which seabirds obtained food from fishing boats around Shetland was studied in the mid 1980s by Hudson (1986). Whitefish trawlers provided huge quantities of discarded fish for seabirds but Herring Gulls were relatively rare and were forced to compete with Great Black-backed Gulls, Gannets and Great Skuas for discarded fish. Over half (52%) of the fish Herring Gulls picked up were dropped or stolen from them (Hudson and Furness 1988). By contrast, boats fishing in the Clyde and on adjacent coasts caught mainly Norway Lobsters in the 1980s. Furness *et al.* (1988) found that the fish discarded from these catches were generally small enough for Herring Gulls to swallow with ease, especially as there was less competition from larger scavengers. The increase in the legal minimum mesh size for whitefish nets in the North Sea in 1987 resulted in a decrease in the amount of discarded fish but an increase in their average size. This, it was predicted, would put smaller scavenging species such as the Herring Gull at a further competitive disadvantage and so reduce the food available to them behind fishing boats in the North Sea (Furness *et al.* 1988). The ease with which Herring Gulls collect food from fishing boats in the Clyde and adjacent areas, compared with the effort required to exploit similar food sources in Shetland, may be one reason why numbers of breeding Herring Gulls have continued to increase in the former area but have declined in the latter.

Human persecution is certainly less now than it was in the nineteenth century, but Herring Gulls are still killed by man and prevented from breeding successfully in Britain and Ireland and a number of other European countries. For instance, between 50,000 and 100,000 gulls were shot off Norway each winter during the 1970s (Barrett and Vader 1984). In Spain, the collection of Herring Gulls and their eggs for food was sufficiently widespread in the 1980s to be considered a threat to the population (Bárcena *et al.* 1984, de Juana 1984). Even in Britain and Ireland, the three species of large gull are specifically excluded from some aspects of the legislation to protect wildlife, making it legal (in Britain, for an "authorised person") to kill birds or take eggs at any time of year. No records are available of how many birds are shot on private land each year, or how many are prevented from breeding by egg collecting.

POPULATION CONTROL MEASURES FOR LARGE GULLS

During their population expansion, Herring, Lesser Black-backed and Great Black-backed Gulls have come into conflict with other birds sharing their breeding sites. Each of these gulls is capable of behaving as a predator of eggs and chicks, but evidence of serious damage by gulls to other nesting birds is scarce (Thomas 1972). Nevertheless, breeding productivity of Puffins in Newfoundland, for example, was clearly affected by piracy and interference from Herring Gulls in the late 1960s (Nettleship 1972). In most cases, Herring Gulls appear to influence other birds breeding nearby more by usurping space for nesting than by direct predation (Thomas 1972). Increasing gull numbers were held responsible for past declines in numbers of breeding terns at a number of colonies in Britain, Ireland and the USA (Nisbet 1973, Lloyd *et al.* 1975, Thomas 1982) although evidence was largely circumstantial.

Herring Gulls can be a problem to man in several ways. They have been accused of spreading disease through washing and defecating in water supplies (both reservoirs and catchment areac), although evidence of any actual harm to human populations is scarce. Gulls may also pose a threat to aircraft through bird-strike, but this problem is rare away from colonies and feeding areas such as rubbish tips. Their presence on town roofs can cause considerable disturbance to residents, particularly during the early morning in spring and summer when birds are establishing and defending their territories.

As a result of these real or perceived threats, Herring Gulls and other large gulls were culled regularly and prevented from breeding at colonies, mostly on nature reserves, in many parts of Britain and Ireland during the 1980s. Little is known about the overall effect this has had, or will have, upon the size of their breeding populations.

The most detailed study of the effects of culling has been made on the Isle of May in southeast Scotland, where gulls were killed in larger numbers and for a longer period than anywhere else in Britain or Ireland. Herring gulls on the Isle of May increased by 13% a year from about 1907 to 1972 when an annual programme of culling breeding adults was started by the Nature Conservancy Council. Nearly 44,000 Herring and Lesser Black-backed Gulls were removed from the island during the first five years and the colony declined from 42,000 pairs to 6650 pairs (Duncan 1978). It was estimated that a further 27,000 birds were deterred from joining the colony during this period and that many of these found their way into other breeding colonies, mainly in east Scotland and northeast England (Duncan and Monaghan 1977). Culling continued on the Isle of May until 1986.

Up to 6000 pairs of terns bred on the Isle of May from 1927 to 1957, but they abandoned the island at the time when the Herring and Lesser Black-backed Gull colony reached 3000 pairs (Wanless 1988). In 1982, when gull numbers had been reduced to between 3000 and 4000 pairs by ten years of culling, Common Terns once again began breeding on the island. Arctic Terns also nested there in the mid 1980s and Sandwich Terns were seen displaying over it. As Wanless points out, the terns' absence from the island coincided with the time when the gulls exceeded 3000 pairs, but other factors such as variation in local food stocks and vegetation changes on the island associated with declining numbers of rabbits also may have affected the terns.

The culling of large gulls does not always have the desired effect upon numbers of other birds breeding in the colony, although it is usually aimed at encouraging sensitive species such as terns, waders or ducks to nest. Some gull colonies declined or disappeared with the repeated removal of breeding birds in the 1970s and 1980s, but this was sometimes followed by habitat changes as vegetation grew more thickly than before and plants such as nettles and brambles flourished. In tern colonies such as that on the RSPB reserve on Coquet Island in Northumberland, additional habitat management was then required to preserve suitable nesting space. A reduction in numbers of large gulls on another RSPB reserve on Horse Island off the Ayrshire coast in the 1970s was accompanied by the disappearance of the terns themselves, probably due to other, unrelated environmental factors (Monaghan and Zonfrillo 1986).

Surveys of gull colonies for the Seabird Colony Register suggested that emigration from gull colonies where regular culling of adults or nest destruction took place may have caused widespread redistribution of the breeding population. Contrary to the trend in numbers elsewhere in eastern Scotland from 1969–70 to 1985–87, Herring Gull numbers increased at undisturbed colonies near the Isle of May (Table 35) and on the coast further north (e.g. Redhead Cliffs, Angus: 589 pairs 1969, 2125 pairs 1986). Similarly, about 1400 Herring Gull nests were destroyed each year on islands in the National Trust for Northern Ireland's reserve on Strangford Lough in the 1970s and 1980s. Meanwhile, the gull colonies off the coast of Down (Copeland Islands, Gun's Island, Burial Island) increased considerably in size from 1969–70 to 1985–87. In Suffolk, the growth of the mixed Herring and Lesser Black-backed Gull colony on the Suffolk coast at Orfordness (see above) can be explained only by immigration (Thomas *et al.* 1982), although it is not known where the new birds came from. Apart from southwest Scotland and northwest Ireland, the only colonies to have increased in size during the last 10–15 years are the ones that appear to have been attracting birds displaced from elsewhere.

Table 33. *Estimated world population of the Herring Gull including the Yellow-legged Herring Gull.*

	No. of pairs	Comments
USSR—Baltic Sea	10,000–100,000	
USSR—Barents Sea	10,000–100,000	Increasing, e.g. Ainov Island
USSR—White Sea	>5000	Tenfold growth 1958–74
USSR—Laptev and Bering Seas	?	
China	?	Breeds W Xinjiang and W Heilongjiang provinces
USA—Alaska	<2000	Unknown numbers inland, declining New Brunswick
SE Canada	156,600	
USA—Great Lakes	>35,000	Local declines, e.g. Long Island
USA—East coast	92,000	Irregular breeding
Svalbard	<50	First bred 1920, little expansion since 1940, interbreeds with Glaucous Gull *L. hyperboreus*
Iceland	10,000	
Faroe Islands	1200–1500	Recent decline in south, increased up to 1971 in north
Norway	260,000	
Sweden	66,000	Increased up to 1975, then stable
Finland	30,000	Increased 1930s–1980
Poland	>500 1978:	First bred 1960s, no complete census
East Germany	1000 1979:	Controlled
Denmark	50,000	Declined since 1974
West Germany	45,200	90% on North Sea coast, spreading inland

Table 33. *Estimated world population of the Herring Gull including the Yellow-legged Herring Gull – cont.*

	No. of pairs	Comments
Britain	161,100	Decreased since 1969, includes c. 15,000 inland and urban
Ireland	44,700	Decreased since 1969, includes c. 500 inland and urban
Netherlands	53,000 1977:	Controlled 1930–60, then increased until 1977
Belgium	>50,000	First bred 1968 inland
France	85,100	Increased since 1976, spread inland
Switzerland	<10	
Atlantic Iberia	40,000	97% in Spain, most on 3 offshore island groups, increased and spread up to 1981
Azores	2000	Includes inland colonies
Madeiran Islands	?	
Canary Islands	?	
Salvage Islands	<50	
Spanish Mediterranean	50,700	Increased since 1960s. Hunted legally and eggs collected
Italy	24,300	Probably increasing
Malta	140	
Yugoslavia	>2900 1974:	No complete census, first bred inland 1979
USSR—Black and Azov Seas	22,000	More than half on roofs
Bulgaria	2250	
Turkey	?	
Cyprus	75	
Greece and Albania	?	
USSR—Lake Baykal and Transbaykal	>6000	
USSR—Caspian Sea	>10,000	
Syria and Lebanon	?	
Israel	5	
Egypt	20–50	
Algeria	2500	
Tunisia	600–700	
Morocco and Chafarinas	4700	Mostly on Chafarinas Islands
Mauritania	<10	Occasional breeder
Approximate total	1.75–2 million pairs	

Sources: Cramp and Simmons (1983), Croxall *et al.* (1984), Røv (1985), MEDMARAVIS and Monbailliu (1986), Hémery *et al.* (1988), Ilyichev and Zubakin (1988), Paterson (1989), Blokpoel and Scharf in press, Kondratiev in press, P.G.H. Evans pers. comm., Seabird Colony Register.
NB: Total of 76,100 pairs reported recently in west Mediterranean outside Spain (Paterson 1989).
? = Breeds, numbers unknown.
Figures in brackets are for year of most recent count if pre-1980.

Table 34.   Numbers of Herring Gulls breeding in coastal colonies in Britain and Ireland 1969–87.

	1985–87		1969–70	
	Pairs	Birds	Pairs	Birds
Shetland Islands	4392[b]	1136	9273	—
Orkney Islands	911	3717	7831	—
Nairn	—	—	300	—
Moray	364	—	1043	—
Banff and Buchan	6700	—	27,748	—
Gordon	3330	—	4037	—
Aberdeen	84	—	93	75
Kincardine and Deeside	8392	—	10,682	—
Angus	4825	5750	1571	—
Dundee	100	—	—	—
Northeast Fife	6191	—	15,808	—
Dunfermline	1090	—	55	—
Edinburgh	110	—	10	—
East Lothian	3456	—	7371	—
Berwickshire	1831	—	1516	—
Western Isles	2519	1593	3750	80
Caithness	10,052	—	22,298	370
Sutherland	2302	71	7035	—
Ross and Cromarty	1322	173	12,983	—
Inverness	137	—	3	—
Skye and Lochalsh	2476	99	1329	196
Lochaber	3639	—	3130	40
Argyll and Bute	13,180	8043[b]	10,479	1050
Cunninghame	4250	—	1250	—
Kyle and Carrick	2385	—	1909	—
Wigtown	499	—	1523	—
Stewartry	1157	—	5305	—
Scotland total	85,700	20,600	158,300	1800
Combined units	96,000[a]		159,200[a]	
Birds converted to pairs	11%		<1%	
Northumberland	268[c]	—	452	—
Tyne and Wear	300	—	80	—
Durham	—	—	11	—
Cleveland	327	—	1016	—
North Yorkshire	752	375	1059	—
Humberside	1151	—	1265	—
Lincolnshire	10	—	—	—
Norfolk	44	—	—	—
Suffolk	3390	6	151	—

Table 34.   *Numbers of Herring Gulls breeding in coastal colonies in Britain and Ireland 1969-87 – cont.*

	1985-87		1969-70	
	Pairs	Birds	Pairs	Birds
Kent	1389	—	663	—
East Sussex	727	—	857	—
West Sussex	24	4	1	—
Hampshire	—	—	3	—
Isle of Wight	160	—	1221	—
Dorset	489	—	2125	—
Devon	2296	121	12,752	—
Cornwall	2694	—	8871	1519
Scilly Isles	1279	—	1000	—
Somerset	68	—	3207	—
Avon	1260	—	5990	—
Gloucester	—	—	49	—
Lancashire	85	—	2	—
Cumbria	11,131	10	20,580	—
Isle of Man	8602	8	9977	—
Channel Islands	3348	30	3970	—
England, Isle of Man and Channel Isles total	39,800	550	75,300	1500
Combined units[a]	40,000[a]		76,100[a]	
Birds converted to pairs	1%		1%	
Gwent	24	—	199	—
South Glamorgan	172	10	211	—
Mid Glamorgan	20	—	196	—
West Glamorgan	13	—	189	—
Dyfed	5275	59	15,394	—
Gwynedd	5136	—	31,160	1000
Clwyd	95	—	727	—
Wales total	10,700	70	48,100	1000
Combined units[a]			48,600[a]	
Birds converted to pairs			1%	
Derry	17	—	—	—
Antrim	5773[d]	—	6757	150
Down	11,659	—	9170	—
Dublin	6857	—	13,407	—
Wicklow	141[d]	—	374	—
Wexford	1600	—	6590	—
Waterford	1638	—	4060	—

Table 34. *Numbers of Herring Gulls breeding in coastal colonies in Britain and Ireland 1969–87 – cont.*

| | 1985–87 | | 1969–70 | |
	Pairs	Birds	Pairs	Birds
Cork	2117[d]	—	3511	—
Kerry	493[d]	—	4458	2
Clare	4	64	788	1276
Galway	464[d]	—	1643	402
Mayo	687[d]	—	1981	195
Sligo	14[d]	400[d]	451	320
Donegal	2058[d]	43	5324	55
Ireland total	33,500	500	58,500	2400
Estimated total	44,200[e]		59,700[a]	
Proportion estimated/converted	24%		2%	
Britain and Ireland total	190,900[a]		335,100[a]	

Totals rounded, <100 to nearest 5, 100–1000 to nearest 10, >1000 to nearest 100.

[a] Includes counts of birds divided by 2 to provide estimate of pairs; details in text.

[b] Excludes Herring/Lesser Black-backed Gulls: 61 pairs Hascosay, 510 birds Gunna.

[c] Includes estimated 260 pairs for Farne Islands; 1283 pairs Lesser Black-backed/Herring Gulls counted. Estimate assumes 4:1 ratio, as in 1969.

[d] In these counties, at least 10% more pairs are estimated to occur at colonies not visited in 1985–87.

[e] This total includes estimates for colonies not counted recently. It is based on the proportional change in numbers at colonies in each region where counts were conducted in both surveys.

Table 35. *Changes in pairs of Herring Gulls breeding in the Firth of Forth.*

	1985–88	1969–70
Inchkeith	4090	750
Isle of May[a]	2100	15,000
Car Craig and Haystack	50	50
Inchcolm	1040	5
Inchgarvie	110	10
Inchmickery[a]	50	30
Eyebroughty	170	140
Fidra[a]	410	100
Lamb	220	550
Craigleith	2280	5500
Bass Rock	325	1050
Siccar Point—Broadhaven	815	450
St Abb's Head	700	920
Total	12,360	24,560

[a] Colonies where adults are or were culled.

Great Black-backed Gull

Larus marinus

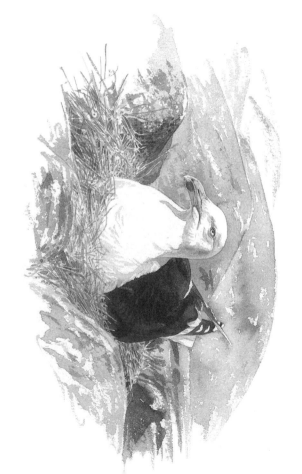

The Great Black-backed Gull is the largest of the gulls nesting in Britain and Ireland and has a wing-span of 152–167 cm. The species is a predator, scavenger and pirate, and feeds on any vertebrate or invertebrate of suitable size, as well as eggs and offal. It is an opportunist, adapting its feeding methods to each situation. Food is obtained by foraging at sea, in the intertidal zone, or by scavenging behind fishing boats, in fields, at rubbish tips or at fish-processing plants. The birds are sometimes seen far from land when following fishing boats (Tasker *et al.* 1987). Most breeding colonies are on islands or on top of rocky stacks and many birds nest as isolated pairs. A few pairs nest inland in Scotland and Ireland on lakes and moorland.

DISTRIBUTION AND INTERNATIONAL STATUS

The Great Black-backed Gull is confined to the North Atlantic. Its breeding range stretches from eastern Canada and the USA to Svalbard and the Barents Sea and south to Britain, Ireland and France (Table 36). It is not known exactly how many Great Black-backed Gulls breed in the USSR and Iceland, but the world population is probably under a quarter of a million pairs, making it considerably rarer than the Herring Gull and only slightly more numerous than the Lesser Black-backed Gull. Britain and Ireland have about 23,300 pairs of Great Black-backed Gulls, or roughly an eighth of the European breeding population.

In common with many other species of seabirds in the North Atlantic, the Great Black-backed Gull has expanded its breeding range during the present century. It colonised Svalbard, Denmark and France in the 1920s and 1930s, and recently has spread further north to the North West Territories of Canada (Brown and Nettleship 1984a). Numbers on both sides of the Atlantic have increased considerably this century although the breeding population in Britain and Ireland appeared to be stable in the 1970s and 1980s. Great Black-backed Gulls on Ainov Island in the Barents Sea increased tenfold between 1958 and the 1980s, to 6000 pairs (Golovkin 1984). The largest North American colony, on Gardiner's Island off Long Island, New York, held over 2000 pairs in 1983 (Buckley and Buckley 1984). The largest British one, by comparison, (Calf of Eday, Orkney) had 800 pairs in 1986 although in 1969 both North Rona (over 1900 pairs) and the Burn of Forse, Hoy (1200 pairs) were larger than this.

Ringing recoveries show that most British and Irish Great Black-backed Gulls remain within 100 km of their breeding colonies even outside the nesting season (Harris 1962b). Birds in the Gulf of Finland are also mainly sedentary (Kilpi and Saurola 1984), but those from further north migrate south. Many Norwegian and Russian birds have been recovered in Britain and Ireland in winter (Coulson *et al.* 1984b).

CENSUS METHODS AND PROBLEMS

Great Black-backed Gulls nest either in colonies or in groups of a few pairs. Colonies are sometimes big and always conspicuous because of the birds' large size and deep voices compared with other gulls. Many colonies are also virtually inaccessible, which can make counting occupied nests difficult. Isolated pairs can be easily overlooked, although most nest near or among other species of breeding seabirds.

The problems in censusing Great Black-backed Gulls are very similar to those for the Herring Gull (see chapter on Herring Gull). A single annual nest count, for example, gives only the roughest estimate of colony size because of the spread of laying, but even less information is available than for Herring or Lesser Black-backed Gulls on the size of the potential error.

During the recent surveys for the Seabird Colony Register, some Great Black-backed Gulls were counted as birds present in the colony, rather than as apparently occupied nests. This was a particular problem in Scotland where a majority (71%) of the counts from Orkney and up to a third of those from Shetland, the Western Isles, Ross and Cromarty, and Argyll and Bute were recorded as birds. In order to use all available counts and to obtain complete population estimates, the counts of birds were divided by two and combined with the counts of occupied sites. The proportion of each count converted from birds, especially those for Scotland, must be considered when comparing the totals in Table 37.

THE GREAT BLACK-BACKED GULL IN BRITAIN AND IRELAND

There appeared to be almost no difference in the number of Great Black-backed Gulls breeding in coastal colonies in 1969–70 (22,500 pairs) and 1985–87 (23,300 pairs) although the latter included a large proportion (28%) of birds converted to pairs. About 70% of the 1985–87 total bred in Scotland. The rest of the population was divided almost equally between England (plus the Isle of Man and the Channel Islands), and Ireland; only 2% of pairs bred in Wales. The largest colonies were found during 1985–87 in Orkney; these were the Calf of Eday (see above), the Burn of Forse area of Hoy (1227 breeding birds) and Rothiesholm Head on Rousay (750 breeding birds). Outside Orkney, only three colonies had more than 200 pairs—North Rona (733 pairs), the Duvillaun Islands off Mayo (217 pairs) and Inishtooskert in the Blasket Islands off Kerry (225 pairs).

The problems in counting gulls already referred to make it clear that counts are not accurate enough to detect changes in the size of the breeding population of less than about 10%. Numbers of Great Black-backed Gulls breeding on most parts of the coast apparently altered by little more than this from 1969–70 to 1985–87 (Figure 26). Small declines may have occurred in the Channel Islands and north Scotland, and some small increases in Northern Ireland, Cumbria and the Isle of Man. The few colonies in northwest Ireland counted in both surveys increased by 60–70%, but this figure is based on a very incomplete sample of colonies. In the Isles of Scilly, numbers remained between 1200 and 1600 pairs from 1969 until 1983, but declined to 1000 pairs by 1987 (Birkin and Smith 1987).

Numbers of Great Black-backed Gulls in the small Welsh breeding population declined by more than half during this period. This was most conspicuous in the big Dyfed colonies of Midland, Skomer and St Margaret's, each with over 100 pairs in 1969–70; these had shrunk to 20–40 pairs each by 1985–87. In fact, in 1969–70 over half of the birds in Wales bred in small colonies of less than 100 pairs. Many of these had disappeared by 1985–87 (e.g. St David's Head, Stack Rocks, Strumble Head, Bardsey, Newborough Warren), their loss being mainly responsible for the decline.

Elsewhere in Britain and Ireland, the majority of the breeding population in 1969–70 was found in colonies with over 100 pairs; many of these also declined by 1985–87 (e.g. Shiants, Am Balg, North Sutor of Cromarty, Mullion Island, Saltee Islands and Inishvickillane). However, many small colonies increased in size so that overall numbers remained reasonably stable. Examples include numerous small colonies on offshore islands such as Tiree (15 to 45 pairs), Staffa (1 to 12 pairs), northwest Colonsay (4 pairs to 86 birds), Cara Island off Islay (8 to 30 pairs), Little Cumbrae (37 to 80 pairs) and Ailsa Craig (6 to 42 pairs). Great Black-backed Gull numbers in the Firth of Clyde were estimated to have grown by 2–3% a year from 1969 to the early 1980s (Monaghan and Zonfrillo 1986).

A few Great Black-backed Gulls breed inland in Scotland and the north of England. Sharrock (1976) mentioned 35 pairs breeding on Tambrook Fell (or Abbeystead) in Lancashire; following the culling there, only one or two pairs survive (Thomas and Tasker 1988). In northwest Ireland, eight pairs of Great

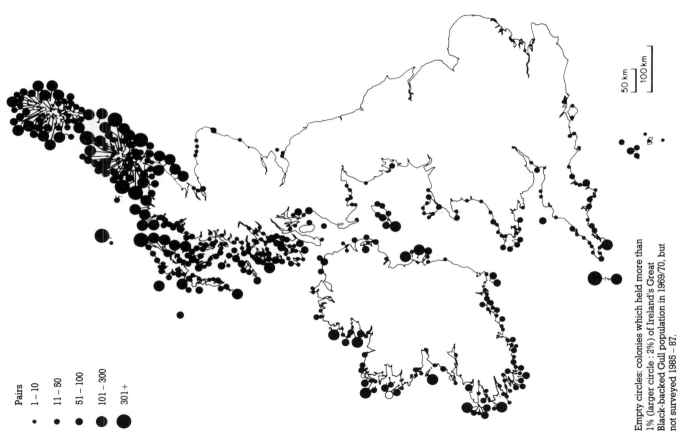

Pairs

·   1 – 10

•   11 – 50

●   51 – 100

⬤   101 – 300

⬤   301+

Empty circles: colonies which held more than
1% (larger circle : 2%) of Ireland's Great
Black-backed Gull population in 1969/70, but
not surveyed 1985 – 87.

*Figure 25.   Distribution and size of coastal Great Black-backed Gull colonies (and
grouped colonies), 1985–87.*

(a)

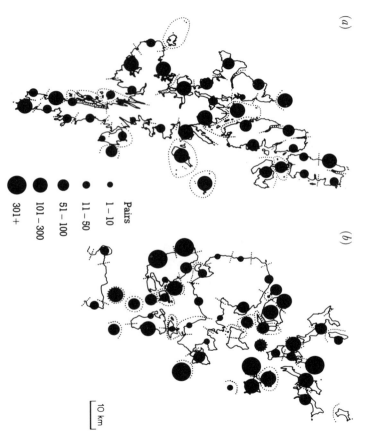

(b)

Pairs

- 1 – 10
- 11 – 50
- 51 – 100
- 101 – 300
- 301 +

10 km

Figure 25a. Detail of distribution and size of coastal Great Black-backed Gull colonies (and grouped colonies) in Shetland, 1985–87.

Figure 25b. Detail of distribution and size of coastal Great Black-backed Gull colonies (and grouped colonies) in Orkney, 1985–87.

Black-backed Gulls nested on Upper and Lower Lough Erne in 1985 and a census of all inland gull colonies from Donegal to Galway in 1977–78 recorded only 50 birds (Whilde 1977). A repeat survey of the main colonies in 1983 suggested that Great Black-backed Gulls had decreased, possibly by nearly a half (Whilde 1983). The only Great Black-backed Gulls reported nesting on buildings in 1974 were seven pairs in Cornwall (Monaghan and Coulson 1977). Thus the total population away from coastal areas is likely to be very small.

REASONS FOR CHANGE IN NUMBERS

In common with many other seabirds, Great Black-backed Gulls have increased in numbers and extended their breeding range in the present century (Cramp *et al.* 1974). The cause of this is unknown but the availability

Figure 26. Regional changes in numbers of coastal breeding Great Black-backed Gulls 1969–87. See Table 37 for counts, and Figure 1 for regional divisions. No figure is given if more than 10% of a county/regional total was derived from counts made as individuals rather than pairs or where totals were less than 400 pairs. Orfordness excluded from SE England total.
* Excludes Sligo.

of artificial foods, such as rubbish, discarded fish and offal has increased during the last 30–40 years. Great Black-backed Gulls can vary their foraging methods to take advantage of artificial food supplies and they switch between foods in response to prevailing feeding conditions. This has probably helped to support the increase (Harris 1970).

The Great Black-backed Gull's size gives it an advantage over smaller birds in a number of feeding situations. Great Black-backed Gulls were observed to feed more successfully than either Herring or Black-headed Gulls on freshly dumped, undisturbed rubbish at tips in northeast England (Greig *et al.* 1986). When foraging around bulldozers burying rubbish, however, they fared less well than the lighter and more agile Black-headed Gulls. During Greig's study, the numbers of Great Black-backed Gulls feeding at rubbish tips were inversely related to the amount of fish offal landed at local ports, suggesting that when fish offal was not available, the gulls switched to rubbish as an alternative food source.

The marked decline of Great Black-backed Gulls in south Wales has been attributed to their habit of feeding on rubbish in conditions which favour the spread of botulism (see chapter on Herring Gull) (Sutcliffe 1986). Corpses and dying birds with symptoms of botulism were picked up at breeding colonies, especially Skokholm and Skomer, in the late 1970s. All measures previously taken to control numbers, such as destruction of nests, were stopped, but the decline has continued. Botulism outbreaks have not been reported among Great Black-backed Gulls elsewhere in Britain, but were suspected to have occurred regularly on Great Saltee in southeast Ireland from 1985 to 1988 (O.J. Merne pers. comm.).

Where Great Black-backed Gulls nest close to other seabirds, predation can provide most of the food for the breeding birds and their young for several months of the year (e.g. Harris 1965); cannibalism is also quite common. The huge expansion of most seabirds in Britain and Ireland this century has undoubtedly increased this particular supply of food for Great Black-backed Gulls although not all of them take advantage of it. On Great Saltee off southeast Ireland, for example, the gulls appeared to be divided into specialist predators and marine feeders. About 400 pairs of gulls bred on the island in 1980 and three-quarters of these nested in a concentrated colony on the summit; the rest were scattered around the clifftops in relatively isolated nest sites (Lloyd 1982a). The food remains in pellets regurgitated at the nest sites showed that the colonial nesting birds fed almost exclusively on fish or crab, whilst it was only the few solitary nesters which collected most of their food by predation, mainly of the auks and gulls breeding near their nests (Hudson 1982).

The enactment of bird protection laws around the turn of the century reduced the amount of persecution and egg collecting that had kept numbers of Great Black-backed Gulls and other seabirds low during the nineteenth century. However, they are still regarded by farmers as a threat to sheep and other livestock, and on nature reserves as possible predators of rarer species such as terns. In fact there is little evidence to suggest that Great Black-backed Gulls have a significant effect on population sizes of other seabirds. Despite this they are controlled at many colonies in Britain (e.g. Farne Islands, Coquet) and Ireland (e.g. Lady's Island Lake, Keeraghs) in an attempt to reduce their alleged impact on other nesting birds nearby (Thomas 1972), or to prevent the hazard of airstrikes at airports (e.g. Lambay). Fewer Great Black-backed Gulls than Lesser Black-backed or Herring Gulls have been killed or prevented from breeding successfully, but their breeding population is considerably smaller than those of the other two species. Roughly nine times more Herring Gulls and four times more Lesser Black-backed Gulls bred in

Britain in the 1980s. Thus the effect of culling on Great Black-backed Gulls is proportionally just as great or even more severe. Great Black-backed Gull numbers were controlled extensively in the 1970s and early 1980s, and this may be one of the reasons why numbers appear not to have increased since 1969.

Table 36. *Estimated world breeding population of the Great Black-backed Gull.*

	No. of pairs	Comments
USSR—Barents Sea	10,000–100,000	Some colonies increasing
USSR—White Sea	50–500	
USSR—Baltic Sea	<1000	
Canada	>15,000	Spreading north in 1970s
USA, Eastern	17,500	Increasing
Greenland	1000–10,000	
Svalbard	<50	First bred 1930, increasing and spreading
Bear Island	30–50	First bred 1921, little change since 1932
Jan Mayen	60–100	Probably increasing
Iceland	500–5000	Increasing up to 1950s, now declining
Faroe Islands	900–1200	
Norway	40,000–50,000	Stable or increasing
Sweden	7,300	Probably increasing
Finland	2000–3000	Increased since 1950s
Denmark	600	First bred 1929, increasing and spreading
Britain	18,900	Stable, includes 100 pairs inland and urban
Ireland	4500	Increasing, includes 50 pairs inland and urban
France	990	First bred 1925
Approximate total	120,000–240,000 pairs	

Sources: Cramp and Simmons (1983), Croxall *et al.* (1984), Røv (1985), P.G.H. Evans pers. comm., Seabird Colony Register.

Table 37. *Numbers of Great Black-backed Gulls breeding in Britain and Ireland 1969–88.*

	1985–87		1969–70	
	Pairs	Birds	Pairs	Birds
Shetland Islands	2156	2038	2674	—
Orkney Islands	1761	8027	5999	—
Nairn	3	—	20	—
Moray	15	—	4	4
Banff and Buchan	12	—	16	—
Gordon	3	—	2	—
Kincardine and Deeside	—	—	23	—
Angus	—	—	1	—
Northeast Fife	2	—	4	—
East Lothian	3	—	1	—
Western Isles	2809	717	2979	32
Caithness	1038	—	936	225
Sutherland	1092	30	1360	—
Ross and Cromarty	137	128	660	—
Inverness	47	—	1	—
Skye and Lochalsh	368	22	214	8
Lochaber	241	2	156	2
Stewartry	19	—	55	—
Argyll and Bute	742	604	586	31
Cunninghame	125	—	82	—
Kyle and Carrick	42	14	30	—
Wigtown	2	2	14	—
Scotland total	10,600	11,600	15,800	300
Combined units	16,300ª		16,000ª	
Birds converted to pairs	35%		1%	
Isle of Wight	1	13	6	—
Dorset	5	—	16	—
Devon	206	30	106	—
Cornwall	285	—	261	2
Isles of Scilly	1030	—	1200	—
Somerset	—	—	17	—
Avon	14	—	42	—
Channel Islands	165	46	200	—
Lancashire	—	—	1	—
Cumbria	45	—	26	—
Isle of Man	349	18	275	—
England, Isle of Man and Channel Islands total	2100	107	2200	2

	1985–87		1969–70	
	Pairs	Birds	Pairs	Birds
Gwent	10	—	33	—
West Glamorgan	2	—	—	—
Dyfed	310	—	700	—
Gwynedd	88	14	172	—
Wales total	410	15	910	—
Antrim	113	—	91	—
Down	152	—	149	—
Dublin	396	—	230	—
Wicklow	2	—	7	1
Wexford	247	—	505	—
Waterford	97	—	72	7
Cork	305	—	381	—
Kerry	628[b]	47	514	26
Limerick	1	—	—	—
Clare	33[b]	—	70	130
Galway	282[b]	—	484	3
Mayo	494[b]	—	388	57
Sligo	75[b]	162	82	—
Donegal	530[b]	34	323	—
Ireland total	3200	240	3300	220
Estimated total	4500[c]		3400[a]	
Proportion estimated/converted	28%		3%	
Britain and Ireland total	23,300[a]		22,500	

Totals rounded, <100 to nearest 5, 100–1000 to nearest 10, >1000 to nearest 100.
[a] Includes counts of birds divided by 2 to provide rough estimate of pairs; details in text.
[b] In these counties, at least 10% more pairs are estimated to occur at colonies not visited in 1985–87.
[c] This total includes estimates for colonies not counted recently. It is based on the proportional change in numbers at colonies in each region where counts were conducted in both surveys.

Kittiwake

Rissa tridactyla

The Kittiwake is a small gull (wing-span 90–92 cm) and is the most oceanic of those which breed in Britain and Ireland. Kittiwakes are often seen far from land but rarely occur inland unless blown there by stormy weather. Most breeding colonies are on coastal cliffs and islands, but some are on buildings and cliffs in coastal towns. Kittiwakes feed on small marine or, more rarely, estuarine fish and invertebrates which they catch near the surface. They forage usually in flocks, especially in the summer months, and typically gather where shoals of fish rise to the surface. They swoop to the surface and grab food or duck underwater after it. Kittiwakes also scavenge for offal from fishing boats (Cramp and Simmons 1983).

DISTRIBUTION AND INTERNATIONAL STATUS

The Kittiwake has a broad circumpolar distribution in the temperate and low arctic zones of the northern hemisphere. Breeding colonies are found at all latitudes from Portugal, the Gulf of St Lawrence and the southern Kuril

Islands in the south, to northeast and northwest Greenland and the islands of the Arctic Ocean. *Rissa tridactyla* is known as the Black-legged Kittiwake in North America to distinguish it from the Red-legged Kittiwake *R. brevirostris* found in the Bering Sea and Aleutian Islands.

The numbers of Kittiwakes breeding in many parts of the species' range are unknown (Table 38), but northern breeding populations are obviously very large. Probably about half the world total breed in Svalbard, Iceland and the Faroe Islands which together may hold up to three million breeding pairs; a further 1.25 million pairs nest in Alaska. Britain and Ireland have slightly over half a million pairs, which is about half the population of Europe excluding Svalbard, Iceland and the Faroes. Some Kittiwake colonies reach enormous size; 150,000 birds nested on Middleton Island in the Gulf of Alaska in the early 1980s and a few of the colonies in the Bering Sea were even larger (Lensink 1984). Information on the size of Kittiwake colonies in the USSR is abundant compared with that available for other species although most counts date from the 1960s and early 1970s. For example, 19,000 pairs bred on the Yama Islands in the Sea of Okhotsk in 1974 (Golovkin 1984). The largest colony in Britain or Ireland, on the Bempton–Flamborough cliffs in East Yorkshire, held 83,700 pairs in 1986 and may be the biggest in the North Atlantic.

The Kittiwake's breeding range extended southwards between the late 1930s and mid 1970s. Kittiwakes colonised Denmark, Sweden and more recently Spain and Portugal (Table 38). They also recolonised Helgoland and spread south in France (Cramp and Simmons 1983). In Canada new colonies formed on the coasts of Labrador and Nova Scotia (Brown and Nettleship 1984a). Breeding numbers have probably increased in all parts of the range this century though there are signs that the increase is slowing down or stopping in Alaska, Denmark, the Faroe Islands, Britain and Ireland.

The birds' range outside the breeding season is known from recoveries of ringed birds and from observations of birds at sea. A majority of recoveries are of birds ringed in Scotland, on the Farne Islands and in southeast Ireland. These show that after the breeding season some birds move south into the Bay of Biscay and immature birds disperse into the North Atlantic. Some Kittiwakes, mainly immatures, move as far west as Newfoundland and Nova Scotia (Coulson 1966, S.R. Baillie *in litt.*). Many Kittiwakes, mainly immature birds, have been shot off west Greenland. Birds in the North Sea in winter are often found around trawlers (Tasker *et al.* 1987).

CENSUS METHODS AND PROBLEMS

Kittiwakes are colonial breeders and their colonies are easy to find. A census of visible occupied nests is also relatively straightforward to carry out. However, nests in some colonies are difficult to see or count accurately as Kittiwakes tend to breed low down on high cliffs (Coulson 1963) and they often nest in sea caves. A majority of the Kittiwake colonies in Shetland in 1980, for example, could only be seen completely from the sea (Pritchard 1981).

An apparently occupied nest site (AOS) was used as the counting unit for Kittiwakes during both the national surveys although there was some confusion during Operation Seafarer as to the exact definition of this, specifically whether or not birds should be present on the nest at the time of the count (Appendix III and IV). Inevitably some birds from the breeding population were absent from the colony at the time of the counts in 1969–70 and 1985–87 although most counts were made in June to coincide with the annual peak in occupied nests. Birds which lost their eggs early in the season and abandoned the colony were excluded from a count in June (though some failed breeders continue to occupy nests). Also excluded were birds in the breeding population which did not attempt to nest in the year of the count.

A fifth of the Kittiwake counts made in 1985–87 in Angus, and a very few of those in Orkney and in Argyll and Bute were recorded as birds rather than pairs. In order to be able to use all the data collected and to obtain a complete estimate of the breeding population, counts of birds were divided by two and combined with counts of nests.

THE KITTIWAKE IN BRITAIN AND IRELAND

Over half a million (543,600 pairs) Kittiwakes nested in Britain and Ireland in 1985–87, making it one of the commonest breeding seabirds. About two-thirds of the birds bred in Scotland, nearly a quarter in England, Wales, the Channel Islands and the Isle of Man, and less than 10% in Ireland. Numbers increased overall by 22% since 1969–70 when 446,700 pairs were counted. The median colony size in both national surveys was 200–300 pairs (depending on the definition of colony, see Coulson 1963 and Richardson 1985).

Kittiwakes have been increasing since the turn of the century (Coulson 1983). As numbers expanded, colonies were established on low cliffs and even at ground level, and existing ones spread lower down than previously (Coulson 1963). Kittiwakes also began nesting on man-made "cliffs" such as the castle walls at Dunbar in southeast Scotland, where nearly 400 nests were recorded in 1987. There are similar colonies on warehouses at North Shields and a flour mill at Gateshead, over 16km from the mouth of the River Tyne; in 1986 these held 70 and 104 nests respectively. Kittiwakes also once nested on a pier and disused coal straithes in Hartlepool dock, while at Lowestoft in Suffolk they nest on derelict buildings, advertising hoardings, a pier pavilion and recently on the pier itself (Brown 1985). When the pavilion was demolished in 1989, a specially designed wall with ledges suitable for nesting Kittiwakes was constructed by the pier's owners. Ten nests, two with clutches of eggs, were already present in June 1989 (B.J. Brown pers. comm.). Up to three nests with eggs have been recorded on the sand dunes at Scolt Head in Norfolk, whilst at Dunmore East, in southeast Ireland, nearly 1200 pairs of Kittiwakes nest on cliffs and occasionally even street lamps or buildings around a busy fishing harbour (O'Meara 1979, McGrath and Walsh 1985).

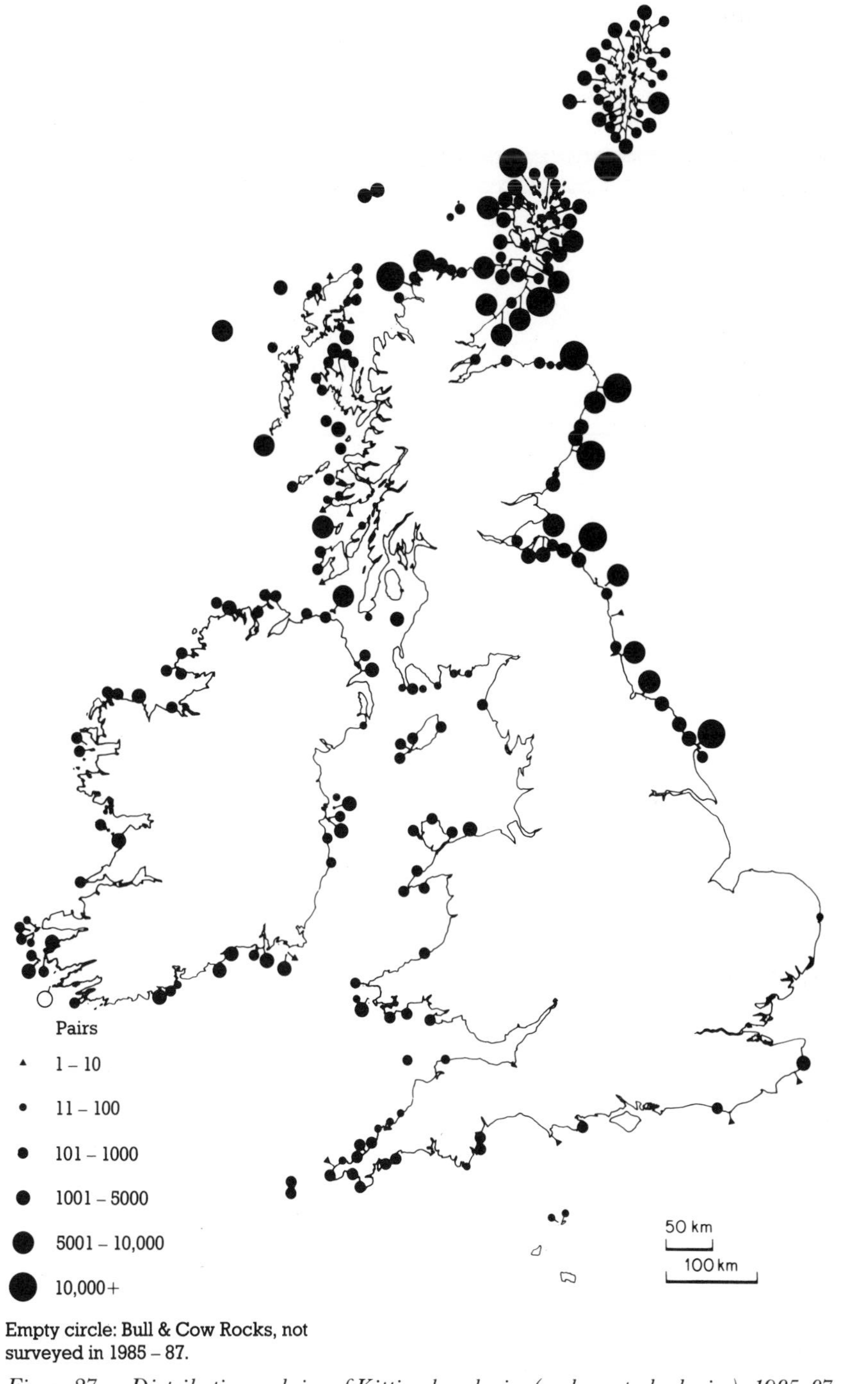

Empty circle: Bull & Cow Rocks, not
surveyed in 1985 – 87.

Figure 27.   Distribution and size of Kittiwake colonies (and grouped colonies), 1985–87.

Pairs

- 1 – 10
- 11 – 100
- 101 – 1000
- 1001 – 5000
- 5001 – 10,000
- 10,000+

50 km

100 km

Plate 21. Kittiwake nesting in boarded window ledge, St Johns church, Lowestoft (B.J. Brown)

At first, as Kittiwake numbers grew, existing colonies expanded but from 1920 onwards new colonies began to be formed. In 1959, the BTO organised a national enquiry into the status of Kittiwakes in Britain and Ireland (Coulson 1963). The total breeding population of England, Wales and the Isle of Man, for which coverage was sufficiently detailed to obtain a reliable estimate, was 37,000 pairs with just over half of these nesting at Flamborough Head. Numbers had apparently increased by 3–4% per annum since 1900. By extrapolating from the figure for England and Wales and from the number of known Kittiwake colonies in Scotland and Ireland, Coulson estimated the total British and Irish breeding population was 170,000–180,000 pairs.

The first complete census of Kittiwakes breeding in Britain and Ireland was made in 1969–70 by Operation Seafarer. This showed that breeding numbers had continued to grow by 3–4% a year in England and Wales between 1959 and 1969. The total population for Britain and Ireland was well over 400,000 pairs with three-quarters of the birds nesting on the east coast and in Shetland and Orkney (Coulson in Cramp *et al.* 1974). The Bempton and Flamborough cliffs colony had increased to 30,800 pairs.

Another Kittiwake survey took place in 1979 (Coulson 1983). Coverage was best in England, Wales and parts of east Scotland, and poor elsewhere. Numbers had increased overall by 7% per annum since 1969, but most of this was due to a massive increase at the largest colony, on the Bempton–Flamborough cliffs. This had grown to 83,000 pairs, equivalent to growth of 10% per annum between 1969 and 1979, whilst elsewhere in England, Wales and the Isle of Man Kittiwake numbers increased by less than 1% a year. Almost all colonies covered on the south and west coasts of Britain and south and east coasts of Ireland had decreased in size during this period (Coulson 1983).

A second complete census of Kittiwakes was carried out in 1985–87. Results showed that the total breeding population increased by about a fifth between 1969 and 1987 (see above) with larger changes in some areas. For example, numbers in Scotland remained approximately stable overall because decreases in Orkney, the Moray Firth, and Dumfries and Galloway were offset by increases virtually everywhere else (Figure 28). These results were consistent with increase in breeding Kittiwakes previously recorded in the Firth of Forth (Harris *et al.* 1987) and the decrease in the Firth of Clyde (Monaghan and Zonfrillo 1986).

In Ireland, some of the coastline in Donegal where Kittiwake colonies were found during Operation Seafarer was not surveyed in 1985–87. Even allowing for this, Kittiwakes in the northwest of Ireland appeared to have declined between 1969–70 and 1985–87, but on the east coast, especially in Antrim, numbers increased during the same period so that overall numbers in Ireland increased.

Counts of Kittiwake in colonies in England, Wales and the Isle of Man can now be compared for 1959, 1969, 1979 and 1986—when almost all the counts for 1985–87 were made (Table 40). Little change was detected at the huge Bempton–Flamborough Kittiwake colony between 1979 and 1986, but growth in all other colonies was about 8% a year during the same period. The overall increase at Bempton–Flamborough of 0.2% per annum was the lowest recorded since 1950. The reason for the apparent sudden spurt in growth of the Bempton–Flamborough colony between 1969 and 1979 is not known.

Coulson (1983) reported a significant decline in the number of occupied nests in a non-random sample of Kittiwake colonies in the south and west of Britain between 1969 and 1979. This decline is not evident in a comparison of the counts for 1969–70 and 1985–87 in these areas (Table 39) although it is possible that numbers declined and then rose again after 1979. Regular counts are not available for any colonies on this area. However, on the Isles of Scilly, Birkin and Smith (1987) recorded a decline in Kittiwake nests from 861 counted in 1983 to 584 in 1987. Colonies in Men-a-vaur and St Helen's were nearly deserted or completely abandoned, but new colonies formed on Samson and Gugh.

The Kittiwake's steep increase in numbers appears to have continued between 1969–70 and 1985–87 on the east coast of Britain, between the Moray Firth and the Isle of Wight, where nest counts almost doubled overall. Large increases occurred at some colonies, particularly in Cleveland, Humberside and Kent. The only other part of Britain or Ireland where increases of similar size appeared to take place during the same period was northeast Ireland. Two

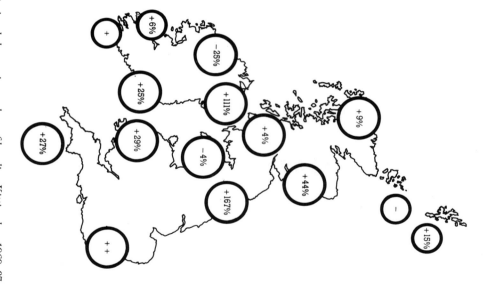

Figure 28.   Regional changes in numbers of breeding Kittiwakes, 1969–87. See Table 39 for counts and Figure 1 for regional divisions.
No figure is given if more than 10% of a county/regional total was derived from counts made as individuals rather than pairs or where totals were less than 100 pairs.

Several studies have monitored numbers of nests, in sample plots, of selected Kittiwake colonies since the early 1970s (see Second Chapter in Part 1). Most of these were not designed to detect changes due to dispersive movement of nesting birds within or between colonies from year to year, whether dispersal from the sample plots to an adjacent cliff face or dispersal right out of the study colony (Heubeck et al. 1985, Mudge 1988). Thus the results of monitoring

examples there were Rathlin, where Kittiwake nest counts on the island's distinctive chalk cliffs increased from 3176 to 6822, and Lambay, where nest totals were 1464 and 3005 respectively.

schemes for Kittiwakes around Britain and Ireland (Table 41) differ slightly from the overall trends in numbers between 1969–70 and 1985–87 (Figure 28).

REASONS FOR CHANGE IN NUMBERS

Much of the increase and spread of the Kittiwake during the twentieth century may have been made possible by the ending of human hunting pressures and egg collecting (Coulson 1963), but food supplies have undoubtedly played a vital role in determining how numbers changed. Kittiwakes forage regularly around fishing boats where they feed on offal. The expansion of the fishing industry since the 1940s in the waters around Britain and Ireland and in their winter quarters in the North Atlantic must have been to their advantage (Cramp *et al.* 1974).

In many areas, Kittiwakes feed their young on small to medium-sized sandeels (Pearson 1968, Cramp and Simmons 1983, Coulson and Thomas 1985). Kittiwakes were one of the species worst hit by the disruption in sandeel supplies around Shetland in the 1980s (see Second Chapter in Part 1). Breeding success at 35 Kittiwake colonies throughout Britain and southeast Ireland was monitored from 1986 to 1988 (Harris and Wanless 1990). This study detected a reduction in chick productivity at colonies in the North Sea which started in Shetland in 1986 and spread southwards during the next two breeding seasons. By 1988 the situation in Shetland had become so bad that only 0.09 chicks/nest were assumed to have fledged (Heubeck 1989b). Evidence presented by Harris and Wanless, although largely circumstantial, strongly suggested that food shortage was responsible for the spreading reduction in breeding success in the North Sea.

Information from other studies on the effect of food shortage upon Kittiwake breeding performance or colony size is scarce. Coulson and Thomas (1985) linked a gradual decline in the Kittiwake colony at North Shields, northeast England (one of Britain's longest-studied seabird colonies) with low breeding productivity and reduced adult survival. Food shortage for breeding birds during the eight to ten months of the year when they occupy this colony was thought to be a possible cause of the changes recorded by their study. In southeast Ireland, numbers of Kittiwakes breeding in east Waterford and the size of the Celtic Sea stock of Herring (assumed to be an important food for adult Kittiwakes) both peaked in the early 1970s and subsequently declined (McGrath and Walsh 1985).

Table 38. *Estimated world breeding population of the Kittiwake.*

	No. of pairs	Comments
USSR—White Sea	?	Unknown
USSR—Barents Sea	66,900	Increased in Seven Islands archipelago and on Murmansk coast
USSR—West Novaya Zemlya	>29,200	Increased in south
USSR—Franz Josef Land	10,000	
USSR—Kara Sea	?	

Table 38.   *Estimated world breeding population of the Kittiwake – cont.*

	No. of pairs	Comments
USSR—Laptev Sea	>44,000	
USSR—East Siberian Sea	c. 40,000	
USSR—Chuckchi Sea	c. 19,000	
USSR—Bering Sea	>300,000	Main colony, Cape Waring, Wrangel Island 10,000 pairs 1960
USSR—Kamchatka	381,000	Increasing at several colonies especially east Kamchatka
USSR—Kuril Islands, Komandorskie Islands and Sakhalin	>56,000	
USSR—Sea of Okhotsk	c. 100,000	Probably stable
USA—Alaska	1,250,000	Probably increasing in Arctic, increasing further south
Canada, Eastern	204,000	Increasing on west coast
Greenland	140,000–1,150,000	Increased, at least up to 1980
Jan Mayen Island	5000–10,000	Order 6
Bear Island	>200,000	
Svalbard	100,000–1,000,000	
Iceland	400,000	
Faroe Islands	50,000–100,000	
Norway	510,000	80% of population and largest colonies above Arctic Circle, increasing; decreased in south
Sweden	24	First bred 1967, peaked 1976 at 55 pairs
Denmark	400	First bred 1941, stable/fluctuating since 1970
West Germany	2500	Recolonised Helgoland 1938, increasing but more slowly than in 1950s
Britain	493,300	Increasing but more slowly than before 1969
Ireland	50,200	Increasing but more slowly than before 1969
France	4000	Increased, and spread since 1930s
Spain	200	First bred 1975 Sisargas Islands, also nests Cape Vilan; increasing
Portugal	3	1978: First bred 1973 Berlengas Islands, increasing
Approximate total	6–8 million pairs	

Sources: Cramp and Simmons (1983), Croxall *et al.* (1984), Vyatkin (1986), Ilyichev and Zubakin (1988), Litvinenko and Shibaev in press, P.G.H. Evans pers. comm., Seabird Colony Register.

Date of most recent count, if pre-1980, given in brackets.

? = Breeds, numbers unknown.

Table 39. *Numbers of Kittiwakes breeding in Britain and Ireland 1969–87.*

	1985–87		1969–70	
	Pairs	Birds	Pairs	Birds
Shetland Islands	50,105		43,475	
Orkney Islands	64,014	77	107,177[b]	
Moray	115		600	
Banff and Buchan	30,837		21,677	
Gordon	6284		6701	
Aberdeen	496		—	
Kincardine and Deeside	46,105		37,932	
Angus	3310	1700	1713	
Northeast Fife	6765		3282	
East Lothian	4460		2820	
Berwickshire	23,219		9951	
Western Isles	28,482		24,758	
Caithness	46,656		54,771	
Sutherland	25,906		16,234	
Ross and Cromarty	329		400	
Skye and Lochalsh	2086		883	
Lochaber	3270		1299	
Argyll and Bute	9690	36	3983	
Kyle and Carrick	3063		7742	
Wigtown	467		672	
Stewartry	60		27	
Scotland total	335,700	1813	346,100	
Combined units[a]	356,600[a]			
Birds converted to pairs	<1%			
Northumberland	6699		2935	
Tyne and Wear	7874		3559	
Durham	—		10	
Cleveland	10,181		1809	
North Yorkshire	7498		4276	
Humberside	83,694		30,797	
Norfolk	—		3	
Suffolk	93		32	
Kent	2686		50	
East Sussex	979		—	
Isle of Wight	—		8	
Dorset	242		262	
Devon	1663		2228	
Cornwall	3270		839	
Isles of Scilly	593		1400	

Table 39. *Numbers of Kittiwakes breeding in Britain and Ireland 1969–87 – cont.*

	1985–87		1969–70	
	Pairs	Birds	Pairs	Birds
Channel Islands	34		12	
Cumbria	995		1468	
Isle of Man	1296		908	
England, Isle of Man and Channel Islands total	127,900		50,600	
West Glamorgan	388		560	
Dyfed	4253		3078	
Gwynedd	4279		3253	
Wales total	8900		6900	
Antrim	9980		4750	
Down	60		3	
Dublin	5419		3853	
Wicklow	1560		21	
Wexford	2951		3759	
Waterford	3876		3417	
Cork	2764[c]		3025	
Kerry	4688		5041	
Clare	4859		4380	
Galway	664		820	
Mayo	3609		3454	
Sligo	678		1000	
Donegal	6935[c]		10,860	
Ireland total	48,000		44,400	
Estimated total	50,200[d]			
Proportion estimated	4%			
Britain and Ireland total	543,500		446,700	

Totals rounded, <100 to nearest 5, 100–1000 to nearest 10, >1000 to nearest 100.
[a] Includes counts of birds divided by 2 to provide estimate of pairs; see text for details.
[b] Includes estimate of 10,000 pairs for Marwick Head, recorded as Order 5 (10,001–100,000 pairs) in 1969; 4741 pairs counted in 1986.
[c] In these counties, at least 10% more pairs are estimated to occur at colonies not visited in 1985–87.
[d] This total includes estimates for colonies not counted recently. It is based on the proportional change in numbers at colonies in each region where counts were conducted in both surveys.

Table 40. *Numbers of Kittiwakes (pairs) breeding in England, Wales and the Isle of Man 1959–86.*

	1959	1969	1979	1986
East coast England including Kent	30,400	43,400	100,800	118,730
South coast England including Devon and Cornwall	700	3,800	3,200	5,440
South Wales and Lundy	2,900	4,600	4,450	5,360
North Wales, Cumbria and Isle of Man	3,000	5,570	4,500	6,570
Total	37,000	57,370	113,000	136,100
Change per annum		+4% (1959–69)	+7% (1969–79)	+3% (1979–86)
Bempton–Flamborough	c. 19,000	30,800	83,000	83,700
Change per annum		+4% (1959–69)	+10% (1969–79)	<1% (1979–86)

Sources: Coulson (1983), Seabird Colony Register.

Table 41. *Trends in Kittiwake numbers at colonies or parts of colonies monitored regularly.*

Site	Trend	Reference
Shetland	Decreasing 1976–86, increasing 1986–87, 5 colonies excluding Foula and Fair Isle	M. Heubeck pers. comm.
Foula	Decreasing early 1970s–1982	Furness (1983)
Fair Isle	Increasing 1971–79	Stowe (1982)
Orkney	Decreasing 1976–85, 5 colonies	Benn *et al.* (1987)
Caithness	Approximately stable 1980–87, 5 colonies	Mudge (1988)
Troup Head	Increasing 1979–83, decreasing 1983–85	Lloyd and North (1987)
Firth of Forth	Increasing 4% per annum 1959–86	Harris *et al.* (1987)
St Abb's Head	Increasing 1976–85	da Prato (1985)
Handa	Stable 1971–79	Stowe (1982)
Canna	Increasing 1971–79	Stowe (1982)
Farne Islands	Increasing 1971–79	Stowe (1982)
Bempton	Increasing/stable 1971–79	Stowe (1982)
Southeast Kent	Stable/increasing 1971–79	Stowe (1982)
Lundy	Decreasing 1981–86	Davies and Price (1986)
Woody Bay	Increasing 1971–79	Stowe (1982)
South Wales	Stable 1971–79, 4 colonies	Stowe (1982)
Little Orme	Stable 1971–79	Stowe (1982)
Isle of Man	Approximately stable 1971–79	Stowe (1982)
Rathlin	Decreasing 1971–79	Stowe (1982)
Northwest Ireland	Increasing, 3 colonies 1971–79	Stowe (1982)
Cliffs of Moher	Stable 1971–79	Stowe (1982)
Waterford	Increase up to 1974, general decrease 1974–84, fairly stable 1984–87, 7 colonies	McGrath and Walsh (1985)

Sandwich Tern

Sterna sandvicensis

The Sandwich Tern is the largest of the five species of terns which breed regularly in Britain and Ireland (wing-span 91–94 cm). Sandwich Terns feed by plunge-diving into shoals of small fish, such as sandeels. Their colonies are on low islands, sandbanks or shingle spits on or near the coast, in saltwater lagoons or, sometimes, on islands in inland lakes. Nests are grouped together at very high density, often in among other terns and Black-headed Gulls.

INTERNATIONAL DISTRIBUTION AND STATUS

The Sandwich Tern nests in almost all coastal European countries from the Baltic and North Sea, down the Atlantic coast, through the Mediterranean and in the Aegean, Adriatic, Black and Caspian Seas and the Sea of Azov. About 75,000–80,000 pairs are estimated to breed in the USSR (Ilyichev and Zubakin 1988) compared with about 55,000 pairs in other parts of Europe. Slightly fewer than the European total of Sandwich Terns nests on the other side of the Atlantic Ocean, in the northeast USA, from Virginia south to Louisiana; in the Caribbean, Venezuela, Brazil and Argentina (Cramp 1985).

194

Plate 22.   Sandwich Tern colony (C.H. Gomersall/RSPB)

There are three subspecies, with the nominate one breeding throughout Europe. The British and Irish breeding population is nearly 19,000 pairs, representing about a tenth of the world total, but more than 40% of the European total (excluding USSR). The Sandwich Tern is listed on Annex 1 of the EC Birds Directive 1979.

Sandwich Terns are migrants. Up to the end of 1987, over 132,000 Sandwich Terns had been ringed in Britain and Ireland, making it the most ringed British and Irish tern. Nearly 4000 recoveries of ringed birds were reported up to 1987, a recovery rate of 2.8%, which was easily the highest of the tern species breeding in Britain and Ireland. Ringing recoveries have shown that, after breeding, the birds moved south to the West African coast, from Morocco to South Africa. Most have been reported from Ghana, Senegal, the Ivory Coast, Sierra Leone and Liberia. In West Africa, British and Irish birds occupy the same wintering grounds as those from the Netherlands, Denmark and West Germany (Møller 1981a and b). In Ghana, Sandwich Terns can be seen feeding offshore from many parts of the coast. Numbers peak in September/October and relatively few are seen later in the winter (January to March). Large numbers of Sandwich Terns congregate at sites such as lagoons, harbours, estuaries and saltworks, particularly to roost at night (Grimes 1987). Ringing recoveries suggest that less than half of birds in their second and third summers return to the colonies to breed (Møller 1981a and b); the remaining young Sandwich Terns move northwards in summer but do not reach the breeding grounds.

CENSUS METHODS AND PROBLEMS FOR TERNS

In general, terns are easier to count than many other seabirds since they usually nest in the open, on flattish ground and are present in the colony by day, but each species has its own peculiarities and problems. Care must be taken when counting all terns to ensure that disturbance is kept to a minimum, i.e. at a level where breeding success is not harmed and which does not cause desertion. Visits by observers to a tern colony have to be brief and must be avoided completely in bad weather. The most critical stage is the beginning of the season, when breeding birds are becoming established, since disturbance at this time may lead to desertion of the colony. However, there are few documented cases of the effects of disturbance on breeding terns and it is possible that some movements of birds which have been attributed to disturbance were really due to other factors.

One problem for national tern surveys, like those for Operation Seafarer and the Seabird Colony Register, is that there are a very large number of tern colonies in Britain and Ireland; nearly 1200 sites were used by at least one species in the years 1969–88. The numbers of terns at a colony can change dramatically from year to year because birds change breeding sites so that it is difficult to combine data from different years with much confidence. This will have affected the results of the two national censuses made in 1969–70 and 1985–87.

Because of the large number of tern colonies, total coverage is difficult to achieve, especially within a single breeding season. Coverage in 1985–87 surveys was complete for the relatively rare Roseate Tern, for the Sandwich Tern and for coastal colonies of Common and Arctic Terns on the mainland of Britain; coverage was also good for the Little Tern. Complete coverage was not attempted in Ireland because the All Ireland Tern Survey had been carried out in 1984. Counts from 1984 were used for colonies where no more recent counts were available. Coverage for terns was also poor in Shetland and Orkney, where many terns, including large numbers of Arctic Terns, nested away from the coast and were not covered thoroughly by either the 1969–70 or the 1985–87 surveys. However, a thorough census of the colonies on these islands was made in 1989 and its results are summarised here. Recommended counting techniques for terns involve a census of all occupied nests in a colony. However, the ease and accuracy with which this can be carried out depends on the size, terrain and accessibility of each colony. Nest density varies from the scattering of nests along a beach in numerous small Little Tern colonies, to the packed nests of a Sandwich Tern colony, and to Arctic Tern colonies which cover entire hillsides. The colony on Papa Westray in northern Orkney, for example, once held 17,500 pairs of Arctic Terns and occupied more than a square kilometre.

Large tern colonies are easy to find but those with only a few pairs are easily missed, especially if the terns are breeding among gulls. Breeding may be difficult to prove since non-breeding birds can loaf at the same site (often potential nesting habitat) day after day through the summer. Distinguishing the different tern species in a mixed colony of gulls and terns may add further confusion. In any case, a single count of nests in the season can give a very misleading estimate of the size of a colony since the timing of the breeding season and the degree of nesting synchrony vary from year to year.

Nearly all the Roseate Terns and about 80% of the Sandwich Terns breeding in Britain and Ireland nest on nature reserves. These birds were counted regularly and fairly accurately (or at least consistently) both during and after Operation Seafarer. Where methods have not been standardised, however, changes in wardening personnel may contribute to apparent changes in colony sizes.

During the 1984–87 surveys, the majority of terns were counted as pairs. Most of the counts for Orkney, and some of those for other parts of Scotland, were of individual birds present in breeding colonies. Bullock and Gomersall (1980) studied attendance of Arctic Terns at several colonies in Shetland and Orkney in 1980 and concluded that the number of birds present per occupied nest varied throughout the season and between colonies. They found that attendance was also likely to vary from year to year, but that on average, 1.5 Arctic Terns were present per occupied nest. Thus conversion of counts of birds to pairs cannot be made accurately but, in order to use all the tern counts made in 1985–87, those referring to birds rather than pairs have been divided by 1.5. The proportion of each total converted in this way must be taken into account when comparing totals in the tables for each species. In addition, some counts were submitted in both 1969–70 and 1985–87 as unidentified Common/Arctic Terns; these are listed in Table 48 and are not included in Tables 47 or 50.

THE SANDWICH TERN IN BRITAIN AND IRELAND

Sandwich Terns nest in scattered locations throughout Britain and Ireland, from Orkney to the Channel Islands and from Suffolk to the northwest of Ireland. The 1985–87 count found 18,400 pairs on the coasts, compared with 12,000 in 1969–70. Nearly two-thirds (64%) of the birds nested in colonies in the east of Britain, between Grampian in northeast Scotland and Kent. Despite breeding widely in both Britain and Ireland, Sandwich Terns are concentrated into a relatively small number of colonies.

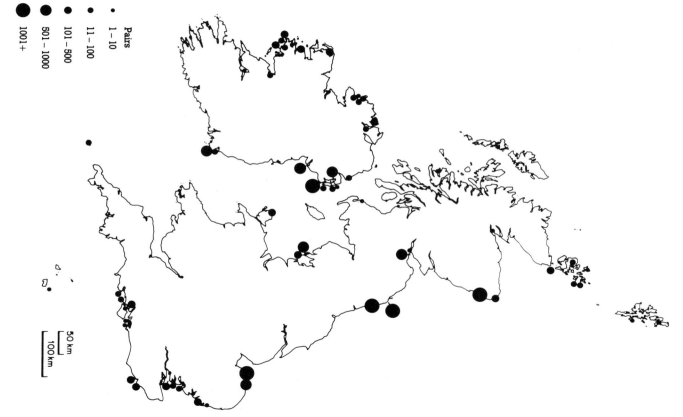

Pairs

· 1 – 10

· 11 – 100

● 101 – 500

● 501 – 1000

● 1001+

50 km

100 km

Figure 29. Distribution and size of Sandwich Tern colonies, 1985–87.

In 1985–87 England held just over 60% of all Sandwich Terns; almost as many as were recorded throughout Britain and Ireland in Operation Seafarer. The four main colonies were Scolt Head (3100 pairs), Blakeney (1000 pairs), the Farne Islands (3500 pairs) and Coquet Island (1600 pairs). Together these colonies contained about half of the British and Irish total. The other large colony was at the Sands of Forvie (1200 pairs) in Grampian, whilst 2100 pairs nested on five small islands in Strangford Lough in Northern Ireland in 1987.

Sandwich Terns were counted regularly between 1969–70 and the most recent surveys at a number of colonies in Britain and Ireland as part of the RSPB Annual Tern Monitoring Scheme (Lloyd *et al.* 1975, Thomas 1982, Thomas *et al.* 1990). Numbers of Sandwich Terns at many of these colonies in 1987 were at almost their highest level since 1969. For example, on Coquet Island counts had increased fivefold, and on Inchmickery the increase was approximately eightfold. Several large new colonies have been established such as those on Brownsea Island and at Loch of Strathbeg. Some colonies were deserted between 1969 and 1987; for example, Tern Island in Wexford Harbour, which once held several thousand nesting terns, was gradually washed away by the sea during the early 1970s.

Sandwich Tern colonies fluctuate in size from year to year more markedly than those of other tern species. Changes at a number of adjacent colonies appear to be linked. The two main Norfolk colonies, Scolt Head and Blakeney Point, for example, appear to exchange birds. From 1969 to 1976, most of the Norfolk birds nested at Scolt Head (in 1972–74 large numbers also nested at Stiffkey Binks), but from 1977 to 1984 most birds apparently switched nesting site to Blakeney. More recently Scolt Head appeared again to be in favour, at Blakeney's expense. Other colonies where the terns have behaved in a similar way include the RSPB reserves of Minsmere and Havergate; the Cumbria colonies of Foulney, Ravenglass and South Walney; the Sands of Forvie and Loch of Strathbeg in northeast Scotland; and Inchmickery and Fidra in the Firth of Forth. In each case, decrease in Sandwich Tern numbers at one of the sites appears to have been closely matched by increases at the other.

Sandwich Terns appear to have increased in numbers by about 50% between 1969–70 and 1985–87. At the same time, there has been a shift in the centre of the population – colonies on the south and east coasts of Britain have increased, in some cases dramatically, while those in the north and west have declined (although many were not very large anyway, Figure 30, Table 43), Wales and southwest England have been recolonised since 1969–70. Colonies in most parts of Ireland have increased in size, although there were declines in some smaller colonies on the west coast.

REASONS FOR CHANGE IN NUMBERS

Discovering the causes of increase in a species is sometimes considered less urgent than finding out reasons for decline. However, in order to be prepared to cope with any reverse in fortunes which might occur in future, it is worth speculating on why numbers of Sandwich Terns have increased. A large proportion of the birds nest on protected sites or nature reserves which are

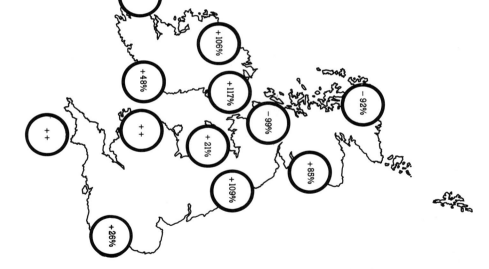

Figure 30. *Regional changes in numbers of Sandwich Terns at regularly counted sites, 1969–87.*
No figure is given if more than 10% of a county/regional total was derived from counts made as individuals rather than pairs or where totals were less than 100 pairs.

wardened (e.g. Scott Head, Blakeney, Farne Islands, Coquet Island, Sands of Forvie, Strangford Lough). Increased protection from disturbance and from predators such as foxes (e.g. Forster 1975), may have been a factor in the expansion of these colonies. Some new colonies (Loch of Strathbeg, Brownsea Island and Chichester Harbour) are located where nesting habitat and protection have recently been improved. On the other hand, little is known about what determines nesting success for this species, or about how its food stocks may have altered in the last 20 years.

British and Irish Sandwich Terns winter in West Africa where they are trapped by man (see Roseate Tern chapter). Sandwich Terns occur in the same areas as Roseate Terns in Ghana and yet their British and Irish numbers are increasing, unlike those of the Roseate Tern. Does this mean that trapping is less significant for Sandwich Terns? Recent analysis of ringing recoveries (Green *et al.* in press) suggests that trapping of first-year Sandwich Terns in West Africa may determine how many birds survive to breeding age and the size of breeding colonies in future years.

Dunn and Mead (1982) showed that the incidence of trapping of Sandwich Terns increased in years when landings of sardines were high in Ghana. It is possible that there is a complicated interrelationship between fisheries in West Africa, winter survival of Sandwich Terns and breeding numbers in Britain and Ireland. Added to this are the effects of variations in breeding productivity at British and Irish colonies, and of any immigration or emigration involving other European Sandwich Tern colonies. In conclusion, the population dynamics of Sandwich (and other breeding terns) is so poorly understood that it would be foolish for conservationists to claim credit for the rise in numbers of Sandwich Terns, whilst blaming the decline in numbers of Roseate Terns on factors beyond their control in West Africa.

Many of the British and Irish Sandwich Tern colonies in 1985–87 were located in or very near Black-headed Gull colonies; the two species nest in a particularly intimate association. It is perhaps not surprising that changes in Sandwich Tern numbers at some colonies were closely related to changes in numbers of Black-headed Gulls. In Norfolk, for example, the fluctuations in size of the Sandwich Tern colonies between Scolt Head and Blakeney Point mirrored those of the Black-headed Gulls. Sandwich Terns seem actually to choose to nest with the gulls since they lay after the gulls and therefore appear to have the option of moving to areas without gulls. Veen (1977) showed that Sandwich Terns in the Netherlands gained an advantage by nesting with Black-headed Gulls, despite the loss of some of their chicks through gull predation. The more aggressive gulls drove off other predators and the presence of the gulls' eggs provided an alternative food for any predators which did manage to reach the colony. These findings have obvious consequences for any programme of Black-headed Gull control carried out at Sandwich Tern colonies.

CONTRIBUTED BY MARK AVERY

Table 42. *Approximate world breeding population of the Sandwich Tern.*

	No. of pairs	Comments
USSR	75,000–80,000	Breeds inland, Black Sea plus Sea of Azov c. 40,000, Caspian Sea 33,000–40,000
USA	<45,000	140 Virginia, colonised 1912 and 1968, nest with Royal Terns; 20,400 in single colony Louisiana
Caribbean	2000	Few colonies, biggest in Bahamas has 400 pairs
South America	?	Breeds from islands off Venezuela to Patagonia
Norway	<50	First bred 1970s, south coast
Sweden	4000	First bred 1975, increasing
Finland	1100	
Poland	300	
East Germany	1350	
Denmark	4000	Fluctuating
West Germany	7150	Fluctuating
Britain	14,000	Increased since 1969
Ireland	4600	Includes 200 inland; increased since 1969
Netherlands	11,800	Decreased 1957–65 because of poisoning; now increasing
France	5900	Increasing since 1970s mainly in south; decreasing Brittany
Spain	25–350	Fluctuating. Breeds in Mediterranean; has bred north coast; may breed Andalucia
Italy	150	Increasing
Greece	50	
Romania	?	Decreased since 1800s
Approximate world total	180,000–230,000 pairs	

Sources: Croxall *et al.* (1984), Cramp (1985), Whilde (1985), Hémery *et al* (1988), Rooth (1989), P.G.H. Evans pers. comm., O.J. Merne pers. comm., Seabird Colony Register.
? = Breeds, numbers unknown.

Table 43. *Numbers of Sandwich Terns breeding in Britain and Ireland 1969–87.*

	1985–87		1969–70	
	Pairs	Birds	Pairs	Birds
Shetland Islands	4		—	
Orkney Islands	25	402	293	—
Banff and Buchan	130		—	
Gordon	1082		740	
Dunfermline	6		—	
East Lothian	655		270	

Table 43.   Numbers of Sandwich Terns breeding in Britain and Ireland 1969–87 – cont.

	1985–87		1969–70	
	Pairs	Birds	Pairs	Birds
Western Isles	72	—	—	
Ross and Cromarty	7		1000	
Argyll and Bute		1		—
Kyle and Carrick	3		162	
Scotland total	2,000	400	2500	—
Combined units[a]		23,000[a]		
Birds converted to pairs		<1%		
Northumberland	5088		2428	
Norfolk	4089		3947	
Suffolk	201		163	
Essex	291		17	
Kent	350		—	
East Sussex	160		—	
West Sussex	28		—	
Hampshire	354		228	
Isle of Wight	2		—	
Dorset	25		—	
Isles of Scilly	20		—	
Channel Islands	2		—	
Cumbria	735		609	
England and Channel Islands total	11,300		7400	
Gwynedd	451		—	
Wales total	450		—	
Antrim	74		—	
Down	2553		1211	
Wexford	704		475	
Kerry	—		63	
Clare	7		—	
Galway	413	—	185	37
Mayo	221		56	
Donegal	305	20	201	—
Ireland total[b]	4400	20	2100	40
Britain and Ireland total	18,400		12,000	

Totals rounded, <100 to nearest 5, 100–1000 to nearest 10, >1000 to nearest 100.
[a] Includes counts of birds divided by 1.5 to provide estimate of pairs; see text for details.
[b] Data from All Ireland Tern Survey 1983–84 (Whilde 1985) used where no more recent (including zero) counts were available.

Roseate Tern

Sterna dougallii

The Roseate Tern is about the same size (wing-span 76–79 cm) as the more numerous Arctic and Common Terns with which it often nests. It is by far the rarest of the seabirds breeding in Britain and Ireland and is the only one currently in danger of extinction in northwest Europe. Like other terns, the Roseate Tern fishes by plunge-diving from the air into shoals of small fish. The commonest prey during the breeding season are sandeels and Sprats.

INTERNATIONAL DISTRIBUTION AND STATUS

Roseate Terns have a more cosmopolitan breeding distribution than any other seabird nesting in Britain and Ireland. Large parts of the breeding population occur in tropical regions such as the Caribbean, East Africa, the Indian Ocean and Australia. In contrast to these scattered breeding locations in the tropics, Roseate Terns also breed in the northern temperate zone including the USA, Canada, France, Britain and Ireland. There are four

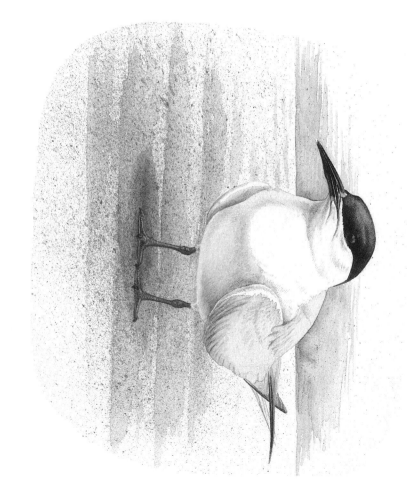

204

(possibly five) subspecies of Roseate Tern and the nominate one is found in Europe and the Macronesian islands (Cramp 1985).

The Roseate Tern is one of Europe's rarest breeding seabirds and is restricted to Britain, Ireland and France (Dunn 1989). The species also breeds on the Azores, Salvages and perhaps on Madeira (Le Grand *et al.* 1984). Occasionally pairs breed in tern colonies outside the main range, for example, in the Ebro delta in Spain, the Camargue in the south of France, the Netherlands, Denmark and West Germany (Nisbet 1980). The species is listed in Annex 1 of the EC Birds Directive 1979.

The Roseate Tern is officially a "threatened species" in the western Atlantic (Buckley and Buckley 1981, Kirkham and Nettleship 1987). Its numbers declined during the 1980s in Canada, apparently because of the loss of breeding habitat to gulls and the effects of predators on the terns' breeding success, coupled with heavy mortality from trapping in the winter quarters (Kirkham and Nettleship 1987). In the USA, Roseate Terns were almost completely restricted to three major colonies by the 1980s, but by then their decline in numbers had slowed and perhaps stopped or even reversed (Nisbet 1980, Buckley and Buckley 1984). Small numbers (c. 80 pairs) nest in southeast USA including about 40 pairs on a roof top in Key West (Clapp and Buckley 1984). By contrast, the Caribbean breeding population of Roseate Terns may not be decreasing; the combined breeding numbers of Puerto Rico and Virgin Islands were around 2500 pairs in the early 1980s (van Halewyn and Norton 1984).

The world breeding population of Roseate Terns is probably about 25,000 and 50,000 pairs (Gochfeld 1983), of which the birds in Britain and Ireland form approximately 1–2%, or about 82% of those breeding in Europe outside the Azores (Table 44). However, the British and Irish breeding population has been in serious decline for at least the past 20 years.

Outside the breeding season, the Roseate Tern is rarely seen on migration and, at all seasons, is one of the most marine of British and Irish terns. Recoveries of ringed birds during winter have been reported from France, Spain, Portugal, and the West African coast from Morocco to Nigeria; but two-thirds of all ringing recoveries come from Ghana. The Ghanaian recoveries were reported from the whole coastline and from all types of locality including rocky and sandy shores. Most first-summer Roseate Terns remain in the tropics, perhaps moving slightly north. Some first- and second-summer birds return to the breeding grounds, but few of them breed. Most birds nest for the first time at three years of age (Langham 1971).

Up to the end of 1987, 22,513 Roseate Terns had been ringed in Britain and Ireland and there had been 308 recoveries (Mead and Clark 1988). The vast majority were ringed as chicks (for example, all but two of 1622 birds ringed in 1983–87). Two-thirds of all rings returned come from the Ghanaian coast. There are no recoveries of foreign-ringed birds in Britain and Ireland but few have been ringed until recently in France, Portugal or the Azores.

It is not known whether ringing recoveries represent an accurate picture of the winter distribution of this species. Because most of the recoveries probably result from birds which were deliberately trapped, it is clear that human activities have a great deal to do with the numbers of ringed birds being reported from different places. For example, the countries near Ghana on the northern shores of the Gulf of Guinea (Ivory Coast, Togo and Benin) are all primarily French-speaking, which may reduce the likelihood of British and Irish rings being reported. However, compared with Sandwich and Common Terns, which also winter in West Africa, a larger proportion of Roseate Tern ringing recoveries are reported from Ghana, suggesting that Roseate Terns concentrate there in winter. Interestingly, the peak of ringing recoveries is in the period December to February (Hepburn 1986) when recent observations suggest that very few terns of any species, including Roseate Terns, are present on the Ghanaian coast (Y. Ntiamoa-Baidu, A. del Nevo pers. comms.).

It is unlikely that the emigration of Roseate Terns from Ghana in December is a recent phenomenon, but it is still not known where the species spends the period between December and February. There are a few observations of small numbers of Roseate Terns in Nigeria in January.

Roseate Terns are difficult to find in the early winter in Ghana because their numbers are swamped by the abundance of other terns, particularly Black, Common, Sandwich and Royal. However, Roseate Terns have been seen at numerous points on the Ghanaian coast, often at lagoons, saltworks, harbours and small estuaries. A total of more than 1300 birds was counted along the Ghanaian coast in November 1988 (A. del Nevo pers. comm.). Several flocks of about 90 Roseate Terns were seen, including ten birds ringed as chicks in Britain and Ireland during the previous summer (probably on Rockabill off the coast of Co. Dublin) and seven ringed as chicks in the Azores in 1984 (A. del Nevo pers. comm.). As with other species of terns, the peak numbers of Roseate Terns occurred at night-time roosts.

CENSUS METHODS AND PROBLEMS

In addition to the general problems involved in censusing breeding terns (see chapter on Sandwich Tern), the chances of either misidentifying or over-looking Roseate Terns are probably higher than for most other species of seabird. Roseate Terns are most likely to be confused with Common Terns, with which they usually nest in Britain and Ireland.

The species' rare and declining status has led to some observers being excessively cautious about disturbing Roseate Terns. Certainly unnecessary disturbance (and any disturbance at all at the beginning of the nesting season) should be avoided, but this does not mean that opportunities to collect useful information on nesting numbers and breeding success should be ignored. In the USA, programmes of intensive study of the Roseate Terns have involved ringing of chicks and large-scale trapping of adults on their nests but have had no deleterious effects. In fact, intensively studied colonies have fared better than ones which were not visited regularly by researchers (Nisbet 1980).

Numbers of Roseate Terns are likely to be underestimated in large, mixed-species tern colonies unless special care is taken when counting nests or adults. Even nest counts may still underestimate the breeding population because Roseate Terns often breed with less synchrony than other terns (Nisbet 1980).

Counting nests of this species is also particularly difficult. Untrained observers will have trouble in distinguishing Roseate eggs from those of other species. Clutch size (smaller in Roseate than Common Tern), appearance of the nest (any nest with copious nest material is likely to be that of a Common Tern), and type of nest site (Roseate Terns more often nest in crevices and sites overhung with vegetation) can give clues to the species' identity. The covert nature of Roseate Terns typically makes them more difficult to find than other species.

Chicks of all ages are readily separated from other species (except Sandwich Tern which is much larger) by black legs (pinkish grey at hatching) and spiky down. However, as with all tern species, the numbers or ratio of chicks of each species in a colony are unlikely to give good measures either of breeding numbers of Roseate Terns or of their relative numbers compared with other nesting terns.

Most regular Roseate Tern colonies were wardened during the 1970s and 1980s and so were censused regularly. However, small numbers of Roseate Terns nesting elsewhere, particularly in Common Tern colonies, could have been missed in 1985–87. The inclusion in the present analysis of data from the All Ireland Tern Survey in 1984 (Whilde 1985) for this rapidly declining species might be thought to have inflated the overall totals; in fact, only 11 pairs bred in 1984 in colonies not resurveyed more recently.

Each of the main colonies has its own special survey problems which hamper any rigorously standardised survey methods. For example, at Europe's largest Roseate Tern colony on Rockabill, 250 pairs nested in 1987 (306+ in 1988), with a smaller number of Common Terns, in walled gardens around the lighthouse and on the adjoining slopes below the lighthouse accommodation. All the nesting areas were thickly vegetated with Tree Mallow *Lavatera arborea* which grew to a height of two metres by the end of the nesting season. Nests could not be counted without entering the gardens and disturbing the birds. Fortunately the birds at this colony were accustomed to people, probably because of the continuous presence of sympathetic lighthouse keepers over the years. The colony could therefore be surveyed by nest counts towards the end of laying.

At the main Welsh colony on Anglesey, Gwynedd, the island used by Roseate Terns could only be viewed from some distance and gaining access to the colony caused considerable disturbance. Uneven terrain, thick vegetation and the need to minimise disturbance have meant that standardised or very accurate counts have never been undertaken at this site.

On Coquet Island, Northumberland, a few Roseate Terns nested in a colony containing several thousand pairs of Common, Arctic and Sandwich Terns and Black-headed Gulls. Good views of the whole colony could only be obtained from the top of the lighthouse tower where access was restricted and visibility was sometimes reduced by spray on the windows. On the Farne Islands nearby, small numbers of Roseate Terns bred with very large numbers of other terns.

At Inchmickery in the Firth of Forth, which had no permanent warden, the Roseate Terns often nested in a part of the island which could not easily be overlooked and where walking was likely to dislodge material onto nesting birds.

THE ROSEATE TERN IN BRITAIN AND IRELAND

The Roseate Tern was first described for science as recently as 1813 after being discovered in the Firth of Clyde (where it no longer breeds). Numbers of Roseate Terns breeding in Britain and Ireland appear to have fluctuated widely in the past one hundred years. By the end of the nineteenth century, numbers had declined to a very low level and the species may have been near to extinction in Britain. There was a dramatic rise in numbers earlier this century, followed by an equally dramatic fall which is still continuing. Numbers probably peaked in the 1950s and early 1960s when about 3000–3500 pairs of Roseate Terns nested in Britain and Ireland (Parslow 1967). Nearly 2400 pairs were found during Operation Seafarer and the numbers have continued to fall ever since; only 470 pairs were counted during the complete survey in 1985–87 and the 1988 total was about 500 pairs (Table 45). Annual counts at RSPB reserves have shown that numbers have declined almost every year since Operation Seafarer (Lloyd et al. 1975, Thomas 1982, Everett et al. 1987, Thomas et al. 1990).

The distribution of Roseate Tern breeding colonies has changed little since 1969–70. In 1985–87, the main colonies were along the east coast of Britain (Inchmickery, Farne Islands, Coquet Island) and around the Irish Sea (Anglesey, Swan Island, islands in Strangford Lough, Green Island, Rockabill, Lady's Island Lake). Roseate Terns rarely nest anywhere other than on small islands so that the number of sites available to them is fairly small. A few Roseate Terns were found breeding or summering in various tern colonies throughout Britain and Ireland including Orkney, southern England and Western Ireland, but none of these sites have ever held many birds in the 1980s.

The decline in breeding numbers occurred in all areas, but some colonies were worse affected than others. During Operation Seafarer, the largest Roseate Tern colony in Britain or Ireland was on Tern Island, a sandbar in the mouth of Wexford Harbour, where about 1350 pairs bred. The island was gradually eroded by winter storms during the early 1970s until, by 1978, it became impossible for the Roseates or any other terns to continue nesting. A colony became established in the early 1970s, presumably by terns displaced from Wexford Harbour, at Lady's Island Lake on the coast nearby. The birds fared well at first, but badly in the early 1980s, due to changing water levels, human disturbance and predation by rats, mink, foxes, and large gulls. Roseate Tern numbers slumped from 275 pairs in 1981 to only ten pairs the following year and eight pairs in 1987. Some birds then appear to have moved up the coast to the island of Rockabill off Co. Dublin where the tern colony increased substantially in size from 1982 onwards. Other Roseate Terns may have arrived on Rockabill at the same time from declining colonies in Northern Ireland (Thomas et al. 1990).

Rockabill is the main ray of hope in an otherwise rather gloomy picture for the Roseate Tern in Britain and Ireland. Numbers nesting there increased during the 1980s from 30 to over 300 pairs by 1988 and breeding success was

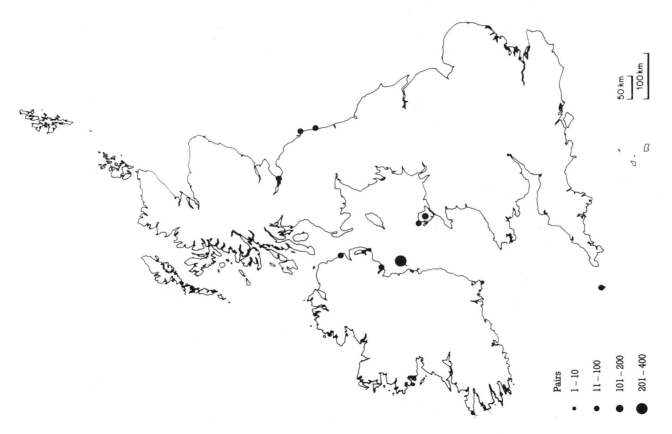

Pairs

· 1 – 10

• 11 – 100

● 101 – 200

⬤ 201 – 400

Figure 31. Distribution and size of Roseate Tern colonies, 1985–87. Note changes recorded in 1988, given in footnote to Table 45.

high (D. Cabot and RSPB *in litt.*). Rockabill has been the only colony in Europe recently where large numbers of Roseate Terns have bred successfully and where they outnumber the other species nesting at the site (in this case Common Terns). The fate of the Roseate Tern in Europe must depend to a significant extent on the continuing success of this colony, which now holds about one-third of the eastern Atlantic breeding population. Rockabill has recently been declared a statutory Refuge for Fauna and a Special Protection Area under the EC Bird Directive by the Irish government. From 1989, the tern colony has received full-time wardening through a joint project between the Irish Government and the Irish Wildbird Conservancy (IWC), with support from the Irish Heritage Council and the RSPB.

In Northern Ireland, three sites were of major importance for Roseate Terns in the 1970s and 1980s: Swan Island in Larne Lough, several islands in Strangford Lough and Green Island in Carlingford Lough. All three are on nature reserves, but numbers of breeding Roseate Terns fell steadily between 1969 and 1988 (Thomas *et al.* 1990 and Seabird Colony Register). Green Island, like Tern Island mentioned above, is eroding seriously. Elsewhere in Ireland, the IWC is carrying out an imaginative experiment on the Keeragh Islands off the coast of Wexford in order to create conditions suitable for Roseate Terns. The number of gulls breeding on the island has been reduced by culling, and models of terns with tape-recordings of their calls have been used to try and attract breeding terns. Since the project began in 1986, Sandwich Terns in particular have shown increasing interest in the island. It is hoped that, if a tern colony of any species could be established on the Keeraghs, Roseate Terns might colonise this site.

The most northerly regularly occupied colonies of Roseate Terns anywhere in the world are in the Firth of Forth in Scotland. In 1969–71 Fidra was the most important site for Roseate Terns, but none has nested there since; instead Inchmickery has taken over as the main colony in the Firth of Forth. Unfortunately this colony also declined rapidly from a peak of 100 pairs in 1976, to just two pairs in 1981 although numbers have since risen again to 20 pairs in 1987. Roseate Tern numbers also fell in northeast England where the colonies on Coquet Island and the Farne Islands now hold only a very few pairs.

Roseate Terns have bred at several sites on Anglesey, where precise locations are not publicised in order to avoid the risk of disturbance. A total of 69 pairs were present in 1987; this declined to only 45 pairs in 1988. Roseate Terns returned to The Skerries (an RSPB reserve off Anglesey) in 1987, for the first time since the 1950s, and 21 pairs nested, apparently successfully, on the edge of a colony of 260 pairs of Arctic Terns. It was hoped that this would herald a recolonisation of this former Roseate Tern site and provide an escape from predation by Peregrines at another Anglesey colony (see below). The following year, although terns were present at the beginning of the season, none of either species stayed to nest. The RSPB has provided nest boxes and has planted Tree Mallow on the island in order to provide a range of nesting opportunities for Roseate Terns.

The decline in Roseate Tern colonies indicates how greatly seabird breeding populations can change and the importance of effective monitoring of breeding numbers. In spite of several problems, Roseate Tern numbers have been monitored effectively as almost all the birds breed in a few wardened colonies. However, although the decline has been comparatively well-documented, its causes are poorly understood.

REASONS FOR CHANGE IN NUMBERS

Numbers of Roseate Terns breeding in Britain and Ireland clearly declined between 1969–70 and 1985–87, probably by 70–75%. This is the only one of the six species of seabird for which Britain and Ireland hold over 80% of the European breeding population, which has decreased steadily over this period.

The accuracy of the Operation Seafarer total of 2400 pairs depends on how precisely the largest colony, Tern Island in Wexford Harbour, was counted. It was thought to contain about 1350 (1200–1500) pairs of Roseate Terns in 1969. However, a large, mixed-species colony such as this, where avoidance of excessive disturbance is essential, cannot be accurately censused.

There is no indication from monitored colonies that Roseate Tern breeding success in Britain and Ireland has been particularly low in the past 20 years, but evidence is meagre. There is at least no evidence to suggest massive breeding failures in Roseate Terns. However, it is possible that either breeding success or survival or both may have been slightly lower during the past twenty years than earlier this century and that this has been partly to blame for the decline in numbers.

Adult Roseate Terns have been killed by various predators in their breeding colonies, especially those in the main colony on Anglesey. Predators suspected or proved to have affected this colony since wardening by the RSPB started in 1970 include Foxes, Brown Rats, Herring Gulls, egg collectors and Peregrines. For example, in 1987 a Fox gained access to the island one night at the very beginning of the season, before egg-laying, and killed at least 57 roosting terns including 12 adult Roseates. Peregrines have killed many adults and chicks each year since 1979 and also caused a great deal of disturbance. In 1980, the wardens estimated that 36 adult Roseate Terns were taken by Peregrines, which represented a very high rate of loss in a colony of only 140 pairs. Despite these and other problems, numbers of Roseate Terns nesting in this colony remained relatively stable, at around 175 pairs, throughout the late 1970s and early 1980s. Perhaps losses of breeding birds were balanced by immigration, in which case the Anglesey colony may have drawn in birds from other colonies nearby.

Could some British and Irish Roseate Terns have emigrated? Changes in nesting sites between years is common behaviour for many terns and there is no reason why the birds should respect international boundaries. However, the only places where Roseate Terns breed regularly in the east Atlantic, other than Britain and Ireland, are in Brittany (France) and the Azores (small numbers may breed annually on Madeira and the Salvage Islands). The French colonies have been monitored since 1970 and are known to have suffered a similar decline in numbers to that of the British and Irish colonies (Henry and Monnat 1981, A. Thomas pers. comm.). The Azores archipelago was surveyed for Roseate Terns in 1984 when 645 pairs were located, whereas another survey in 1989 located just under 1000 pairs. The discrepancy between the two counts is more likely to be due to the greater coverage (particularly late in the season) in 1989 than in 1984 (Dunn 1989, A del Nevo pers. comm.). Some birds may have moved there from further north in Europe, but there are no ringing recoveries to prove this. Thus it seems unlikely that large-scale emigration is an explanation for the decline in Roseate Tern breeding populations in Britain, Ireland and France.

It is also rather unlikely that Roseate Terns have moved to colonies which are still unknown, although some small sites may have been overlooked. However, until the 1984 expedition to the Azores (Dunn 1989), the importance of these islands for Roseate Terns was not appreciated. It is possible that more terns could be found breeding in other sites such as in Tunisia which is a former breeding area. In view of the threatened status of this species, any records of Roseate Terns in suitable breeding location anywhere in the Western Palaearctic would be of interest to the author.

British and Irish Roseate Terns travel to West Africa in the winter, when most ringed birds are reported from Ghana. Observations by British ornithologists in the 1970s and 1980s (notably Alistair Smith and Euan Dunn), added greatly to knowledge of the behaviour and the fate of terns in West Africa. In 1985, the RSPB began a joint programme of research and education with the Ghanaian government and the International Council for Bird Preservation. The 'Save the Seashore Birds Project—Ghana' has carried out surveys of terns and waders all along the Ghanaian coast. These showed that the numbers of terns, including Roseate Terns, peaked in September and October but fell off in December and remained low for the rest of the winter (Y. Ntiamoa-Baidu pers. comm.). The peak in tern numbers coincides with the arrival in inshore waters of shoals of small fish (*Sardinella*). Their presence probably attracts the terns; in addition the fish caught by fishermen are spread out in the sun to dry. Some of these fish are then used as bait to catch terns. Tern trapping for fun, or sometimes for food, occurs at many places on the coast of Ghana and in other West African countries too (Dunn and Mead 1982).

'Trapping takes a variety of forms. Fish, with hooks inside them, are inflated by blowing into the swim bladder, attached to fishing lines and used to catch birds from jetties and piers. Terns feeding inshore are knocked from the air with stones, apparently with some success. Nooses held open with small pieces of wood are set over fish placed on open ground; the bird is caught by the neck when it dips to pick up the fish (Bourne and Smith 1974, Dunn and Mead 1982, E.J. Dunn, A. del Nevo and I.R. Hepburn pers. comms.). Trapping is not directed at any particular species of tern, and Roseate Terns form a very small proportion of the total tern population in West Africa. Thus any suggestion that trapping is the cause of the decline in Roseate Tern numbers must explain why this species seems particularly susceptible to trapping. Mead (*in litt.*) has shown from analysis of ringing recoveries of British and Irish terns that Roseates have a much higher chance of being recovered in West Africa than do Common and Sandwich Terns, but was unable to suggest why. Research is in progress to try to measure trapping intensity on the coast of Ghana. However, the finding (see earlier) that all terns apparently spend only the months September–November in

Ghana weakens the idea that trapping there is responsible for the decline in numbers.

In order to investigate causes of the decline in Roseate Terns, colour-ringing of chicks at all major British and Irish colonies has recently been organised by the RSPB. Studies of the species' breeding biology are being carried out, both on Rockabill in a joint project by the IWC, the Irish Wildlife Service and the RSPB; and in the Azores in a joint RSPB and Universidade dos Açores project. Survey work, coupled with an education campaign against trapping of terns in Ghana, is being continued by the RSPB and Ghanaian government.

The Roseate Tern appears to have been close to extinction in Britain and Ireland in the late nineteenth century due to large-scale egg collecting and shooting of adults for the plume trade. Following cessation of these activities, numbers increased again to a peak of perhaps 3500 pairs in 1962 (Parslow 1967). It is imperative that conservation measures throughout the species' eastern Atlantic range, from Europe to West Africa, are made as effective as possible in order to give the birds a chance of repeating such a resurgence.

CONTRIBUTED BY MARK AVERY

Table 44. *Estimated world breeding population of the Roseate Tern.*

	No. of pairs	Comments
Canada	103–127	Breeds east Long Island to southeast Massachusetts, decreasing; 80 pairs Florida
USA	3400–3600	
Bahamas	500–1000	Decreasing
Caribbean	3000–3500	2500 pairs Puerto Rico and US Virgin Islands, apparently stable; elsewhere disappeared from several islands this century, e.g. Belize, St Croix
Venezuela	100–300	"Several hundred" pairs
Britain	130	Decreased since 1969
Ireland	340	Decreased since 1969
France	80–120	Decreasing/fluctuating
Portugal	?	
Azores	c. 1000	
Madeira and Salvages	<20	Discovered on 2 islands in the Salvages, 1982
Southern Africa	<100	Decreasing
East Africa	8500+	Decreasing
Madagascar	4100	Most on islands off Kenya
Oman	<200	On offshore islands
Indian Ocean Islands	<1000	Amirantes 100+, Seychelles 100–1000, Mascarenes <10, also nest St Brandon, Maldives, Chagos, Andamans
India, Sri Lanka, Burma	500–2000	
Indonesia	?	Breeds in 2 localities, may breed in 4 others
Australia	?	11 sites Western Australia, 6 sites Queensland
New Caledonia and Solomon Islands	?	May also breed in Fiji
China	?	
Japan	?	Breeds in "large numbers" in Ryukyu Islands
Approximate world total	25,000–50,000 pairs	

Sources: Croxall *et al.* (1984), Cramp (1985), Kirkham and Nettleship (1987), A. del Nevo pers. comm., Seabird Colony Register.
? = Breeds, numbers unknown.

Table 45. *Numbers of Roseate Terns breeding in Britain and Ireland 1969–87.*

	1985–87 Pairs	1969–70 Pairs	Birds
Orkney Islands	—	3	
Angus	—	1	
Dunfermline	2	5	
East Lothian	20	107	
Western Isles	1	—	
Argyll and Bute	—	3	
Kyle and Carrick	—	15	
Scotland total	23	134	
Northumberland	35	332	
Hampshire	—	2	
Isles of Scilly	6	20	
Cumbria	—	1	
England total	41	355	
Gwynedd	69[a]	202	
Wales total	69[a]	202	
Antrim	25	—	20
Down	44	251	
Dublin	250[b]	60	
Wexford	8	1352	
Cork	—	10	
Kerry	1	1	
Galway	6	—	
Donegal	3	6	
Ireland total	337	1701	
Britain and Ireland total	470	2392	

[a] Reduced to 45 pairs in 1988.
[b] Increased to 306–332 pairs in 1988. 1988 total for Britain and Ireland was at least 490 pairs.

Common Tern

Sterna hirundo

The Common Tern is similar in size (wing-span 77–90 cm) and shape to the Arctic Tern. Common Terns nest both on the coast and at inland sites, and feed on marine and freshwater fish and aquatic invertebrates. Some terrestrial insects may also be taken. Like other terns, they fish by plunging to the water's surface, often from a hovering position.

INTERNATIONAL DISTRIBUTION AND STATUS

Common Terns nest throughout temperate Europe and Asia. To the north, their distribution extends into arctic Asia and North America and, to the south, there are a few colonies in West Africa and the Middle East. The estimated world population may be between 250,000 and 500,000 pairs (Table 46) but it should be noted that nothing is known about population size for large parts of the range. There are three subspecies, of which the nominate breeds in Britain and Ireland.

In Europe, Common Tern populations are declining generally. In the Netherlands, a large decline occurred in the 1960s due to organochlorine poisoning of the Rhine (Dunker and Koeman 1978). Pollution and land-claim on inland water bodies have also affected populations. The species is listed on Annex 1 of the EC Birds Directive 1979.

Common Terns arrive in Britain in early to mid April and are present in British and Irish waters up to late October, although this species has been recorded in all months of the year (Hudson 1973). Up to the end of 1987,

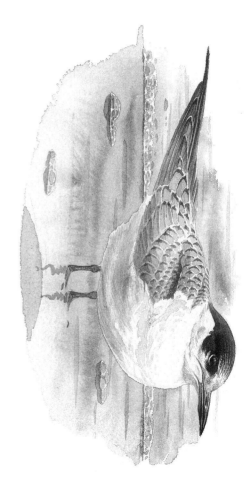

87,078 Common Terns had been ringed in Britain and Ireland. The majority were ringed as chicks (for example, all but 755 of 15,931 birds ringed in 1983–87). This effort has resulted in 1497 recoveries, a rate of 1.7%, the second highest of our five breeding terns. These ringing recoveries show that at least some British and Irish birds travel quickly to West Africa: birds have been recovered in Ghana as early as the end of August. Most recoveries in Europe have come from France, Spain and Portugal, and others come from all countries on the Western African coast from Morocco to Nigeria inclusive, and from Gabon, Congo Brazzaville, Angola, Namibia and South Africa. Most recoveries are from Ghana (95) and Senegambia (72). These recoveries suggest that British and Irish birds winter mostly along the northern shores of the Gulf of Guinea, and that rather few venture further south across the equator. Common Terns therefore seem to winter further north than Sandwich Terns. The species has been seen regularly 600 km offshore from Ghana in the Gulf of Guinea (Urban *et al.* 1986). One wholly exceptional bird was recovered in Australia. Sixty-two foreign-ringed birds have been recovered in Britain from many of the European breeding localities. Most have come from Germany (19), Finland (11) and Norway (9). Four recoveries have come from Mauritania.

CENSUS METHODS AND PROBLEMS

Census methods are similar to those for other terns (see Sandwich Tern chapter, for general methods and problems). Few Common Tern colonies hold more than 1000 pairs; since 1969, only Coquet Island, Blakeney Point and Needs Ore Point have exceeded this figure. Many colonies are only a handful of pairs and counting of nests is feasible. In mixed colonies, with both Common and Arctic Terns, it can be difficult to estimate the relative numbers of nesting pairs. Good estimates of the numbers of adults of each species may be difficult to obtain and there is no guarantee that head-counts will be the same as nest ratios. Nevertheless, this is often the only way of estimating breeding numbers of each species. Identification of either chicks or eggs is not simple in mixed colonies with Roseate or Arctic Terns.

An unknown proportion (possibly 10%) of birds breed inland, particularly at gravel pits in southern England but also at lakes in the west of Ireland and along river valleys in Scotland (Sharrock 1976). The inland population of Common Terns was not counted during 1985–87. Numbers inland have never been surveyed properly although Thomas *et al.* (1990) analysed counts recorded in local bird reports and found a total of over 500 pairs inland in 1984. The size and location of inland Common Tern colonies alters greatly between years; a single year census would be necessary to avoid the problems caused by this habit.

THE COMMON TERN IN BRITAIN AND IRELAND

About 14,700 pairs of Common Terns nest on the coasts of Britain and Ireland. The largest proportion of these (42%) breed on Scottish coasts, but

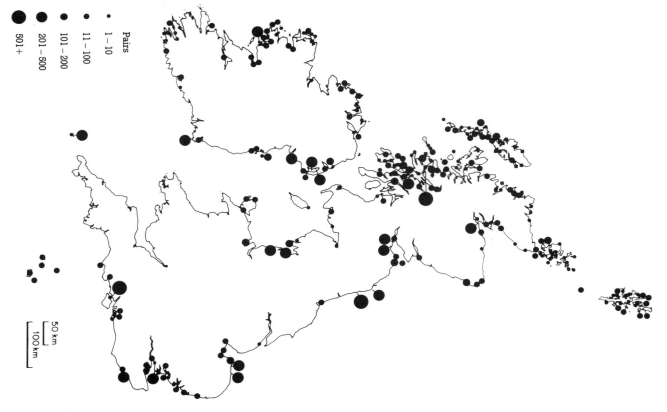

Figure 32. *Distribution and size of coastal Common Tern colonies (and grouped colonies), 1985–87 and distribution of undifferentiated Common/Arctic Tern colonies (squares).*

Pairs

- ·   1 – 10
- •   11 – 100
- ●   101 – 200
- ●   201 – 500
- ●   501+

50 km
100 km

there is a considerable degree of uncertainty over numbers in Shetland at present (see below), and the total of 6200 pairs for the whole of Scotland may be too high.

The Common Tern is considerably rarer than the Arctic Tern, and now somewhat less numerous than the Sandwich Tern in Britain and Ireland so its name belies its status. However, it breeds at a much larger number of sites than the Sandwich Tern and has a more widespread distribution in Britain than the Arctic Tern.

There has been little overall change in the coastal population, but this disguises a decline in England and Ireland which is mostly offset by an increase in Scotland. The Scottish increase between 1969–70 and 1985–87 was of about 1900 pairs (44%) but almost 600 pairs of this apparent rise are on Shetland where the 1980 Arctic Tern survey located about 1000 pairs of Common Terns. The figures used for Shetland derive from the 1980 census there. There was considerably improved coverage in 1980 compared with Operation Seafarer, and it is likely that the 1969–70 figure was low (Bullock and Gomersall 1980). Similarly, the large rise in recorded numbers in Argyll and Bute seems likely to be due, at least in part, to increased coverage by one active worker.

In Ireland, there has been a decline in Common Tern numbers from 4100 to 2700 pairs even though the counts used here are mainly from the 1984 All Ireland Tern Survey (Whilde 1985). The coverage attained by that survey probably exceeded that of Operation Seafarer, strongly suggesting that the decline was real. The largest colony in Ireland in Operation Seafarer was on Tern Island, Wexford, which held 800 pairs in 1969, but fewer in every subsequent year until the island finally disappeared.

The largest Common Tern colony in Britain in most of the past 20 years has been Coquet Island in Northumberland. Over a thousand pairs bred there in every year from 1969 to 1982 (peak of 1725 in 1973), but since then numbers have decreased to 725, 526 and 676 pairs in 1985–87 respectively. In 1987, the largest British colony, of 728 pairs, was near Mull in western Scotland.

Numbers at the main Norfolk colonies have declined: at Scolt Head between 300 and 600 pairs bred in the 1970s but there was a decline to a range from 0 to 280 pairs in the 1980s. At Blakeney Point numbers ranged from 850 to 1800, and 175 to 575 for the same periods.

The problem of undifferentiated Common/Arctic ("Commic") Terns complicates any assessment of change. In England and Wales the number of undifferentiated birds in both surveys was trivial (Table 48), so the totals were unaffected (though, of course, not all birds may have been correctly identified!). In both Scotland and Ireland the numbers of Commic Terns were much larger in Operation Seafarer than in the present survey, suggesting that the current figures may be more accurate than those for Operation Seafarer. In Scotland, there could have been an underestimate of 23% in numbers of Common Terns due to non-identification during Operation Seafarer; however, if the Commic Terns are divided in proportion to the numbers of specifically identified terns there would only have been a 3% undercount of Common Terns. The equivalent figure for the 1985–87 counts is under 1%. The problem in Ireland is larger and it seems likely that around 20% of

Plate 23.   Common Terns at nest, Co. Wexford (Richard T. Mills)

Common Terns were not identified during Operation Seafarer, and 4% in the recent surveys. If these "extra" terns are added, overall trends are not altered, however, but there is some effect on magnitude of change.

REASONS FOR CHANGE IN NUMBERS

There appears to have been little overall change in the Common Tern breeding population as outlined above. However, there are several problems in assessing population levels accurately and Common Terns are susceptible to many of the same pressures that affect other terns.

Common Terns appear to be able to tolerate human presence near their nesting colonies better than many other species. In addition to the many small colonies at gravel pits and reservoirs, a large colony has grown up in the industrial Leith Docks in southeast Scotland. From 50 pairs in 1971, the colony had grown to 382 pairs by 1987. The colony is isolated on a stone platform to which human access is impossible except by boat, and the nesting terns can be observed quite closely without disturbing them. However, the colonies in gravel pits have been susceptible to in-filling of the pits, and massive change in use from, for instance, an angling water to a power-boating area.

There has been a change in distribution and decline in absolute numbers of

Common Terns on the west coast of Scotland in the 1980s (J.C.A. Craik pers. comm.). Previously, there were numerous small colonies on small islands off the coast; many of these are now extinct, leaving fewer large colonies on islands further offshore. This has been accompanied by several instances of mass deaths of chicks in apparently flourishing colonies. Examination of corpses reveals that most have been killed by American Mink, a relatively new arrival in the area. Presumably, the small inshore islands are vulnerable to this predator, and the birds are now being driven to breed on islands further offshore, where feeding conditions may be sub-optimal. Mink reached the largest Common Tern colony in Britain and Ireland in 1989, killing a minimum of 129 juvenile terns and causing the birds to desert the colony (J.C.A. Craik pers. comm.).

Common Terns do not appear to have suffered to the same extent as Arctic Terns from reduced food availability in Shetland waters. This may partly be due to differences in foraging and breeding strategy. Common Terns tend to feed closer inshore than Arctic Terns, and in northeast England at least, have been found to be less dependent on sandeels (Dunn 1972). In Shetland, Uttley *et al.* (1989) found that Common Terns were able to rear their young on Saithe, while Arctic Tern chicks died through lack of their preferred food, sandeels. Food supply has affected Common Terns elsewhere; Becker & Frank (1988) compared Common Tern colonies on an offshore island and the mainland coast of the Wadden Sea. Breeding performance varied from year to year. In years with poor weather conditions (rain and wind) the birds did not forage so effectively in marine areas. Those nesting on the coast could move inland to feed on relatively low energy fish, while those offshore had no alternatives. In these poor years, the coastal birds were more productive. In good years, the offshore birds could feed for longer on high-energy fish, and chick growth was higher on the islands. Thus it appears that perhaps Common Terns are more adaptable to times of varying food availability than are Arctic Terns.

It is impossible to assess the full impact of these various pressures on Common Tern populations in Britain and Ireland as there is insufficient information to say how the British and Irish Common Tern population has changed over the past 20 years.

Contributed by Mark Avery

Table 46. *Estimated world breeding population of the Common Tern.*

	No. of pairs	Comments
USSR—Baltic Sea	9900	Also breeds inland in USSR
USSR—Belorussia	18,600	
USSR—Black Sea plus Sea of Azov	>25,000	
USSR—Caspian Sea	c. 40,000	
USSR—Kamchatka	c. 80,000	
Canada, Eastern	?	Breeds Newfoundland to Gulf of Maine, also inland eg <1000 Lake Ontario 1987

Table 46.   *Estimated world breeding population of the Common Tern – cont.*

	No. of pairs	Comments
USA, Eastern	31,000+	Breeds Maine to Louisiana, 28,000; bred Long Island, New York 1983, increasing
Caribbean	< 1000	
Faroe Islands	1–10	Occasional breeder
Norway	13,000	
Sweden	22,000	
Finland	5000	Stable/declining
Poland	2000	Increasing in some areas
East Germany	2600	Fluctuating, decreasing inland
Denmark	600–900	Decreasing since 1970
West Germany	6000	Decreasing inland and on coast
Britain	12,900	Includes estimated 900 inland, approx. stable since 1969
Ireland	3100	Includes estimated 400 inland, decreased since 1969
Netherlands	10,000–15,000	Decreased 1954–71 because of poisoning, slight recovery since
Azores	2000	Increased since 1969
Salvage Islands	< 50	Decreasing in some areas
Canary Islands	?	May breed Tenerife and Gran Canaria
Belgium	200	Most in Mediterranean, decreasing
France	4000	Decreased since late 1960s
Spain	2500–3000	
West Africa	400 (1970s)	Banc d'Arguin, Mauritania
Czechoslovakia	?	Decreasing
Austria	< 500	
Hungary	> 200	
Switzerland	> 300	
Italy	2800	Decreasing
Yugoslavia and Albania	100–1000	
Romania	100–200	
Greece	1100	Decreasing
Turkey	1000–10,000	
Lebanon	?	
Israel	300–475	Fluctuating
Tunisia	500	
Iran	?	Breeds in wetlands and on islands in Arabian Gulf
China	?	Breeds inland
Approximate world total	250,000–500,000 pairs	

Sources: Croxall *et al.* (1984), Cramp (1985), Whilde (1985), Hémery *et al.* (1988), Ilyichev and Zubakin (1988), Blokpoel and Scharf in press, P.G.H. Evans pers. comm., Seabird Colony Register.
? = Breeds, numbers unknown.

Table 47. *Numbers of Common Terns breeding in coastal colonies in Britain and Ireland 1969–87.*

	1985–87		1969–70	
	Pairs	Birds	Pairs	Birds
Shetland Islands	1000[d]	82	404[a]	—
Orkney Islands[e]	111	129[a]	213[a]	—
Nairn	—		12	
Moray	5	6	43	—
Banff and Buchan	172	9	33	—
Gordon	163		475	
Angus	80		9[a]	
Northeast Fife	68		55[a]	
Dunfermline	60		55	
Edinburgh	382		—	
East Lothian	339	—	865	4
Western Isles	437[a]	204[a]	56[a]	
Caithness	11	—	47[a]	—
Sutherland	303[a]	1	91	—
Ross and Cromarty	120	15[a]	152[a]	—[a]
Inverness	350[a]		106	
Skye and Lochalsh	7	56	214[a]	45
Lochaber	319[a]		69	
Argyll and Bute	1895[a]	68[a]	755[a]	50[a]
Inverclyde	—	—		2
Cunninghame			98	
Kyle and Carrick	4		184	
Wigtown	—[a]		48	
Stewartry	—		99	
Nithsdale	1		138	
Scotland total	5800	570	4200	100
Combined units[a]	6200[b]		4300[b]	
Birds converted to pairs	5%		1%	
Northumberland	997		1765	
Durham	16		30	
Cleveland	1		—	
Lincolnshire	83		122	
Norfolk	841		1904	
Suffolk	102		313	
Essex	407		53	
Kent	502	17	419	—
East Sussex	75		118	
West Sussex	61	1	33	—
Hampshire	785		254	
Isle of Wight	1		1	
Dorset	122		74	
Isles of Scilly	171		150	

Table 47. *Numbers of Common Terns breeding in coastal colonies in Britain and Ireland 1969–87 – cont.*

	1985–87		1969–70	
	Pairs	Birds	Pairs	Birds
Channel Islands	223	2	107	
Lancashire	715		572	
Cumbria	131[a]		291	
Isle of Man	7		1	
England, Isle of Man and Channel Islands total	5200		6200	
Combined Units	5300[b]	20		
Gwynedd	346		222	
Clwyd	200[a]		70	
Wales total	550		300	
Derry	8		—	
Antrim	159		385	
Down	1088		917	
Dublin	170		68	
Wicklow	—		15	
Wexford	280		1038[a]	
Cork	83[a]		579[a]	
Kerry	48		533[a]	
Clare	16		—	
Galway	500		184[a]	7
Mayo	180[a]		118[a]	1
Sligo	—		—	200
Donegal	174[a]		130[a]	
Ireland total	2700		4000	210
Combined units			4100	
Britain and Ireland total	14,700		14,900	

Totals rounded, < 100 to nearest 5, 100–1000 to nearest 10, > 1000 to nearest 100.

[a] Excludes Common/Arctic Terns listed in Table 48.

[b] Includes counts of birds divided by 1.5 to provide estimate of pairs; details in text.

[c] Data from All Ireland Tern Survey 1983–84 (Whilde 1985) used where no other counts were available.

[d] Shetland total for 1980 (Bullock and Gomersall 1980), 77 pairs + 82 birds found by incomplete survey 1985–87.

[e] Survey incomplete in 1985–87; total of only 118 pairs present in 1980 (Bullock and Gomersall 1980).

Table 48. Numbers of undifferentiated Common/Arctic Terns breeding in Britain and Ireland 1969–87.

	1985–87 Pairs	1969–70 Pairs
Shetland Islands	—	5
Orkney Islands[b]	180[a]	85
Angus	—	30
Northeast Fife	—	163
Western Isles	162[a]	2[a]
Caithness	—	2000
Sutherland	10	—
Ross and Cromarty	89[a]	512[a]
Skye and Lochalsh	—	61
Lochaber	20	—
Argyll and Bute	184[a]	39[a]
Wigtown	22	—
Scotland total	670[a]	2900[a]
Cumbria	91	—
Clwyd	15	—
England and Wales total	110	—
Down	—	770
Wexford	—	13
Cork	122	54
Kerry	—	65
Clare	—	20
Galway	—	193[a]
Mayo	28	33[a]
Donegal	9	45
Ireland total	200[c]	1200[a]
Britain and Ireland total[a]	980[c]	4100[a]

These counts are not included in Tables 47 and 50.
[a] Includes counts of birds divided by 1.5 to provide estimate of pairs.
[b] Survey of Orkney incomplete 1985–87.
[c] Data from All Ireland Tern Survey 1983–84 (Whilde 1985) included where no other (including zero) counts were available.

Arctic Tern

Sterna paradisaea

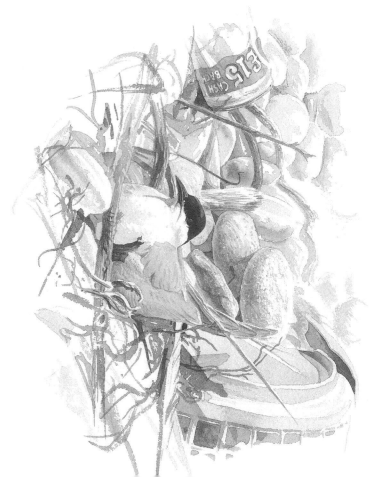

This is one of the three medium-sized terns nesting in Britain and Ireland (wing-span 75–85 cm). Arctic Terns often form large colonies and use a wide variety of nesting habitats including grassland, dunes and moorland near the coast, offshore islands and inland lochs, and even fields of barley or potatoes. They feed by plunge-diving into shoals of fish and crustaceans just below the surface of the water. They prey almost entirely on marine species and rely mainly on sandeels during the breeding season. They sometimes steal food from other terns. Breeding birds defend their nests vigorously with shrill calls and accurate dive-bombing against potential predators, wandering cattle and sheep, and unsuspecting seabird counters. The intruder may be harassed and hit repeatedly by the swooping terns.

INTERNATIONAL DISTRIBUTION AND STATUS

The Arctic Tern has a circumpolar breeding distribution in the northern hemisphere. The largest breeding populations are in arctic Russia, Canada,

226

Plate 24.   Arctic Tern with sandeel at nest site, near Point of Ayr, Isle of Man (Richard T. Mills)

Alaska, Greenland and Iceland. The most southerly breeding sites are in Britain, Ireland and France (Brittany) in the eastern Atlantic, and in Massachusetts in the western Atlantic (Table 49).

The estimated world breeding population is between 0.75 and 1 million pairs but this is a very approximate figure since it is possible that nearly a million pairs may breed in Greenland alone. The British and Irish population of at least 81,000 pairs is approximately 10% of the world total or about 45% of the European numbers outside Iceland. This species is listed on Annex 1 of the EC Birds Directive 1979.

The Arctic Tern is an impressive long-distance migrant. At least some of the birds "winter" in the sub-Antarctic as far as 60 degrees south. Those breeding in the Arctic may therefore see more daylight than almost any other species. Most one-year-old Arctic Terns probably remain in the southern hemisphere; second-summer birds move north but arrive too late to breed. Breeding does not start until the third summer after fledging although first-summer birds have been recorded on breeding grounds (Langham 1971, Cramp 1985).

The first Arctic Terns usually return to British and Irish waters in mid to late April and some remain until late October, although there are records from all months except January and February (Hudson 1973). Up to the end of 1987, nearly 108,000 Arctic Terns had been ringed in Britain and Ireland; the second highest total of the five breeding terns but they have provided the lowest recovery rate (1.1%). Arctic Terns move quickly south to antarctic waters where the chances of recovery are slim. Recoveries of ringed birds show that at least some of those from Britain and Ireland travel directly to West Africa in autumn; birds have been recovered from Ghana and Liberia immediately after the breeding season, in late August and early September. Recoveries have been reported from all but a few countries on the western African coast from Morocco to South Africa, with Ghana, Liberia, Angola and South Africa supplying most records. Three birds have been recovered in Australia, but only one in Antarctica.

In addition to the general problems in counting breeding terns already mentioned (see chapter on Sandwich Tern), an Arctic Tern census in Britain and Ireland is complicated by the fact that most of the population breeds in Orkney and Shetland. Nearly all of those islands are suitable for nesting Arctic Terns (some pairs are found up to 7 km from the sea), and so the area which has to be surveyed for a complete count is immense. In addition, many colonies are situated on small stacks and islets which are difficult to reach. In 1980, an RSPB survey of Arctic Terns located 214 colonies in Orkney and 396 in Shetland (Bullock and Gomersall 1981). Approximately half of all known British and Irish tern colonies are Arctic Tern colonies in Orkney or Shetland.

Arctic Terns can easily be confused with Common Terns and their ranges overlap in Britain and Ireland. Approximately 4100 pairs of terns counted in "Operation Seafarer and 1000 pairs in the 1985–87 survey were counted as "Commic" Terns (undifferentiated Common or Arctic). The eggs are also not easily distinguishable from those of Common Tern and the chicks are also rather difficult to separate.

For the Arctic Tern, there are additional problems in counting nests in very large colonies. In 1985–87 there were seven colonies with over 1000 birds in Orkney and Shetland, two with over 500 pairs elsewhere in Scotland, and a further 4000 pairs on the Farne Islands. In tern colonies of this size, nest counts are usually confined to sample areas, and the breeding population is estimated by extrapolation from the recorded nest densities and the total area covered by the colony. An observer's concentration is likely to be improved (and the count more accurate) if protective headgear is worn when counting Arctic Terns at their colonies!

Nearly 65,000 pairs of Arctic Terns bred in Shetland and Orkney in 1980 (Bullock and Gomersall 1981), and a further 15,300 pairs (including counts of birds converted to pairs) were counted elsewhere on the coasts of Britain and Ireland in 1985–87. Tern colonies in the Northern Isles were not completely covered in 1985–87 but were censused again in 1989 in a survey organised by the RSPB. That survey showed that since 1980, Arctic Tern numbers had

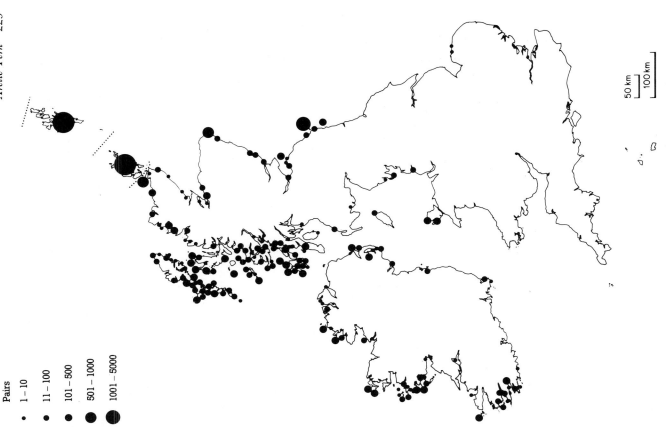

Pairs

1–10
11–100
101–500
501–1000
1001–5000

50 km
100 km

Figure 33.   Distribution and size of coastal Arctic Tern colonies (and grouped colonies) outside Shetland and Orkney, 1985–87. Orkney and Shetland plotted centrally as total 1980 figures.

fallen by about 60% in Shetland and by about 40% in Orkney. About 52,300 pairs of Arctic Terns (with an additional 4100 pairs of Common/Arctics) were recorded in coastal colonies by Operation Seafarer in 1969–70.

Only 10% of the Arctic Tern breeding population of Britain and Ireland nested outside Scotland in the 1980s. Arctic Tern numbers in England and Wales remained remarkably constant between 1969–70 and 1985–87. Almost all the birds nested in Northumberland where the Farne Islands are the major stronghold. These islands had 3200 pairs of Arctic Terns in 1969 but, in the subsequent years, counts dropped to a low of 1100 in 1975 and rose again to around 4000 pairs in the 1980s. Nearby Coquet Island held between 500 and 800 pairs during the same period. Nearly 700 pairs of Arctic Terns bred on the coast of North Wales, mainly on Anglesey, compared with 440 pairs in 1969–70, and small numbers nested in Lancashire at Foulney and Walney Islands. There were also a few pairs in Common Tern colonies elsewhere, such as at Blakeney Point and Scolt Head in Norfolk.

This is probably the most difficult of all our terns to monitor effectively, simply because there are so many colonies and they are mostly in Scotland where observers are relatively few. The figures given in Table 50 are likely to be biased to an unknown extent by lack of information in both Operation Seafarer and the 1985–87 fieldwork. Operation Seafarer covered only coastal seabird colonies and so missed many Arctic Terns nesting inland; only 12,300 pairs were recorded in Orkney and 7700 in Shetland (Cramp *et al.* 1974). The Orkney figure was later revised, on the basis of a reassessment of the large Papa Westray colony, to give a total of 32,179 pairs (Lloyd *et al.* 1975). The Shetland figure was revised to 7300 pairs. Since no complete survey of tern colonies in the Northern Isles was carried out in 1985–87, the totals from the survey in 1980 (Bullock and Gomersall 1981) are used in Table 50.

Similarly, Arctic Tern counts from the All Ireland Tern Survey in 1984 (Whilde 1985) were used where no more-recent counts were available. The apparent increase in Irish Arctic Tern numbers especially on the west coast may be due to increased effort rather than a real increase in the breeding population. The number of Irish Arctic Tern colonies where counts appeared to have declined after Operation Seafarer is similar to those whose size had increased. The rise in numbers is due largely to new colonies, some of which may have been overlooked during Operation Seafarer.

REASONS FOR CHANGE IN NUMBERS

Arctic Tern numbers were not adequately counted in either Operation Seafarer or for the Seabird Colony Register because of the practical difficulties involved. However, it is clear that numbers have fallen by about 50% overall in Orkney and Shetland since 1980. This period has been one when Arctic Terns have experienced very low breeding success in Shetland (Monaghan *et al.* 1989) and when some Orkney colonies have failed too. The low breeding success has been shown to be due to the lack of sandeel prey (Monaghan *et al.* 1989); chicks have starved and adults have deserted their breeding colonies.

The cause of the lack of sandeels is not known. Concern has been expressed that over-fishing by the sandeel fishery around Shetland may have played a major part in the lack of sandeels (Avery and Green 1989) but fisheries biologists have tended to favour other factors such as the rise in Herring stocks or oceanographic changes (see Second Chapter, Part 1 and Kunzlik 1989, Bailey 1989). Whatever the cause, it seems almost certain that the Arctic Tern population will continue to fall since there have been very few chicks fledged in the last few years that could now join the breeding population.

Arctic Terns are likely to suffer from many of the same pressures as Common Terns. Luckily Mink farming has been banned in the Arctic Tern's stronghold on the northern isles, so the species is unlikely to suffer the fate of some Common Terns on the west coast of Scotland. However, other predators (many introduced) can have an effect. Hedgehogs have been recorded taking eggs of Arctic Terns on Shetland from a colony that abandoned its breeding attempt shortly afterwards (Uttley *et al.* 1990). Elsewhere, Foxes have proved to be a problem. In general, it is possible to protect terns from the attacks of predators if sufficient resources are available. It is probably not possible to influence food resources to the same extent, and it seems likely that in future tern populations will be affected much more by food than by predators.

CONTRIBUTED BY MARK AVERY

Table 49. *Estimated world breeding population of the Arctic Tern.*

	No. of pairs	Comments
USSR	Several 100,000s	c. 10,000 Estonia, c. 10,000 on Murmansk coast, c. 25,000 White Sea, colony of 2500 on Harlov Island, Barents Sea; breeds east to Bering Sea
USA—Alaska	Several 100,000s	
Canada, Eastern	10,000–1 million	25,000 birds in coastal colonies
USA—Maine to Massachusetts	1300	Breeds high arctic to Gulf of Maine Decreased since 1930s
Greenland	0.1–1 million	
Jan Mayen	500–1000	Order 4–6
Svalbard	10,000	
Iceland	>100,000	Order 4–5
Faroe Islands	2,000	Stable
Norway	25,000–50,000	Dramatic decrease recently
Sweden	25,000	Fluctuating, especially in north
Finland	10,000–20,000	
East Germany	2000	Fluctuating/declining
Denmark	6000–8000	Fluctuating
West Germany	6000–8000	Stable Decreasing

Table 49.   *Estimated world breeding population of the Arctic Tern – cont.*

	No. of pairs	Comments
Britain	78,200	Includes estimated 500 inland
Ireland	2600	Includes 100 inland, increased since 1969
Netherlands	1200–1500	Decreasing
Belgium	<10	
France	<5	
Approximate world total	0.75–1 million pairs	

Sources: Croxall *et al.* (1984), Cramp (1985), Whilde (1985), Ilyichev and Zubakin (1988), P.G.H. Evans pers. comm., Seabird Colony Register.
? = Breeds, numbers unknown.

Table 50.   *Numbers of Arctic Terns breeding in Britain and Ireland 1969–87.*

	1985–87		1969–70	
	Pairs	Birds	Pairs	Birds
Shetland Islands	31,800[d]	—	7288[a]	10
Orkney Islands	33,100[e]		32,535[a]	—
Nairn	1		2	—
Moray	12	45	89	—
Banff and Buchan	493	52	45	—
Gordon	49		125	
Kincardine and Deeside	20		2[a]	
Angus	94		70[a]	
Northeast Fife	112		—[a]	
East Lothian	99		38	
Western Isles	918[a]	641[a]	1133[a]	66
Caithness	222		2073[a]	57
Sutherland	285[a]	16[a]	549	—[a]
Ross and Cromarty	74		257[a]	
Inverness	200[a]		6	—[a]
Skye and Lochalsh	1216	63	220[a]	92
Lochaber	403[a]	190	139	
Argyll and Bute	1623[a]	1526[a]	1182[a]	549[a]
Cunninghame	—		12	
Kyle and Carrick	16		66	
Wigtown	—[a]		13	
Stewartry	—	16	23	
Nithsdale	—		2	
Scotland total	70,700	2500	45,900	780
Combined units[a,b]	72,400		46,400	
Birds converted to pairs	2%		<1%	—

Table 50.   *Numbers of Arctic Terns breeding in Britain and Ireland 1969–87 – cont.*

	1985–87		1969–70	
	Pairs	Birds	Pairs	Birds
Northumberland	4510		4256	
Norfolk	3		14	
Lancashire	20		1	
Cumbria	45[a]		198	
Isle of Man	13		29	
England and Isle of Man total	4600		4500	
Gwynedd	678		436	
Wales total	680		440	
Antrim	—	—	35	5
Down	363		83	
Dublin	30[a]		129	
Wexford	34	—	75[a]	
Cork	142[a]		64[a]	77[a]
Kerry	343		51[a]	
Galway	699		188	
Mayo	369[a]		125[a]	6[a]
Sligo	—	120	—	—[a]
Donegal	440[a]		161[a]	
Ireland total[c]	2400	120	910	90
Combined units[a]	2500		970	
Birds converted to pairs	2%		5%	
Britain and Ireland total	80,200		52,300	

Totals rounded, <100 to nearest 5, 100–1000 to nearest 10, >1000 to nearest 100.
[a] Excludes Common/Arctic Terns listed in Table 48.
[b] Includes counts of birds divided by 1.5 to provide estimate of pairs; details in text.
[c] Data from All Ireland Tern Survey for 1983–84 (Whilde 1985) used where no recent (including zero) counts were available.
[d] Shetland total for 1980 (Bullock and Gomersall 1980, 4221 pairs + 12,773 birds counted in incomplete survey in 1985–87.
[e] Orkney total for 1980 (Bullock and Gomersall 1980), 1396 pairs + 18,832 birds counted in incomplete survey in 1985–87.

Little Tern

Sterna albifrons

This is the smallest of the terns nesting in Britain and Ireland, with a wing-span of only 48–55 cm, about two-thirds the size of a Common Tern. Like other terns, it feeds by plunging to take small fish and invertebrates from near the surface. Little Terns tend to feed very close inshore and sometimes in estuaries. The species nests in small groups on sand, gravel or shingle beaches or islands. This habit has led to much colony disturbance, to which the terns may respond by dive-bombing the intruder.

The Little Tern breeds in Europe, Asia and Africa. In Europe it nests around the Baltic and North Seas, and along Atlantic and Mediterranean coasts. The largest European populations are in Italy, Britain and Spain. It breeds on the North African coast and in western Africa (*S.a. guineae*) between Mauritania and Gabon and inland at Lake Turkana, Kenya (Urban *et al.* 1986, Grimes 1987, Y. Ntiamoa-Baidu pers. comm.). Elsewhere, the species breeds across Asia from Iraq to Japan and in Australia. There are three subspecies of which the nominate one breeds in Europe. The Nearctic Least

234

Tern *Sterna antillarum* was formerly regarded as another subspecies, but is now generally considered a separate species, forming a superspecies with *S. albifrons* and other allied forms.

The world population is estimated to lie between 70,000 and 100,000 pairs (Table 51). The British and Irish total of 2800 pairs is around 3% of the world population, and 15% of the European total. The Little Tern is listed on Annex 1 of the EC Birds Directive 1979.

Little Terns are summer visitors to Britain and Ireland and usually arrive around mid April with a very few remaining until mid October. It is presumed that first-year birds remain in winter quarters during their first summer and that at least some breed at two years old (Cramp 1985).

Up to the end of 1987, 8500 Little Terns had been ringed in Britain and Ireland, from which 116 recoveries have resulted (1.4%). The vast majority were ringed as chicks (for example, all but 53 of 1413 birds ringed in 1983–87). Recoveries come from around the North Sea (Denmark, Germany and the Netherlands) and western Europe (France, Spain and Portugal). Two birds have been recovered from each of Morocco and Senegal, and one from Italy. The Senegal recoveries provide the only evidence that British and Irish birds winter in West Africa. No British or Irish birds have been recovered in the Gulf of Guinea, in spite of the high recovery rates of other terns in that area. Little Terns ringed elsewhere in western Europe have been recovered in Ivory Coast and Ghana (Urban *et al.* 1986).

CENSUS METHODS AND PROBLEMS

Most Little Tern colonies are in southeast England where birdwatching activity is high, and it is unlikely that many colonies are missed. As with other terns there is a risk of undercounting if some birds fail or desert early in the season, and of double-counting birds who then move to new colonies (see Sandwich Tern for general description of tern counting).

Little Terns are most often found nesting away from other species of terns, but, even where other species are present, identification of this species should pose no real problems. Colonies tend to be rather loosely packed so that finding all nests in even moderately large colonies can take time. A high incidence of nest failure and re-laying at many colonies makes it difficult to know how many pairs are actually attempting to nest. A high proportion of English and Welsh Little Terns nest at wardened sites where there will have been plenty of opportunity to make repeated estimates of breeding numbers. In Scotland and Ireland most sites are not wardened and therefore many estimates will have come from single visits. At least this species does not inflict injury on counters, thus making the task of counting a colony less nerve-racking.

LITTLE TERNS IN BRITAIN AND IRELAND

Little Terns breed around much of the British and Irish coasts, but are absent from southwest England, south Wales, and Orkney and Shetland. The

Pairs

· 1 – 10
• 11 – 50
● 51 – 100
● 101 – 250

50 km
100 km

Figure 34.   Distribution and size of Little Tern colonies, 1985–87.

population of Britain and Ireland is about 2800 pairs. Over 70% of the pairs counted in both Operation Seafarer and the Seabird Colony Register were in England, and on both occasions over half the British and Irish total were found in southeast England from Lincolnshire to Hampshire. This is the one seabird that has its stronghold in southeast England where it can be enjoyed by the maximum number of people!

The Scottish total of 370 pairs is widely scattered with no very large colonies. Overall the Scottish population in 1985–87 was very similar to that of Operation Seafarer whereas the English, Welsh and Irish populations increased more markedly.

Larger colonies which have held more than 100 pairs in at least one year since Operation Seafarer are: Foulness (maximum of 360 pairs in 1983), Blakeney Point (208, 1975), Great Yarmouth (140, 1988), South Binness (138, 1987), Chesil Beach (125, 1971), Tetney Marshes (120, 1977), Holkham (c. 120, 1988), Orfordness (115, 1986), Scolt Head (110, 1984), Chichester Harbour (102, 1975) and Needs Ore Point (100, 1977).

At Great Yarmouth beach, a colony has grown up in recent years to be one of the major British colonies. No Little Terns nested there in 1969 and through the 1970s the only breeding was of five pairs in 1977. The next breeding record was of six pairs in 1982. Only four pairs bred the next year but since then the colony has increased to 140 pairs in 1988 (17, 1984; 27, 1985; 55, 1986; 70, 1987) and has been wardened by the RSPB from 1986 onwards. As well as the large number of breeding pairs the productivity of this colony has been high: an annual average of over one and a quarter chicks per pair has fledged over the past three years. This really is a success story—large numbers of birds breeding successfully on the edge of a busy town and being seen by large numbers of people.

A success story similar to that at Great Yarmouth has occurred on the North Bull Island in Dublin Bay. There, within sight of thousands of people travelling to work every day, a Little Tern colony has thrived under protection from the Irish Wildbird Conservancy. In 1969 only seven pairs nested, but in 1987 a total of 88 pairs was present, Ireland's largest Little Tern colony in any of the past 20 years.

Not all wardening schemes for Little Terns are immediately successful. At St Cyrus in Scotland 106 pairs nested in 1972 when the site was not wardened and fledged only 25 chicks. Full-time wardening by NCC began in 1975 when 83 pairs nested and raised only six young. The worst year on record for 1969–87 was the glorious summer of 1976 when only 10 pairs actually nested even though the warden for that year (the author of this account) was keenly expecting more! Since then numbers have increased (though never reaching the 1972 figure) but nesting success has been low in all but recent years.

REASONS FOR CHANGE IN NUMBERS

The most obvious threat to Little Terns is disturbance at their nesting sites. The Little Tern's preferred habitat puts it into direct conflict with man. This species is not very aggressive, and it is sometimes possible for people to cause serious disturbance at colonies of Little Terns without knowing that they are doing so.

Many protection schemes have been established and some have had spectacular success in allowing birds to stay and breed at sites where for years before they had been unsuccessful. One such protection scheme on the beach at Minsmere, Suffolk has had mixed success. Birds have occasionally nested in quite large numbers but nesting success has been very variable; sometimes predation has wiped out most of the eggs and chicks. At Gronant in north Wales, protection from disturbance has allowed the birds some years of high nesting success. This colony may have attracted birds from other, less-protected Welsh colonies. Many of the latter have shrunk in numbers while Gronant has grown and then maintained its numbers at around 35 pairs since 1976.

At some colonies failure due to human disturbance has simply been replaced by failure due to predation. This is a problem for Little Terns at many of their colonies, but it is unclear how serious it is in national terms. The main predators appear to be Fox, Kestrel and Carrion Crow (Haddon and Knight 1983) although this list is possibly biased towards birds because their daylight depredations are more obvious to observers. Even individual predators can cause havoc in a short time. For example, one Oystercatcher destroyed 12

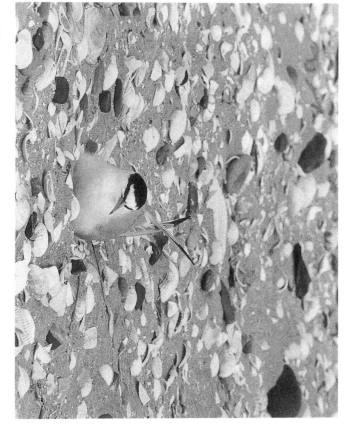

Plate 25.   *Little Tern at nest, Bull Island, Dublin Bay (Richard T. Mills)*

clutches in half an hour, and in a similar period a Stoat took 12 eggs. Foxes can often be discouraged with electric fencing.

Flooding is a hazard for any bird nesting close to the high-water mark, and Little Terns nest closer to it than any others. About half of British Little Tern colonies suffer losses due to tidal flooding and a third of these losses were recorded as being serious (Haddon and Knight 1983). Various methods have been used to raise favoured nesting areas above the high-water mark with varying degrees of success. These schemes include major undertakings to raise areas of beach in order to rescue individual nests. Such attempts are often expensive both in time and money. It is questionable whether they have a large effect in Britain on overall breeding success. However, the effects of tidal flooding on Little Tern colonies can be dramatic; the largest colony in Britain and Ireland in 1988 was that at Langstone Harbour where flooding prevented 162 pairs from raising any young at all.

It would be very satisfying to think that the increase in numbers of Little Terns since 1969 was due to organisations such as the RSPB, NCC, National Trust and county naturalists' trusts who have erected and manned fences around Little Tern colonies to reduce disturbance. Despite some apparent successes (see above) this case is not really proven. It is clear that the rapid rise in numbers of birds at some protected sites is due to movement of birds rather than to the high productivity at those sites. For example, at the Great Yarmouth colony (see above) the rise in numbers of pairs breeding could not possibly be due to recruitment of young raised at that colony. Thus one effect of protection schemes is to draw birds into more concentrated colonies. Here they may suffer increased predation or increased competition for food. The provision of protected sites could even have deleterious effects if those sites attracted Little Terns to areas where predation is high or where they are more likely to be flooded out.

The real test of protection schemes is whether the productivity (and survival) of Little Terns is enhanced by them overall. Data do not exist to allow assessment of this for the whole British and Irish population and without such evidence it is difficult to be sure what effect the protection schemes are having on the overall population. In short, it is not known whether Little Tern productivity has risen nationally due to protection schemes or not.

The reasons why Little Terns move colonies are not known. Disturbance is almost certainly a factor in some cases but at some protected sites the number of birds has not remained high. This may perhaps mean that food availability varies from year to year. Little Terns eat small fish and crustaceans, often caught within sight of the colony. There is no information about how food availability has changed in recent years and there has been no detailed study of breeding biology in Britain or Ireland.

Although Little Terns probably winter in West Africa in areas where tern trapping occurs, there are virtually no ringing recoveries because Little Terns, while they may inspect baited snares, generally shun them, being far too wary to get caught (E.K. Dunn pers. comm.).

CONTRIBUTED BY MARK AVERY

Table 51. *Estimated world breeding population of the Little Tern.*

	No. of pairs	Comments
USSR total	<50,000	Breeds inland
USSR—Baltic and Belorussia	<1300	Increasing
USSR—Black Sea and Sea of Azov	>5000	
USSR—Caspian	several 1000s	
USSR—Far East	c. 1500	
Sweden	550	Stable
Finland	<50	First bred early 1960s, increasing
Poland	800	Mostly inland
East Germany	150	Fluctuating
Denmark	400	Decreasing slightly
West Germany	500	Decreasing, especially in Baltic
Britain	2400	Increased since 1969
Ireland	390	Increased since 1969
Netherlands	400	
Belgium	5	Irregular breeder
France	1100	Now concentrated into a few areas, fluctuating numbers in Camargue
Spain	1000–3000	90% in southwest Spain, e.g. Coto de Doñana where colonies have moved from coast to inland marshes
Portugal	200–300	
Italy	6000	
Hungary	<50	
Albania	?	
Greece	3000	
Turkey	400	
Israel	10	Decreasing
Egypt	<100	Breeds on Nile delta
Libya	?	
Tunisia	700	Increasing
Algeria	<50	
Morocco	?	
Mauritania and Senegambia	<200	Bred Banc d'Arguin and Senegal delta in 1970s
West Africa	?	Breeds Ghana, Togo, Benin, Nigeria, Cameroun, Equatorial Guinea and Gabon
Iran	?	Breeds in inland wetlands and delta marshes
Iraq	?	
Saudi Arabia	?	
India	?	Breeds in 3 localities and may breed at 3 others
Indonesia	?	

Table 51.   *Estimated world breeding population of the Little Tern – cont.*

	No. of pairs	Comments
Australia	?	Breeds at 38 sites from Coral Sea to Tasmania, recent decline in New South Wales
New Caledonia	?	May breed
China	?	
Japan	?	Breeds in "large numbers" in Honshu, Kyushu and Shikoku, also in N Ryukyu Islands; recent decrease

Approximate world total   70,000–100,000 pairs

Sources: Cramp (1984), Croxall *et al.* (1984), Urban *et al.* (1986), Ilyichev and Zubakin (1988), P.G.H. Evans pers. comm., Seabird Colony Register.
? = Breeds, numbers unknown.

Table 52.   *Numbers of Little Terns breeding in Britain and Ireland 1969–87*

	1985–87		1969–70	
	Pairs	Birds	Pairs	Birds
Nairn	1			
Moray	—		11	
Banff and Buchan	—		3	
Gordon	27		21	
Kincardine and Deeside	16		32	
Angus	58	12	55	—
Northeast Fife	—	—	2	9
East Lothian	23		22	
Western Isles	63	68	56	2
Caithness	10		3	
Sutherland	22		6	
Inverness	4		—	
Skye and Lochalsh	—	1	5	1
Argyll and Bute	96	—	74	1
Kyle and Carrick	4		6	
Wigtown	—		1	
Nithsdale	—		2	
Scotland total	320	80	300	15
Combined units[a]		370[a]		310[a]
Birds converted to pairs		14%		2%
Northumberland	29		20	
Durham	—		2	
Cleveland	44		—	
Humberside	—		4	
Lincolnshire	206		63	

Table 52. *Numbers of Little Terns breeding in Britain and Ireland 1969–87 – cont.*

	1985–87		1969–70	
	Pairs	Birds	Pairs	Birds
Norfolk	458		416	
Suffolk	356		80	
Essex	339		163	—
Kent	94		55	
East Sussex	66		70	
West Sussex	12		62	
Hampshire	221		82	
Isle of Wight	1		5	
Dorset	22		120	
Cumbria	75		105	
Isle of Man	60		19	
England and Isle of Man total	2000		1300	
Gwynedd	11	—	14	15
Clwyd	47		4	
Wales total				
Combined units[a]	60	20	20	15
Birds converted to pairs			30%[a]	33%
Derry	2		6	
Dublin	88		8	
Wicklow	25		49	
Wexford	69		99	
Cork	2		2	
Kerry	22		11	
Galway	85	—	38	40
Mayo	72		26	
Donegal	19	20	49	—
Ireland total[b]	380	20	280	40
Combined units[a]	390[a]		310[a]	30%[a]
Birds converted to pairs	3%		10%	33%
Britain and Ireland total	2800[a]		2000[a]	

Totals rounded, < 100 to nearest 5, 100–1000 to nearest 10, > 1000 to nearest 100.
[a] Includes counts of birds divided by 1.5 to provide estimate of pairs, see text.
[b] Data from All Ireland Tern Survey in 1983–84 (Whilde 1985) used where no more recent (including zero) counts were available.

Guillemot

Uria aalge

The Guillemot is the largest of the four species of auks which breed in Britain and Ireland, and has a wing-span of about 71 cm. Most birds breed in large colonies on steep mainland cliffs, usually over 30 metres high, and on cliffs or more level parts of rock stacks and offshore islands. They build no nest but lay their single eggs on rock ledges, also sometimes in caves or amongst boulders.

Guillemots feed on fish and some marine invertebrates. Sandeels, Sprat, Herring and Capelin each form the diet of birds in various parts of the species' range but the first two species are the commonest in diets of birds in Britain and Ireland (Cramp 1985). The birds fish by diving from the surface and swimming underwater, propelling themselves by flapping their wings. They usually dive to about 20 metres, but can swim down to 180 metres or more after bottom-dwelling species (Piatt and Nettleship 1985). Most breeding birds feed within 50 km of their colony although their foraging range just prior to egg laying can be up to 200 km (Tasker *et al.* 1987). Single fish are brought back to the breeding ledges held lengthways in the bill to be fed either to the mate during pre-laying courtship or, later in the season, to the chick. In North America, the Guillemot is called the Common Murre.

Plate 26. Guillemot colony at Sumburgh Head, Shetland (Dr M.P. Harris)

DISTRIBUTION AND INTERNATIONAL STATUS

The Guillemot has a wide breeding range in both the North Atlantic and in the northern Pacific. There are eight subspecies (Tuck 1960). In the Pacific, the Guillemot breeds as far south as Hokkaido (Japan) and southern California, and north to the Bering Sea. In the Atlantic, it breeds south to the

Gulf of St Lawrence and Portugal, and north to Labrador, southwest Greenland, western Novaya Zemlya and Jan Mayen. The Guillemot's world breeding population is probably between eight and ten million birds with about half of these found in the Pacific Ocean and northeast USSR (Table 53). Britain and Ireland have about 1.2 million birds or about two-thirds of the European population outside Iceland.

The Guillemot has increased in most of its European range this century. The main exceptions are the Faroe Islands (and probably Iceland), where there has been a recent decline, and northern Norway, where there has been a major crash in numbers in the 1980s (Vader *et al.* in press). The tiny Iberian breeding population at the southern edge of the species' Atlantic range has declined also. Little is known about the Guillemot's status in the Pacific. At the southern edge of its Pacific range, numbers have increased since the turn of the century in California, but have declined in the small Japanese population.

The Guillemot's distribution away from the colonies in the northeast Atlantic is comparatively well known. A large number of recoveries of birds ringed at colonies in Scotland, northeast England, south Wales and southern Ireland were reported up to the early 1970s (Birkhead 1974, Mead 1974), and a detailed study of the species at sea in the North Sea and off western Britain was made in the 1980s (Tasker *et al.* 1987, Webb *et al.* 1990). Guillemots do not breed until they are at least four or five years old (Hudson 1979), and for most of their immature years they spend less time than the adults on land in the breeding colonies.

Many first-year birds ringed in colonies in Scotland and northeast England have been shot, netted or oiled off the coast of southern Norway and in the Kattegat soon after fledging. Observations of birds at sea show that adults from the most northerly colonies move into the North Sea after breeding and join those from the rest of east and north Scotland and eastern England. Large flocks of moulting Guillemots were found off the east coast of Britain in August by Tasker *et al.* (1986). Birds from colonies in northwest Scotland gather to moult in the Minch (Webb *et al.* 1990). These moulting flocks had dispersed by autumn and, in the North Sea, some birds move south or east to the coast of Norway. Guillemots ringed at colonies around the Irish Sea have been recovered to the south in the Bay of Biscay and the English Channel during their first winter of life. Older immature birds have been recovered between these areas and the breeding colonies. Most breeding adults remain within the Irish Sea throughout the year, with a few moving south as far as northwest France in winter.

CENSUS METHODS AND PROBLEMS

Guillemot colonies are usually large, noisy and obvious during the breeding season but most are also inaccessible. Guillemots prefer to breed at very high density and they crowd together, shoulder to shoulder, on broad nesting ledges or flat tops of stacks. Despite the apparent chaos which prevails in a busy colony of Guillemots, paired birds return to the same area of rock to nest each year. Pairs of birds are, rather difficult to count, as this requires identification of all sites with eggs, young or incubating adults. This takes hours of observation,

Plate 27.   Guillemot colony, Isle of May (Dr M.P. Harris)

usually from a hide, even for a specially selected study colony. The usual count unit is therefore of individual birds. Fortunately, most birds on land in a Guillemot colony can be counted or their numbers estimated with reasonable ease, especially if large colonies are separated into sub-units for counting purposes.

There are problems with this method, however. First, the number of Guillemots in a colony varies with time of day and during the breeding season. For this reason, the recommended counting period is during the middle part of the day during the first three weeks of June when the birds' attendance at the colony is least variable. Secondly, some parts of a colony are often difficult to see from a safe counting point on the cliff top, or from the low angle of view obtained from a boat below the cliffs. Numbers of birds in these areas have to be estimated rather than counted. Estimates also have to be made for birds hidden from view among rocks in boulder colonies or in caves.

The difference between counting units used for auks (birds) and for other species (pairs or apparently occupied sites (AOS)) has led to considerable confusion in the literature on the size of auk populations. During Operation Seafarer, observers were asked to count all birds in the colony, excluding those on the sea and in non-breeding loafing areas on land. Most of the Guillemot counts were probably of birds, but unfortunately some of these were recorded as apparently occupied sites (due partly to the design of the recording card). All were expressed as "pairs" in subsequent publications (e.g. Cramp *et al.* 1974). It has been assumed for the present analysis that the majority of observers during Operation Seafarer counted Guillemots as birds and not AOS, despite the entries on the record cards. Thus, in order to be able to compare counts from Operation Seafarer with those collected in 1985–87, figures recorded as either AOS or birds on the original record cards for 1969–70 have been combined and expressed as birds.

During surveys for the Seabird Colony Register in 1985–87, observers were asked to count Guillemots as adult birds on land, using the methods recommended by the Seabird Group (Evans 1980). However, about 3% of the total count for England, the Isle of Man and the Channel Isles were of AOS and not birds (Table 54). Observations by Harris (1989b) and others at many Guillemot colonies over a number of years have shown that the ratio of breeding pairs to total number of birds in June is about 0.67. In order to be able to include the counts recorded in the "wrong" unit in population totals in Table 54, figures for AOS were divided by 0.67, to provide a rough estimate of the number of birds they would have represented.

THE GUILLEMOT IN BRITAIN AND IRELAND

The Guillemot is one of the most numerous breeding seabirds in Britain and Ireland (Table 1). A total of 1,203,000 birds were present during the surveys in 1985–87 and numbers overall were 119% higher than in 1969–70, when 550,400 birds were recorded. A large majority of the breeding birds (79%) were found in Scotland, 13% were in Ireland and 8% elsewhere.

The main concentration of breeding Guillemots in 1985–87 was in the north of Scotland, with the biggest colony in Britain and Ireland in the magnificent mixed seabird colony on the island of Handa (98,700 birds). The next largest colonies were at Fowlsheugh, on the mainland of east Scotland (52,350 birds) and, in Ireland, on the islands of Lambay (44,500 birds) and Rathlin (41,900

Individuals

▲ 1 – 10

· 11 – 100

• 101 – 1000

● 1001 – 5000

● 5001 – 10,000

● 10,000+

Empty circle: Bull & Cow Rocks not surveyed
in 1985 – 87.

Figure 35. Distribution and size of Guillemot colonies (and grouped colonies), 1985–87.

birds). The largest colony in Wales, by comparison, was at Carreg y Llam (incomplete count of 4700 birds in 1987, 7550 birds in 1989) and the largest in England was at Flamborough/Bempton (32,300 birds).

Guillemot numbers in almost all parts of Britain and Ireland were higher in 1985–87 than they had been during Operation Seafarer (Figure 36). In Scotland, the median or midpoint of colony size had shifted from 100–200 birds in 1969–70 to 400–500 birds in 1985–87 (Figure 37). This was not the case in other parts of Britain or in Ireland where the median colony size was less than 100 birds in both 1969–70 and 1985–87.

The only place where a decrease in Guillemot numbers may have occurred is in northwest Ireland. This is almost entirely due to uncertainty about the size of the Horn Head, Donegal, colony in 1969–70. The size of this colony was only estimated from the sea, evidently by two overawed observers. Their estimates varied from 50,000 to 150,000 birds. The ratio of Razorbills to Guillemots seen on the sea and in flight (3:1) was used to estimate total numbers of breeding birds for each species (45,000 and 10,000 birds respectively). However, when the cliffs were thoroughly surveyed in 1980, 5550 Guillemots and 12,400 Razorbills were found. No conclusion can be drawn about whether or not the numbers of breeding auks had really declined (Watson and Radford 1982). The Guillemots on Horn Head were counted again in 1987 giving a total of 4800 birds; this suggests a decline of 14% had occurred since 1980. An 8% net increase between 1969 and 1987, as in northwest Ireland as a whole, would suggest a 1969 population of 4400 birds (see Table 54). This figure was used for estimating the Irish total for 1969–70.

The Operation Seafarer counts and those made in 1985–87 give only the beginning and end points for the changes which have taken place since 1969–70, although numbers are undoubtedly higher now than they were 16–18 years ago. Fortunately, Guillemots are one of the species whose numbers have been monitored regularly in a sample of colonies around Britain (see First chapter in Part 1), so that information is available on how numbers have fared in the years between the two national censuses.

Monitoring counts in Scotland and northeast England since the mid 1970s confirm the general trend for increase but the picture is more confused elsewhere (Table 55). However, counts of birds in sample plots are not always representative of changes in the whole colony (e.g. Harris *et al.* 1983, Mudge 1988). For example, in several colonies in England and Wales where Guillemot numbers were monitored and considered stable throughout the 1970s and early 1980s (Stowe 1982), there was an overall increase in total numbers between 1969–70 and 1985–87.

Monitoring at Guillemot colonies in north and east Scotland showed that numbers increased up to the late 1970s and early 1980s and then stabilised or declined slightly (Mudge 1986, Benn *et al.* 1987, Lloyd and North 1987, Wanless and Kinnear 1988). Guillemots at a few of the colonies monitored in the southwest of Britain also declined in size between 1975 and 1982; these included Lundy (−10% per annum), Skokholm (−3% per annum) and South Stack, Anglesey (−2% per annum) (Rothery *et al.* 1988). Harris (1989a) pointed out that, in the North Sea, a plateau in Guillemot numbers was reached first in the northernmost colonies monitored; counts at plots in

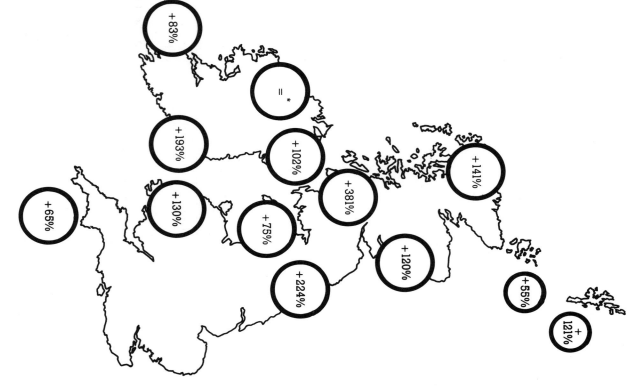

Figure 36.   Regional changes in numbers of breeding Guillemots, 1969–87. See Table 54 for counts and Figure 1 for regional divisions.
* Excludes Horn Head.
No figure is given if more than 10% of a county/regional total was derived from counts made as individuals rather than pairs or where totals were less than 400 pairs.

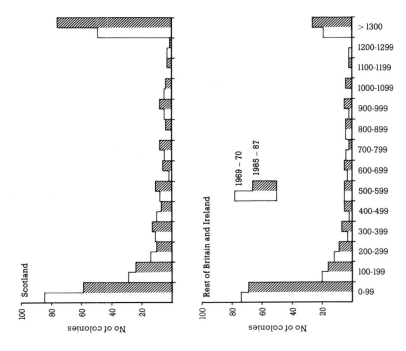

Figure 37. Frequency distribution of Guillemot colony sizes, 1969–70 and 1985–87.

Shetland increased up to the late 1970s and then declined (M. Heubeck pers. comm.). Colonies further south reached a turning point slightly later. On the Isle of May, Guillemot numbers increased until about 1984 and then began to decline (Wanless and Kinnear 1988). Even further south, on the Farne Islands for example, Guillemot numbers were still increasing in 1988.

Without the data collected by monitoring studies, little would be known about the changes in Guillemot numbers in the years between 1969–70 and 1985–87. On the other hand, the one-off censuses have given a comprehensive picture of change, and will be more likely to be representative of the population as a whole than are the monitoring counts. This demonstrates the need for combined long-term monitoring counts and regular total censuses if changes in Guillemot breeding population are to be detected and tracked.

REASONS FOR CHANGE IN NUMBERS

Guillemots, like many other seabirds in Britain and Ireland, probably benefited from bird protection laws enforced at the turn of the century. Bourne and Vauk (1988) estimated that in the 1880s up to 35,000 eggs were being collected annually from Guillemots at Flamborough Head in Humberside. However, there are few records of Guillemot numbers at colonies in Britain and Ireland before 1969 (e.g. Cramp *et al.* 1974), and no firm conclusions on how numbers have changed can be drawn from them because of the difficulty in estimating numbers in large colonies. Nevertheless following Operation Seafarer, Cramp *et al.* (1974) suggested that, at colonies for which earlier counts were available, Guillemots had declined in both England and Wales and in southwest Scotland; but that numbers had increased at some other Scottish colonies.

As stated above, numbers of Guillemots increased in the 1970s; this growth was estimated by Stowe and Harris (1984) to be about 5% per annum. The increase appears to have slowed, halted, or even to have been reversed since the late 1970s in the North Sea. On the Isle of May, survival of immature Guillemots declined as numbers levelled off in the mid 1980s, whilst adult survival and breeding productivity remained high (Harris and Wanless 1988). The reasons for this change in survival are not known but it helps explain why numbers of Guillemots breeding on the Isle of May, and perhaps elsewhere, are no longer increasing.

Food availability has probably played a major role in the ten years or more of growth in the Guillemot breeding population throughout Britain and Ireland, and possibly in the recent declines (see Second chapter, Part 1). No single factor known to cause mortality in Guillemots seems able to explain the changes in numbers that have taken place in the 1970s and 1980s. There have been few oiling incidents in Europe involving large numbers of Guillemots apart from that following the grounding of the "Torrey Canyon" in 1967 and the incident in the Skagerrak in January 1981. Oil spills during the 1970s off southeast Canada and New England have also killed many Guillemots (Powers and Rumage 1978, Brown and Johnson 1980), but monitoring of breeding populations in Canada began too recently to detect any effects of these incidents (Brown and Nettleship 1984a).

During the 1970s, between 30% and 90% of Guillemots found dead in Britain and Ireland each year were oiled (Baillie and Stowe 1984). However, neither numbers of oiled birds found by the RSPB/Seabird Group Beached Bird Surveys nor recoveries of ringed birds reported oiled showed significant increase during the 1970s. Numbers of Guillemots reported by Beached Bird Surveys and those involved in oil pollution incidents affecting birds were also generally lower in the 1970s than in the 1960s (Stowe and Underwood 1984).

Since 1981, the numbers of Guillemots killed by oil and in other mortality incidents around the North Sea may have increased again (Baillie and Mead 1982, Harris and Wanless 1984, Underwood and Stowe 1984). A combination of adverse weather conditions and changes in the distribution of the birds' food may have been partly responsible for the increase in mortality (Blake 1984). Baillie and Mead (1982) suggested a decline in Guillemots would be a likely result of severe oiling incidents in the Skagerrak and off Norfolk during the winter of 1980–81 which involved many immature birds. They predicted that the increase in mortality due to this oiling would cause a 6–9% decrease in breeding populations of Guillemots from Shetland, Orkney and eastern Britain over a five-year period (1981–85), but mostly in 1985 when the group of immatures most affected by the oil would be reaching breeding age. In fact, counts of birds at some colonies in northern Scotland stopped increasing before 1985, and those at the colonies furthest south in the North Sea continued to increase up to at least 1988.

Other marine pollutants seem to have had little effect on Guillemots. Derivatives of organochlorine pesticides, heavy metals, PCBs and other toxic chemicals have been detected in high concentrations in Guillemot eggs from some parts of Britain (Parslow 1973, Parslow and Jefferies 1973) and Norway (Barrett *et al.* 1985), but possible interference with the birds' breeding performance has not been detected. Toxic chemical pollution may have been partly to blame for the large wreck of auks which occurred in the Irish Sea in the autumn of 1969 (Holdgate 1971) although evidence for this was largely inconclusive.

Fishing nets are now the biggest artifical threat to Guillemots in the seas of northwest Europe (Mead 1989). This mortality is especially heavy in gill-nets off Denmark, Norway and Sweden. Numbers of birds netted in the southeast Kattegat increased in the early 1980s as birds shifted their wintering grounds from further north (Oldén *et al.* 1985). About 12,000 birds, 95% of them Guillemots including ringed birds from northeast Scotland, Orkney and Shetland, were killed annually in the winters of 1982–83 and 1983–84. More birds become entangled in large-meshed cod-nets than in herring-nets. The toll was lower when ice conditions restricted fishing activities in the winter of 1984–85 and only 1600 birds died in gill-nets. Many seabirds including Guillemots were caught in salmon drift-nets elsewhere on the Norwegian coast in the early 1980s (Barrett and Vader 1984). Salmon nets (mostly illegal) set close inshore off northwest Ireland are thought to have caused declines in numbers of auks during the 1970s and 1980s at some nearby colonies (Whilde 1979, O.J. Merne pers. comm.). Netting has also caused heavy mortality to Guillemots in the Faroe Islands, off the Atlantic coasts of northern Iberia and around Newfoundland (Croxall *et al.* 1984).

Until recently, many Guillemots were shot for sport off northwest Europe. Hunting and disturbance throughout the year in the Baltic colonies almost caused their extinction there during the last century, and numbers in Finland, Sweden, Denmark and West Germany have increased only with protection (Evans 1984). During the 1970s, 30,000–40,000 auks, including Guillemots from British breeding colonies, were shot each winter off southwest Norway although, since 1979, Guillemots have received complete protection (Barrett and Vader 1984). Shooting of auks has declined particularly around the Faroes where hunting has been restricted by law for the past decade (Mead 1989). Elliot (1985) estimated that 100,000 Guillemots were shot annually off Newfoundland in the 1970s, mainly for sport rather than subsistence. Lastly, in Spain, in addition to oiling, netting and shooting, Guillemots were collected for food and, incredibly, their chicks taken to be kept as pets (Bárcena *et al.* 1984).

Table 53. Estimated world breeding population of the Guillemot (pairs unless otherwise stated).

	Pairs/individuals	Comments
USA—Alaska	3,840,000 Birds	Most colonies probably stable
Canada—British Columbia	5600 Birds	
USA—Oregon and California	363,000 Birds	Decreasing
USSR—Bering Sea	?	5000+ pairs of *Uria* spp., mostly Brünnich's Guillemot *U. lomvia*
USSR—Chukchi Sea	?	35,000 pairs of *Uria* spp., about half *U. aalge*, in the main (stable) colony
USSR—Laptev Sea	?	35,000 pairs of *Uria* spp. in two colonies
USSR—Kamchatka	139,300 Birds	Decreasing
USSR—Kuril Islands and Sakhalin	450,000 Birds	
USSR—Sea of Okhotsk	800,000	
USSR—Novaya Zemlya	750	
USSR—Murmansk	4000	
Japan	1000 Birds	
Canada—southeast	600,000 Birds	Increased since 1940s in Labrador and Newfoundland
Norway	100,000–120,000	70% of population in one colony, status unknown; increased at four other colonies and decreased at one.
Greenland—southwest	300–500	Large decline in mid 1980's
Jan Mayen	600	Two colonies
Svalbard	40,000–100,000	Large decline in north
Iceland	800,000–1,600,000	Declined 1953–79 in two largest colonies
Faroe Islands	175,000	Declined 1972–83 in study colonies
Sweden	7800	Increased this century
Finland	50	Increased this century
Denmark	1600	Increased this century
West Germany	2400	Helgoland; increased 1973–81
Britain	1,050,100 Birds	Increased between 1969–70 and 1985–87
Ireland	153,000 Birds	Increased between 1969–70 and 1985–87
France	250	Increased 1930s, decreased 1970s

Table 53. *Estimated world breeding population of the Guillemot (pairs unless otherwise stated) – cont.*

	Pairs/individuals	Comments
Spain	78 Birds	Declined 1930s–1960, present status unknown
Portugal	75	Declined from 6000 pairs in 1948, present status unknown

Approximate totals (combined units): Pacific   c. 5.5 million birds
                                       Atlantic   3–5 million birds

Sources: Croxall *et al.* (1984), Nettleship and Evans (1985), Vyatkin (1986), Vader *et al.* in press, Litvinenko and Shibaev in press, Rodeway in press, Seabird Colony Register. ? = Breeds, numbers unknown.

Table 54. *Numbers of Guillemots breeding in Britain and Ireland 1969–87.*

	1985–87		1969–70	
	AOS	Birds	AOS	Birds
Shetland	—	162,652	5333	68,195
Orkney	—	182,613	18,142	99,937[b]
Banff and Buchan	—	25,290	10,483	1546
Gordon	—	3829	1667	—
Aberdeen	—	4	—	—
Kincardine and Deeside	—	57,731	32,912	290
Angus	—	2608	3	174
Northeast Fife	—	17,585	—	9008
East Lothian	—	5601	15	1217
Berwickshire	—	29,301	15	7199
Western Isles	—	140,350	42,619	36,013
Caithness	—	147,056	12,255	44,805
Sutherland	—	115,656	30,790	4257
Ross and Cromarty	—	933	—	750
Skye and Lochalsh	2290	365	364	—
Lochaber	—	11,117	—	2159
Argyll and Bute	—	36,848	1643	1604
Kyle and Carrick	—	4988	4177	—
Wigtown	—	4347	1200	712
Stewartry	—	604	8	387
Scotland total	2300	949,500	161,600	278,300
"converted" totals[a]		952,900[a]		439,900
Combined units				
% of total in AOS		<1%		38%
Northumberland	—	17,250	2935	—
North Yorkshire	416	290	—	23
Humberside	—	32,288	10,950	1620
Isle of Wight	—	300	65	—

Table 54. Numbers of Guillemots breeding in Britain and Ireland 1969–87 – cont.

	1985–87		1969–70	
	AOS	Birds	AOS	Birds
Dorset	—	744	35	498
Devon	8	3287	212	2157
Cornwall	246	844	301	—
Isles of Scilly	99	—	60	—
Channel Islands	14	342	61	110
Cumbria	—	4908	—	—
Isle of Man	213	1178	2602	1050
England, Isle of Man and Channel Islands total	1000	61,400	17,200	5700
1980s "converted" total	62,900^d			
Combined units			22,900	
% of total as AOS	<1%		75%	
West Glamorgan	—	178	—	140
Dyfed	—	16,830	4654	2424
Gwynedd	4	17,282	84	7603
Wales total	5	34,300	4700	10,200
Combined units			14,900	
% of total as AOS			32%	
Antrim	—	45,047	22,267	—
Dublin	—	46,510	—	11,438
Wicklow	—	83	—	—
Wexford	—	16,419	—	9729
Waterford	—	1236	631	162
Cork	—	4455^c	2432	2445
Kerry	—	6745	3987	—
Clare	—	16,510	—	8526
Galway	—	1713	250	1271
Mayo	—	2278	—	2211
Sligo	—	1012	2000	—
Donegal	—	6195	852^c	146^c
Ireland total	—	148,200	32,400	35,900
Estimated total		153,000^d		72,500^c
% estimated		3%		51%
Britain and Ireland total		1,203,100		550,400

AOS = apparently occupied site. Totals rounded, <100 to nearest 5, 100–1000 to nearest 10, >1000 to nearest 100.

[a] Counts of AOS in 1985–87 divided by 0.67 to provide estimate of number of birds. Both units used in 1969–70 combined to provide estimate of number of birds; details in text.

[b] Includes estimated 13,300 birds for Marwick Head, recorded as Order 5 (10,000–100,000 pairs) in 1969; 25,220 birds in 1986, assumes 90% increase as in rest of Orkney.

[c] In these counties, at least 10% more birds are estimated to occur at colonies not visited in 1985–87.

[d] This total includes estimates for colonies not counted recently. It is based on the proportional change in numbers at colonies in each region where counts were

conducted in both surveys (4170 birds for Bull and Cow Rocks, Co. Cork and a total of 670 birds for colonies in Kerry, Clare, Mayo and Donegal).

*Includes estimate of 4200 birds for Horn Head, Donegal in 1969–70 (4528 birds counted in 1987; 1969–70 estimate assumes an 8% increase between 1969 and 1987 at other colonies in NW Ireland).

Table 55. *Trends in numbers at Guillemot colonies or study plots monitored regularly.*

Site	Trend	Recent Reference
Shetland	Increased 1976–early 1980s in 6 colonies, then decreased up to 1988	M. Heubeck pers. comm.
Fair Isle	Increased 1971–87	Fair Isle Bird Observatory reports
Orkney	Increased 1976–80/81, then stable/decreasing in 5 colonies up to 1988	Benn *et al.* (1987)
Caithness	Stable 1980–87 in 5 colonies	Mudge (1986)
Troup Head	Increased 1979–82, then approx. stable up to 1985	Lloyd and North (1987)
Isle of May	Increased up to 1982, then decreased up to 1988	Wanless and Kinnear (1988)
St Abb's Head	Increased 1977–88	da Prato (1985), Walsh (1990)
Handa	Increased/stable 1971–79	Stowe (1982)
Shiant Isles	Increased 1971–79	Stowe (1982)
Canna	Increased 1974–83, then declined slightly to 1987	Walsh (1990)
Farne Islands	Increased 1971–88	Stowe (1982), Walsh (1990)
Bempton	Increased 1971–79	Stowe (1982)
Berry Head, South Devon	Increased 1976–87	Walsh (1990)
North Devon and Cornwall	Stable 1971–79, 3 colonies	Stowe (1982)
Lundy	Stable 1981–86 in whole colony	Davies and Price (1986)
South Wales	Stable 1971–79, 3 colonies	Stowe (1982)
Skokholm	Stable 1971–79 in whole colony	Stowe (1982)
Skomer	Decreased 1971–78, then increased up to 1987	Stowe (1982), Walsh (1990)
Lochtyn	Increased 1971–79	Stowe (1982)
New Quay Head	Stable 1971–79	Stowe (1982)
Bardsey	Increased 1976–87	Walsh (1990)
North Wales	Stable 1971–79, 4 colonies	Stowe (1982)
Isle of Man	Stable 1971–79	Stowe (1982)
Rathlin	Increased/stable 1971–79	Stowe (1982)
Aughris Head	Increased 1971–79	Stowe (1982)
Creevagh Head	Decreased/stable 1971–79	Stowe (1982)
Downpatrick Head	Decreased 1971–79	Stowe (1982)
Cliffs of Moher	Approx. stable 1971–79	Stowe (1982)
Great Saltee	Increased 1978–88	Lloyd (1982a), Merne *in litt.*

Razorbill

Alca torda

The Razorbill (wing-span 63–66 cm) is one of the four species of auks which breed in Britain and Ireland. Razorbills build no nests but lay their single eggs in crevices or under boulders, usually sharing a colony with other seabirds. Even in the biggest colonies, the density of Razorbill nest sites is never as high as that of Guillemots.

Razorbills eat fish, especially sandeels and Sprat, and some invertebrates. They dive from the surface with a flick of their wings and swim underwater to catch fish at depths of usually about 5–7 metres but sometimes as deep as 120 metres (Piatt and Nettleship 1985). Breeding birds can forage 20–30 km from the colony although most feed within a few kilometres of it (e.g. Webb *et al.* 1985). Flight-lines of birds moving to and from the feeding grounds are a characteristic sight at breeding colonies during the summer months, and Razorbills can also sometimes be watched from land as they fish underwater below the breeding cliffs. Adults usually carry several fish crosswise in their bills when returning with food for the young.

DISTRIBUTION AND INTERNATIONAL STATUS

The Razorbill breeds only in the North Atlantic with the centre of its distribution in Iceland. Hundreds of thousands of pairs, possibly up to a million pairs, breed in Iceland but numbers and status are unknown. Just under a quarter of a million pairs of Razorbills breed elsewhere in the northeast Atlantic. The world breeding population of the Razorbill is probably between 500,000 and 700,000 pairs, of which about 20% breed in Britain and Ireland, and less than 5% in North America (Table 56). Over 80% of the Razorbills in Europe outside Iceland breed in Britain and Ireland. There are two subspecies: the birds nesting in Britain and Ireland belong to *A.t. islandica*, which is also found in Iceland, the Faroes, West Germany and France.

Outside Iceland, the largest Razorbill colonies are in northwest Scotland. Three sites each had more than 10,000 birds in 1985–87. The biggest colony in Norway, by comparison, is Nord-Fugløy with 10,000 pairs (Barrett and Vader 1984); and in Canada, the Gannet Islands off Labrador have 5500 pairs (Nettleship and Evans 1985).

Razorbill colonies in the Baltic were severely reduced in size earlier this century by egg collecting, disturbance and cold weather. Numbers have increased only in about the last ten years since protection was introduced. Elsewhere Razorbills are known to have declined since the 1960s in west Greenland, the Gulf of St Lawrence, Norway and France, but appear to have increased between 1969–70 and 1985–87 in Britain and much of Ireland.

In the northeast Atlantic, the Razorbills' distribution outside the breeding season is relatively well-known from recoveries of birds ringed in Britain and Ireland (Lloyd 1974, Mead 1974), and from observations of birds at sea in the North Sea and off western Britain during the 1980s (Tasker *et al.* 1987, Webb *et al.* 1990). Most Razorbills breed for the first time at four or five years of age (Lloyd and Perrins 1977). Young birds move away from the breeding colonies during their first autumn and winter. Prior to the mid-1970s, many first-year birds from colonies in north and east Scotland were shot or netted in the fjords of the Norwegian coast. With the introduction of legal protection at the end of the 1970s, the numbers of birds shot declined. However, as relatively few Razorbills were seen at sea off southern Norway in the 1980s (Tasker *et al.* 1987), it is possible that Razorbills no longer move to Norwegian waters. Ringing has shown that other immature birds from colonies in the North Sea and the Irish Sea move south and west of Britain and Ireland, to the Bay of Biscay, Iberia, Morocco, the western Mediterranean, the Azores and even southwest Greenland. Many of the birds probably remain in the southern areas throughout their second year of life. In August and September, adult razorbills from colonies in Shetland, Orkney and Caithness gather into large moulting flocks which have been seen in the outer Moray Firth and to east of the Orkney Islands (Tasker *et al.* 1986). In winter, most recoveries of adult Razorbills come from the North Sea, the Irish Sea and the Bay of Biscay; some recoveries have been reported from as far south as Iberia and the west Mediterranean.

CENSUS METHODS AND PROBLEMS

Breeding Razorbills can be difficult to find in a seabird colony and numbers are easily underestimated when only one or two visits a year are made to a colony. Often they nest on open cliffs scattered between ledges of Guillemots or else hidden in boulder scree. Many nest sites are out of view and, moreover, the number of birds visiting a colony varies even more widely than in the Guillemot. As with the Guillemot, many of the visible birds in a colony are non-breeders.

The birds visible on land in a Razorbill colony can be counted with reasonable ease and this provides a measure of colony size. The effects on census results of variations in colony attendance by breeding and non-breeding birds can be minimised by using specially developed counting methods (Evans 1980). These recommend a count in June, between 0700 and 1500 GMT on days without heavy rain, mist or strong winds. Interpretation of Razorbill counts in terms of the actual number of pairs nesting is difficult. Even in open cliff colonies, where all birds on land can be seen, the ratio of known breeding sites to birds present during June, when attendance is least variable, can range from 0.59 to 0.77 (Harris 1989b). Comparative values of this ratio for Guillemots in the same colony (Isle of May) were 0.62 to 0.68.

During Operation Seafarer and the surveys in 1985–87, most observers counted Razorbills as birds on land in June. A few of the counts in 1969–70 were made late in the breeding season, in July, or even August, when most birds would have left the colonies; and some Razorbill counts were recorded as apparently occupied sites (AOS). Counts in different units in 1969–70 cannot be combined as many of the counts recorded as pairs on record cards may in fact have been of individuals; counts in the different units are kept separate in Table 57. This problem hinders comparisons of the two censuses.

Some of the counts in 1985–87 were also recorded in AOS despite the request for counts of birds (see Appendix III), but at least there was little confusion about which unit was used. The largest proportions of counts in the "wrong" unit were in England, the Isle of Man and the Channel Islands (14%) and in Scotland (4%). In order to obtain complete estimates for the size of the Razorbill breeding population, the same ratio of breeding sites to birds present suggested by Harris (1989b) for the Guillemot was used to convert one unit to the other; counts of AOS in 1985–87 were divided by 0.67 and combined with counts of birds.

THE RAZORBILL IN BRITAIN AND IRELAND

Over 179,900 Razorbills bred in Britain and Ireland in 1985–87, compared with 81,600 AOS and 46,000 birds counted in 1969–70. Numbers obviously increased in the intervening period but it is impossible to say by how much. In 1985–87, 70% of the Razorbills were found at colonies in Scotland and 19% in Ireland. The main breeding concentrations were in the north of Scotland (the

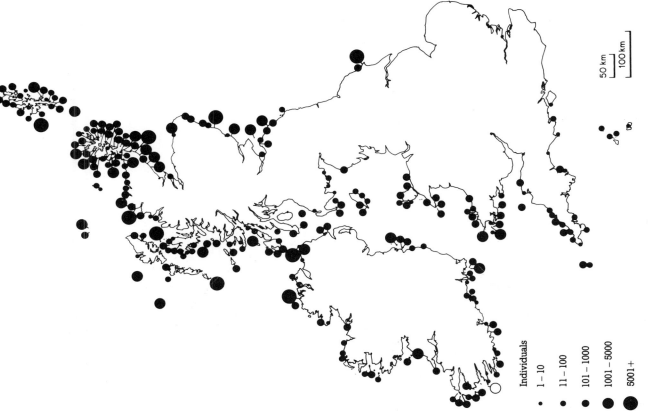

Individuals

·	1 – 10
•	11 – 100
●	101 – 1000
●	1001 – 5000
●	5001+

Empty circle: Bull & Cow Rocks, not surveyed
in 1985 – 87.

Figure 38.   Distribution and size of Razorbill colonies (and grouped colonies), 1985–87.

Western Isles, Shetland, Caithness and Sutherland). The three largest sites were Handa (16,400 birds), Berneray (11,900), and the Shiants (10,900). Foula had 6200 birds and Mingulay, 5000 birds. Elsewhere there were large colonies at Bempton (7700 birds) and Skomer (3600); and at Rathlin (8900), Horn Head (5100) and Great Saltee (4100) in Ireland.

It is impossible to estimate from the counts made in 1969–70 and 1985–87 the percentage change in numbers for different parts of Britain and Ireland. Differences in counting units and some later (July–August) counts during Operation Seafarer prevent comparison of data for 1969–70 and 1985–87. However, many individual Razorbill colonies were censused in both of the national surveys using the same unit and these give an indication of how numbers may have changed on a wider scale.

The number of Razorbills counted in Shetland, for example, increased from 7347 birds in 1969–70 to 13,159 in 1985–87, with another 1200–1300 apparently occupied sites recorded on both occasions. Counts of Razorbills in northeast Scotland were also higher in the 1985–87 census than during Operation Seafarer. Two new colonies were found within Aberdeen city limits, and 137 birds were present in colonies just north of the city where only 10 AOS had been counted in 1969–70.

Comparison of counts for the north and west of Scotland is confused by more thorough coverage of Caithness, Skye, Lewis and Harris during 1985–87 than for Operation Seafarer. In the larger colonies, both increases (Shiants, Berneray, Handa, Faraid Head, Gaeilavore Islands, Canna, northwest Colonsay, Mull of Galloway) and decreases (Flannan Isles, Sula Sgeir, Hirta, Ailsa Craig) were recorded, whilst others showed remarkably little change in size (Mingulay, Rhum and Muck). During Operation Seafarer, there was confusion over the size of the Razorbill colony at Clo Mor, in northwest Sutherland, partly because at least three different observers attempted to estimate numbers, and also because of the cliff's great height and length. The colony was recorded in the species summary list for Razorbills as "Order 4–5" (1000–100,000 pairs or c. 10,000 pairs?), making it one of the largest in Britain and Ireland in 1969–70. About 5500 pairs appear to have been included for Clo Mor in the total for West Sutherland given by Cramp et al. (1974). Examination of the original record cards showed that in fact only about 1500 birds were counted or estimated on the cliffs in 1969; 1800 Razorbills were estimated to be present in the same colony in 1988.

Increase in Razorbill numbers can also be detected at some colonies further south. In northeast England, counts on the Farne Islands increased from 7 to 65 AOS between 1969 and 1987, on the Bempton–Flamborough cliffs from 1700 AOS to 7700 birds, and at St Bees Head, in the northwest, from 55 AOS to 210 birds. Numbers may have remained more stable in the south of Britain. Razorbill counts increased at several of the larger Cornish colonies such as Trevose Head, Gull Rock (off Nare Head), The Mouls, Lye Rock and Carter's Rocks, but declined at others including those near Porthtowan and on Bound's Cliff. Colonies in the southwest were comparatively small. All of those in Cornwall had less than 100 birds in 1985–87 and most were under 50. Numbers of Razorbills in colonies on the Isles of Scilly appeared to have decreased between 1969 and 1986 (400 pairs to 157 pairs), whilst those in the small Channel Islands colonies increased during the same period (42 pairs to 88 birds + 2 pairs). Most Welsh Razorbill colonies either hardly changed in size from 1969–70 to 1985–87, or declined a little.

Razorbill numbers declined slightly during the same period in Ireland as a whole, although on the east and northeast coasts there was a marked increase. The largest Razorbill colony recorded in Britain or Ireland during Operation Seafarer was at Horn Head in northern Donegal. The number of Razorbills was estimated from the auks seen during boat trips below these splendid cliffs in 1969, from the length of cliff face occupied by seabirds, and from the density of breeding ledges (R.A.O. Hickling *in litt.*). A "provisional figure" of 45,000 Razorbills was entered on the record card, but because the accuracy of the estimate was known to be low by the observer and the organisers of Operation Seafarer, the Razorbill total for Donegal given by Cramp *et al.* (1974) was only 27,160 pairs. Razorbills at Horn Head were counted for the first time in June 1980 when 12,400 birds were seen on land (Watson and Radford 1982). By 1987 these had apparently declined by 58% to 5140 birds. Razorbills in the only other large colonies in Donegal, Tory Island (615 birds) and Tormore (362 birds), also declined between 1969 and 1987.

Counts of Razorbills appear to have decreased elsewhere in the west and south of Ireland between 1969–70 and 1985–87. On Clare Island in south Mayo, numbers dropped from 1700 to 200 birds, and on Inishmore in the Aran Islands from 300 to 180 birds. The decline in Razorbills counted on Inishtearaght in the Blasket Islands has been the source of some controversy. Evans and Lovegrove (1974) found 5000–7000 pairs of birds (although how pairs were assessed was not stated) in June 1968. Only 500 pairs of Razorbills were found in mid July 1969 during a count for Operation Seafarer, but 600–800 pairs were counted the following year and 700 pairs in 1973. The reason for this apparent crash in breeding numbers was never proved, but it may have been associated with an unusually heavy tick infestation (Evans and Lovegrove 1974). This was not believed by Kelly and Walton (1977), who felt that such changes may have been due to the rather late count in 1969. Only about 120 Razorbills were counted on Inishtearaght in 1988, and numbers of birds on nearby Inishnabro were also found to have decreased (528 pairs to 193 birds) between 1969 and 1988. Few Guillemots breed on Inishtearaght, but Puffin numbers also declined steeply between 1968 and 1969, and had not recovered by 1988. On Great Saltee, off the Wexford coast, Razorbill numbers fell from 6650 birds in 1969 to 4117 birds in 1985, although on Little Saltee a couple of kilometres away they increased from 75 to 300 AOS in the same period.

In contrast with the south and west coasts, a large increase in Razorbill numbers occurred between 1969–70 and 1985–87 on the east and northeast coasts of Ireland. Several new colonies appear to have been formed, for example at Little Skerry and Larrybane Head on the Antrim coast and Maggy's Leap in Down. In the large colony on Lambay, 1400 Razorbills were counted in 1970 and 3648 in 1987. Growth in the relatively few east coast Razorbill colonies between 1969–70 and 1985–87 compensated for the widespread decline elsewhere so that overall the total number of birds in Irish colonies was little changed.

Monitoring counts of Razorbills in study plots at colonies in different parts of Britain and Ireland provided information on trends in numbers between the two national surveys (Table 58). These counts in Shetland and Orkney, at Troup Head and Lion's Head in northeast Scotland, and on the Isle of May in the Firth of Forth showed that numbers of Razorbills increased up to the early 1980s and then stabilised or declined (see chapter on Guillemot). In plots at colonies in Wales, southern England and western Ireland, numbers appear to have remained stable or declined.

REASONS FOR CHANGE IN NUMBERS

Razorbills, like most other seabirds, were killed in large numbers and had their eggs taken by man during the nineteenth century. Counts at several British breeding colonies in the 1880s to early 1900s suggest that Razorbill numbers may have been higher then than they have been at any time since (Cramp *et al.* 1974). Bird protection laws became effective for seabirds early in the present century but, in all but seven of the 32 colonies for which informa- tion on numbers for 1900–1969 is available, numbers generally declined or showed little change (Cramp *et al.* 1974).

Changes in Razorbill numbers both before and since 1969 must have been greatly influenced by availability of the birds' food (see Second chapter in Part 1). Little is known about how Razorbill food stocks, particularly those of sandeels and Sprat, have fared during the last 40 years. However, Razorbills were relatively unaffected by the scarcity of sandeels which caused breeding failure amongst some seabirds in Shetland in the 1980s (Heubeck 1989b, see also Second chapter in Part 1). The exact reasons for the recent general increase in Razorbill numbers in many parts of Britain and the east of Ireland are unknown.

Fishing nets caused especially heavy mortality among Razorbills off the west and south coasts of Ireland from at least the 1960s onwards. This was most severe in the northwest where birds become tangled in salmon drift-nets set near their breeding colonies (Bibby 1972, Melville 1973, Whilde 1979, O.J. Merne pers. comm.). It seems unlikely to be a coincidence that the only colonies in Ireland where Razorbill numbers, almost without exception, were higher in 1985–87 than in 1969–70 were on the east and northeast coasts where drift-nets are not widely used to catch salmon. Razorbills were also trapped in fishing nets on their wintering grounds, particularly in gill-nets in the Kattegat (Oldén *et al.* 1985) and off the coast of Iberia (Lloyd 1974, Teixeira 1986). This may now be the most important artificial mortality factor for Razorbills (Mead 1989).

The deaths of Razorbills and other auks from oil pollution increased during the 1950s and 1960s (e.g. Cramp *et al.* 1974). The wreck of the "Torrey Canyon" in 1967, for example, reduced the number of Razorbills breeding on Les Sept Îles off Brittany from 450 to 50 pairs (Yeatman 1976). The RSPB/ Seabird Group Beached Bird Survey in the 1970s showed that a large propor- tion of the Razorbill corpses washed ashore were oiled, but that there was no significant increase in Razorbill mortality due to oil during this time (Andrews and Standring 1979). In the western Atlantic, where the total Razorbill population is relatively small, various oil pollution incidents off Newfoundland and New England are also known to have killed large numbers of birds, but the effect upon breeding populations is not clear (Brown and Nettleship 1984a).

Organochlorines and mercury found in Razorbill eggs from colonies in northern Norway and the Gulf of St Lawrence (Canada) were not at levels considered likely to affect breeding performance (Chapdelaine and Laporte 1982, Barrett *et al*. 1985). Similar conclusions were drawn for Danish Razorbills breeding in the relatively confined and heavily polluted waters of the southern Baltic and Kattegat (Salomonsen 1979).

Between 30,000 and 40,000 auks were shot each winter in Norwegian waters during the 1970s (Barrett and Vader 1984); these probably included Razorbills from British breeding colonies (see above). Both Razorbills and Guillemots have been protected in Norwegian waters since 1979. Numbers of Razorbills breeding at many Norwegian colonies had been decreasing during the 1970s (Brun 1979), but have since stabilised or increased slightly (Nettleship and Evans 1985).

Table 56. *Estimated world breeding population of the Razorbill.*

	No. of pairs	Comments
USSR—Murmansk	2000–2500	
USSR—White Sea	1700	
Canada—Southeast	15,000	Increased Labrador 1952/3–78/81, decreased N Gulf of St Lawrence 1960–82
USA—Maine	300	Two colonies
Greenland—South and Southwest	1500–5500	Decreased 1965–74 at six main colonies
Jan Mayen	10–100	
Bear Island	50	
Iceland	450,000	
Faroe Islands	1000–5000	60–75% decrease 1960–80, now stable increasing with protection
Norway	30,000	Decreased 1964–76
Sweden	4300	Stable/increasing with protection
Finland	4000	Stable/increasing with protection
Denmark	200–250	Stable/increasing with protection
West Germany	5–10	Occasional breeding on Helgoland since 1975
Britain	147,700 Birds	Increased 1969–87
Ireland	34,200 Birds	Increased 1969–87 in NE, declined elsewhere
France	70	Decreased 1965–80
Approximate total	500,000–700,000 pairs	

Sources: Croxall *et al*. (1984), Nettleship and Evans (1985), Hémery *et al*. (1988), P.G.H. Evans pers. comm., A. Gardarsson *in litt*., Seabird Colony Register.

Table 57. *Numbers of Razorbills breeding in Britain and Ireland 1969-87.*

	1985-87		1969-70	
	AOS	Birds	AOS	Birds
Shetland	1200	13,159	1347	7347
Orkney	68	9792	3973	4538
Banff and Buchan	304	1809	896	128
Gordon	6	137	10	—
Aberdeen	—	8	—	—
Kincardine and Deeside	—	6558	5632	143
Angus	—	1163	41	88
Northeast Fife	—	1937	1	350
East Lothian	—	260	50	16
Berwickshire	423	1557	257	—
Western Isles	—	39,180	17,525	4405
Caithness	—	17,564	17,317	292
Sutherland	146	18,937	8618	1729
Ross and Cromarty	4	104	3	60
Skye and Lochalsh	844	136	260	69
Lochaber	—	1957	454	1065
Argyll and Bute	—	6230	1562	406
Kyle and Carrick	—	1001	2276	—
Wigtown	35	622	248	—
Stewartry	—	116	82	12
Scotland total	3500	121,700	60,600	20,600
1980s "converted" total[a]		126,900[a]		
Pairs converted to birds		4%		
Northumberland	65	—	7	—
North Yorkshire	104	26	—	11
Humberside	—	7662	1724	—
Isle of Wight	—	8	6	—
Dorset	—	33	6	13
Devon	4	1230	922	120
Cornwall	115	490	225	269
Isles of Scilly	157	3	400	—
Channel Islands	4	81	42	—
Cumbria	340	307	601	—
Isle of Man	—	210	55	—
England, Isle of Man and Channel Islands total	790	10,000	4000	410
1980s "converted" total[a]		11,200[a]		
Pairs converted to birds		10%		

	1985–87		1969–70	
	AOS	Birds	AOS	Birds
West Glamorgan	—	50	—	70
Dyfed	—	7422	4475	506
Gwynedd	47	2130	704	1010
Wales total	50	9500	5200	1600
1980s "converted" total[a]		9600[a]		
Pairs converted to birds		< 1%		
Antrim	—	11,027	3493	—
Dublin	—	4189	—	1762
Wicklow	—	99	12	—
Wexford	300	4174	130	6650
Waterford	—	176	1135	6
Cork	7[b]	674[b]	1872	144
Kerry	—	2365	2981	—
Clare	—	2349	1658	—
Galway	—	198	—	317
Mayo	15[b]	262	147	2042
Sligo	—	133	55	—
Donegal	—	6196	300	857
Ireland total	320	33,300	11,800	11,800
Estimated total		34,200[c]		23,400[b]
Proportion estimated/converted		1%		
Britain and Ireland total		181,900[a]		81,600 +46,000

AOS = apparently occupied sites. Totals rounded, < 100 to nearest 5, 100–1000 to nearest 10, > 1000 to nearest 100.

[a] Counts of AOS divided by 0.67 to provide estimate of numbers of birds; details in text.

[b] In these counties, at least 10% more birds are estimated to occur at colonies not visited in 1985–87.

[c] Includes estimate of 1600 birds for Bull and Cow Rocks, not covered in 1985–87; 1500 pairs in 1970.

[d] Includes estimate of 11,600 birds for Horn Head, Donegal (rough estimate of 45,000 birds in 1969–70, not used by Cramp *et al.* 1974); 5139 birds in 1987. Assumes 55% decline as in rest of NW Ireland.

Table 58. *Trends in numbers of Razorbills at colonies or study plots monitored regularly.*

Site	Trend	Recent Reference
Shetland	Increased 1976–81 in 5 colonies decreased 1982–83, stable 1984–88	Heubeck (1988)
Fair Isle	Increased 1971–87	Fair Isle Bird Observatory reports
Orkney	Increased 1976–82 in 5 colonies decreased 1983–88	Benn et al. (1987)
Caithness	Stable/decreased in 5 colonies 1980–87	Mudge (1988)
Troup Head	Increased/stable 1979–82	Lloyd and North (1987)
Isle of May	Increased 1970–83, stable 1983–86 then decline in 1987	Wanless and Kinnear (1988) Harris and Wanless (1989)
St Abb's Head	Increased 1976–85	da Prato (1985)
Handa	Increased/stable 1971–79	Stowe (1982)
Shiant Isles	Stable in 6 out of 7 plots, one increased 1971–79	Stowe (1982)
Farne Islands	Increased 1971–79	Stowe (1982)
Bempton	Increased 1971–79	Stowe (1982)
North Devon and Cornwall	Stable 1971–79, 3 colonies	Stowe (1982)
Lundy Island	Decreased 1981–86 in whole colony	Davies and Price (1986)
South Wales	Stable 1971–79, 2 colonies	Stowe (1982)
Skokholm	Decreased 1971–79	Stowe (1982)
Skomer	Stable 1971–79	Stowe (1982),
North Dyfed	Stable 1971–79, 2 colonies	Stowe (1982)
North Wales	Stable 1971–79, 4 colonies	Stowe (1982)
Aughris Head	Stable 1971–79	Stowe (1982)
Creevagh Head	Stable/decreased 1971–79	Stowe (1982)
Downpatrick Head	Decreased 1971–79	Stowe (1982)
Cliffs of Moher	Decreased/stable 1971–79	Stowe (1982)
Great Saltee	Approximately stable 1970s–80s	Lloyd (1982a)

Black Guillemot

Cepphus grylle

The Black Guillemot is known in Shetland as the Tystie after the Scandinavian form of its name. With a wing-span of about 58 cm, it is one of the two small auks breeding in Britain and Ireland, and the only species to lay a clutch of two eggs. Unlike the other auks, Black Guillemots in Britain and Ireland nest at low density and in many places can hardly be considered colonial. Nest sites are hidden in cavities on cliffs or in boulder scree and storm beaches.

The birds have a particularly varied diet with regional, seasonal and individual differences in the commonest food species. Black Guillemots in Britain and Ireland feed mainly on fish and some crustaceans. They take mostly species living on the bottom close inshore including Butterfish, blennies, Lumpsuckers and sandeels (Cramp 1985). The birds dive from the surface and swim underwater after fish which they collect usually within 8 metres of the surface although dives can go down to at least 50 metres (Piatt and Nettleship 1985). Most breeding birds feed within a few kilometres of the colony and, when feeding chicks, return with whole fish held in their bills.

DISTRIBUTION AND INTERNATIONAL STATUS

The Black Guillemot has a circumpolar breeding distribution but is absent from long sections of coastline in northern USSR and Canada. Breeding occurs as far north as northwest Greenland, the east Canadian Arctic and the Taimyr Peninsula, and as far south as Maine in the eastern USA and the south coast of Ireland. There are three subspecies, of which *C. g. arcticus* is found in Britain and Ireland. The world population is probably about a third of a million pairs (Table 59), but estimates must be treated with caution since breeding censuses for this species are more difficult than for the other auks. With an estimated total of around 40,500 birds, the Black Guillemot is the rarest of the six species of auk which breed in Britain and Ireland. It is also the rarest of the four species of auk which breed in the North Atlantic (Nettleship and Birkhead 1985). British and Irish birds probably represent about a third of those breeding in Europe.

The largest concentration of breeding birds are in colonies in the north of the range. The USSR, Greenland and the east Canadian Arctic together probably hold over 200,000 pairs of Black Guillemots, but little recent information is available for the large Soviet breeding population or on how numbers might have changed there in the past. In Alaska and the west Canadian Arctic, the species' range extended eastwards into the Beaufort Sea during the 1970s (Divoky et al. 1974, Kuyt et al. 1976). Numbers also increased during the 1960s in Denmark, possibly following immigration of birds from Swedish islands invaded by American Mink, but they declined in the late 1960s and early 1970s because of heavy oil pollution in the Kattegat (Asbirk 1978).

In the southern part of their range, Black Guillemots generally nest in small scattered colonies, with few colonies of over 200 pairs. One example is the largest colony in the eastern USA, on Great Duck Island which has 400 pairs (Buckley and Buckley 1984). In Britain, the Monach Islands (Western Isles) had 850 birds in 1988. Some Black Guillemot colonies at high latitudes are considerably larger. Four of those in Lancaster Sound and Jones Sound in the Canadian Arctic held a total of about 20,000 pairs (Brown and Nettleship 1984a).

Most breeding Black Guillemots in Britain and Ireland remain near their colonies throughout the year, unlike other auks which mostly move away from the nesting grounds after breeding. Adults gather to moult in traditional sites, such as in bays or among islands, close inshore near the colonies (Ewins and Kirk 1988). Birds from remote and isolated colonies, like those on Fair Isle and Foula in the Shetland Islands, move to these more sheltered waters, often involving journeys of up to 100 km. Adults spend the winter in sheltered inshore waters and may visit the breeding colonies regularly (e.g. Greenwood 1987).

CENSUS METHODS AND PROBLEMS

Black Guillemots are probably the most difficult of the auks to census, mainly because they breed at such low density. Their nest sites are usually hidden deep under boulders or in burrows and crevices, and breeding birds can be very secretive. Thus it is often impossible to find all breeding areas or nests during general seabird surveys. Whatever method is used, some isolated pairs are probably missed.

Operation Seafarer in 1969–70 only provided "an indication of numbers and distribution" for the Black Guillemot (Cramp *et al.* 1974) and generally underestimated the population. Almost all counts of Black Guillemots were made at the same time as other seabirds, mostly during June. Slightly over half the final count was recorded as AOS rather than birds on the Operation Seafarer cards and figures in both units were added together and expressed as pairs by Cramp *et al.* (1974).

During surveys for the Seabird Colony Register in 1985–87, observers were asked where possible to make a separate census of Black Guillemots during the pre-breeding season in April using the method recommended by Ewins (1985a) (see Appendix III). This method was also used to make similar censuses in various parts of Scotland and elsewhere from 1982 onwards (Table 60). Areas not yet covered by pre-breeding surveys include southwest Scotland and most of southern Ireland. Some estimates of breeding birds or apparently occupied sites were made in these areas during general seabird surveys in June 1985–87. No special attempt was made to search these coasts thoroughly looking for isolated Black Guillemot sites so coverage in June 1985–87 was probably no more complete than for Operation Seafarer (and was less complete in the west of Ireland).

There is no way in which counts of birds present near the colony during the pre-breeding season can be converted to nest sites occupied in June, or vice versa. Because of the different census methods and units used, counts of Black Guillemots during Operation Seafarer and in the 1980s cannot be compared directly. It is likely, however, that counts of pairs during either survey are equivalent to *at least* twice that number of individual birds.

THE BLACK GUILLEMOT IN BRITAIN AND IRELAND

The stronghold of the Black Guillemot is in north and west Scotland. Of 34,900 birds counted in Scotland during pre-breeding surveys in the 1980s, just over half (54%) were in Shetland and Orkney and 19% in Skye and the Western Isles. Black Guillemots breed no further south than about Aberdeen in eastern Scotland, but in the west of Britain they extend to north Wales. Breeding colonies occur all around Ireland and those in Cork are the most southerly in the east Atlantic.

Black Guillemots were often scattered singly or in small groups along coastline with suitable nesting habitat so division of counts into colonies was done mainly for convenience. Density of birds during the pre-breeding season was highest in Shetland and Orkney where many sections of coastline and individual islands had over 300 birds each. Examples include Fair Isle with 383 birds, Out Skerries also in Shetland with 393, the large island of Westray in Orkney which had 923 birds and the Holm of Papa nearby with 629 birds.

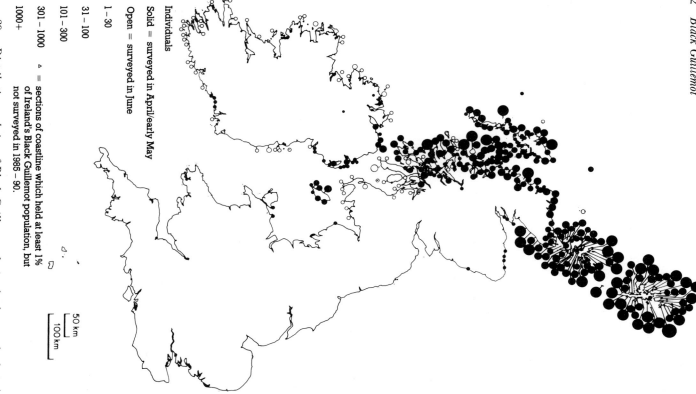

Individuals

Solid = surveyed in April/early May

Open = surveyed in June

·   1–30

•   31–100

●   101–300

⬤   301–1000

⬤   1000+

▵ = sections of coastline which held at least 1%
     of Ireland's Black Guillemot population, but
     not surveyed in 1985–90.

50 km
100 km

Figure 39.   Distribution and size of Black Guillemot colonies (and grouped colonies),
1982–90.

In the Western Isles the largest group of pre-breeding Black Guillemots was on the Monach Islands (850 birds), while on Skye, the biggest concentration was on Waiy (129 birds). The density of birds was also high in parts of east Caithness in April; for example, 1077 birds along the coast between Helmsdale and Lybster. Large numbers of Black Guillemots also probably bred further south in western Scotland in areas not yet surveyed during the pre-breeding season.

The main breeding area outside Scotland was on the Isle of Man; 101 Black Guillemots were counted at Peel Hill in April 1987. The largest colony in Northern Ireland was on Rathlin Island, off the north Antrim coast, where there were 144 birds in April 1987.

Unfortunately comparison between pre-breeding counts of Black Guillemots and those made mostly in June during Operation Seafarer gives no indication of how much numbers may have changed in the last 15 years. However, since counts in almost all areas of Britain and in Northern Ireland were higher in 1982–90 than in 1969–70, it seems probable that Black Guillemots have increased since 1969. (Coverage of the rest of Ireland was too incomplete to show whether or not Black Guillemot numbers had changed.) For example, a total of 32,200 birds were counted in pre-breeding surveys in the north and northwest of Scotland where Operation Seafarer recorded about 3100 birds and 3500 additional occupied sites. On the Isle of Man 23 birds and 13 sites were counted in 1969 compared with 395 birds in April 1986–87; and in Northern Ireland the population estimate increased from nine birds and 136 sites to 514 birds and 28 pairs during the same period.

Black Guillemots appear to have colonised several areas in southwest Scotland and around the Irish Sea since 1969, continuing an expansion which began earlier this century (Cramp *et al.* 1974). On the Clyde and in many harbours in Northern Ireland, including Belfast, they have colonised abandoned wharves and docks. Black Guillemots nest in old lighthouse buildings off the coast of Down, and at Bray in Wicklow they nest in the culverts of a railway embankment. Numbers have also continued to increase in the east of Scotland where only one pair nested south of Caithness in the 1950s (Baxter and Rintoul 1953). Single birds were found at three sites in east Grampian during Operation Seafarer surveys, but were only proved to breed at Redhythe Point. During the 1970s and early 1980s, breeding was proved at five other sites and suspected at two more, and in 1986 a total of 19 birds was counted in a pre-breeding survey of Grampian and Nairn.

REASONS FOR CHANGE IN NUMBERS

Almost nothing is known about how the Black Guillemot's food stock changed in the 1970s and 1980s but it seems probable that breeding numbers are linked to food availability. Many of the birds' food species are of no commercial value and have been unaffected by man's fishing industry; Black Guillemots only rarely make use of fish discarded from fishing boats (e.g. Ewins 1987). Nevertheless the Black Guillemot breeding population in

Scotland and probably in Ireland increased between 1969–70 and 1985–87 at the same time as those of other seabirds.

Without the protection of large colonies, Black Guillemots suffer more than many other seabirds from ground-predators. They are therefore especially vulnerable to mammals deliberately or accidentally introduced onto islands where they breed. The presence of Rats, Cats, Stoats and Hedgehogs was thought to have affected the distribution of Black Guillemots in Shetland and Orkney in the 1980s (Ewins and Tasker 1985); Otters also killed a few birds in Shetland (Ewins 1985b). Brown Rats have been observed killing adult and young Black Guillemots on Papa Westray (Orkney) (Gray 1988). The problem of introduced predators was even worse elsewhere in the species' range. In Iceland, Sweden and Norway, American Mink which have escaped from fur-farms take eggs and kill chicks and adults in sufficient quantities to cause populations to decline (e.g. Barrett and Vader 1984). Black Guillemots disappeared from all but the furthest offshore islands in southwest Sweden following heavy predation of their colonies by Mink in the 1960s (Asbirk 1978).

Black Guillemots in Britain and Ireland are sedentary and spend all their lives near the breeding colony. As a result they are also vulnerable, at all times of year, to oil pollution from sources both onshore and at sea. For example, mortality following an oil spill by the "Esso Berricia" in Sullom Voe, Shetland

Plate 28. Black Guillemots, Queens Parade, Bangor, Co. Down. The birds nest in artificial nest sites within the seawall (Julian G. Greenwood)

during December 1978 almost wiped out the breeding colonies of Black Guillemots in neighbouring Yell Sound (Heubeck and Richardson 1980). Similarly, birds breeding in Danish colonies decreased by 20% between 1965 and 1972 following a series of oil pollution incidents in the Kattegat (Asbirk 1978a).

The use of artificial nest sites, in the form of holes in man-made structures such as harbour walls and piers and even of specially provided nest boxes, may have helped Black Guillemots to spread and increase around southwest Scotland and the Irish Sea where this habit seems most common (e.g. Carnduff 1981). Flexibility in choice of nest sites has also enabled Black Guillemots to extend their breeding range in northern Alaska and to colonise northwest Canada. Faced with a scarcity of natural nest sites, the birds bred in deserted buildings and used artificial debris on beaches as nesting cover (Divoky *et al.* 1974, Kuyt *et al.* 1976). In Denmark, the birds nested under old fish-boxes and on piers, and in the southern Kattegat, where no rocky nesting habitat was available, they used nest burrows in clay cliffs or took over abandoned nest holes of Sand Martins and Starlings (Asbirk 1978).

Table 59.   *Estimated world breeding population of the Black Guillemot.*

	Pairs	Comments
USSR—Baltic to Chukchi Sea	60,000–100,000	Most counts 1950–1960
USA—Alaska	200	"A few hundred birds"
Canada	71,500	Almost all in east
USA—Maine and New Hampshire	5000 (1977)	
Greenland	23,000–61,000	
Jan Mayen	100–1000	Order 3
Bear Island	300	
Svalbard	10,000–20,000	
Iceland	50,000	
Faroe Islands	1000–2000	
Norway	11,000–19,000	
Sweden	11,000–12,000	
Finland	10,000	
Denmark	400–450	
Britain	c. 37,500 Birds	
Ireland	c. 3000 Birds	
Approximate minimum total	300,000–350,000 pairs	

Sources: Croxall *et al.* (1984), Ewins and Tasker (1985), Nettleship and Birkhead (1985), Seabird Colony Register.

Table 60. *Pre-breeding censuses of Black Guillemots 1982–90.*

Area	Year of survey	Reference
Shetland Islands	1982–84	Ewins (1985a), Ewins and Tasker (1985)
Orkney Islands	1983–84	Tasker and Reynolds (1983), Tasker and Webb (1984), Ewins and Tasker (1985)
Grampian	1986	Lloyd and Tasker (1987)
Inverness—Caithness	1985	Seabird Colony Register
North Sutherland	1986–87	Seabird Colony Register
West Sutherland—Wester Ross	1989	Tasker and Webb in prep.
Skye	1987	Tasker and Webb in prep.
Lewis and North Uist	1988	Tasker and Webb in prep.
South Uist, Small Isles	1989	Tasker and Webb in prep.
Lochaber—North Argyll and Bute	1989	Tasker and Webb in prep.
Central Argyll and Bute	1990	Tasker and Webb in prep.
Isle of Man	1986–87	Moore (1987)
Northern Ireland	1987	Greenwood (1988)
Waterford	1986–87	Seabird Colony Register

Table 61. *Numbers of Black Guillemots breeding in Britain and Ireland 1969–90.*

	1982–90 Pairs	1982–90 Birds	1969–70 Pairs	1969–70 Birds
Shetland	—	12008[a]	1530	581
Orkney	—	6883[a]	1133	1134
Moray	—	2[a]		
Banff and Buchan	—	14[a]	—	1
Kincardine and Deeside	—	3[a]	—	1
Western Isles	—	3749[a]	153	368
Caithness	—	2124[a]	377	60
Sutherland	—	1187[a]	—	368
Ross and Cromarty	—	1645[a]	170	216
Skye and Lochalsh	—	2967[a]	68	171
Lochaber	—	1631[a]	72	226
Argyll and Bute	269	2605[b]	230	326
Inverclyde	12	—	—	—
Cunninghame	2	—	3	—
Kyle and Carrick	9	—	52	—
Wigtown	6	57	16	1
Stewartry	—	4	1	3
Scotland totals April	300	34,900	3800	3500
June	—	550[b]	—	—

Table 61. *Numbers of Black Guillemots breeding in Britain and Ireland 1969-90 – cont.*

	1982–90		1969–70	
	Pairs	Birds	Pairs	Birds
Cumbria	—	13	—	2
Isle of Man	—	395[a]	13	23
England and Isle of Man total	—	410	15	25
Gwynedd	4	8	5	—
Wales total	5	10	5	—
Derry	—	40[a]	—	—
Antrim	—	320[a]	114	9
Down	28[a]	154[a]	22	—
Louth	3	—	—	2
Dublin	7	8	15	6
Wicklow	45	24	41	—
Wexford	—	18	—	12
Waterford	—	61[a]	1	93
Cork	24	32	49	28
Kerry	—	46	32	9
Clare	—	1	—	20
Galway	—	55	6	36
Mayo	—	52	29	119
Sligo	2	18	7	8
Donegal	22	47	117	48
Ireland total (incomplete)	130	890	430	390
Britain and Ireland minimum total	430	36,700	4300	3900

Totals rounded, <100 to nearest 5, 100–1000 to nearest 10, >1000 to nearest 100.
[a] April counts, see Table 60 for sources.
[b] April count incomplete, 482 individuals counted in June in areas not surveyed in April included in total but not Argyll figure.

Puffin

Fratercula arctica

The Puffin is the smallest of the auks breeding in Britain and Ireland (wing-span 53–58 cm), and its colonies are mostly on offshore islands or inaccessible mainland cliffs. Despite this, it is probably one of the best known seabirds breeding in Britain and Ireland and can be seen adorning everything from books to buses. Puffins lay a single egg underground in a burrow dug into turf or under boulders. Especially in the evenings at the height of the breeding season, huge flocks gather at the breeding colonies, standing out on grassy slopes, forming rafts on the sea below the cliffs or wheeling in synchrony over the colony.

Puffins feed on fish and, to a lesser extent, marine invertebrates. In Britain and Ireland during summer their main foods are sandeels, Sprat and Herring. The birds dive from the sea's surface and swim underwater after fish which they catch mostly at depths of less than 15 metres. Loads of small fish are brought back to the nest burrows held crosswise in the adult's bill and it is relatively easy to study the diet of Puffin chicks. The Puffin is sometimes referred to as the Atlantic Puffin to distinguish it from other species of puffins which breed in the Pacific.

278

Plate 29.   Puffin with sandeel, North Rona (Dr M.P. Harris)

DISTRIBUTION AND INTERNATIONAL STATUS

The Puffin breeds only in the North Atlantic and has colonies from the coast of Labrador in Canada eastwards to west Novaya Zemlya, USSR. The most northerly colonies are in Thule, northwest Greenland, and the most southerly are in Maine, USA. The centre of the Puffin's distribution is in Iceland, where there are eight to ten million birds or approximately three million pairs (Table 62). This represents a large part of the world population. Britain and Ireland, by comparison, have more than 500,000 pairs, probably under a quarter of those breeding in Europe outside Iceland. There are three subspecies; Puffins breeding and Britain and Ireland belong to *F.a. grabae.*

Details of the distribution and status of the Puffin outside Britain and Ireland were given by Harris (1984a). In the early part of the last century, Puffins bred on Helgoland (Germany) and up to about 1970 they also bred in several small colonies in Sweden. Numbers of Puffins appear to be about stable in Iceland and the Faroe Islands although many colonies are inaccessible, very large and impossible to census. Puffins are the most numerous seabird in Norway where almost all colonies are situated in the north and northwest of the country. It is not known whether Puffin numbers have changed in Norway during the present century, but studies at the largest colony, on Røst in the Lofoten Islands, showed little change in numbers during the 1970s and early 1980s (Barrett *et al.* 1985).

Similarly, nothing is known of the status of Puffins on Svalbard or in northwest USSR. The most southerly colonies in Europe, on islands off Brittany, have been decreasing or have been deserted in the last 50 years. Two major oil pollution incidents, caused by the "Torrey Canyon" in 1967 and the "Amoco Cadiz" in 1978, killed many seabirds and hastened the decline of French Puffins.

In the west Atlantic, Puffin numbers declined generally in the nineteenth century. The best documented colonies are those in the Gulf of St Lawrence, where numbers increased up to the 1960s and then crashed, but are now mostly stable. Further south, Puffins have been increased with habitat management and protection from persecution, and have been reintroduced to Maine where they now occupy their three colonies. Puffins are extending their breeding range northwards in Labrador and small, undiscovered colonies may exist in the Canadian Arctic (Nettleship and Evans 1985).

Some indication of the Puffin's distribution outside the breeding season is provided by recoveries of ringed birds (Harris 1984b). Only very few of these are reported compared with the other auks, reflecting the Puffins more pelagic nature. In addition, records are biased by the fact that most birds are found dead in the spring, when Puffins moult their wing feathers and become temporarily flightless (which happens in autumn in the other auks). Many birds from colonies in Norway and north and east Britain winter in the North Sea. Observations of seabirds at sea have shown that in winter Puffins are widely dispersed throughout the North Sea, but are present at lower densities than the other auks (Tasker et al. 1987). After breeding, Puffins from colonies in the west of Scotland, and probably those from Ireland, move out into the North Atlantic where ringed birds have little chance of being recovered. They disperse south as far as the Canary Islands and west to southern Greenland. Icelandic Puffins and those from colonies further north regularly reach Greenland and Newfoundland in the winter months.

CENSUS METHODS AND PROBLEMS

Large Puffin colonies are unmistakable and most are found in or near colonies of other breeding seabirds. Where Puffins breed in small numbers, especially if nests are in burrows hidden by vegetation or deep under rocks, colonies can be easily overlooked. For most of the day, even large colonies can appear almost deserted with few birds visible on land or the sea nearby. This can make it difficult to determine whether or not Puffins are actually breeding in an area and often leads to gross underestimates of colony size.

Ideally, a census of breeding Puffins is carried out by counting occupied burrows or nest sites (Evans 1980, Harris 1984a). This is impossible in many colonies because burrows are inaccessible, or because there is no time to check even a sample of potential nest sites for breeding occupancy. Instead the numbers of birds on land and the nearby sea are counted. Attendance at the breeding colony is extremely variable, depending on factors such as the weather, so interpretation of these "head counts" in terms of breeding numbers is unreliable.

The most useful head counts are those made either early or late in the breeding season. When Puffins in rafts on the water around the Isle of May were counted regularly during April, the maximum annual count was found to be roughly equal to the number of birds which later bred on the island (Harris 1977). Alternatively, counts of Puffins in several colonies on a series of calm evenings (20.00 hours to dusk) late in the breeding season (usually July) have shown that the maximum number of birds recorded on land is approximately equal to half the number of breeding adults (Ashcroft 1979, Lloyd 1982a). In general, however, counts of birds cannot be converted satisfactorily to numbers of pairs, or vice versa. If standardisation of units is essential, it has usually been assumed that one bird at the colony is equivalent to a minimum of one apparently occupied site or one breeding pair (Cramp *et al.* 1974, M.P. Harris pers. comm.).

During Operation Seafarer, most Puffin counts were made in June or July at the same time as other seabirds (Appendix IV). A few were as late as August by which time many Puffin chicks would have fledged. The units used to count Puffins were birds on land or apparently occupied sites (AOS). A majority of the counts were of AOS (Table 63) but, because of the time required to identify occupied sites in a Puffin colony, it seems likely that some were counts of birds which were entered on the record cards as AOS. Cramp *et al.* (1974) presented the Operation Seafarer Puffin data as pairs but, because of difficulties in censusing, gave totals for each county in Britain and Ireland only as orders of magnitude (e.g. Order 2: 10–99 pairs).

Most of the Puffin counts during 1985–87 were also recorded as AOS rather than birds on land and sea (Appendix III). Nearly all were made at the same time as those for other seabirds in June. The results of Operation Seafarer for the Puffin cannot be compared directly with those for 1985–87 because of the differences in counting methods and units.

Changes in counts of occupied Puffin burrows are difficult to interpret with confidence. Since many colonies are too large or too inaccessible for all likely Puffin burrows to be examined, censuses of occupied burrows are generally made in sample areas (Harris 1984a). The area of ground used by Puffins for nesting is then estimated and the total number of burrows in the colony calculated by extrapolation from the density of occupied burrows in the areas sampled. In practice, counts of burrows in sample areas can be made with reasonable accuracy and are useful as a tool for monitoring population change, but estimation of total colony size by this method is often very difficult (Harris 1984a).

Descriptions of Puffins at some colonies in past centuries suggest enormous numbers once bred where now relatively few remain. For example, Harris and Murray (1977) list historical documentation of Puffin colonies on St Kilda which includes accounts such as the following by Macaulay (1764):

Incredible flight of these Puffins . . . and sometimes while on the wing, involve everything below them in darkness, like a small cloud of locusts, in another country.

St Kilda still has a very large Puffin colony, but this description would not have applied in the 1980s, even to the highest density nesting slopes and on an evening of maximum attendance. Taking into account the large variation in numbers of birds that can be seen in a Puffin colony, it is safest to regard these old records with caution.

THE PUFFIN IN BRITAIN AND IRELAND

Assuming each bird in a Puffin colony represents a breeding pair, at least 512,000 pairs bred in Britain and Ireland in 1985–87, probably slightly more than were recorded by Operation Seafarer in 1969–70. Harris (1976a) suggested a total of about 550,000 pairs in 1975, and around 700,000 pairs in the early 1980s (Harris 1984a). The recent surveys showed that the large colony on the Clo Mor cliffs in northwest Sutherland contained at least 5900 Puffins (daytime count in June 1988), and not 25,000 to 50,000 pairs as previously assumed. The total for Irish Puffins in 1985–87 was less than 26,000 pairs, rather than 45,000 pairs as estimated by Harris (1984a), partly because of the decline in numbers on Inishtearaght (see below). Otherwise

Plate 30. *Puffins on Cleitean McPhaidean, Boreray, St Kilda. St Kilda holds Britain and Ireland's largest Puffin colony; in the background is Stac Lee, holding part of the world's largest Gannet colony (Peter Moore)*

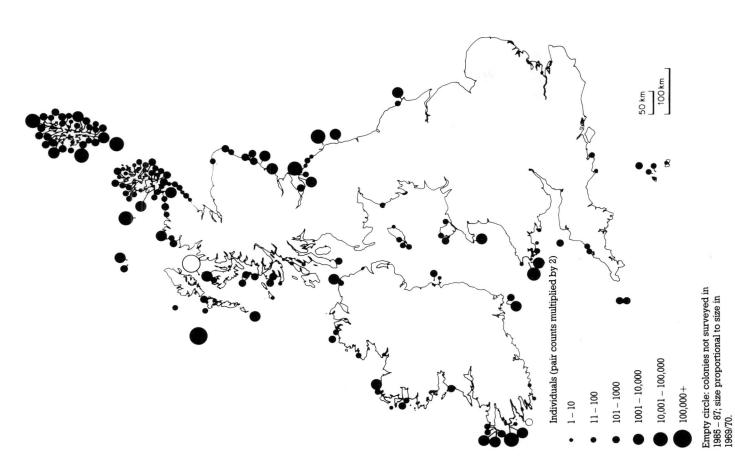

Individuals (pair counts multiplied by 2)

- · 1 – 10
- · 11 – 100
- ● 101 – 1000
- ● 1001 – 10,000
- ● 10,001 – 100,000
- ● 100,000 +

50 km
100 km

Empty circle: colonies not surveyed in
1985 – 87; size proportional to size in
1969/70.

Figure 40.   Distribution and size of Puffin colonies (and grouped colonies), 1985–87.

the results of the 1985–87 surveys and estimates made by Harris are remarkably similar.

Scotland had a large majority of the Puffins in 1985–87; 89% of pairs and 75% of birds counted were in Scottish colonies. The largest of these, with about 155,000 pairs, was on the St Kilda group. Other big colonies were Sule Skerry west of Orkney (47,000 pairs); Fair Isle (20,200 birds) and Foula (48,000 pairs) in Shetland; and the Isle of May (12,000 pairs). The Shetland islands as a whole probably hold about 20% of Britain and Ireland's Puffin population. The Puffins in another large colony, the Shiant Islands in the Minch, have not been censused since 1970, when there were over 76,100 pairs.

About 8% of the Puffin population of Britain and Ireland is in England and Wales. There were relatively few colonies, and none in the southeast on the coast between Flamborough Head and Portland Bill although one or two pairs may still nest on the Isle of Wight. The largest colonies in England were in the northeast, on the Farne Islands (20,700 pairs), Coquet Island (3300 pairs) and on the Bempton–Flamborough cliffs (6900 birds). The Isle of Man held 124 Puffins in 1985–86. At the southern edge of the species' breeding range, there were 124 pairs on the Isles of Scilly and 74 pairs + 1042 birds on the Channel Islands. The main colonies in Wales were on Skomer (7400 pairs), Skokholm (5000 birds) and the Ynys Gwylans (600 pairs).

Most of the Puffins in Ireland bred in the southwest, on the Blasket and Skellig Islands and Puffin Island. Together these colonies had 12,000 pairs of Puffins and nearly 5400 additional birds. The only other large concentrations of breeding Puffins were on Rathlin Island (2400 pairs), Great Saltee (1100 birds), the Cliffs of Moher (940 birds) and Illaunmaster (1900 pairs).

Differences in census unit and the difficulties in interpreting Puffin counts make it difficult to assess how much numbers may have changed between 1969–70 and 1985–87. Evaluation of historical accounts of picturesque masses of Puffins at certain colonies, such as St Kilda, in relation to recent, more modest population estimates, led Harris (1984a) to conclude that many of the apparent dramatic declines in Puffin numbers during the mid twentieth century were actually quite gradual, or were less marked than previously supposed. St Kilda, for example, once had one of the world's largest concentrations of Puffins and, in the 1980s with over 150,000 pairs, was still the biggest colony in Britain and Ireland. Numbers have decreased since earlier this century, probably mainly between 1947 and 1959–60, but without the dramatic population crash inferred when the loss of birds was first discovered (Flegg 1972). Numbers appeared to be more or less stable during the 1970s and 1980s.

The only satisfactory method of detecting change in Puffin colonies is by long-term monitoring of burrow density in sample areas of the colony (Harris 1984a). Such studies have been carried out by Harris and others since the 1970s at seven colonies in Scotland (Figure 41). At those in the north and west there was little change in nest density between 1972 and 1983. Only in the study colony on Dun in St Kilda did numbers change extensively from one year to the next, showing how this could have confused single censuses such as those for Operation Seafarer or the Seabird Colony Register. Occupied

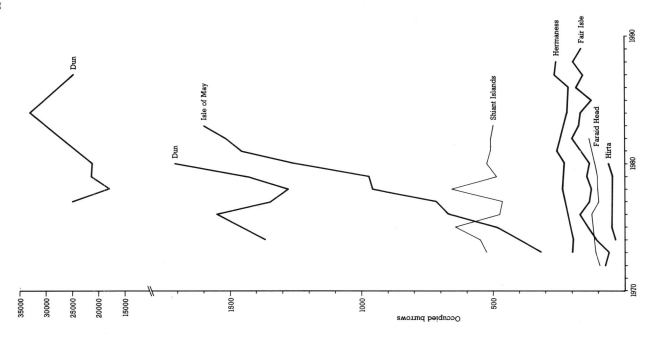

Figure 41. Changes in numbers of occupied Puffin burrows in sample areas of seven Scottish colonies (after Harris 1984a). Note that count method on Dun, St Kilda changed in the late 1970s.

burrow density on Dun fluctuated more than in other colonies, but there was no overall decline. Instead, variations in burrow occupancy may have been caused by birds taking a year off from breeding, behaviour which is not uncommon amongst seabirds.

On the east coast of Scotland, monitoring of Puffin burrows in sample areas of the Isle of May showed that numbers increased fivefold during the 1970s and early 1980s (Harris 1984a). In 1960 there were only a few pairs of Puffins breeding on the island, but by 1970 the total had risen to 2000 pairs and an estimated 12,000 pairs nested in 1985. The 22% annual increase that has occurred since the 1950s is far faster than would be possible without immigration of Puffins from other colonies. Colour-ringing of chicks by Harris and others during the 1970s showed that movement of young birds between colonies occurred more extensively than had previously been supposed (Harris 1976b, 1984a). Some young Puffins were seen at colonies near where they were born and a few may have settled to breed in one of these rather than returning to the natal colony. For instance, there was a two-way exchange of birds between the Isle of May and the Farne Islands 100 km south, and up to 23% of the immature birds from the Isle of May may have changed colony. Some long-distance interchange also occurred, for example, between Scotland and Iceland, and Iceland and northern Norway. Certain colonies at strategic points on the Puffins' flight paths seem to attract passing birds. Unusually high numbers of colour-ringed birds were seen on both Swona in the Pentland Firth between Orkney and the Scottish mainland, and Great Saltee off the southeast tip of Ireland. A few adult Puffins may have paid casual visits to other colonies but in Harris' study no breeding bird was known to have changed its nesting colony.

Puffin counts from colonies on the east coast of England which were censused regularly between the two national surveys showed a pattern of growth in numbers. On the Farne Island, Puffins increased steadily each year from 6800 pairs in 1969 to 20,700 pairs in 1984. On nearby Coquet Island, 400 pairs were estimated in 1969 and numbers appeared to fluctuate between 50 and 1000 pairs in the 1970s before reaching 3300 pairs in 1986. At the six Puffin colonies in Dorset, Devon and Cornwall, counted regularly between 1969–70 and 1985–87, numbers fluctuated from year to year (especially as pairs or birds were used as counting units in different years). One colony in the southwest which probably became extinct in the 1980s was on Lye Rock in north Cornwall. Here Puffin numbers decreased from 200 birds in 1967 to only four in 1972 and then remained between six and 16 birds until 1979. Only two Puffins were seen on Lye Rock in 1981 and more recent surveys have failed to locate any birds ashore.

In Ireland, there were major increases in Puffin numbers on the east coast from Antrim to Wexford between 1969–70 and 1985–87. In Antrim, Puffins were recorded on Rathlin, Muck Island and The Gobbins in 1969, and on Rathlin, Sheep Island and Larrybane Head in 1985; numbers doubled from 1330 to 2400 pairs. Puffin counts also increased in Co. Dublin, from 100 pairs to over 250 birds on Lambay. Further south, Puffin numbers may have increased slightly between 1969–70 and 1985–87 on Great Saltee in Wexford. A large majority of Irish Puffins breed on the Kerry islands. In 1984–88 birds were seen ashore and apparently breeding on Great Blasket and Little

Skellig where none had been recorded by Operation Seafarer, and counts of Puffins on Inishvickillane, Inishnabro and Puffin Island all appeared considerably higher than in 1969–70. On Great Skellig, where there were 6500 pairs in 1969, only 4500 pairs were estimated in 1984. On Inishtearaght there had been a steep decline in numbers of Puffins. In 1968, 20,000 to 30,000 pairs of Puffins were estimated to have bred, but when only 6000–9000 pairs were found the following year much controversy about counting methods ensued (Kelly and Walton 1977, Evans and Bourne 1978). However, there were still only about 8000 pairs of Puffins on the island in 1973 and at most 3365 birds were present in 1988. Few Guillemots breed on Inishtearaght, but Razorbill numbers also declined sharply between 1968 and 1969.

The only other part of Ireland in which Puffin numbers appeared to have declined was the northwest coast. The cliffs of north Mayo, and Tory Island, Tormore and Horn Head in Donegal each held far fewer birds in the 1985–87 survey than during Operation Seafarer counts. The loss of Puffins from Inishtearaght and colonies in the northwest was sufficiently large to cause an overall decline in the Irish totals, despite the increase in numbers of Puffins breeding on the east coast and the apparent stability of most other colonies.

REASONS FOR CHANGE IN NUMBERS

Harris (1984a) reviewed possible causes of past changes in numbers of Puffins and concluded that, at least in some sites, there were specific reasons for decline such as predation by rats, interference by man or oil pollution at sea. The decrease in Puffin numbers earlier this century seems to have occurred naturally and was probably brought about by changes in the birds' food and conditions at sea which were associated with the gradual warming of water in the North Atlantic up to about 1950.

The role of natural fluctuations in the birds' food in determining breeding success was demonstrated by events in Shetland and Orkney during the late 1980s (see Second chapter, Part 1). Sandeels of the right size and at a suitable depth for Puffins appear to have been scarce. Puffins in some Shetland colonies, including the one on the National Nature Reserve at Hermaness on the northern tip of Unst, experienced breeding failure in 1987 and 1988, apparently from lack of food for their chicks (Heubeck 1989b). Similar breeding failure has been recorded among Puffins in Norway and possibly Newfoundland following over-exploitation by man of the birds' food stocks of Herring and Capelin respectively (Lid 1981, Brown and Nettleship 1984b).

In northwest Ireland, decline in numbers of Puffins may be associated with the heavy mortality of Puffins and other seabirds caused by salmon drift-nets set close inshore during May and June (Whilde 1979, O.J. Merne pers. comm.). The reason for the crash of the Puffin colony on Inishtearaght in 1968–69 is unknown but a heavy infestation of ticks may have been partly responsible (Evans and Lovegrove 1974, Evans and Bourne 1978). The light-house keepers' Goats also caused serious soil erosion on the Puffin nesting slopes until the last animal died in the mid 1980s. In 1988, the main Puffin colony was in more rocky ground nearby (Brazier and Merne 1988).

Table 62. *Estimated world breeding population of the Puffin (after Harris 1984a).*

	No. of pairs	Comments
USSR—Murmansk	16,000–17,000	Majority probably on Ainov Island
USSR—W Novaya Zemlya	300	
Canada—southeast	365,000	Three colonies, increasing
USA—Maine	1100	Probably about stable
Greenland	2500–5500	
Svalbard	10,000	
Bear Island	600	
Jan Mayen	1000–10,000	
Iceland	8,000,000–10,000,000 Birds	
Faroe Islands	500,000–750,000 Birds	About stable
Norway	1,300,000	
Britain	500,000–950,000 Birds	Increasing
Ireland	25,000–42,000 Birds	Stable/decreasing
France	470	Decreasing
Approximate total	5.7–6.0 million pairs[a]	

Sources: Croxall *et al.* (1984), Harris (1984a), Nettleship and Evans (1985), Hémery *et al.* (1988), P.G.H. Evans pers. comm., Seabird Colony Register.
[a] Assumes Iceland c. 3 million pairs (Nettleship and Evans 1985), Britain and Ireland 0.5 million pairs (Table 63).

Table 63. *Approximate numbers of Puffins breeding in Britain and Ireland 1969–87.*

	1985–87		1969–70	
	Pairs	Birds	Pairs	Birds
Shetland	73,599	34,411	61,715	3339
Orkney	46,920	5173	62,513	817
Banff and Buchan	124	137	583	53
Gordon	—	71	—	—
Kincardine and Deeside	—	599	62	77
Angus	550	2130	51	130
Northeast Fife	12,000	860	2500	80
East Lothian	89	1369	52	413
Berwickshire	—	110	39	—
Western Isles	245,188[b]	3378	243,453	82
Caithness	—	3190	25,993	2205
Sutherland	—	7326	2727	749
Skye and Lochalsh	616	11	465	37
Lochaber	93	946	80	537
Argyll and Bute	75	3091	1200	39
Kyle and Carrick	—	—	18	—
Wigtown	—	—	2	—
Scotland total	379,300	62,800	401,500	8600

Table 63. *Approximate numbers of Puffins breeding in Britain and Ireland 1969–87 – cont.*

	1985–87		1969–70	
	Pairs	Birds	Pairs	Birds
Northumberland	24,032	—	6800	400
North Yorkshire	—	139	—	—
Humberside	—	6946	812	185
Isle of Wight	—	—	—	4
Dorset	—	21	6	29
Devon	—	39	41	—
Cornwall	—	53	8	225
Isles of Scilly	90	9	100[a]	—
Channel Islands	41	398	74	1042
Cumbria	11	—	6	—
Isle of Man	—	123	51	31
England, Isle of Man and Channel Islands total	24,200	7600	7900	1900
West Glamorgan	—	3	—	—
Dyfed	7453	5040	3610	40
Gwynedd	602	211	9	596
Wales total	8000	5300	3600	640
Antrim	2398	17	1327	1
Dublin	—	264	100	8
Wexford	—	1240	25	750
Cork	—[c]	16	412	—
Kerry	12,000	5354	18,428	—
Clare	—	850	—	646
Mayo	1983	99	3540	216
Donegal	—	724	1825	711
Ireland total	16,400	8600	25,700	2300
Estimated total	16,800[d]			
Proportion estimated	2%			
Britain and Ireland total	428,300	84,300	438,700	13,400
Combined units (birds)	512,600–941,000		452,100–890,800	

Totals rounded, <1000 to nearest 10, >1000 to nearest 100.
Combined units allow 1–2 birds per pair

[a] No record cards exist; Cramp *et al.* (1974) give five colonies of Order 1 (1–9 pairs) and one colony of Order 2 (10–99 pairs).

[b] Includes estimated 80,000 pairs on Shiant Islands; not counted 1985–87, 76,100 pairs 1970.

[c] No adequate coverage.

[d] Includes estimated 320 pairs on Bull and Cow Rocks; not counted 1985–87, 400 pairs 1970, and allows for an apparent 20% decline at other colonies in SW Ireland and an estimated 70 pairs at a colony in Mayo.

Rare Breeders

Several unusual species of seabird either bred or attempted to breed in Britain and Ireland in the 1970s and 1980s. The Mediterranean Gull *Larus melanocephalus* has been a regular attempted breeder since 1968 when the first breeding bird was seen at Needs Ore Point in Hampshire. Up to eight pairs (1983) have been recorded in England but many of them were mixed pairs in which a Mediterranean Gull paired with a Black-headed Gull. In 1986 there were Mediterranean Gulls at five sites. A pair built a nest and laid eggs in Kent, birds were present during the breeding season in Black-headed Gull colonies in Lincolnshire and South Humberside, another pair held a site at a colony in Suffolk, and a single bird was present throughout the summer at a Common Gull colony in central Scotland (Spencer *et al.* 1988). Another site on the south coast has since been colonised by Mediterranean Gulls. A female Lesser Crested Tern *Sterna bengalensis* has attempted to breed with a Sandwich Tern on the Farne Islands (Northumberland) from 1986 to 89. Breeding was successful in 1989 at least, and a hybrid chick was seen being fed on the Firth of Forth by its parents after the breeding season.

There have been unsuccessful attempts to breed in England by Little Gulls *Larus minutus*. A Little Shearwater *Puffinus assimilis* held a burrow on Skomer (Dyfed) for at least two seasons in the early 1980s. Another seabird which occasionally tried to breed in England and Ireland during the 1960s is the Black Tern *Chlidonias niger*, and Gull-billed Terns *Sterna nilotica* bred in Essex in 1949 and 1950 (Cramp *et al.* 1974). One famous non-breeder has been a single Black-browed Albatross *Diomedea melanophris* that has lived among the

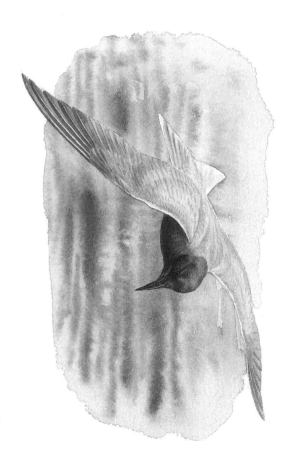

Gannets in Hermaness (Shetland) every summer from the early 1970s to 1987 (it was not seen in 1988 or 1989, but returned in 1990). Possibly the same bird was seen with the Gannets on the Bass Rock in the 1960s (Cramp *et al.* 1974). Wouldn't it be fine if this were our next breeding seabird?

Appendix I

Numbers of seabirds breeding on different parts of the coast of the UK and Ireland in 1985–87. Figures refer to pairs of breeding birds for all species except auks (Guillemot, Razorbill, Black Guillemot and Puffin), where figures are of individual birds.

Species	Scotland	England	Isle of Man	Channel Islands	Wales	Northern Ireland	Republic of Ireland
Fulmar	528,000	6500	2300	160	2500	4100	27,200
Manx Shearwater	110,000+	<1000	<100		140,000+	<1500	30,000+
Storm Petrel	33 + cols.	4 cols.	1 col.	2 cols.	4 cols.		28+ cols.
Leach's Petrel	7 cols.						1 col.
Gannet	127,900	780		4500	30,000		24,700
Cormorant	2900	1450	50	100	1700	640	3600
Shag	32,100	3500	610	1500	770	320	8500
Arctic Skua	3400						
Great Skua	7900						
Black-headed Gull	7900	69,200	90		200	4500	2300
Common Gull	14,800	40				180	720
Lesser Black-backed Gull	18,800	24,500	100	1100	19,000	440	1800
Herring Gull	96,000	28,000	8600	3400	10,700	18,600	25,600
Great Black-backed Gull	16,300	1800	350	170	410	270	4200
Kittiwake	356,600	125,000	1300	30	8900	10,000	40,200
Sandwich Tern	2300	11,300		<10	450	2600	1800
Roseate Tern	25	40			70	70	270
Common Tern	6200	5100	10	220	550	1300	1450
Arctic Tern	72,400	4600	10		680	360	2150
Little Tern	370	1800	60		60	<10	390
Guillemot	952,900	61,400	1500	360	34,300	45,000	108,000
Razorbill	126,900	10,300	810	90	9600	11,000	23,200
Black Guillemot	c. 37,500	<20	400		<20	570	c. 2500
Puffin[a]	821,400	52,200	120	480	21,300	4800	28,800

Counts greater than 1000 are rounded to nearest 100, counts less than 1000 to nearest 10.

col. = colony.

[a] Counts of Puffin pairs have been multiplied by two and added to counts of individuals for this table.

Appendix II

Contributors 1980–1988 to the Seabird Colony Register. We hope this list is complete; we apologise to anyone accidentally omitted.

R.G. Adam, G.R.J. Adams, M. Adcock, S.G. Addinall, J. Addyman, M.D. Alexander, D. Allen, N.V. Allen, G. Anderson, S. Angus, J.S. Armitage, I. Armstrong, D. Arnold, R.W. Arnold, R. Ascroft, S.J. Aspinall, N.K. Atkinson, P. Atkinson.

C. Badenoch, A. Bainbridge, A. Baker, R.M. Baker, A.G. Ball, S. Barber, M.J. Barrett, S. Barrett, C.J.D. Bates, T. Beer, D. Bell, M.V. Bell, P. Bellamy, S. Benn, J. Bennett, T.R.A. Bennett, I. Berry, B.J. Best, M. Betts, F.M. Beveridge, B. Bewsher, H. Bibby, R.R. Birch, M. Birkin, O.H. Black, A.C. Blackburn, N.J. Bleakley, M.A. Blick, M. Bones, B. Bonner, I. Booker, C.J. Booth, M. Borthwick, D.G. Borton, W.R.P. Bourne, B.P. Bower, J.R. Bower, W. Bown, P.R. Boyer, V. Boyle, L.T.A. Brain, P. Branscombe, H. Brazier, T. Breeze Jones, P. Brennan, C. Brewster, D.J. Britton, R.A. Broad, S.D.A. Brogan, D. Bromwich, A.W. Brown, B.J. Brown, C. Brown, C.C. Brown, J. Brown, N.H. Brown, R.A. Brown, T. Brown, D. Browne, K. Bruce, N. Buckley, D. Budworth, R.S.K. Buisson, P.F. Burns, C.A. Burton, I. Buxton, J. Byrne.

D. Cabot, M. Caine, D. Callan, J. Callion, E.J. Cameron, C. Campbell, C.J. Camphuysen, T. Carne, S. Carre, M. Carruthers, T. Carruthers, J. Carson, S. Casey, K.A.H. Cassels, B. Cave, E.A. Chapman, T.D. Charlton, J. Chester, J.M. Cheverton, D.J. Chown, A. Christelow, G. Christer, S.M. Christophers, H. Clark, J. Clark, J. Clarke, P. Clarke, L.T. Colley, P.N. Collin, P. Collins, T. Collins, G. Conway, K.G. Cook, M. Cook, M.J.H. Cook, D.E. Cooke, T. Cooney, Copeland Bird Observatory, M. Corbin, Cornwall Trust for Nature Conservation, R.D. Corran, C.J. Corse, D.C.F. Cotton, D. Cox, S. Cox, J.C.A. Craik, L.V. Cranna, G.C. Crittenden, K.G. Croft, R.P. Cronk, C.H. Crooke, Cumbria Trust for Nature Conservation, D. Cullen, J.P. Cullen, I. Cumming, A. Currie, A. Curtis, D. Curtis, T. Curtis.

S.R.D. da Prato, T. Daniels, P.R. Davey, A. Davidson, I.S. Davidson, R. Davidson, J.A. Davies, M. Davies, P. Davies, P.E. Davis, R. Davis, P. Dean, T. Dean, R.C. Dickson, W. Dickson, B. Dillon, T.J. Dix, I. Dixon, R.H. Dobson, A.F. Dodge, E. Doran, C. Dore, M.T. Dorgan, P. Doughty, A. Dowland, C. Dowling, D. Duggan, J. Dunbar, D.W. Duncan, P. Duncan, M. Dunn, P.J. Dunn, G.M. Dunnet, J.N. Dymond.

R. Eades, C.F. Eagles, J.E. Eagles, J.J. Earley, J. Edelsten, R.D.M. Edgar, R.L. Edwards, T. Edwards, V. Egan, D. Elias, M.M. Elliott, R. Ellis, J.W. Enticott, B. Etheridge, D. Eva, F. Evans, P.G.H. Evans, M.J. Everett, P.J. Ewins.

Fair Isle Bird Observatory, K. Fairclough, P. Farbridge, Farne Islands Watchers, P. Farrelly, J.W. Fennell, K. Ferry, Filey Brigg Ornithological Group, P. Fisher, D.S. Flumm, P. Foley, P. Forrest, J.A. Fowler, S. Fowler, W. Fox, E. Franklin, M.A. Freeman, H.D. Freeth, S.J. Fulford, R.W. Furness.

S. Gallagher, J. Garden, P. Gardiner, J. Gatins, A. Gear, D. Gilbert, B. Goggin, P.R. Gordon, J. Gowencock, E. Grace, S. Grant, M. Green, J.G. Greenwood, J. Grice, G. Guille, P.J. Guille, E. Gynn, G. Gynn.

D. Hall, M. Hancock, B. Haran, S. Hardy, P. Harford, M. Harman, M.P. Harris, P.R. Harris, G. Harrison, N.M. Harrison, A.H.J. Harrop, P.V. Harvey, R. Harvey, T. Harvey, A.C. Hathway, P. Hawke, R.J. Haycock, G.A.H. Heaney, V. Heaney, J. Heath, R. Heath, R.J. Hemsworth, T.W. Henderson, M. Hensey, K. Henshall, M. Heubeck, P. Heyworth, M.C. Higgins, M.G. Hill, J.P. Hillis, K. Hindmarsh, P. Hirst, S. Hiscock, S. Hocking, T.N. Hodge, M.S. Hodgson, D. Hogan, J.L. Hogarth, R. Hollingsworth, P. Holms, N. Holton, P.G. Hopkins, J. Howard, C.F. Howarth, M.A. Howe, G. Howells, A.V. Hudson, H. Huggins, S. Hugheston-Roberts, J. Hurley, M. Hutchings, G.I. Huws.

A.R. Inkster, M. Innes, Irish Wildbird Conservancy, D. Irving.

D.B. Jackson, G. Jackson, S. Jackson, P. James, A. Jennings, A. Johnson, D.B. Johnson, C. Johnstone, P.H. Jones, Jordanthorpe School.

A. Kane, A. Kaye, R. Keats, D.F. Kelley, M. Kemp, R. Kemp, P.R. Kennedy, E.D. Kerruish, F. Kiddie, J. King, P.K. Kinnear, P. Kirkland, A. Knight, A. Kohler, B. Kohler, S. Kruger.

R. Lambert, P. Lamont, R. Lane, E. Larrisey, J.D. Law, B. Lawson, M. Lawson, S. Lawson, G.M. Leaper, D. Leech, M. Legg, A.F. Leitch, M. Lennox, D. Levell, T. Leyland, N. Leys, R.A. Lihou, B.W. Litherland, D. Little, C.S. Lloyd, H. Loates, J.B. Longhurst, A. Lord, M. Lord, R. Lord, J.K. Lovatt, J.A. Love, R. Lovegrove, C. Lowe, B.M. Lynch, H.F. Lyttle.

B. Macdonald, G. Macdonald, R.A. Macdonald, M. Macintyre, S. Mackay, R.N. Macklin, C. Maclean, A. Macquarrie, M. Madders, J. Magee, D. Mainland, C. Manning, Mrs Marsden, J.T. Marshall, R.M.S. Marshall, T.W. Marshall, A.R. Martin, J. Martin, Maryport Natural History Society, J. Matthews, E.W.E. Maughan, F. Mawbey, M. May, W. McAvoy, P. McCartney, J. McCutcheon, R. McCutcheon, G. McElwaine, J. McEvoy, D. McGrath, M. McGregor, E.B. McIntyre, N.D. McKee, D. McLaughlin, A. McMillan, J. McNair, J. McNeil, A.C. Meakin, B. Mearns, C.S. Mearns, R. Mearns, N.F. Medland, A. Mee, E.R. Meek, O.J. Merne, R. Middlemiss, F. Miller, G.R. Miller, G.R. Mills, M. Mills, S. Mills, K. Milton, A.S. Moore, P.R. Moore, A. Moorhouse, A. Moralee, Moray and Nairn RSPB Members Group, D. Morgan, F. Morrell, J. Morton, R. Morton, D. Moss, G. Moss, D. Mower, D. Moxon, G.P. Mudge, H. Murchison, C. Murphy, G. Murphy, T. Murphy, S. Murray.

Nature Conservancy Council, W. Neill, W.N.A. Nelson, Newcastle University Conservation Society, J.A. Newnham, S. Newton, S.G. North.

M.V. O'Brien, D.A. O'Connor, J. O'Connor, L. Oakes, P. Oakley, M.A. Ogilvie, R. O'Haire, D. Okill, M.J. Orchard, K. Osborn, E. O'Sullivan, P. O'Sullivan, D.L. Ovenden, T. Owen.

A. Parker, A.J. Parsons, S.M. Parsons, J. Partridge, K.E. Partridge, A. Patterson, M. Peacock, T.H. Pearson, I.D. Pennie, S. Percival, R.J. Perkins, A. Perry, K. Perry, B.P. Pickess, J. Pickles, S. Pierce, S. Pilbeam, F. Pirie, B. Planterose, P. Pound, R. Powell, M. Preece, D. Price, H.D.V. Prendergast, R. Procter, E.A. Pulford.

A. Quillin.

D. Radford, A.D.K. Ramsay, H. Ramsay, M. Rayment, J. Reed, G.H. Rees, F. Rennie, C. Reynolds, P. Reynolds, I. Rhys Jones, B. Ribbands, C.J. Richardson, D. Richardson, M.G. Richardson, S. Richardson, D.A. Richmond, N. Riddiford, M. Riddy, K.J. Rideout, C. Riley, W.T. Ritchie, C.S. Robbins, I. Robertson, C.K. Robeson, T.M. Robilliard, M. Robinson, P. Rock, H.W. Roderick, M.H. Rodgers, H.E. Rose, D. Rothe, A. Rothwell, P. Rothwell, P.I. Rothwell, J. Rowe, Royal Society for the Protection of Birds.

C. Sampson, J. Sanders, I. Sandison, L.A.H. Sarl, F. Saunders, R.A. Schofield, A. Scott, D. Scott, L. Scully, I. Shaw, K.D. Shaw, K. Shepherd, J.R. Shepherd, S. Shimeld, M. Shorten, A.F. Silcocks, M. Sinclair, R.Q. Skeen, F. Slag, C.A. Slater, M. Slater, P.J.B. Slater, D. Sloss, R. Smalder, P. Smiddy, A. Smith, A.J.M. Smith, D.E. Smith, P. Smith, R.J.W. Smith, A.M. Smout, T.C. Smout, R. Southwood, J. Sorensen, I. Spence, R. Squires, D. Stacey, J. Stafford, R.D. Steele, J. Stenning, M. Stentiford, D. Steventon, A.G. Stewart, J. Stewart, C.W. Stone, J.M. Stratford, S. Street, D. Suddaby, S.J. Sutcliffe, D. Swann, R.L. Swann, F.L. Symonds.

T. Tarpey, M.L. Tasker, A.E. Taylor, C.W. Taylor, M. Taylor, D. Terry, P.G. Terry, C.J. Thomas, D.K. Thomas, D.L. Thomas, D.R. Thompson, K. Thompson, R. Thompson, R.I. Thorpe, D.C. Totty, N. Trigg, M. Tully, R. Tully, C.J. Tyas.

E.T. Urbanski, B.M. Utton.

F. Vandewege, P.J. Vaudin, P. Vaughan, P.K. Veron, K. Verstraalen, M.P. Visick.

E.A. Wace, P. Wakelin, D. Wakley, D. Walker, E. Wallace, A. Walsh, P.M. Walsh, S. Wanless, G. Ward, N. Ward, R.M. Ward, C.E. Warman, S. Warman, A.B. Watson, J. Watson, P.S. Watson, M.S. Weare, D.J. Weaver, G.P. Weaver, A. Webb, B.L. Webb, D. Welford, B.G. Wells, P. Wells, D. Wheeler, J. Whelehan, A. Whilde, N.A. Willcox, E.J. Williams, G.A.

Williams, J.D. Wilson, M. Wilson, P. Wilson, R. Wilson, E. Wiseman, B. Withers, P. Wood, T. Wood, D. Wooldridge, M. Wright, T. Wyatt, T.A. Wyatt, R. Wynde.

B.J. Yates, M. Yeoman, J. Yonge.

B. Zonfrillo.

Appendix III

Instructions and recording forms used for the Seabird Colony Register between 1985 and 1988.

Introduction

Operation Seafarer provided baseline information on the size and distribution of Britain and Ireland's breeding seabirds. Since those counts (1969–70) further surveys have been made at many colonies, and there have been refinements in techniques for counting seabirds. Some of the recent counts have been published and are readily available, but many are in unpublished reports or have not been reported at all.

The Seabird Group is currently attempting to obtain a relatively comprehensive set of data on British and Irish breeding seabirds. The Seabird Colony Register was established in 1985. When complete, this will make accessible summaries for each species and all breeding colonies. Seabird Group members and everyone else interested in seabirds are urged to complete a set of the standard recording forms for sections of coastline, even those at present without nesting seabirds. Britain has been divided into 17 coastal regions, with an eighteenth for the Republic of Ireland. Each has its own regional organiser who will coordinate coverage and collect records.

Important

Please read these instructions carefully and keep them available for reference. If you have any queries, contact your regional organiser. Please be sure to obtain permission before venturing onto private land; this survey does not give you right to enter private property. Your own personal safety is paramount; do not go near the edge of unsafe cliffs. Neither the Seabird Group nor its members will be held responsible for any accidents.

The recording forms

Three forms are provided for the Seabird Colony Register:

i. **Ten km square summary**
This card provides information on the exact position of colonies, and also of areas with no breeding seabirds. Each colony and area with nesting seabirds is named and details given on ii.

ii. **Colony register form**
The relatively permanent features about each site and the current status of its seabird population are given on this sheet. It provides a convenient summary

298

of knowledge about the site, including details of any special work carried out there.

iii. Data sheet

Each count made at the colony is recorded on this sheet. Only one is needed per year, but there is no need to change either the colony register form or the 10 km square summary each year unless the birds' distribution alters.

Instructions on how to use the forms

i. Ten km square summary

Using an O.S. map (preferably scale 1:50,000), locate the 10 km square on the coast you wish to cover. Complete one card for all the coast in that square. Sketch the shoreline on the grid using a black pen, and mark seabird colonies or breeding areas clearly using names given on the O.S. map if possible. Where seabird colonies occur away from the coast, mark the approximate colony limits on the relevant 10 km square. In areas where Fulmars breed extensively inland (eg. Shetland, Orkney), please try and record numbers in each one km square. Use two 10 km square summary cards but one colony register form for sites which overlap two 10 km squares.

ii. Colony register form

We suggest the definition of a colony for this survey should be that if it is possible to walk between two groups of breeding birds without disturbing them, then they are counted as two colonies. This distance should be a minimum of 100 m. However, we feel that the exact definition of colony boundaries is best left to on-site assessment. If in doubt, it is usually best to sub-divide an area so long as this can be done unambiguously.

Colony name: Please use same names as on 10 km square summary.
Location: Fill in O.S. grid references for the start and finish of a cliff section, or for the approximate centre of a flatter colony.
Description: eg. north side of Firth of Forth, near Crail.
Status: eg. National Nature Reserve, SSSI, RSPB reserve.
Description: Details of cliff height & aspect, habitat on island, etc. If possible, sketch map on back of form or enclose photograph(s) of the colony to show where each species nests & to mark features of interest.
Access: eg. ease of access, boatman &/or landowner's name & address, other useful information for anyone wishing to visit the site.
History: Be brief, refer to bibliography if possible.
Seabirds: List breeding seabird species & summary of status (ie. increasing, decreasing or stable) if known, eg. colony expanding rapidly according to local boatman.

Counting problems: Indicate approximately what percentage of the colony can be counted from land, how much can be seen only from sea, & any particular problems encountered, eg. birds nesting in caves etc.

Other notes: Any relevant information on the colony, eg. site of extensive seabird ringing since 1956, site of annual monitoring counts etc.

Bibliography: Give details of any books, journals, reports etc. which mention this colony.

iii. **Data sheet**

Complete one sheet for each year's observations including all counts carried out, even partial ones. If you have data for the colony which does not exactly fit on the form, eg. counts of Puffins on sea, counts of individual Fulmars on land, include them on the back of the sheet.

Colony name: Use same name as on 10km square summary and colony register form with qualifications if necessary, eg. Auskerry, south side.

Year: Year of counts.

Date: Record month and exact dates during which counts were made. If the figures given are the means of counts on several different days, give details on the back of the sheet.

PLEASE READ THE FOLLOWING VERY CAREFULLY.
IT IS THE MOST IMPORTANT PART OF THE INSTRUCTIONS.

Count & estimates: In some seabird colonies, every breeding bird or nest can be seen and counted accurately; in others a careful estimate of numbers (ideally made by sub-dividing the colony into sections) is the only possible way of censusing the breeding birds. Usually the birds in part of the colony can be counted accurately (i.e. with an estimated error of 10% or less), and the remainder must be estimated. For example, sections of a stretch of cliff which are visible from land might give accurate counts whilst the sections that can be counted only from the sea would give estimates.

Fill in what you count and what you estimate separately so that the two parts of the census together give an approximate total for the colony. For example, you count 233 nests (233 in the "Accurate Count" column) and you estimate there were a further 10-25 nests out of sight (10 in the "Minimum Estimate" column and 25 under "Maximum Estimate"). For some colonies only the count column will be needed, for others only one or both of the estimate columns, but for most colonies there will be entries in all 3 columns.

Put "N" against any species which is present on land in the colony but apparently not breeding. For breeding species present but not counted, put "P" but please attempt at least an estimate of numbers for all nesting species.

Unit:

Follow the recommended counting techniques attached, with special attention to the counting unit required. Code the unit you use for your counts as follows.

1 = Individual birds on land, excluding any on non-breeding ledges or loafing areas.
2 = Apparently occupied nest sites.
3 = Apparently occupied breeding territories.
4 = Other, give details in Notes.

Counting method: Record how each species was counted.

1 = From land.
2 = From a boat.
3 = From the air, give details in Notes.
4 = From photo.
5 = From land and sea.
6 = Other, give details in Notes.

Breeding status:

Use the highest code possible to record how certain you were that each species was breeding in the colony. NB. This is unrelated to the unit used for counting. You might count individual Guillemots but give a breeding status of 15, "nest with eggs".

01 = Bird seen in suitable nesting habitat during the breeding season.
02 = Bird singing in suitable nesting habitat during the breeding season, eg. petrels.
03 = Pair of birds seen in suitable nesting habitat during the breeding season.
04 = Birds seen defending territory, two records at least one week apart.
05 = Courtship displays etc. recorded.
06 = Nest site found.
07 = Agitated/anxious parents seen.
08 = Bird seen incubating.
09 = Bird seen building a nest.
10 = Distraction display recorded.
11 = Used nest found, eg. broken eggshell, droppings, food remains etc.

12 = Fledged young present. Do not use for birds which may have travelled some distance eg. petrels.
13 = Occupied nest, contents unknown.
14 = Food seen being brought to young.
15 = Nest with eggs found.
16 = Nest with chicks found.

Comments

As with any survey, it would be surprising if all observations could be fitted into categories. Please do your best. If you are unsure or cannot fit a count into one of the sections of the data sheet, give details of your method and results on the back of the sheets. This is more easily processed than an accompanying letter.

Completed Forms

Mark clearly any records or information you wish to remain confidential. Please return all used and unused forms to your regional organiser as soon as possible after your count. If in doubt about who your regional organiser is, send forms to:

Seabird Colony Register, Nature Conservancy Council,
17 Rubislaw Terrace, Aberdeen, AB1 1XE.

THANK YOU FOR YOUR HELP!

Recommended techniques for counting breeding seabirds

At all times, please be mindful of your own safety, and avoid disturbance to breeding sites.

Do not count seabirds on days with heavy rain, fog or high winds. Most species should be counted in the middle of the day (0900-1600 **BST**), the main exceptions being the auks (see below). Note any departures from these instructions on the back of the data sheet, eg. counts made after 1600.

Fulmar

Count apparently occupied nest sites, ideally late in June but late May to early August will suffice. A site is counted as occupied only when a bird is sitting tightly on a reasonable horizontal area large enough to hold an egg. Two birds on such a site, apparently paired, count as one site.

Manx Shearwater, Storm Petrel, Leach's Petrel

A total census usually involves random sample quadrants and possibly a long-term ringing study. Instructions and advice are available from The Seabird Group if such a census is planned. Otherwise, record the presence/

absence of birds on land at night in suitable habitat, and each species' breeding status. If possible, roughly estimate the size of the colony &/or the number of birds singing in burrows.

Gannet

Count apparently occupied nest sites, either directly or from a good quality photograph. Count all sites occupied by one or two Gannets, irrespective of whether or not any nesting material is present, so long as the site is suitable for breeding. Count in the early to mid nestling period, usually June.

Shag, Cormorant

Count apparently occupied nest sites in the early to mid nestling periods, late May or early June. Include all substantial or well-constructed nests occupied by at least one bird.

Arctic Skua, Great Skua

Count apparently occupied territories ideally when most nests have completed clutches or when eggs have just started to hatch, approximately early June. Choose a suitable vantage point and scan from a distance using binoculars. Beware of counting paired birds standing apart as two territory holders, and of overlooking birds that blend against the background. Ideally repeat the procedure on 3 separate days during the count period, and mark territories on a sketch map.

Black-headed Gull, Common Gull, Lesser Black-backed Gull, Herring Gull, Great Black-backed Gull, all terns

Count apparently occupied nests in the mid incubation to early nestling period (usually late May and June). With all these species, particularly the terns, keep disturbance to a minimum. Large colonies may require the use of a team of counters or sample quadrats, and advice for these should be sought from The Seabird Group.

Kittiwake

Count apparently occupied nest sites. These are substantial or well-constructed nests capable of holding 2-3 eggs, occupied by at least one bird standing on or within touching distance of the nest. Count during the late incubation to early nestling period, early to mid June; easiest if the cliff is divided into sections and each counted separately.

Guillemot, Razorbill

Count individual birds on land during the incubation to early nestling period, normally the first 3 weeks of June. All counts should be made between 0800 and 1600 BST; record the time for counts made outside this period in Notes. It is easiest to divide the cliff face into a series of sections and count the birds in each separately. If possible, estimate numbers of birds nesting in caves, and use photographs from higher adjacent land to count birds on flat-topped stacks.

Black Guillemot

Differs from all other species: counting is recommended in the pre-breeding period, April to early May, and in the very early morning (0500–0900 BST). Count all adult-plumaged birds on sea within 200 m of shore, and note other birds separately. All coastline should be checked but the species is rarely present off low land on coasts and islands accessible to rats.

Puffin

Optimum count is of apparently occupied nest sites, made during laying period (May). Ideally this should cover the whole colony or be based on circular quadrats used to sample larger areas (details available on request). Burrow occupancy is determined by fresh digging, droppings and, during the nestling period, by broken eggshell or fish in the burrow entrance. Rabbit burrows are usually larger with more soil outside, and bare earth and droppings in the entrance. Separation of Puffin and Manx Shearwater burrows is difficult and requires observation of the burrows early in the morning when Puffins bring fish to chicks.
Probably all that can be achieved at cliff colonies is a count of individual birds on land and adjacent sea. Although not absolutely essential, these give best results if carried out just before dusk. Record land and sea counts separately and note the time of day (BST) of the count in Notes. NB. Be sure to record exactly which unit you used when censusing this species.

SEABIRD COLONY REGISTER

Ten km square summary   Square no.   N O 8 6

Observer *P.I. Rothwell*   County/district *Kincardine/Deeside*

Address *NCC*

Date *17 Rubislaw Terrace Aberdeen* *16·6·82*

Please sketch the coastline here; each small square represents a 1 km square on your map. Mark place names, and exact position of any seabird colonies or extent of breeding areas. Indicate any stretches of coast you did NOT survey. Use back of card for remarks and additional details.

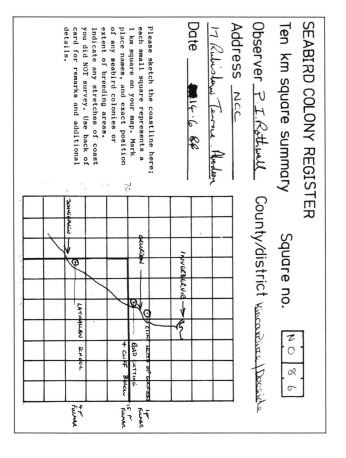

Colony register form

Cliff start

end

or Centre

Colony/sub-colony . . . . Location:
name

Description of Location:

Compiler's name and address:

. . . .

. . . .

. . . .

. . . .

Status . . . . Date of compilation . . . .

Description . . . .

Landing / Access / Ownership:

Ornithological history:

Breeding Seabirds and Status:

Counting problems:

Other notes:

Bibliography:

SEABIRD COLONY REGISTER

Data Sheet

Name: _____   Year: _____

Give address on back of sheet if
different from Colony Register Form

Colony Name: _____

Notes: Use back of sheet

County or District: _____

SPECIES		DATES OF COUNTS	ACCURATE COUNT	RANGE OF ESTIMATE min.	RANGE OF ESTIMATE max.	Unit	Method	Br. Status
Fulmar	022							
Manx shearwater	046							
Storm petrel	052							
Leach's petrel	055							
Gannet	071							
Cormorant	072							
Shag	080							
Arctic skua	567							
Great skua	569							
Black-headed gull	582							
Common gull	590							
Lesser black-back	591							
Herring gull	592							
Great black-back	600							
Kittiwake	602							
Sandwich tern	611							
Roseate tern	614							
Common tern	615							
Arctic tern	616							
Little tern	624							
Guillemot	634							
Razorbill	636							
Black guillemot	638							
Puffin	654							

FILL IN HERE

UNIT
1 = Individual bird on land
2 = Apparently occupied nest
3 = Apparently occupied territory

COUNTING METHOD
1 = From land   4 = From photo
2 = From sea   5 = From land and sea
3 = From air   6 = Other, give details
                      in Notes.

BREEDING STATUS
01 = Bird in habitat   09 = Nest building
02 = Singing in habitat   10 = Distraction
03 = Pair in habitat   11 = Used nest
04 = Territory   12 = Fledged young
05 = Display   13 = Occupied nest
06 = Nest site   14 = Food for young
07 = Anxious parent   15 = Nest + eggs
08 = Incubation   16 = Nest + young

Appendix IV

Instructions and record card used for Operation Seafarer in 1969–70.

OPERATION SEAFARER

A Guide for Observers

'Operation Seafarer', a census of breeding seabirds organised by the Seabird Group, is to take place throughout the summer of 1969. During 1967 and 1968 preliminary surveys were carried out in a wide variety of areas in preparation for the main census in 1969. Many observers and in some cases expeditions are taking part in the survey. The aim is to obtain a really comprehensive account of the numbers and distribution of breeding seabirds around the coasts of Great Britain and Ireland. Although some species breed inland particularly in Scotland, the census committee considers that not enough man-power is available to cover these adequately as well in 1969, and instead will concentrate all its resources on a thorough coastal survey this year.

Because of the number of families and species involved, it has been considered necessary to produce a short guide to the counting methods to be used. It is hoped that all our observers will adhere to the suggested methods outlined below—this being the only way uniform methods can be obtained. We have drawn on the knowledge of the number of experts in this compilation, and to all of them we express our sincere thanks.

Completing the Card

1   Name and Address. The most appropriate person should put his name and address below that of a group or expedition. This will facilitate enquiries should there be any questions concerning records.

2   Date and Time. These are most important, the time particularly so. If spread over a period this should be plainly indicated e.g. 0730 - 1200HRS. If a series of counts are made throughout the day, these should not be averaged together, but recorded on separate cards under the appropriate time, this applies particularly to auk colonies.

3   Grid Reference. A full 6 figure reference should be taken from the 1" (In Ireland ½") Ordnance Survey maps. Immediately in front of the Grid Reference the 100 Km square in which the area lies should be given. This is designated by means of letters e.g. SM, or in Ireland a single letter, and these together with an example of how to take a reference may be found on the lower

307

margin of the map. A single Grid Reference may be provided where the record card relates to a whole island, or small section of coast. In other cases references should be given showing the extent of the area surveyed.

4   Locality. Names used should be those found on Ordnance Survey Maps, not other local names which can lead to difficulties, though these should not occur if Grid References are given.

The question does arise, how much of a section of coast should be included on one card? Should for instance a small island, which may have a total coastline of several miles be recorded on a single card? It may be, but if the coast can be divided into sectors by the use of permanent and easily found landmarks it is much better to complete several cards. This means that any future population changes may be followed in greater detail. The same system should if possible be applied to sections of mainland coast and that of larger islands. Permanent landmarks together with Grid References should always be given as boundaries.

5   Description of Colony. As much information as possible should be given in this section, and ancillary notes such as "Razorbills confined to boulder beach area" or "Kittiwakes only on offshore stack" should be provided where necessary.

6   Weather. A complete description of the weather at the time of the count should be given. If there have been any marked changes in conditions in the previous 48 hours these should be noted. Wind-observers should follow the Beaufort Scale to save space on the card and to allow a more accurate interpretation of the weather note. The Scale to Force 9 is as follows:

Scale

0 - 1	Light Airs	Sea like mirror, or with scale like ripples.
2 - 3	Gentle Breeze	Wavelets form, a few scattered "White Horses."
4 - 5	Fresh Breeze	Small to moderate waves, numerous "White Horses"
6 - 7	Near Gale	Sea heaps up, foam blown from breaking waves
8 - 9	Gale	High waves, foam blown in well marked streaks down wind

7   Extent of Census. As much information as possible should be included here, if necessary on an attached sheet. With concise information available this will ensure that in future years other observers can make surveys which will be instantly comparable with those made in 1969. Details supplied by observers will be particularly important when assessing the information received.

As an aid to future surveys sketch maps showing the limits of colonies in relation to natural features on the cliff such as gullies and fault lines etc are most valuable, and observers are asked to supply these wherever possible. Photographs on which the limit of colonies are marked can be also used. Outline maps taken from the 2½" map are useful in marking areas.

COUNTING METHODS

Where possible, and particularly if the colony involved includes less than 2,000 pairs, an attempt should be made to count the birds present. If the colony is larger, it may be possible to count well defined sample areas and to include an estimate based on these for the whole colony. If this method is used it is essential that complete details concerning the numbers in each sample area are given. In other cases when it is not possible to make an accurate count an estimate only may be made, together with a note on the estimated accuracy. This may be given in orders of abundance - Order 1 (under 10 pairs), 2 (10 - 99 pairs), 3 (100 - 999 pairs), 4 (1000 - 9999 pairs) and 5 (10,000 pairs upwards).

What needs to be counted also varies from species to species. With Kittiwakes for instance the unit is the nest, with Guillemots it is the number of birds present at a colony, and the information required is given under the species headings.

Although many of our seabirds are present at their colonies for quite a considerable part of the year, it is possible to carry out census work only during the breeding season. This may be short, particularly in the case of the auks, where the first ones are already leaving the cliffs in early July, and the vast majority have left by the end of the month. As the best time for carrying out the survey varies from species to species more details are given in the appropriate sections. It is hoped that whenever possible observers will work on these lines, though we quite understand that this will not be possible in the case of observers on holiday or special expeditions.

If time is limited an observer may be unable to count all the species in a given area. Priority should be given to Fulmars and Kittiwakes (in view of the existing 10 year survey of these), and then to the auk family as it is important that accurate surveys are made of these species which are so prone to oil pollution, gull predation and disturbance. Censuses of other species should follow in the order given overleaf, though it should always be possible for an observer to give an indication of all species present at a colony and the relative order of abundance.

THE ATTENTION of observers is drawn to the fact that DISTURBANCE to seabird colonies should be avoided at all costs. It is better to have an estimate made from a distance than an accurate count made of a disturbed colony, for the damage done may change the colony so that the count will be relatively worthless. Some groups, in particular the TERNS and AUKS are prone to disturbance and we stress again that GREAT CARE MUST BE TAKEN by all "Seafarer" observers.

FULMAR: - The survey may be carried out at any time from the end of May to mid August as a count or estimate of the number of occupied sites but the best time for counting is late June when brooding birds sit tight and many pairs are together. In the majority of cases it is impossible to discover whether a sitting bird is incubating or not, hence the need to record occupied sites. Late counts of nestlings do not take into account egg and chick losses but should be noted when other details are impossible to obtain.

KITTIWAKE: - Present at colonies from February onwards, nest building commences early in April and counts are possible from early May until mid August. With this species only actual nests should be counted, these being easy to recognise present no difficulty to the observer. A useful definition of a nest is 'where there is sufficient nesting material to allow eggs to be retained'. Care should also be taken, particularly towards the end of the season, not to confuse 'whitewash' with nests.

RAZORBILL AND GUILLEMOT: - These species have probably the most restricted breeding season of all our seabirds. Although they visit their colonies at intervals throughout the winter and spring, the numbers present during these occupations may be highly variable. Egg-laying usually commences in early to mid May, so that counts can be made from the third week onwards. In southern colonies at least, the first young are leaving the cliffs before the end of June, so counts after this time quickly lose their accuracy. Even in the far north, counts will be reduced after the first week of July. For both species the ideal month for counting is June with extensions into late May and early July, though these limits may be extended a little earlier in the south and later in the north. However counts or records made before or after this period should not be ignored but should be noted on the card. They will be of value in the preparation of distribution maps.

RAZORBILL: - These usually nest as scattered pairs, sometimes among Guillemots rather than as distinct colonies. If they are using niches and cliff-crevices the individual pairs may usually be observed and counted with little difficulty. Problems arise when the birds are nesting in enlarged burrow entrances or crevices under boulders and in broken cliffs. Here the incubating and brooding birds are completely invisible from a distance and the majority are inaccessible. In some colonies of this type an egg count may be feasible, but great care should be taken to avoid disturbance, especially if predatory species such as Jackdaws are in the vicinity. At the moment more research is required into the breeding biology of Razorbills nesting in such situations so any figures of birds standing around in the colony are difficult to interpret. However well documented information is urgently required for full analysis when more knowledge is available.

GUILLEMOT: - While it is generally possible to pick out incubating birds in undisturbed colonies since they face the cliff in half-crouching fluffed out manner, owing to egg-losses the number seen will not represent a true picture of the total breeding pairs present. It is better to count all birds in the colony, excluding those on the sea, and from this the strength of the colony may be calculated by the organisers. Several counts made at different times of the day are valuable, and should be recorded on separate cards together with the time. When the ledges are deep or the birds nesting in crevices care must be taken to allow for those standing at the rear. Groups standing idly on low rocks just above the water mark should not be included in the survey, nor should non-breeders which may gather at favourite places away from the main colony.

"BRIDLED GUILLEMOTS": - Counts of the "bridled" variety of the Common Guillemot have been made over the whole of its Atlantic range in 1938 - 39, 1948 - 49 and 1958 - 59. The first survey revealed an intriguing pattern of distribution with "bridles" rare in the south of the range but increasing northwards to over 50% in Iceland. The first repeat survey showed a considerable decline in the percentage of "bridles" at some colonies and an increase at a few. The second repeat after 20 years showed that these changes had been more or less neatly cancelled and the distribution of "bridles" was back to the 1938 level. It should be very interesting now that a further 10 years have passed, to survey the scene again.

Counts at any colonies are valuable but particularly at those north of the Forth-Clyde line. These have a "bridled" proportion of 5% or more and many have been counted in previous surveys. It is most important that a sketch map is made of the whole colony showing roughly the separation between sub-colonies and to give an estimate of the total numbers. Counts preferably of some hundreds of birds, should be made of each sub-colony and kept separate, because sub-colonies sometimes vary in the "bridled" percentage considerably.

Counts made from the sea are not dependable. With counts made from the land, the golden rule is never make a count unless you are near enough to pick out "bridled" birds instantly and unerringly with optical aids. Counts made looking steeply down on to ledges are difficult and it may be best to wait for birds to turn their heads for a positive identification and be content with a smaller sample.

Any queries concerning "bridled" Guillemots may be addressed to H. N. Southern, Animal Research Group, Botanic Garden, High Street, Oxford, who has been responsible for organising the previous surveys.

PUFFIN: - Used Puffin burrows, like those of Manx Shearwaters, are pretty obvious at close quarters, though care should be taken if the colony is mixed or when Rabbits are present in the area. If the colony is accessible these may be counted, or in the case of large numbers sample areas counted in order to give some idea of the total population. Weather conditions seem to play a vital role in the attendance of Puffins at their colonies, while peak numbers, which may vary considerably from day to day, come ashore only in the evening. It is desirable that any counts of birds standing in the colony should be made as early as possible before too many non-breeders arrive. This usually occurs from the end of June until the colony is deserted during August. Perhaps the most satisfactory way of carrying out a census is to count the rafts of Puffins on the sea towards the end of April and in early May to the onset of the breeding season.

BLACK GUILLEMOT: - This is rather a difficult species to count. Nests are hidden away among boulder beaches, in crevices and sometimes caves. The best time to attempt a survey seems to be about the second week of May when the pairs are displaying on the sea. During incubation the peak of visible activity seems to be in the early morning and evening with very little during the remainder of the day. When the chicks have hatched the adults flying in with food can provide an assessment of the successful population. However this is a species of which the most we can reasonably expect from observers is a rough indication of numbers. Observers are asked to pay particular attention to this species in the Irish Sea area where there is evidence of a recent expansion of range.

HERRING GULL. - These normally nest in such situations as cliff slopes where methods used for other gull species cannot be employed, though nests can be searched for in accessible colonies. If the ground is not too broken and providing that tall vegetation is absent, incubating birds may be observed at a distance from late April until the end of May, after which the chicks start hatching. Orders of abundance may be estimated from the number of adults flying overhead, particularly when the colony is disturbed.

Observers are requested to provide as much information as possible concerning nesting on rooftops in coastal towns. This habit which has been growing in recent years urgently requires documentation, particularly in view of the health hazard and nuisance these birds may create in such situations. Stanley Cramp, 32 Queens Court, London W.C.1 is collecting all information concerning the roof nesting habit and will be pleased to receive any details available from previous years.

GREATER BLACK BACKED GULL. - This tends to be a solitary nester, or in loose knit colonies which may occasionally be very large. Nests may be located by searching or watching from a distance. When the young have hatched the alarm calls of the parent birds still indicate the territory, while discarded food remains litter the nest site. Care should be taken not to overlook the occasional pair nesting among other gulls, or those tucked away on cliff slopes and offshore stacks. Extra information concerning predation by this species on other seabirds would be most valuable to receive.

LESSER BLACK BACKED and BLACK HEADED GULLS: - Here it is impossible to obtain accurate counts once the young have hatched, usually by about mid June. This is because both species nest in such dense colonies that separating territories is quite out of the question.

One method which may be used in a large colony when enough observers can be mustered, is for the party to walk slowly through. Each observer counts the area between himself and the next person (this distance can be decided in advance depending on the terrain). Marker posts such as white-topped canes may be set up in advance as guide-lines indeed this is essential in large colonies.

It would be an advantage if colony boundaries can be plotted on suitable scale maps, and this can be done even when the young have hatched. An estimate of the order of abundance of the colony may also be obtained at this late stage from the adults flying above it, particularly when they are disturbed.

COMMON GULL: - This tends to nest in smaller and less dense colonies than the above two species. Nests may usually be found by searching, or when the eggs have hatched an estimate can be made by watching from a distance. To aid the counting of nests the colony may be divided up into sub-colonies by the use of natural features.

TERNS: - Together with the Auk family this is a group where great care should be taken by observers to avoid disturbance, and not to draw the attention of casual onlookers to the area. Visits to the colony should be for short periods only and should not exceed 20 minutes. If the colony is large it may be safe to work in one sector without putting the birds off their nests in another. Small colonies should be treated with great caution as their members are very easily deterred.

A survey of Sandwich Terns organised by Nigel Langham, Marine Labs, Victoria Road, Torry, Aberdeen, is in progress, and observers are already arranged for the well documented colonies. However, there is a possibility that new colonies will be discovered during 1969 particularly in remote regions and these should be counted.

Egg-laying varies with the locality and the number of terns in the colony. If new colonies are discovered it will probably be after the chicks have hatched, which if disturbed tend to hide away from the vicinity of the nests, though these are frequently obvious by the faecal squirtings and remains of shells. As Sandwich Terns are usually associated with Black-headed Gulls and/or other terns, a careful note should be made of these associated species.

In Britain the Roseate Tern usually nests under vegetation, in crevices or Rabbit burrows and it is often impossible to get an accurate figure of the colony without causing disturbance. If the colony is scattered or sub-divided it may still be possible, otherwise the estimate should be made by observation from a distance.

Where mixed colonies of Common and Arctic Terns occur observers should endeavour to survey the colony from a vantage point using binoculars. It should then be possible to determine the bounds of each species for rarely are they completely integrated. The Common Tern is found mostly in areas of tall or dense vegetation, while the Arctic Tern occurs in areas of short turf, bare sand or rock. Once the young have hatched faecal deposits are a good guide to occupied nest sites.

The Little Tern was the subject of a special enquiry into its status in 1967, in view of concern for its safety and continuation as a breeding species in many counties. Wherever possible we are asking observers to count specific colonies rather than making a general appeal for information. This will mean that disturbance is kept to a minimum. Observers in western Ireland and northern Scotland may however discover small new Little Tern colonies and counts or estimates should be made of their size. Once again as with the other Tern species we emphasise that GREAT CARE SHOULD BE TAKEN.

GREAT SKUA and ARCTIC SKUA: - The number of territories in an area may be assessed fairly, easily, by walking over the nesting grounds on several occasions. Both species are best surveyed during the incubation period which lasts until late June. It is important with these species that we get good cover in the area at the southern edge of their range, where both are still increasing.

CORMORANT: - This usually nests in open and conspicuous sites, often in large colonies. Accurate nest counts are possible all through the breeding season, and perhaps after the young have departed, for the adults still frequent the "white-washed" site. Both Cormorant and Shag can have a protracted breeding season and a colony in July may contain both fully-fledged young and nests containing eggs.

SHAG: - More difficult to census than the Cormorant. Many nest in caves often at a considerable distance from the entrance and the only indication of their presence is the birds flying to and fro. Others nest under boulders on scree or grassy slopes, or the heads of beaches. If the colony is small or well scattered it should be easy to locate nests providing the terrain is not too difficult. However, if the colony is dense intrusion of observers may create a disturbance above an acceptable level, and so should be avoided and an estimate made from a distance. Counts of adult Shags on the sea, or resting on rocks may be recorded, provided that full details are given for sites where nesting is suspected.

MANX SHEARWATER: - This is present at the colonies from March to October. Because of its burrow nesting and nocturnal habits when on land it is one of the most difficult of seabirds to count accurately. The number of birds visiting a colony in late summer is swelled considerably by the arrival of non-breeders in early July, so that false impressions of the breeding population may be obtained.

It would seem that unless there is considerable man-power and time available it is not practicable to attempt a census of a large shearwater colony. Those wishing to embark upon such an exercise should consult the Skokholm Birds Obs. Report for 1967.

When such an extensive survey cannot be carried out, the extent of the colony may be mapped, and its density noted, if only in general terms. A good indication of the presence and size of a shearwater colony may be gained from observing the "rafts" offshore in the late evening. It is preferable if several watches can be made on different days in case a particular watch is biased by some weather factor or other.

STORM PETREL and LEACH'S PETREL: - These are again difficult to count by conventional methods. If the colony is of a single type and readily accessible, for instance a boulder beach, it may be possible to mark and count the sites where the singing birds can be heard. However in most cases all we can expect from an observer is an indication that Storm or Leach's Petrels are present in a given area, and possibly their order of abundance. Disturbance of nesting birds should be avoided whenever possible as both easily desert, indeed examination of a nest need only be carried out to prove a new breeding record and then extreme caution should be used.

SUMMARY

These instructions have been prepared as a guide to observers. Where precise methods are outlined observers are asked to follow these in order that the interpretation of results may be simplified. With several species more work is urgently required on their breeding biology and behaviour when ashore to discover good census techniques. The information gathered during "Seafarer" will assist with counts in future years.

It will be appreciated if observers can send their records to the organiser as soon after the observations are completed as possible, so that we can check on outstanding problems.

If observers find they are suddenly unable to carry out the survey in their area will they please inform the organiser immediately. It may be possible for alternative arrangements to be made.

"SEAFARER" ORGANISER

David Saunders
"Tom the Keepers"
Marloes
Haverfordwest
Pembrokeshire   Tel DALE 202

PHOTOGRAPHS

Many observers during the course of their surveys will be taking photographs of the colonies they are working on. The Seabird Group would be very pleased to examine any such photographic records, whether black and white or colour transparencies. If the photographs provide a good record of the colonies counted and can be used to effect comparisons in future years the Group would like to have reproductions made.

SPECIMEN CARD

Observer's Name BARRY SPENCE   Date 1969   Grid reference TA 398.108

Address SPURN BIRD OBSERVATORY,   County YORKSHIRE

via PATRINGTON, HULL, E.YORKS   Vice-County No. 61

KILNSEA   Locality SPURN POINT.

HU 12 045

	No. apparently occupied nests	Accuracy		No. apparently occupied nests	Accuracy
Fulmar			Kittiwake		
Manx Shearwater			Sandwich Tern		
Storm Petrel			Common Tern		
Leach's Petrel			Arctic Tern		
Gannet			Roseate Tern		
Cormorant			Little Tern	4	Acc.
Shag			Razorbill		
Great Skua			Guillemot		
Arctic Skua			Black Guillemot		
Black-headed Gull			Puffin		
Lesser Black-back			Others:		
Herring Gull					
Greater Black-back					
Common Gull					

NOTES: 1. Enter figures only for those species you KNOW are breeding in the locality. Otherwise "?" and give details of suspected breeding in "general" space overleaf.

2. Enter "ACC" here if an accurate count was made; otherwise indicate the accuracy of your estimate; e.g., if correct to ± 1000 enter 1000 here, if to ± 100 enter 100, etc., if present but not estimated show if many or few.

Description of Colony: (e.g., sheer cliff, broken scree, boulder or sandy beach, etc.)

Weather during count:

Extent of census: a) Was any section of the colony missed because of overhanging cliffs, dead ground, lack of time, etc.? If so, please indicate extent to which nests may have been missed, and why.

b) Could a boat have been used to cover parts of colony missed from land, or to get a better count? If so, can you say where one can be hired?

General: Please give details of any species suspected of, but not proved to be, breeding. If auks, shearwaters, or petrels are present please say how the numbers given were estimated.

N. omy fludged.

NOTES: A. Please attempt to estimate the numbers of all species present. If this is not possible please give priority to counting i) Fulmar and Kittiwake, ii) the auks, iii) other species.

B. With very large colonies please try to estimate to the nearest thousand; with colonies of less than 500 please try for complete counts.

C. Please indicate clearly the limits of the area counted; e.g., do not send in this card marked only "Skokholm" unless you have counted all the colonies on the island; instead give grid references of the colony or colonies actually counted.

Appendix V

Scientific names of vertebrate and invertebrate animals mentioned in the text.

Goose Barnacle *Balanus balanoides*
Norway Lobster *Nephrops norvegicus*
Portuguese Man O'War Jellyfish *Physalia physalis*

Blennies *Blennidae*
Brown Trout *Salmo trutta*
Butterfish *Pholis gunnellus*
Capelin *Mallotus villosus*
Cod *Gadus morhua*
Dab, Long-rough *Hipploglossoides platessoides*
Haddock *Melanogrammus aeglefinus*
Herring *Clupea harengus*
Lumpsucker *Cyclopterus lumpus*
Mackerel *Scomber scombrus*
Norway Pout *Trisopterus esmarkii*
Perch *Perca fluviatilis*
Pike *Esox lucius*
Plaice *Pleuronectes platessa*
Poor Cod *Trisopterus minutus*
Roach *Rutilus rutilus*
Saithe *Pollarchius virens*
Salmon *Salar salar*
Sandeels *Ammodytes* spp., main seabird food *A. marinus*
Sea Trout *Salmo trutta*
Sprat *Sprattus sprattus*
Whiting *Merlangius merlangus*
Wrasse *Labridae*

Loggerhead Turtle *Caretta caretta*

317

BIRDS

Arctic Skua *Stercorarius parasiticus*
Arctic Tern *Sterna paradisaea*
Australian Gannet *Sula serrator*
Avocet *Avocetta curvirostra*
Blackbird *Turdus merula*
Black Guillemot *Cepphus grylle*
Black Tern *Chlidonias niger*
Black-browed Albatross *Diomedea melanophris*
Black-headed Gull *Larus ridibundus*
Brunnich's Guillemot *Uria lomvia*
Cape Cormorant *Phalacrocorax capensis*
Common Gull *Larus canus*
Common Tern *Sterna hirundo*
Cormorant *Phalacrocorax carbo*
Double-crested Cormorant *Phalacrocorax auritus*
Fulmar *Fulmarus glacialis*
Gannet *Sula bassana*
Great Auk *Alca impennis*
Great Black-backed Gull *Larus marinus*
Great Skua *Catharacta skua*
Gull-billed Tern *Sterna nilotica*
Guillemot *Uria aalge*
Herring Gull *Larus argentatus*
Hooded/Carrion Crow *Corvus corone*
Kestrel *Falco tinnunculus*
Kittiwake *Rissa tridactyla*
Leach's Petrel *Oceanodroma leucorhoa*
Lesser Black-backed Gull *Larus fuscus*
Lesser Crested Tern *Sterna bengalensis*
Little Gull *Larus minutus*
Little Shearwater *Puffinus assimilis*
Little Tern *Sterna albifrons*
Long-tailed Skua *Stercorarius longicaudus*
Manx Shearwater *Puffinus puffinus*
Mediterranean Gull *Larus melanocephalus*
Oystercatcher *Haematopus ostralegus*
Peregrine *Falco peregrinus*
Pomarine Skua *Stercorarius pomarinus*
Puffin *Fratercula arctica*
Raven *Corvus corax*
Razorbill *Alca torda*
Red-legged Kittiwake *Rissa brevirostris*
Robin *Erithacus rubecula*
Roseate Tern *Sterna dougallii*
Royal Tern *Sterna maxima*
Sand Martin *Riparia riparia*

Sandwich Tern *Sterna sandvicencis*
Sea Eagle *Haliaeetus albicilla*
Shag *Phalacrocorax aristotelis*
South African Gannet *Sula capensis*
Starling *Sturnus vulgaris*
Storm Petrel *Hydrobates pelagicus*

MAMMALS

Cat *Felis domesticus*
Dog *Canis familiaris*
Ferret *Mulstela putorius*
Fox, Red *Vulpes vulpes*
Goat *Capra hircus*
Hedgehog *Erinaceus europaeus*
Lemming *Lemmus* spp.
Mink, American *Mulstela vison*
Otter *Lutra lutra*
Rabbit *Oryctolagus cuniculus*
Rat, Black *Rattus rattus*
Rat, Brown *Rattus norvegicus*
Sheep *Ovis aries*
Stoat *Mustela erminea*

References

Aebischer, N.J. 1986. Retrospective investigation of an ecological disaster in the Shag *Phalacrocorax aristotelis*: a general method based on long-term marking. *J. Anim. Ecol.* 55:613–629.

Alexander, M. and Perrins, C.M. 1980. An estimate of the numbers of shearwaters on the Neck, Skomer 1978. *Nature in Wales* 17:43–46.

Allen, R. 1974. Gulls and other seabirds in the Isles of Scilly, April to August 1974. *Nature Conservancy Council Report*, SW England Region, Taunton.

Allen, R. 1977. Population trends of seabirds in Scilly. *Nature Conservancy Council Report*, SW England Region, Taunton.

Anderson, A. 1982. Establishment and growth of a new Fulmar colony on sand dunes. *Bird Study* 29:189–194.

Anderson, D.W., Gress, F., Mais, K. and Kelly P.R. 1980. Brown Pelicans as anchovy stock indicators and their relationships to commercial fishing. *CalCOFI Rep.* 21:54–61.

Andrews, J.H. and Standring, K.T. (eds.) 1979. *Marine pollution and birds.* Royal Society for the Protection of Birds, Sandy.

Armstrong, I.H., Coulson, J.C., Hawkey, P. and Hudson, M. 1978. Further mass seabird deaths from paralytic shellfish poisoning. *Brit. Birds* 71:58–68.

Asbirk, S. 1978. Breeding numbers and habitat selection of Danish Black Guillemots *Cepphus grylle. Dansk Orn. Foren. Tidsskr.* 72:161–178.

Ashcroft, R.E. 1979. Survival rates and breeding biology of Puffins on Skomer Island, Wales. *Ornis Scand.* 10:100–110.

Ashmole, N.P. 1963. Regulation of numbers of tropical oceanic birds. *Ibis* 103:458–473.

Ashmole, N.P. and Ashmole, M.J. 1967. Comparative feeding ecology of seabirds of a tropical oceanic island. *Bull. Peabody Mus. Nat. Hist.* 24:1–131.

Avery, M. and Green, R. 1989. Not enough fish in the sea. *New Scientist* 1674:28–29.

Bailey, R.S. 1983. The sandeel fisheries. *Fishing Prospects* 1983:37–41.

Bailey, R.S. 1989. Shetland's sandeels. *New Scientist* 1678:64–65.

Baillie, S.R. and Mead, C.J. 1982. Effect of severe oil pollution during the winter of 1980–81 on British and Irish auks. *Ringing and Migration* 4:33–44.

Baillie, S.R. and Stowe, T.J. 1984. A comparison between the percentage of seabirds reported as oiled from ringing recoveries and from the Beached Bird Survey. *Seabird* 7:47–54.

Baker, R.B. 1980. The significance of the Lesser Black-backed Gull to models of bird migration. *Bird Study* 27:41–50.

Bárcena, F., Teixeira, A.M. and Bermejo, A. 1984. Breeding seabird populations in the Atlantic sector of the Iberian peninsula, pp 335–346 in Croxall, J.P., Evans, P.G.H. and Schreiber, R.W. (eds.) *Status and conservation of the world's seabirds.* ICBP Tech. Pub. No. 2, Cambridge.

Barrett, R.T. 1979. Changes in the population of Gannets *Sula bassana* in North Norway. *Fauna Norv. Ser. C, Cinclus* 2:23–26.

Barrett, R.T., Skaare, J.U., Norheim, G., Vader, W. and Frøslie, A. 1985. Persistent organochlorines and mercury in eggs of Norwegian seabirds. *Envir. Poll. A* 39:79–93.

Barrett, R.T. and Strann, K-B. 1987. Two new breeding records of the Storm Petrel *Hydrobates pelagicus* in Norway. *Fauna Norv. Ser. C, Cinclus* 10:115–116.

Barrett, R.T. and Vader, W. 1984. The status and conservation of breeding seabirds in Norway, pp 323–334 in Croxall, J.P., Evans, P.G.H. and Schreiber, R.W. (eds.) *Status and conservation of the world's seabirds*. ICBP Tech. Pub. No. 2, Cambridge.

Barth, E.K. 1975. Taxonomy of *Larus argentatus* and *Larus fuscus* in northwest Europe. *Ornis Scand.* 6:49–63.

Baxter, E.V. and Rintoul, L.J. 1953. *The birds of Scotland. Their history, distribution and migration*, Vol. 2. Oliver and Boyd, Edinburgh.

Becker, P.H. and Frank, D. 1988. Feeding strategies of Common Terns in the Wadden Sea, pp 8–10 in Tasker, M.L. (ed.) *Seabird food and feeding ecology*, Proc. 3rd Int. Conf. of the Seabird Group, Sandy.

Bell, M.V. (ed.) 1985. Herring Gull. *North-East Scotland Bird Report 1984*: 22.

Belopol' skii, L.O. 1957. *Ecology of sea colony birds of the Barents Sea*. (English translation, Israel Program for Scientific Translations, Jerusalem 1961).

Benn, S., Burton, C.A., Tasker, M.L., Webb, A. and Ward, R.M. 1988. Seabird distribution on the north-west Scottish shelf. *Nature Conservancy Council Chief Scientist Directorate Report* no. 803.

Benn, S., Tasker, M.L. and Reid, A. 1987. Changes in numbers of cliff-nesting seabirds in Orkney, 1976–1985. *Seabird* 10:51–57.

Berry, R.J. and Davis, J.W.F. 1970. Polymorphism and behaviour in the Arctic Skua. *Proc. Roy. Soc. Lond.* 175B:255–267.

Bibby, C.J. 1971. Auks drowned in fishing-nets. *Seabird Report* 2:48–49.

Bibby, C.J. 1972. Net loss to auks. *Birds* 4:248.

Birkhead, T.R. 1974. Movements and mortality rates of British Guillemots. *Bird Study* 21:241–254.

Birkin, M. and Smith, A. 1987. Breeding seabirds, Isles of Scilly 1987. *Nature Conservancy Council Report*, SW England Region, Taunton.

Blake, B.F. 1984. Diet and fish stock availability as possible factors in the mass death of auks in the North Sea. *J. Exp. Mar. Biol. Ecol.* 76:89–103.

Blokpoel, H. and Scharf, W.C. in press. Status and conservation of seabirds nesting in the Great Lakes of North America, in Croxall, J.P. (ed.) *Supplement to Status and conservation of the world's seabirds*. Cambridge University Press/ICBP, Cambridge.

Bourne, W.R.P. 1976. Seabirds and pollution. pp 403–502 in Johnston, R. (ed.) *Marine Pollution*. Academic Press, London.

Bourne, W.R.P. 1979. Herring Gulls nesting on buildings in eastern Scotland. *North-East Scotland Bird Report 1978*: 45–46.

Bourne, W.R.P. 1988. Herring and Lesser Black-backed Gulls nesting in Rosyth dockyard. *Sea Swallow* 37:64–65.

Bourne, W.R. and Currie, A. 1983. A seabird survey of the Western Isles in 1977. *Hebridean Naturalist* 7:9–16.

Bourne, W.R.P. and Smith, A.J.M. 1974. Threats to Scottish Sandwich Terns. *Biol. Conserv.* 6:222–224.

Bourne, W.R.P. and Vauk, G. 1988. Accumulation by birds. In Salomons, W., Bayne, B.L., Duursma, E.K. and Förstner, U. (eds.) *Pollution of the North Sea—an assessment.* Springer-Verlag, Heidelberg.

Bourne, W.R.P., Smith, A.J.M. and Dowse, A. 1978. Gulls and terns nesting inland in northeast Scotland. *Scot. Birds* 10:50–53.

Boyd, H. 1954. The 'wreck' of Leach's Petrels in the autumn of 1952. *Brit. Birds* 47:137–163.

Brazier, H. 1980. A report on an expedition to Puffin Island, Little Skellig and Inishvickillane, Co. Kerry, June–July 1980. *Irish Wildbird Conservancy Report*, Greystones.

Brazier, H. and Merne, O.J. 1988. *The Blasket Islands expedition, 1988.* Irish Wildbird Conservancy/Wildlife Service, Dublin.

Broad, R.A. 1974. Contamination of birds with Fulmar oil. *Brit. Birds* 67: 297–301.

Brooke, M. 1978a. Some factors affecting the laying date, incubation and breeding success of the Manx Shearwater *Puffinus puffinus. J. Anim. Ecol.* 47:477–495.

Brooke, M. 1978b. Sexual differences in voice and individual vocal recognition in Manx Shearwaters (*Puffinus puffinus*). *Anim. Behav.* 26:622–629.

Brooke, M. 1990. *The Manx Shearwater.* T. and A.D. Poyser, London.

Brooke, R.K., Cooper, J., Shelton, P.A. and Crawford, R.J.M. 1982. Taxonomy, distribution, population size, breeding and conservation of the Whitebreasted Cormorant, *Phalocrocorax carbo*, on the southern African coast. *Gerfaut* 72:188–220.

Brown, A.W. 1983. The Fulmars of Holyrood Park, Edinburgh. *Scot. Birds* 12:228–229.

Brown, B.J. 1985. A history of the Kittiwake in Suffolk. *Suffolk Bird Report 1984*: 66–71.

Brown, R.G.B. 1970. Fulmar distribution: a Canadian perspective. *Ibis* 112:44–51.

Brown, R.G.B. 1980. Seabirds as marine animals. pp 1–39 in Burger, J., Olla, B.L. and Winn, E.B. (eds.) *Behavior of Marine Animals*, Volume 4. Plenum Press, New York.

Brown, R.G.B. and Johnson, B.C. 1980. The effects of "Kurdistan" oil on seabirds. In Vandermeulen, J. (ed.) *Scientific studies during the "Kurdistan" tanker incident: proceedings of a workshop.* Bedford Institute of Oceanography Report Series BI–R–80–3, Dartmouth, Nova Scotia.

Brown, R.G.B. and Nettleship, D.N. 1984a. The seabirds of northeastern North America; their present status and conservation requirements, pp 85–100 in Croxall, J.P., Evans, P.G.H. and Schreiber, R.W. (eds.) *Status and conservation of the world's seabirds.* ICBP Tech. Pub. No. 2, Cambridge.

Brown, R.G.B. and Nettleship, D.N. 1984b. Capelin and seabirds in the northwest Atlantic, pp 184–196 in Nettleship, D.N., Sanger, G.A. and Springer, P.F. (eds.) *Marine Birds: their feeding ecology and commercial fisheries relationships*, Canadian Wildlife Service Special Publication, Ottawa.

324 *References*

Brun, E. 1972. Establishment and population increase of the Gannet *Sula bassana* in Norway. *Ornis Scand.* 2:27–38.

Brun, E. 1979. Present status and trends in populations of seabirds in Norway, pp 289–301 in Bartonek, J.C. and Nettleship, D.N. *Conservation of marine birds of northern North America*. U.S. Fish and Wildl. Serv. Wildl. Res. Rep. vol. 11.

Buckley, N.J. and O'Halloran, J. 1986. Mass mortality of gulls in west Cork attributed to botulism. *Irish Birds* 3:283–285.

Buckley, P.A. and Buckley, F.G. 1981. The endangered status of North American Roseate Terns. *Colonial Waterbirds* 4:166–173.

Buckley, P.A. and Buckley, F.G. 1984. Seabirds of the north and middle Atlantic coasts of the United States: their status and conservation, pp 101–133 in Croxall, J.P., Evans, P.G.H. and Schreiber, R.W. (eds.) *Status and conservation of the world's seabirds*. ICBP Tech. Pub. No. 2, Cambridge.

Bullock, I.D. and Gomersall, C.H. 1980. Breeding terns in Orkney and Shetland 1980. *Royal Society for the Protection of Birds Report*, Sandy.

Bullock, I.D. and Gomersall, C.H. 1981. The breeding populations of terns in Orkney and Shetland in 1980. *Bird Study* 28:187–200.

Buxton, N. 1985. A new breeding site for the Atlantic Gannet. *Scot. Birds* 13:187–188.

Carnduff, D. 1981. Black Guillemots breeding in the inner Clyde estuary. *Scot. Birds* 11:195–196.

Castro, M. 1984. Auks drown in Spanish nets. *BTO News* 132:1.

Chabrzyk, G. and Coulson, J.C. 1976. Survival and recruitment in the Herring Gull. *J. Anim. Ecol.* 44:187–203.

Chapdelaine, G. 1980. Onzième inventaire et analyse des fluctuations des populations d'oiseaux marins dans les refuges de la côte nord du Golfe Saint-Laurent. *Can. Field-Nat.* 94:34–42.

Chapdelaine, G. and Laporte, P. 1982. Populations, reproductive success, and analysis of contaminants in Razorbills *Alca torda* in the estuary and Gulf of St. Lawrence, Quebec. *Canadian Wildlife Service Progress Notes* 129:1–10.

Chapdelaine, G., Laporte, P. and Nettleship, D.N. 1987. Population, productivity and DDT contamination trends of Northern Gannets (*Sula bassanus*) at Bonadventure Island, Quebec, 1967–1984. *Can. J. Zool.* 65:2922–2926.

Chapman, A. 1976. Seabirds breeding on RSPB reserves. *Royal Society for the Protection of Birds Report*, Sandy.

Clapp, R.B. and Buckley, P.A. 1984. Status and conservation of seabirds in the southeastern United States, pp 135–155 in Croxall, J.P., Evans, P.G.H. and Schreiber, R.W. (eds.) *Status and conservation of the world's seabirds*. ICBP Tech. Pub. No. 2, Cambridge.

Collins, T.S. 1985. A partial census of the cliff-breeding birds of Cape Clear Island 1983. *Cape Clear Bird Observatory 1983–84*:60–70.

Corkhill, P. 1973. Manx Shearwater numbers on Skomer: population and mortality due to gull predation. *Brit. Birds* 66:136–143.

Coulson, J.C. 1961. Movements and seasonal variation in mortality of Shags and Cormorants ringed on the Farne Islands, Northumberland. *Brit. Birds* 54:225–235.

Coulson, J.C. 1963. The status of the Kittiwake in the British Isles. *Bird Study* 10:147–179.

Coulson, J.C. 1966. The movements of Kittiwakes. *Bird Study* 13:107–115.

Coulson, J.C. 1983. The changing status of the Kittiwake *Rissa tridactyla* in the British Isles, 1969–1979. *Bird Study* 30:9–16.

Coulson, J.C. 1985. Reply to Wanless and Harris. *Ornis Scand.* 16:74–75.

Coulson, J.C. and Brazendale, M.G. 1968. Movements of Cormorants ringed in the British Isles, and evidence of colony-specific dispersal. *Brit. Birds* 61:1–21.

Coulson, J.C. and Butterfield, J. 1985. Movements of British Herring Gulls. *Bird Study* 32:91–103.

Coulson, J.C., Butterfield, J., Duncan, N., Kearsey, S., Monaghan, P. and Thomas C. 1984b. Origin and behaviour of Great Black-backed gulls wintering in northeast England. *Brit. Birds* 77:1–11.

Coulson, J.C., Deans, I.R., Potts, G.R., Robinson, J. and Crabtree, A.N. 1972. Changes in organochlorine contamination of the marine environment of eastern Britain monitored by Shag eggs. *Nature* 236:454–456.

Coulson, J.C., Duncan, N. and Thomas, C.S. 1982. Changes in the breeding biology of the Herring Gull (*Larus argentatus*) induced by reduction in the size and density of the colony. *J. Anim. Ecol.* 51: 739–756.

Coulson, J.C. and Horobin, J.M. 1972. The annual re-occupation of breeding sites by the Fulmar. *Ibis* 114:30–42.

Coulson, J.C., Monaghan, P., Butterfield, J.E.L., Duncan, N., Ensor, K., Shedden, C. and Thomas, C. 1984a. Scandinavian Herring Gulls wintering in Britain. *Ornis Scand.* 15:79–88.

Coulson, J.C., Potts, G.R., Deans, I.R. and Fraser, S.M. 1968. Exceptional mortality of Shags and other seabirds caused by paralytic shellfish poison. *Brit. Birds* 61:381–404.

Coulson, J.C. and Thomas, C.S. 1985. Changes in the biology of the Kittiwake *Rissa tridactyla*: a 31-year study of a breeding colony. *J. Anim. Ecol.* 54:9–26.

Counsell, D. 1983. A colony of Cormorants at a freshwater loch in North Uist. *Hebridean Naturalist* 7:25–26.

Cramp, S. 1971. Gulls nesting on buildings in Britain and Ireland. *Brit. Birds* 64:476–483.

Cramp, S. (ed.) 1985. *Birds of the Western Palearctic*, Vol. 4. Oxford University Press, Oxford.

Cramp, S., Bourne, W.R.P. and Saunders, D. 1974. *The seabirds of Britain and Ireland*. Collins, London.

Cramp, S. and Simmons, K.E.L. (eds.) 1977. *Birds of the Western Palearctic*, Vol. 1. Oxford University Press, Oxford.

Cramp, S. and Simmons, K.E.L. (eds.) 1983. *Birds of the Western Palearctic*, Vol. 3. Oxford University Press. Oxford.

Croxall, J.P., Evans, P.G.H. and Schreiber, R.W. (eds.) 1984. *Status and conservation of the world's seabirds*. ICBP Tech. Pub. No. 2, Cambridge.

Cushing, D.H. 1952. Echo-surveys of fish. *J. Cons. Int. Explor. Mer.* 18:45–60.

Cushing, D.H. 1982. *Climate and fisheries*. Academic Press. London.

da Prato, S.R.D. 1985. St Abb's Head National Nature Reserve seabird census 1985. *Nature Conservancy Council Report*, SE Scotland region, Edinburgh.

Davies, J.C. 1980. The birds of Scariff, Deenish and neighbouring islands, Co. Kerry. *Irish Birds* 1:535–539.

Davies, M. and Price, D. 1986. Lundy census of breeding seabirds (1981, 82 & 86): site register and summary of counts. *Royal Society for the Protection of Birds Report*, Sandy.

Davidson, R. 1987. Breeding birds of Lough Neagh, 1987. *Department of the Environment (Northern Ireland) Report*, Craigavon.

Davis, J.W.F. 1974. Herring Gull populations and Man. *Nature in Wales* 14:85–90.

de Juana, E.A. 1984. The status and conservation of seabirds in the Spanish Mediterranean, pp 347–362 in Croxall, J.P., Evans, P.G.H. and Schreiber, R.W. (eds.) *Status and conservation of the world's seabirds*. ICBP Tech. Pub. No. 2, Cambridge.

de Juana, E.A., Varela, J. and Witt, H-H. 1984. The conservation of seabirds at the Chafarinas Islands. pp 363–370 in Croxall, J.P., Evans, P.G.H. and Schreiber, R.W. (eds.) *Status and conservation of the world's seabirds*. ICBP Tech. Pub. No. 2, Cambridge.

Debout, G. 1987. Le Grand Cormoran, *Phalacrocorax carbo*, en France: les populations nicheuses littorales. *Alauda* 66:35–54.

Divoky, G.J., Watson, G.E. and Bartonek, J.C. 1974. Breeding of the Black Guillemot in Northern Alaska. *Condor* 76:339–343.

Dott, H.E.M. 1975. Fulmars at colonies: time of day and weather. *Bird Study* 22:255–259.

Drury, W.H. and Kadlec, J.A. 1974. The current status of the Herring Gull population in the northeastern United States. *Bird-Banding* 45:297–306.

Duinker, J.C. and Koeman, J.H. 1978. Summary report on the distribution and effects of toxic pollutants (metals and chlorinated hydrocarbons) in the Wadden Sea, pp 45–54 in Essink, K. and Wolff, W.J. *Pollution of the Wadden Sea area*. Report 8: Wadden Sea Working Group, Leiden.

Duncan, N. 1978. Effects of culling Herring Gulls (*Larus argentatus*) on recruitment and population dynamics. *J. Appl Ecol.* 15:697–713.

Duncan, N. 1981a. The Abbeystead and Mallowdale gull colonies before control. *Bird Study* 28:133–138.

Duncan, N. 1981b. The Lesser Black-backed Gull on the Isle of May. *Scot. Birds* 11:180–188.

Duncan, N and Monaghan, P. 1977. Infidelity to natal colony by breeding Herring Gulls. *Ringing and Migration* 1:166–172.

Dunn, E.K. 1972. *Studies on terns with particular reference to feeding ecology*. Ph.D. Thesis, University of Durham.

Dunn, E.K. 1989. *The 1984 Azores Roseate Tern expedition*. Unpub. report to Royal Society for the Protection of Birds, Sandy.

Dunn, E.K. and Mead, C.J. 1982. Relationship between sardine fisheries and recovery rates of ringed terns in West Africa. *Seabird* 6:98–104.

Dunnet, G.M., Anderson, A. and Cormack, R.M. 1963. A study of survival of adult Fulmars with observations on the pre-laying exodus. *Brit. Birds* 56:2–18.

Dunnet, G.M. and Ollason, J.C. 1978. Survival and longevity in the Fulmar *Fulmarus glacialis*. *Ibis* 120:124–125.

Dunnet, G.M. and Ollason, J.C. 1982. The feeding dispersal of Fulmars *Fulmarus glacialis* in the breeding season. *Ibis* 124:359–361.

Dunnet, G.M., Ollason, J.C. and Anderson, A. 1979. A 28-year study of breeding Fulmars *Fulmarus glacialis* in Orkney. *Ibis* 121:293–300.

Elliot, J.E., Norstrom, R.J. and Keith, J.A. 1988. Organochlorines and eggshell thinning in Northern Gannets (*Sula bassanus*) from eastern Canada 1968–1984. *Env. Pollut.* 52:81–103.

Elliot, R.D. 1985. The Newfoundland turr hunt. p 23 in Tasker, M.L. (ed.) *Population and monitoring studies of seabirds*. Proc. 2nd Int. Conf. of the Seabird Group, Sandy.

Evans, P.G.H. (ed.) 1980. *Seabird counting manual: auks*. Seabird Group, Oxford.

Evans, P.G.H. 1984. Status and conservation of seabirds of northwest Europe (excluding Norway and the U.S.S.R.), pp 293–322 in Croxall, J.P., Evans, P.G.H. and Schreiber, R.W. (eds.) *Status and conservation of the world's seabirds*. ICBP Tech. Pub. No. 2, Cambridge.

Evans, P.G.H. and Bourne, W.R.P. 1978. Auks on Inishtearaght, 1968–1973, and the occurrence of disease in terns. *Irish Birds* 1:239–243.

Evans, P.G.H. and Lovegrove, R.R. 1974. The birds of the south west Irish islands. *Irish Bird Report 1973*: 33–64.

Evans, P.G.H. and Nettleship, D.N. 1985. Conservation of the Atlantic Alcidae, pp 428–488 in Nettleship, D.N. and Birkhead, T.R. (eds.) *The Atlantic Alcidae*. Academic Press, London.

Everett, M.J. 1982. Breeding Great and Arctic Skuas in Scotland in 1974–5. *Seabird Report* 6:50–58.

Everett, M.J., Hepburn, I., Ntiamoa-Baidu, Y. and Thomas, G.J. 1987. Roseate Terns in Britain and West Africa. *RSPB Conservation Review* 1: 56–58.

Ewins, P.J. 1985a. Colony attendance and censusing of Black Guillemots *Cepphus grylle* in Shetland. *Bird Study* 32:176–185.

Ewins, P.J. 1985b. Otter predation on Black Guillemots. *Brit. Birds* 78: 663–664.

Ewins, P.J. 1987. Opportunistic feeding of Black Guillemots *Cepphus grylle* at fishing vessels. *Seabird* 10:58–59.

Ewins, P.J., Ellis, P.M., Bird, D.R. and Prior, A. 1988. The distribution and status of Arctic and Great Skuas in Shetland 1985–86. *Scot. Birds* 15:9–20.

Ewins, P.J. and Kirk, D.A. 1988. The distribution of Shetland Black Guillemots *Cepphus grylle* outside the breeding season. *Seabird* 11:50–61.

Ewins, P.J. and Tasker, M.L. 1985. Breeding distribution of Black Guillemots *Cepphus grylle* in Orkney and Shetland, 1982–84. *Bird Study* 32:186–193.

Fasola, M. 1986. *Laridae* and *Sternidae* breeding in Italy: a report on the 1982–84 census project, pp 3–18 in MEDMARAVIS and Monbaillu, X. (eds.) *Mediterranean marine avifauna: population status and conservation*. NATO Adv. Sci. Insts., Ser. G: Ecol. Sci., Vol. 12, Springer-Verlag, Heidelberg.

Ferns, P.N. and Mudge, G.P. 1981. Accuracy of nest counts at a mixed colony of Herring and Lesser Black-backed Gulls. *Bird Study* 28:244–246.

Ferns, P.N. and Mudge, G.P. 1982. The feeding ecology of five species of gulls (*Aves: Larini*) in the inner Bristol Channel. *J. Zool., Lond.* 197:497–510.

Fisher, J. 1952a. *The Fulmar*. Collins, London.

Fisher, J. 1952b. A history of the Fulmar *Fulmarus* and its population problems. *Ibis* 94:334–54.

Fisher, J. 1966. The Fulmar population of Britain and Ireland, 1959. *Bird Study* 13:5–76.

Fisher, J. and Lockley, R.M. 1954. *Sea-birds*. Collins, London.

Fisher, J. and Waterston, G. 1941. Breeding distribution, history, and population of the Fulmar (*Fulmarus glacialis*) in the British Isles. *J. Anim. Ecol.* 10:204–272.

Flegg, J.M. 1972. The Puffin on St. Kilda. *Bird Study* 19:7–17.

Flegg, J.M. and Morgan, R.A. 1976. Mortality in British gulls. *Ringing and Migration* 1:65–74.

Forster, J.A. 1975. Electric fencing to protect Sandwich Terns against foxes. *Biol. Conserv.* 7: 85.

Fossi, C., Focardi, S. and Rezoni, A. 1984. Trace-metals and chlorinated hydrocarbons in birds' eggs from the Delta of the Danube. *Envir. Conserv.* 11:345–350.

Fowler, J.A. 1982. Leach's Petrels present on Ramna Stacks, Shetland. *Seabird Report* 6:93.

Furness, B.L. 1980. *Territoriality and feeding behaviour in the Arctic skua (Stercorarius parasiticus (L.))*. Ph.D. thesis, University of Aberdeen.

Furness, B.L. 1981b. Feeding strategies of the Arctic Skua *Stercorarius parasiticus* at Foula, Shetland, Scotland, Scotland, pp 89–98 in Cooper, J. (ed.) *Proc. Symp. Birds of the Sea and Shore. South African Seabird Group*, Cape Town.

Furness, R.W. 1977. Effects of Great Skuas on Arctic Skuas in Shetland. *Brit. Birds* 70:96–107.

Furness, R.W. 1978. Movements and mortality rates of Great Skuas ringed in Scotland. *Bird Study* 25:229–238.

Furness, R.W. 1981a. Colonisation of Foula by Gannets. *Scot. Birds* 11:211–213.

Furness, R.W. 1982. Methods used to census skua colonies. *Seabird Report* 6:44–47.

Furness, R.W. 1983. *The birds of Foula*. Brathay Hall Trust, Ambleside.

Furness, R.W. 1986. The conservation of Arctic and Great Skuas and their impact on agriculture. *Nature Conservancy Council Chief Scientist Directorate Report no. 642.*

Furness, R.W. 1987. *The skuas*. T. and A.D. Poyser, Calton.

Furness, R.W. 1988. Effects of changes in white-fish net-mesh size on scavenging seabird ecology. *Nature Conservancy Council Chief Scientist Directorate Report no. 799.*

Furness, R.W. 1989. Changes in diet and feeding ecology of seabirds on Foula, 1971–88, pp 22–23 in Heubeck, M. (ed.) *Seabirds and sandeels*. Proceedings of a seminar held in Lerwick, Shetland, 15–16 October 1988. Shetland Bird Club, Lerwick.

Furness, R.W. and Ainley, D.G. 1984. Threats to seabird populations presented by commercial fisheries, pp 701–708 in Croxall, J.P., Evans, P.G.H. and Schreiber, R.W. (eds.) *Status and conservation of the world's seabirds*. ICBP Tech. Pub. No. 2, Cambridge.

Furness, R.W. and Baillie, S.R. 1981. Factors affecting capture rates and biometrics of Storm Petrels on St. Kilda. *Ringing and Migration* 3:137–148.

Furness, R.W. and Birkhead, T.R. 1984. Seabird colony distributions suggest competition for food supplies during the breeding season. *Nature* 311:655–656.

Furness, R.W. and Hislop, J.R.G. 1981. Diets and feeding ecology of Great Skuas *Catharacta skua* during the breeding season in Shetland. *J. Zool., Lond.* 195.1–23.

Furness, R.W., Hudson, A.V. and Ensor, K. 1988. Interactions between scavenging seabirds and commercial fisheries around the British Isles, pp 232–260 in Burger, J. (ed.) *Seabirds and other marine vertebrates: competition, predation and other interactions.* Columbia University Press, New York.

Furness, R.W. and Monaghan, P. 1987. *Seabird ecology.* Blackie, Glasgow.

Furness, R.W. and Todd, C.M. 1984. Diets and feeding of Fulmars *Fulmarus glacialis* during the breeding season: a comparison between St Kilda and Shetland colonies. *Ibis* 126: 379–387.

Galbraith, H., Baillie, S.R., Furness, R.W. and Russell, S. 1986. Regional variations in the dispersal patterns of Shags *Phalacrocorax aristotelis* in northern Europe. *Ornis Scand.* 17:68–74.

Galbraith, H., Russell, S. and Furness, R.W. 1981. Movements and mortality of Isle of May Shags as shown by ringing recoveries. *Ringing and Migration* 3:181–189.

Gardarsson, A. 1982. Status of Icelandic seabird populations. *Viltrapport* 21:23.

Gardarsson, A. 1989. (A survey of gannet *Sula bassana* colonies in Iceland.) *Bliki* 7:1–22.

Gibson, J.A. 1985. Population studies of Clyde seabirds, part four. *Trans. Buteshire Nat. Hist. Soc.* 22:85–105.

Gibson, J.A. 1986. Recent changes in the status of some Clyde vertebrates. *Proc. Roy. Soc. Edinburgh* 90B:451–467.

Gochfeld, M. 1983. World status and distribution of the Roseate Tern, a threatened species. *Biol. Conserv.* 25:103–125.

Golovkin, A.N. 1984. Seabirds nesting in the USSR: the status and protection of populations, pp 473–486 in Croxall, J.P., Evans, P.G.H. and Shreiber, R.W. (eds.) *Status and conservation of the world's seabirds.* ICBP Tech. Pub. No.2, Cambridge.

Goodlad, J. 1989. Industrial fishing in Shetland waters, pp 50–56 in Heubeck, M. (ed.) *Seabirds and sandeels.* Proceedings of a seminar held in Lerwick, Shetland, 15–16 October 1988. Shetland Bird Club, Lerwick.

Gorke, M., Hartwig, E. and Schrey, E. 1988. Feeding ecology of Black-headed Gull *Larus ridibundus* in German coastal areas—a review, p 21 in Tasker, M.L. (ed.) *Seabird food and feeding ecology.* Proc. of Third Int. Conf. of the Seabird Group, Sandy.

Gray, M. 1988. *Some aspects of the breeding biology of the Black Guillemot* (Cepphus grylle [L.]) *in the Orkney Islands.* B.Sc. thesis, University of Ulster, Coleraine.

Green, R.E., Baillie, S. and Avery, M.I. in press. Can ringing recoveries help explain the population dynamics of British terns? *The Ring*.

Green, R.E. and Hirons, M.G.J. 1988. The effect of nest failure and spread of laying dates on counts of breeding birds. *Ornis Scand.* 19:76–78.

Greenwood, J.G. 1987. Winter visits by Black Guillemots *Cepphus grylle* to an Irish breeding site. *Bird Study* 34:135–136.

Greenwood, J.G. 1988. The Northern Ireland Black Guillemot survey 1987. *Irish Nat. J.* 22:490–491.

Greig, S.A., Coulson, J.C. and Monaghan, P. 1986. A comparison of foraging at refuse tips by three species of gull (*Laridae*). *J. Zool., Lond.* 210:459–472.

Gribble, F.C. 1976. A census of Black-headed Gull colonies. *Bird Study* 23:135–145.

Grimes, L.G. 1987. *The birds of Ghana; an annotated checklist*. British Ornithologists Union, London.

Gurney, J.H. 1913. *The Gannet. A bird with a history*. Witherby, London.

Gurnewy, J.H. 1919. Breeding stations of the Black-headed Gull in the British Isles. *Trans. Norfolk Nat. Soc.* 10:416–447.

Guyot, I. 1988. Relationships between Shag feeding areas and human fishing activities in Corsica (Mediterranean Sea), pp 22–23 in Tasker, M.L. (ed.) *Seabird food and feeding ecology*. Proc. of Third Int. Conf. of the Seabird Group, Sandy.

Haddon, P.C. and Knight, R.C. 1983. *A guide to Little Tern conservation*, RSPB, Sandy.

Hamer, K.C. Furness, R.W. and Caldow, R.W.G. in press. The effects of changes in food availability on the breeding ecology of Great Skuas *Catharacta skua* in Shetland. *J. Zool., Lond.*

Hamilton, F.D. 1962. Census of Black-headed Gull colonies in Scotland, 1958. *Bird Study* 9:72–80.

Harris, M.P. 1962a. Migration of the British Lesser Black-backed Gulls as shown by ringing data. *Bird Study* 9: 174–182.

Harris, M.P. 1962b. Recoveries of ringed Great Black-backed Gulls. *Bird Study* 9:192–197.

Harris, M.P. 1964. Recoveries of ringed Herring Gulls. *Bird Study* 11:183–191.

Harris, M.P. 1965. The food of some *Larus* gulls. *Ibis* 107:43–53.

Harris, M.P. 1966a. Age of return to colony, age of breeding and adult survival in Manx Shearwaters. *Bird Study* 13:84–95.

Harris, M.P. 1966b. Breeding biology of the Manx Shearwater *Puffinus puffinus*. *Ibis* 108:17–33.

Harris, M.P. 1970. Rates and causes of increases of some British gull populations. *Bird Study* 17:325–335.

Harris, M.P. 1972. Inter-island movements of Manx Shearwaters. *Bird Study* 19:167–171.

Harris, M.P. 1976a. Present status of the Puffin in Britain and Ireland. *Brit. Birds* 69:239–264.

Harris, M.P. 1976b. Inter-colony movements of Farne Islands Puffins. *Trans. Nat. Hist. Soc. Northumbria* 42:115–118.

Harris, M.P. 1977. Puffins on the Isle of May. *Scot. Birds* 9:285–290.

Harris, M.P. 1984a. *The Puffin*. T. and A.D. Poyser, Calton.

Harris, M.P. 1984b. Movement and mortality patterns of North Atlantic Puffins as shown by ringing. *Bird Study* 31:131–140.

Harris, M.P. 1989a. Development of monitoring seabird populations and performance. *Nature Conservancy Council Chief Scientist Directorate Report* no. 941.

Harris, M.P. 1989b. Variations in the correction factor used for converting counts of individual Guillemots *Uria aalge* into breeding pairs. *Ibis* 131:85–93.

Harris, M.P. and Forbes, R. 1987. The effect of date on counts of nests of Shags *Phalacrocorax aristotelis*. *Bird Study* 34:187–190.

Harris, M.P. and Hislop, J.R.G. 1978. The food of young Puffins, *Fratercula arctica*. *J. Zool., Lond.* 185:213–236.

Harris, M.P. and Murray, S. 1977. Puffins on St. Kilda. *Brit. Birds* 70:50–65.

Harris, M.P. and Murray, S. 1978. *Birds of St. Kilda*. Institute of Terrestrial Ecology, Cambridge.

Harris, M.P. and Wanless, S. 1984. The effect of the wreck of seabirds in February 1983 on auk populations on the Isle of May (Fife). *Bird Study* 31: 103–110.

Harris, M.P. and Wanless, S. 1988. The breeding biology of the Guillemot *Uria aalge* on the Isle of May over a six year period. *Ibis* 130:172–192.

Harris, M.P. and Wanless, S. 1989. The breeding biology of Razorbills *Alca torda* on the Isle of May. *Bird Study* 36:105–114.

Harris, M.P. and Wanless, S. 1990. Breeding success of British Kittiwakes *Rissa tridactyla* in 1986–88: evidence for changing conditions in the northern North Sea. *J. Appl. Ecol.* 27:172–187.

Harris, M.P., Wanless, S. and Rothery, P. 1983. Assessing changes in the numbers of Guillemots *Uria aalge*. *Bird Study* 30:57–66.

Harris, M.P., Wanless, S. and Smith, R.W.J. 1987. The breeding seabirds of the Firth of Forth. Scotland. *Proc. Roy. Soc. Edinburgh* 93B: 521–533.

Harvey, P. 1983. Breeding seabird populations, Isles of Scilly. *Nature Conservancy Council Report* SW England Region, Taunton.

Harvie-Brown, J.A. 1912. The Fulmar: its past and present distribution as a breeding species in the British Isles. *Scot. Nat.* 1912:97–102, 121–132.

Hatch, J.J. 1984. Rapid increase of Double-crested Cormorants nesting in southern New England. *Amer. Birds* 38:984–988.

Hémery, G., d'Elbee, E. and Terrasse, J-F. 1986. Régulation d'une population de Pétrels-tempête *Hydrobates pelagicus* par reproduction intermittente. *C.R. Acad. Sci. Paris* 303:353–356.

Hémery, G., Pasquet, E. and Thibault, J.-C. 1988. Réflexions sur les populations d'oiseaux marins en France. *Alauda* 56:1–7.

Henry, J. and Monnat, J.Y. 1981. *Oiseaux marins de la façade atlantique Française*. Société pour l'Etude et al Protection de la Nature en Bretagne, Brest.

Hepburn, I.R. 1973. *Aspects of the breeding biology of the Fulmar* Fulmarus glacialis *on the Monach Islands and Heisker in 1973, with particular reference to behaviour*. B.Sc. thesis, University of Ulster, Coleraine.

Hepburn, I.R. 1986. In search of Roseate Terns. *BTO News* 146:12–13.

Hepburn, I.R. and Randall, R. 1975. Nest site distribution of the Fulmar (*Fulmarus glacialis*) within the Monach Isles National Nature Reserve, Outer Hebrides, U.K. *J. Biogeog.* 2:223–228.

Heubeck, M. (ed.) 1989a. *Seabirds and sandeels: proceedings of a seminar held in Lerwick, Shetland, 15–16 October 1988.* Shetland Bird Club, Lerwick.

Heubeck, M. 1989b. Breeding success of Shetland's seabirds: Arctic Skua, Kittiwake, Guillemot, Razorbill and Puffin, pp 11–18 in Heubeck, M. (ed.) *Seabirds and sandeels: proceedings of a seminar held in Lerwick, Shetland, 15–16 October 1988.* Shetland Bird Club, Lerwick.

Heubeck, M. and Richardson, M. 1980. Mortality following the 'Esso Bernicia' oil spill, Shetland, December 1978. Shetland Bird Club, Lerwick.

Heubeck, M., Richardson, M.G. and Dore, C.P. 1985. Monitoring numbers of Kittiwakes *Rissa tridactyla* in Shetland. *Seabird* 9:32–42.

Hickling, R.A.O. 1977. Inland wintering of gulls in England and Wales, 1973. *Bird Study* 24:79–88.

Hickling, R.A.O. 1986. Herring Gull, pp 240–241 in Lack, P. *The atlas of wintering birds in Britain and Ireland.* T. and A.D. Poyser, Calton.

Hildén, O. 1988. Recent changes in the seabird populations in Finland. Proc. 5th conf. Baltic Birds.

Hislop, J.R.G. and Harris, M.P. 1985. Recent changes in the food of young Puffins *Fratercula arctica* on the Isle of May in relation to fish stocks. *Ibis* 127:234–239.

HMSO 1981. Wildlife and Countryside Act 1981, as amended in 1985. HMSO, London.

Holdgate, M. (ed.) 1971. The Seabird wreck in the Irish Sea, autumn 1969. *NERC Public. Ser. C*, No. 4.

Horton, N., Brough, T., Fletcher, M.R., Rochard, J.B.A and Stanley, P.I. 1984. The winter distribution of foreign Black-headed Gulls in the British Isles. *Bird Study* 31:171–136.

Hudson, A.V. 1982. Great Black-backed Gulls on Great Saltee Island, 1981. *Irish Birds* 2:167–175.

Hudson, A.V. 1986. *The biology of seabirds utilising fishery waste in Shetland.* Ph.D. Thesis, University of Glasgow.

Hudson, A.V. and Furness, R. 1988. Utilization of discarded fish by scavenging behind whitefish trawlers in Shetland. *J. Zool., Lond.* 215:151–166.

Hudson, A.V. and Furness, R. 1989. The behaviour of seabirds foraging at fishing boats around Shetland. *Ibis* 131:225–237.

Hudson, P.J. 1979. *The behaviour and survival of auks.* D.Phil. thesis, University of Oxford, Oxford.

Hudson, R. 1973. *Early and late dates for summer migrants.* BTO Guide 15. BTO, Tring.

Hunt, G.L., Eppley, Z.A. and Schneider, D.C. 1986. Reproductive performance of seabirds: the importance of population and colony size. *Auk* 103:306–317.

Hurford, C. 1985. *Gull trends in Glamorgan 1970–84.* Cardiff Nat. Soc., Orn. Section, Cardiff.

Hutchinson, C. 1989. *Birds in Ireland.* T. and A.D. Poyser, Calton.

Ilyichev, V.D. and Flint, V.E. 1982. *The birds of the USSR: Divers, grebes, tubenoses.* Nauka, Moscow.

Ilyichev, V.D. and Zubakin, V.A. 1988. *The birds of the USSR: Lari.* Nauka, Moscow.

Isenmann, P. and Czajkowski, M.A. 1978. Note sur un recensement de Laridés entre Nice et Naples en décembre 1977. *Riv. Ital. di Orn.*, 48:143–148.

James, P.C. 1984. The status and conservation of seabirds in the Mediterranean, pp 371–376 in Croxall, J.P., Evans, P.G.H. and Schreiber, R.W. (eds.) *Status and conservation of the world's seabirds.* ICBP Tech. Pub. No.2, Cambridge.

James, P.C. and Robertson, H.A. 1985. The use of playback recordings to detect and census nocturnal burrowing seabirds. *Seabird* 8:12–20.

Jehl, J.R. 1984. Conservation problems of seabirds in Baja California and the Pacific northwest, pp 41–48 in Croxall, J.P., Evans, P.G.H. and Schreiber, R.W. (eds.) *Status and conservation of the world's seabirds.* ICBP Tech. Pub. No.2, Cambridge.

Johansen, O. 1975. (The relation between breeding grounds and wintering grounds in the Shag *Phalacrocorax aristotelis* in Norway as shown by ringing recoveries.) *Sterna* 14:1–21.

Jones, P.H. and Tasker, M.L. 1982. *Seabird movements around the coasts of Great Britain and Ireland.* Nature Conservancy Council/Seabird Group, Aberdeen.

Kelly, T.C. and Walton, G.A. 1977. The auk population crash of 1968–69 on Inishtearaght: a review. *Irish Birds* 1:16–36.

Kilpi, M. 1987. Annual variations in the efficiency of adult Herring Gull *Larus argentatus* counts. *Ornis Fenn.* 64:76–77.

Kilpi, M. and Saurola, P. 1984. Migration and wintering strategies of juvenile and adult *Larus marinus*, *Larus argentatus* and *Larus fuscus* from Finland. *Ornis Fenn.* 61:1–8.

Kirkham, I.R. and Nettleship, D.N. 1987. Status of the Roseate tern in Canada. *J. Field Ornithol.* 58:505–515.

Knox, A.G. and Bell, M.V. 1979. Systematic list, pp 6–31 in Knox, A.G. (ed.) *North-East Scotland Bird Report 1978.* North-East Scotland Bird Club, Aberdeen.

Kondratiev, A.J. in press. The status and conservation of seabirds nesting in north-east USSR, in Croxall, J.P. (ed.) *Supplement to Status and conservation of the world's seabirds.* Cambridge University Press/ICBP, Cambridge.

Kunzlik, P. 1989. Small fish around Shetland, pp 38–47 in Heubeck, M. (ed.) *Seabirds and sandeels*: proceedings of a seminar held in Lerwick, Shetland 15–16 October 1988. Shetland Bird Club, Lerwick.

Kuyt, E., Johnson, B. E., Taylor, F.S. and Barry, T.W. 1976. Black Guillemots' breeding range extended into the western Canadian arctic. *Can. Field-Nat.* 90:75–76.

Lack, D. 1948. Notes on the ecology of the Robin. *Ibis* 90:252–279.

Lack, D. 1966. *Population studies of birds.* Clarendon Press, Oxford.

Lack, P. 1986. *The atlas of wintering birds in Britain and Ireland.* T. and A.D. Poyser, Calton.

Langham, N.P.E. 1971. Seasonal movements of British terns in the Atlantic Ocean. *Bird Study* 18: 155–175.

Langham, N.P.E. 1972. Chick survival in the terns (*Sterna* spp.) with particular reference to the Common Tern. *J. Anim. Ecol.* 41:385–395.

Lebreton, J.D. and Isenmann, P. 1976. Dynamique de la population camarguaise de Mouettes rieuses (*Larus ridibundus*): un modèle mathématique. *Terre et Vie* 30:529–549.

le Grand, G., Emmerson, K. and Martin, A. 1984. The status and conservation of seabirds in Macaronesian Islands, pp 377–392 in Croxall, J.P., Evans, P.G.H. and Schreiber, R.W. (eds.) *Status and conservation of the world's seabirds*. ICBP Tech. Pub. No.2, Cambridge.

Lensink, C.J. 1984. The status and conservation of seabirds in Alaska, pp. 13–28 in Croxall, J.P., Evans, P.G.H. and Schreiber, R.W. (eds.) *Status and conservation of the world's seabirds*. ICBP Tech. Pub. No.2, Cambridge.

Lid, G. 1981. Reproduction of the Puffin on Røst in the Lofoten Islands in 1964–1980. *Fauna Norv. Ser. C, Cinclus* 4:30–39.

Litvinenko, N. and Shibaev, Y. in press. The status and conservation of seabirds nesting in south-east USSR, in Croxall, J.P. (ed.) *Supplement to Status and conservation of the world's seabirds*. Cambridge University Press/ICBP, Cambridge.

Lloyd, C.S. 1974. Movement and survival of British Razorbills. *Bird Study* 21:102–116.

Lloyd, C.S. 1975. Timing and frequency of census counts in cliff-nesting auks. *Brit. Birds* 68:507–513.

Lloyd, C.S. 1982a. The seabirds of Great Saltee. *Irish Birds* 2:1–37.

Lloyd, C.S. 1982b. An inventory of seabird breeding colonies in the Republic of Ireland. *Forest and Wildlife Service Report*, Dublin.

Lloyd, C.S. 1985. *The travelling naturalists*. Croom Helm, Beckenham.

Lloyd, C.S., Bibby, C.J. and Everett, M.J. 1975. Breeding terns in Britain and Ireland in 1969–74. *Brit. Birds* 68:221–237.

Lloyd, C.S. and North, S.G. 1987. The seabirds of Troup and Pennan Heads 1979–86. *Scot. Birds* 14:199–204.

Lloyd, C.S. and Perrins, C.M. 1977. Survival and age at first breeding in the Razorbill (*Alca torda*). *Bird-Banding* 48:239–252.

Lloyd, C.S. and Tasker, M.L. 1987. Seabirds breeding on the coast of north-east Scotland. *North-east Scotland Bird Rep.* 1986:42–50.

Lloyd, C.S., Thomas, G.J., Macdonald, J.W., Borland, E.D., Standring, K. and Smart, J.L. 1976. Wild bird mortality caused by botulism in Britain, 1975. *Biol. Conserv.* 10:119–129.

Lockley, R.M. 1942. *Shearwaters*. Dent, London.

Lockley, R.M. 1983. *Flight of the Storm Petrel*. David & Charles, Newton Abbott.

Macaulay, K. 1764. *The history of St Kilda*. Beckett and de Hondt, London.

MacDonald, J.W. and Standring, K.T. 1978. An outbreak of botulism in gulls on the Firth of Forth, Scotland. *Biol. Conserv.* 14:149–155.

Macdonald, M.A. 1977a. An analysis of recoveries of British-ringed Fulmars. *Bird Study* 24:208–214.

Macdonald, M.A. 1977b. Pre-laying exodus of the Fulmar (*Fulmarus glacialis*). *Ornis Scand.* 8:33–37.

Macdonald, R.A. 1987. The breeding population and distribution of the Cormorant in Ireland. *Irish Birds* 3:405–416.

McGrath, D. and Walsh, P.M. 1985. Population decline and current status of breeding Kittiwakes in east Waterford. *Irish Birds* 3:75–84.

Maguire, E.J. 1978. Breeding of the Storm Petrel and the Manx Shearwater in Kintyre, Argyll. *Western Naturalist* 7:63–66.

Maguire, E.J. 1980. The status of storm petrels in the Clyde and Forth. *Scot. Birds* 11:51–53.

Mainwood, A.R. 1975. Leach's Petrels breeding on Foula. *Scot. Birds* 8:321–323.

Martin, A.R. 1989. The diet of Atlantic Puffin *Fratercula arctica* and Northern Gannet *Sula bassana* chicks at a Shetland colony during a period of changing prey availability. *Bird Study* 30:170–180.

Massa, B. and Catalisano, A. 1986. Status and conservation of the Storm Petrel in Sicily, pp 143–152 in MEDMARAVIS and Monbailliu, X. *Mediterranean marine avifauna; population studies and conservation*. NATO Adv. Sci. Insts., Ser. G: Ecol. Sci., vol. 12, Springer-Verlag, Heidelberg.

Matthews, J. and North, S.G. 1989. Gannets breeding on mainland Scotland. *Scot. Birds*. 15:132–133.

Mead, C.J. 1974. Results of ringing auks in Britain and Ireland. *Bird Study* 21:45–86.

Mead, C. 1989. Mono-kill and Auk netfax. *BTO News* 163:1 & 8.

Mead, C.J. and Clark, J.A. 1988. Report on bird ringing in Britain and Ireland for 1987. *Ringing and Migration* 9:169–204.

MEDMARAVIS and Monbailliu, 1986. *Mediterranean marine avifauna; population studies and conservation*. NATO Adv. Sci. Insts., Ser. G: Ecol. Sci., vol. 12, Springer-Verlag, Heidelberg.

Meek, E.R., Booth, C.J., Reynolds, P. and Ribbands, B. 1985. Breeding skuas in Orkney. *Seabird* 8:21–33.

Melville, D. 1973. Birds and salmon nets. *Seabird Report 1971:* 47–50.

Mills, D.H. 1969. The food of the Cormorant at two breeding colonies on the east coast of Scotland. *Scot. Birds* 5:268–276.

Møller, A.P. 1978. (Distribution, population size and changes in gulls *Larinae* breeding in Denmark, with a review of the situations in other parts of Europe.) *Dansk Orn. Foren. Tidsskr.* 72:15–39.

Møller, A.P. 1981a. Migration of European Sandwich Tern, *Sterna s. sandvicencis* I. *Die Vogelwarte* 31:74–94.

Møller, A.P. 1981b. Migration of European Sandwich Tern, *Sterna s. sandvicensis* II. *Die Vogelwarte* 31:149–168.

Monaghan, P. 1979. Aspects of the breeding biology of Herring Gulls *Larus argentatus* in urban colonies. *Ibis* 121:475–481.

Monaghan, P. and Coulson, J.C. 1977. The status of large gulls nesting on buildings. *Bird Study* 24:89–104.

Monaghan, P., Shedden, C.B., Ensor, K., Fricker, C.R. and Girdwood, R.W.A. 1985. Salmonella carriage by Herring Gulls in the Clyde area of Scotland in relation to their feeding ecology. *J. Appl. Ecol.* 22:669–680.

Monaghan, P. and Uttley, J. 1989. Breeding success of Shetland's seabirds: Arctic Tern and Common Tern, pp 3–4 in Heubeck, M. (ed.) *Seabirds and sandeels*: proceedings of a seminar held in Lerwick, Shetland, 15–16 October 1988. Shetland Bird Club, Lerwick.

Monaghan, P., Uttley, J.D., Burns, M.D., Thaine, C. and Blackwood, J. 1989.

The relationship between food supply, reproductive effort and breeding success in Arctic Terns *Sterna paradisaea*. *J. Anim. Ecol.* 58:261–274.

Monaghan, P. and Zonfrillo, B. 1986. Population dynamics of seabirds breeding in the Firth of Clyde. *Proc. Roy. Soc. Edinburgh* 90B: 363–375.

Montevecchi, W.A., Kirkham, I.R., Purchase, R. and Harvey, B.D. 1980. Colonies of northern gannets in Newfoundland. *Osprey* 11:2–8.

Moore, A.S. 1985. The Fulmar in the Isle of Man 1927–84. *Peregrine* 6:47–59.

Moore, A.S. 1987. The numbers and distribution of seabirds breeding on the Isle of Man 1985–86. *Peregrine* 6:64–80.

Mudge, G.P. 1986. Trends of population change at colonies of cliff-nesting seabirds in the Moray Firth. *Proc. Roy. Soc. Edinburgh* 91B:73–80.

Mudge, G.P. 1988. An evaluation of current methodology for monitoring changes in the breeding populations of Guillemots *Uria aalge*. *Bird Study* 35:1–9.

Murray, S. and Wanless, S. 1986. The status of the Gannet in Scotland 1984–85. *Scot. Birds* 14:74–85.

Nelson, J.B. 1978. *The Gannet.* T. and A.D. Poyser, Berkhamstead.

Nelson, J.B. 1980. *Seabirds, their biology and ecology.* Hamlyn, London.

NERC 1983. *Contaminants in marine top predators.* NERC report series C, No. 23.

Nettleship, D.N. 1972. Breeding success of the Common Puffin (*Fratercula arctica*, L.) on different habitats at Great Island, Newfoundland. *Ecol. Mon.* 42:239–268.

Nettleship, D.N. 1974. Northern Fulmar colonies on the south coast of Devon Island. *Auk* 91:412.

Nettleship, D.N. 1975. A recent decline of Gannets *Morus bassanus* on Bonaventure Island, Quebec. *Can. Field-Nat.* 89:125–133.

Nettleship, D.N. 1976. Gannets in Northern America: present numbers and recent changes. *Wilson Bull.* 88:300–313.

Nettleship, D.N. and Birkhead, T.R. (eds.) 1985. *The Atlantic Alcidae.* Academic Press, London.

Nettleship, D.N. and Chapdelaine, G. 1988. Population size and status of the Northern Gannet *Sula bassanus* in North America. *J. Field Ornith.* 59:120–127.

Nettleship, D.N. and Evans, P.G.H. 1985. Distribution and status of the Atlantic Alcidae, pp 54–154 in Nettleship, D.N. and Birkhead, T.R. (eds.) *The Atlantic Alcidae.* Academic Press, London.

Nettleship, D.N. and Lock, A.R. 1973. Tenth census of seabirds in the sanctuaries of the North Shore of the Gulf of St. Lawrence. *Can. Field-Nat.* 87:395–402.

Nisbet, I.C.T. 1973. Terns in Massachusetts: present numbers and historical changes. *Bird-Banding* 44:27–55.

Nisbet, I.C.T. 1980. Status and trends of the Roseate Tern *Sterna dougallii* in North America and the Caribbean. Report to US Fish and Wildlife Service, Office of Endangered Species.

Nørrevang, A. 1986. Traditions of sea bird fowling in the Faroes: an ecological basis for sustained fowling. *Ornis Scand.* 17:275–281.

O'Donald, P. and Davis, J.W.F. 1975. Demography and selection in a population of Arctic Skuas. *Heredity* 35:75–83.

Okill, D. 1985. Update on breeding Cormorants. *Shetland Bird Club Newsletter* 59:2–4.

Okill, D. 1989. Breeding success of Shetland's seabirds: Red-throated Diver, Fulmar, Gannet, Cormorant and Shag, pp 6–10 in Heubeck, M. (ed.) *Seabirds and sandeels*; proceedings of a seminar held in Lerwick, Shetland, 15–16 October 1988. Shetland Bird Club, Lerwick.

Oldén, B., Peters, M. and Kollberg, E. 1985. (Seabird mortality in gill-net fishing, southeast Kattegat, South Sweden.) *Anser* 24:159–180.

O'Meara, M. 1975. Building nesting Herring Gulls (*Larus argentatus*, Pontoppidan) in Co. Waterford. *Irish Nats. J.* 18:152–153.

O'Meara, M. 1979. Kittiwakes nesting on light standards in Co. Waterford. *Irish Birds* 1:407–409.

Parslow, J.L.F. 1967. Changes in status among breeding birds in Britain and Ireland. *Brit. Birds* 60:2–47.

Parslow, J.L.F. 1973. Pollutants in Guillemot and Kittiwake eggs from Lundy. *Lundy Field Soc. Ann. Rep.* 23:1–7.

Parslow, J.L.F. and Jefferies, D.J. 1973. Relationship between organochlorine residues in the livers and whole bodies of guillemots. *Envir. Pollut.* 5: 87–101.

Parslow, J.L.F. and Jefferies, D.J. 1977. Gannets and toxic chemicals. *Brit. Birds* 70:366–372.

Parsons, J. and Duncan, N. 1978. Recoveries and dispersal of Herring Gulls from the Isle of May. *J. Anim. Ecol.* 47:993–1005.

Paterson, A.M. 1989. Second MEDMARAVIS symposium. *Seabird Group Newsletter* 54:7–9.

Peacock, M.A., Beveridge, F.M. and Campbell, L.H. 1985. Shetland moorland breeding birds survey 1985. *Royal Society for the Protection of Birds Report.*

Pearson, T.H. 1968. Feeding biology of sea-bird species breeding on the Farne Islands, Northumberland. *J. Anim. Ecol.* 37:521–552.

Perrins, C.M. 1968. The number of Manx Shearwaters on Skokholm. *Skokholm Bird Observatory Rep. 1967:* 23–29.

Perrins, C.M. 1975. Records from the national census of breeding seabirds 1969–70. *Bird Study* 22:254.

Petersen, A. 1981. *Breeding biology and feeding ecology of Black Guillemots.* D.Phil. thesis, University of Oxford.

Piatt, J.F. and Nettleship, D.N. 1985. Diving depths of four alcids. *Auk* 102: 293–297.

Potts, G.R. 1968. Success of eggs of the Shag on the Farne Islands, Northumberland, in relation to their content of dieldrin and pp'DDE. *Nature* 217: 1282–1284.

Potts, G.R. 1969. The influence of eruptive movements, age, population size and other factors on the survival of the Shag (*Phalacrocorax aristotelis* (L).) *J. Anim. Ecol.* 38: 53–102.

Potts, G.R., Coulson, J.C. and Deans, I.R. 1980. Population dynamics and breeding success of the Shag, *Phalacrocorax aristotelis*, on the Farne Islands, Northumberland. *J. Anim. Ecol.* 49:465–484.

Powers, K.D. and Rumage, W.T. 1978. Effect of the 'Argo Merchant' oil spill on bird populations off the New England coast, 15 December 1976–January

1977, pp 142–148 in: *In the wake of the 'Argo Merchant'*. Center for Oceanographic Management Studies, University of Rhode Island, Kingston.

Preston, K. 1979. Twenty-sixth Irish Bird Report 1978. *Irish Birds* 1:413–499.

Pritchard, D.E. 1981. *Monitoring for conservation: the Kittiwake in Shetland*. M.Sc. thesis, University College, London.

Przybysz, A., Przybysz, J.P. and Przybysz, K. 1985. (The Cormorant (*Phalacrocorax carbo*) in Poland in 1980 and 1981.) *Przegl. Zool.* 29:199–213.

Rand, R.W. 1963. The biology of guano producing seabirds. 4. Composition of colonies on the South West African islands. *Investl. Rep. Div. Sea Fish. S. Afr.* 46:1–26.

Reed, T.M., Langslow, D.R. and Symonds, F.L. 1983. Arctic skuas in Caithness, 1979 and 1980. *Bird Study* 30:24–26.

Rennie, F.W. 1988. The status and distribution of the Great Skua in the Western Isles. *Scot. Birds* 15:80–82.

Reynolds, P. and Booth, C.J. 1987. Orkney Cormorants—an aerial census of the breeding population. *Scot. Birds* 14:131–137.

Richardson, M.G. 1985. Status and distribution of the Kittiwakes in Shetland in 1981. *Bird Study* 32:11–18.

Rodeway, M.S. in press. Status and conservation of breeding seabirds in British Columbia, in Croxall, J.P. (ed.) *Supplement to Status and conservation of the world's seabirds*. Cambridge University Press/ICBP, Cambridge.

Rooth, J. 1989. (Numbers of Sandwich Terns *Sterna sandvicensis* breeding in the Netherlands in 1961–88.) *Limosa* 62:121–124.

Ross, A. 1988. *Controlling nature's predators on fish farms*. Marine Conservation Society, Ross-on-Wye.

Rothery, P., Wanless, S. and Harris, M.P. 1988. Analysis of counts from monitoring Guillemots in Britain and Ireland. *J. Anim. Ecol.* 57:1–19.

Røv, N. 1985. Distribution and numbers of some seabird species breeding on the Norwegian coast with reference to the National Seabird Mapping Programme, pp 15–16 in Tasker, M.L. *Populations and monitoring studies of seabirds*. Proc. 2nd. Int. Conf. of the Seabird Group, Sandy.

Røv, N. 1986. (The breeding population of Lesser Black-backed Gulls (*Larus fuscus*) in Norway with emphasis on *L. f. fuscus*.) *Var Fuglefauna* 9:79–84.

Røv, N. and Strann, K.B. 1986. The present status, breeding distribution and colony size of the Cormorant (*Phalacrocorax carbo carbo*) in Norway. *Fauna Norv. Ser. C, Cinclus* 10:39–44.

Rutledge, R.F. 1966. *Ireland's birds*. Witherby, London.

Salomonsen, F. 1965. Geographic variation of the Fulmar (*Fulmaris glacialis*) and zones of the marine environment in the North Atlantic. *Auk* 85:327–355.

Salomonsen, F. 1979. Marine birds in the Danish Monarchy and their conservation, pp 267–287 in Bartonek, J.C. and Nettleship, D.N. *Conservation of marine birds of northern North America*. U.S. Dept. of the Interior, Fish and Wildl. Serv., Wildlife Research Rep. No. 11, Washington, D.C.

Schaffner, F.C. 1986. Trends in Elegant Tern and Northern Anchovy populations in California. *Condor* 88:347–354.

Schneider, D.C., Harrison, N.M. and Hunt, G.L.Jr. 1987. Variations in the occurrence of marine birds at fronts in the Bering Sea. *Estuarine, Coastal and Shelf Sci.* 25:135–141.

Sharrock, J.T.R. (ed.) 1976. *The atlas of breeding birds in Britain and Ireland.* British Trust for Ornithology and Irish Wildbird Conservancy, Tring and Dublin.

Sherman, K., Jones, C., Sullivan, L., Smith, W., Berrieu, P. and Ejsymont, L. 1981. Congruent shifts in sand eel abundance in western and eastern North Atlantic ecosystems. *Nature* 291: 486–489.

Slater, C. 1987. Fulmar population changes. *Trans. Norfolk Norwich Nat. Soc.* 27:421–423.

Smith, R.W.J. 1976. Forth islands bird counts 1976. *Edinb. Nat. Hist. Soc. J.* 1976: 24–28.

Sowls, A.L., Hatch, S.A. and Lensink, C.J. 1978. *Catalog of Alaskan seabird colonies.* FWS/OBS-78/78. U.S. Fish and Wildl. Serv., Biological Services Program, Anchorage, Alaska.

Spencer, R. and Rare Breeding Birds Panel. 1988. Rare breeding birds in the U.K. in 1986. *Brit. Birds* 81:417–443.

Springer, A.M., Roseneau, D.G., Lloyd, D.S., McRoy, C.P. and Murphy, E.C. 1986. Seabird responses to fluctuating prey availability in the eastern Bering Sea. *Mar. Ecol. Progr. Ser.* 32:1–12.

Stanley, P.I., Brough, T., Fletcher, M.R., Horton, N. and Rochard, J.B.A. 1981. The origins of Herring Gulls wintering inland in south-east England. *Bird Study* 28:123–132.

Steel, T. 1965. *The life and death of St. Kilda.* National Trust for Scotland, Edinburgh.

Stewart, B. 1986. Expansion of roof nesting by Common Gulls in Aberdeen. *Scot. Bird News* 4:2.

Stowe, T.J. 1982. Recent population trends in cliff-breeding seabirds in Britain and Ireland. *Ibis* 124:502–510.

Stowe, T.J. and Harris, M.P. 1984. Status of Guillemots and Razorbills in Britain and Ireland. *Seabird* 7:5–18.

Stowe, T.J. and Underwood, L.A. 1984. Oil spillages affecting seabirds in the United Kingdom, 1966–1983. *Mar. Poll. Bull.* 15:147–152.

Sullivan, M.A. 1985. Common Gulls nesting successfully on a roof in Aberdeen. *Scot. Birds* 13:229.

Sutcliffe, S.J. 1986. Changes in the gull populations of SW Wales. *Bird Study* 33:91–97.

Swann, R.L. and Ramsay, A.D.K. 1984. Long-term seabird studies on Canna. *Scot. Birds* 13:55–56.

Tasker, M.L., Jones, P.H., Blake, B.F. and Dixon, T.J. 1985a. The marine distribution of the Gannet *Sula bassana* in the North Sea. *Bird Study* 32:82–90.

Tasker, M.L., Jones, P.H., Blake, B.F. and Dixon, T.J. 1985b. Distribution and feeding habits of the Great Skua *Catharacta skua* in the North Sea. *Seabird* 8:34–43.

Tasker, M.L., Moore, P.R. and Schofield, R.A. 1988. The seabirds of St Kilda, 1987. *Scot. Birds* 15:21–29.

Tasker, M.L. and Pienkowski, M.W. 1987. *Vulnerable concentrations of birds in the North Sea.* Nature Conservancy Council, Peterborough.

Tasker, M.L. and Reynolds, P. 1983. A survey of 'Tystie (Black Guillemot)

Cepphus grylle distribution in Orkney, April 1983. *Nature Conservancy Council report*, NE Scotland region, Aberdeen.

Tasker, M.L. and Webb, A. 1984. A survey of Tystie (Black Guillemot) *Cepphus grylle* distribution in Orkney, April 1984. *Nature Conservancy Council report*, Chief Scientist Team, Huntingdon.

Tasker, M.L., Webb, A., Hall, A.J., Pienkowski, M.W. and Langslow, D.R. 1987. *Seabirds in the North Sea. Nature Conservancy Council*, Peterborough.

Tasker, M.L., Webb, A., Murray, S. and Holt, R. 1986. The dispersal of auks in the northern North Sea, June to September 1985. *Nature Conservancy Council Chief Scientist Directorate Report* no. 589.

Tasker, M.L. and Webb, A.W. in prep. The size and distribution of the Black Guillemot population in Scotland.

Tasker, M.L., Webb, A. and Matthews, J.M. in prep. A census of the large inland Common Gull colonies of Aberdeenshire.

Taylor, A.M. 1985. Manx Shearwaters on Lundy: ringing information and other observations. *Rep. Lundy Field Soc.* 36:23–24.

Teixeira, A.M. 1985. More auk deaths in Iberian nets. *BTO News* 138:1.

Teixeira, A.M. 1986. Razorbill *Alca torda* losses in Portuguese nets. *Seabird* 9:11–14.

Thom, V. 1986. *Birds of Scotland.* T. and A.D. Poyser, Calton.

Thomas, C.J. and Tasker, M.L. 1988. The Abbeystead gull colony in 1988. *Nature Conservancy Council Chief Scientist Directorate report* no. 844.

Thomas, D.H. 1981. The size of the colony of Manx Shearwaters (*Puffinus puffinus*) on Lundy. *Rep. Lundy Field Soc.* 32:16–20.

Thomas, G.J. 1972. Review of gull damage and management methods at nature reserves. *Biol. Conserv.* 4:117–127.

Thomas, G.J. 1982. Breeding terns in Britain and Ireland, 1975–79. *Seabird Report* 6:59–69.

Thomas, G.J., Partridge, J., Wolstenholme, R.S., Richards, P., Everett, M.J. and Cadbury, C.J. 1982. The increase and feeding habits of Herring and Lesser Black-backed Gulls at Orfordness, Suffolk. *Trans. Suffolk Nat. Soc.* 18:277–285.

Thomas, G.J., Underwood, L.A. and Partridge, J.K. 1990. Breeding terns in Britain and Ireland 1980–84. *Seabird* 12:20–31.

Thompson, D.B.A. and Thompson, P.S. 1980. Breeding Manx Shearwaters *Puffinus puffinus* on Rhum. *Hebridean Naturalist* 4:54–65.

Thomson, A.L. 1974. The migration of the gannet: a reassessment of British and Irish ringing data. *Brit. Birds* 67:89–103.

Tuck, L.M. 1960. *The Murres.* Canadian Wildlife Service, Ottawa.

Underwood, L.A. and Stowe, T.J. 1984. Massive wreck of seabirds in eastern Britain, 1983. *Bird Study* 31:79–88.

Urban, E.K., Fry, C.H. and Keith, S. (eds.) 1986. *The birds of Africa*, Vol. 2. Academic Press, London.

Uttley, J., Monaghan, P. and White, S. 1989. Differential effects of reduced sandeel availability on two sympatrically breeding species of tern. *Ornis Scand.* 20:273–277.

Uttley, J., Monaghan, P. and Blackwood, J. 1990. Hedgehog *Erinaceous europaeus* predation on Arctic Tern *Sterna paradisaea* eggs: the impact on breeding success. *Seabird* 13:2–6.

Vader, W., Barrett, R.T., Erickstad, K.E. and Strann K.-B. Differential responses of Common and Thick-billed Murres to a crash in the Capelin stock in the southern Barents Sea. *Studies in Avian Biology* 14:175–180.

van Eerden, M.R. and Zijlstra, M. (eds.) 1990. Proceedings second International workshop on Cormorants, Lelystad, April 1989. RWS Directorate Flevoland, Lelystad.

van Halewyn, R. and Norton, R.L. 1984. The status and conservation of seabirds in the Caribbean, pp 169–222 in Croxall, J.P., Evans, P.G.H. and Schreiber, R.W. (eds.) *Status and conservation of the world's seabirds*. ICBP Tech. Pub. No.2, Cambridge.

Veen, J. 1977. Functional and causal aspects of nest distribution in colonies of Sandwich Tern (*Sterna s. sandvicensis* Lath.). *Behaviour*, suppl. xx:1–193.

Veldkamp, R. 1986. (Decline and recovery of the Cormorant (*Phalacrocorax carbo*) in northwest Overijssel.) *Limosa* 59:163–168.

Vyatkin, P.S. 1986. Nesting cadastres of colonial birds in the Kamchatka Region, in Litvinenko, N.M. (ed.) *Seabirds of the Far East*. Collection of scientific papers. Acad. of Sci. of the USSR, Vladivostok. (English translation by Canadian Wildlife Service, Ottawa.)

Walsh, P.M. 1990. Seabird numbers and breeding success in 1989. *Nature Conservancy Council Chief Scientist Directorate Report* no. 1071.

Wanless, S. 1987. *A survey of the numbers and breeding distribution of the North Atlantic Gannet* Sula bassana *and an assessment of the changes which have occurred since Operation Seafarer 1969/70*. Research and Survey in Nature Conservation No.4, Nature Conservancy Council, Peterborough.

Wanless, S. 1988. The recolonisation of the Isle of May by Common Terns and Arctic Terns. *Scot. Birds* 15:1–8.

Wanless, S., French, D.D., Harris, M.P. and Langslow, D.R. 1982. Detection of annual changes in the numbers of cliff-nesting seabirds in Orkney 1976–1980. *J. Anim. Ecol.* 51:785–795.

Wanless, S. and Harris, M.P. 1984. Effect of date on counts of nests of Herring Gulls and Lesser Black-backed Gulls. *Ornis Scand.* 15:89–94.

Wanless, S. and Harris, M.P. 1985. Counting gulls—a plea for realism. *Ornis Scand.* 16:75–77.

Wanless, S. and Kinnear, P. 1988. Recent changes in numbers of some cliff-nesting seabirds on the Isle of May. *Bird Study* 35:181–190.

Wanless, S. and Langslow, D.R. 1983. Effects of culling on the Abbeystead and Mallowdale gullery. *Bird Study* 30:17–23.

Warham, J. 1975. Fulmar behaviour. *Scot. Birds* 8: 319–321.

Waring, M. and Davis, S. 1983. Rediscovery of Leach's Petrels breeding in Ireland. *Irish Birds* 2:360–363.

Warman, C.E. 1983. The quinquennial Berwickshire seabird colony survey, 1982. *Nature Conservancy Council Report*. SE Scotland Region, Edinburgh.

Waterston, G. (ed.) 1976. Fair Isle Bird Observatory Report for 1975: 24.

Watson, P.S. 1980. The seabirds of Northern Ireland and adjacent waters. *Irish Birds* 1:462–486.

Watson, P.S. and Radford, D.J. 1982. Census of breeding seabirds at Horn Head, County Donegal in June 1980. *Seabird Report* 6:26–34.

Webb, A. 1987. Petrels and tape luring: where next? *Sula* 1:103–105.

Webb, A., Harrison, N.M., Leaper, G.M., Steele, R.D., Tasker, M.L. and Pienkowski, M.W. 1990. *Seabird distribution west of Britain*. Nature Conservancy Council, Peterborough.

Webb, A., Tasker, M.L., Murray, S. and Best, M.A. 1985. The distribution of Guillemots (*Uria aalge*), Razorbills (*Alca torda*) and Puffins (*Fratercula arctica*) at sea around Flamborough Head, June 1984. *Nature Conservancy Council Chief Scientist Directorate Report* no. 590.

West, B., Cabot, D. and Greer-Walker, M. 1975. Food of the Cormorant (*Phalacrocorax carbo*) at some breeding colonies in Ireland. *Proc. Roy. Irish Acad.* 75B:285–304.

Whilde, A. 1977. A preliminary account of the summer population of gulls on Lough Corrib. *Irish Birds* 1:59–62.

Whilde, A. 1978. A survey of gulls breeding inland in the west of Ireland 1977 and 1978 and a review of the inland breeding habit in Ireland and Britain. *Irish Birds* 1:134–160.

Whilde, A. 1979. Auks trapped in salmon drift-nets. *Irish Birds* 1:370–376.

Whilde, A. 1983. A repeat survey of gulls breeding inland in the west of Ireland. *Irish Birds* 2:344–345.

Whilde, A. 1985. The 1984 All Ireland Tern Survey. *Irish Birds* 3:1–32.

Whitelaw, A. 1987. The Lesser Black-backed Gulls of Flanders Moss. *Scot. Bird News* 5:7.

Williamson, K. 1948. *The Atlantic Islands: the Faeroe life and scene*. Collins, London.

Wilson, J.G. and Earley, J.J. 1986. Pesticide and PCB levels in the eggs of the Shag *Phalacrocorax aristotelis* and Cormorant *Phalacrocorax carbo* from Ireland. *Envir. Pollut. Ser. B* 12:15–26.

Wormell, P. 1976. The Manx Shearwaters of Rhum. *Scot. Birds* 9:103–118.

Wynde, R.M. and Richardson, M.G. 1986. Moorland and coastal bird surveys—NCC 1985. *Nature Conservancy Council Report*. North-east Scotland Region, Aberdeen.

Wynne-Edwards, V.C. 1962. *Animal dispersion in relation to social behaviour*. Oliver and Boyd, Edinburgh.

Yeatman, L. 1976. *Atlas des oiseaux nicheurs de France de 1970 a 1975*. Soc. Ornith. de France, Ministère de la Qualité de la Vie Environment Direction de la Protection de la Nature, Paris.

Zonfrillo, B. 1980. Status of Storm Petrel in Clyde and Forth. *Scot. Birds* 11:52.

Gazetteer

Abberton Reservoir TL9718 90
Abbeystead SD6258 149, 151, 163, 174
Aberdeen NJ90 62, 262, 271
Ailsa Craig NX0299 74, 78, 81, 162, 174, 262
Ainov Island 173
Alaska 37, 49, 68, 183, 270, 275
Aleutian Islands 37
Am Balg NC1866 174
Anglesey 207, 208, 210, 211, 230
Angola 228
Angus 158, 184
Annet SV8609 55, 58, 64, 66
Antarctic 3, 227
Antrim 187, 286
Argyll and Bute 137, 139, 146, 158, 173, 184, 219, 276
Aughris Head G5137 257, 268
Auskerry HY6716 65
Azores 34, 118, 205, 206, 211, 212, 213, 259

Balearic Islands 97, 104
Baltic 265
Bamburgh Castle NU1835 47
Bangor, Co. Down J5081 274
Bank's Marsh, Ribble SD3924 128, 131
Bardsey SH1221 55, 59, 66, 174, 257
Barry Docks ST1167 150
Bass Rock NT6087 74, 78, 79, 81, 171, 291
Bay of Biscay 39, 75, 118, 183, 245, 259
Bear Island 75, 118, 156
Beginish V4178 66
Belfast J37 273
Bermersyde NT53 130
Benwee Head F8245

Bering Sea 37, 38, 183
Berneray NL5680 65, 262
Berry Head SX9456 257
Berwickshire 47
Bigga HU4479 65
Bill's Rocks, Mayo L5593 67
Blackrock, Mayo F4816 67
Blakeney Point TG0047 128, 199, 200–201, 217, 219, 230, 237
Blaskets V29 46, 55, 284, 286
Bonaventure Island 74, 80
Boreray, St Kilda NA1505 69, 79
Boreray, Sound of Harris NF8581
Bottle Island NB9705 121
Bound's Cliff SX0181 262
Braewick HU2478 84
Brannock Islands L7612 67
Bray Head O2917 55, 273
Brazil 3
Bristol Channel 150
Brittany 211, 264, 280
Brother Isle, Shetland HU4281 65
Brownsea SZ0288 199, 200
Bruray HU6972 67
Bull Rock, Cork V4039 66, 81, 257
Burhou, Channel Islands WA5508 64, 66
Burial Island J6763 162, 167
Burn of Forse, Hoy HD2395 173, 174

Caher L6676 67
Caithness 31, 47, 88, 110, 112, 119, 121, 158, 193, 257, 259, 262, 268, 273
Calf of Eday HY5839 85, 88, 173, 174
Calf of Man SC1565 55, 57, 58, 62, 66, 78
California 69, 90, 245
Camargue 131, 205

Canada 173, 183, 205, 252, 270, 275

Canary Islands 34, 60, 118, 280
Canna NG2505 46, 54, 55, 57, 58, 67, 100, 162, 193, 257 262
Cape Clear Island V9522 62, 66
Cape Verde Islands 34, 118
Cara Island NR6444 174
Car Craig and Haystack NT2083 171
Cardiff ST1978 150, 162
Cardigan Island SN1652 57, 59
Caribbean 205
Carmel Head SH2992 55, 59
Carreg y Llam SH3343 249
Carter's Rocks SW7559 262
Causamul NF6670 88
Ceann a'Mhara, Tiree NL9340 162
Chakbeg Stack, Stags of Broadhaven F8448 71
Channel Islands 33, 34, 45, 62, 74, 174
Chesil Beach SY5585 237
Chichester Harbour SU7701 200, 237
Clare Island L6986 59, 67, 78, 81, 263
Cleveland 187
Cliffs of Moher RO492 46, 193, 257, 268, 284
Clo Mor NC3373 31, 262, 282
Clyde (Firth of) xiii, 42, 130, 162, 164, 165, 174, 187, 273
Coll NB4639 112
Colonsay (Northwest Cliffs) NR3895 112, 162, 174, 262
Copeland Islands J5983 59, 140, 158, 162, 167
Copister Brough, Shetland HU4778 65
Coppay, Harris NF9394 65
Coquet Island NU2904 128, 166, 178, 199, 200, 207, 208, 210, 217, 219, 230, 284, 286
Coreen Hills NJ5021 137
Cork (Co.) 131, 164, 271
Cornwall 176, 257, 268, 286
Corsemaul NJ33 137

Craigleith NT5587 46, 171
Craigwatch NJ3835 137
Creevagh Head G1841 257, 268
Culver Cliff SZ6485
Cumbria 158, 174

Daaey, Shetland HU6095 65
Davillaun L5366 59
Deenish V4756 55, 59
Denmark 126, 131, 137, 145, 156, 173, 183, 205, 235, 253, 270, 275
Derry (Co.) 47
Devon 83, 257, 268, 286
Donegal 45, 130, 187
Dorset 46, 286
Dover TR3242 162
Down (Co.) 128, 158, 273
Downpatrick Head G1243 257, 268
Dublin (Co.) 286
Dumfries and Galloway 187
Dun, St Kilda NF1097 43, 284, 285, 286
Dunbar NT6879 184
Dungeness TR0718 141
Dunmore East X6805 184
Dunstanburgh NU2622 47
Durlston—St Alban's Head SZ0077 46
Duvillaun Islands F5816 67, 174
Dyfed 268

East Sussex 45
Ebro Delta 205
Edinburgh NT27 47, 137
Eigg NM4786 58
Eilean A'Chaolais NM6980 89
Eilean An Roin NC1858 121
Eilean Dubh, Summer Isles NB9705 121
Eilean Na Saille NC1833 88
Eilean nan Ron NC6465 65
Eldey 38
Enegars, Hoy HY2004 58
English Channel 6, 21, 245
Essex 290

Eyebroughty NT4986 171
Eynhallow HY3629 39, 46, 47, 65

Fair Isle HZ2172 45, 65, 78, 81, 109, 110, 113, 114, 193, 257, 268, 270, 271, 284, 285
Faraid Head NC3972 67, 262, 285
Farne Islands NU2438 46, 85, 100, 102, 103, 104, 105, 148, 178, 183, 193, 199, 200, 207, 208, 210, 228, 230, 251, 257, 262, 268, 284, 286, 290
Faroes 14, 15, 38, 47, 74, 80, 109, 113, 114, 117, 118, 122, 126, 183, 245, 253, 259, 279
Fastnet Rock V8816 67
Fermanagh 130
Fetlar HU69 110, 121
Fidra NT5187 171, 199, 210
Fife 47
Finland 126, 145, 150, 217, 253
Firth of Forth 151, 164, 171, 187, 193, 210
Fitful Head HU3515 45
Flamborough Head/Bempton TA27 14, 45, 81, 183, 186, 187, 193, 249, 252, 257, 262, 268, 284
Flanders Moss NS6497 149
Flannan Isles NA74 65, 71, 72, 79, 81, 262
Flat Holm ST2265 157
Folkestone TR2235 162
Foula HT9640 22, 23, 31, 39, 45, 47, 49, 58, 62, 65, 71, 72, 78, 81, 100, 109, 110, 113, 114, 118, 119, 121, 122, 193, 262, 270, 284
Foulness Point TR0595 128, 237
Foulney Island SD2564 131, 199, 230
Fowlsheugh NO8880 249
Frampton Marsh TF3838 130
France 54, 74, 90, 97, 145, 156, 173, 183, 205, 217, 235, 245, 259
Franz Josef Land 37

Gacilavore Islands NG3680 262
Galway 130, 139, 162

Gardiner's Island, New York 173
Garnham's Island TM2226 128
Gasker NA8711 88
Gateshead NZ2664 184
Ghana 201, 205, 206, 212, 213, 217, 228, 235
Glamorgan 150, 162
Glasgow NS66 137
Gobbins J4997 286
Godin, Jersey, Channel Islands WV4038 67
Grampian 47, 139, 273, 276
Grand Banks 118
Grassholm SM5909 78, 81
Great Blasket V2797 59, 67
Great Skellig V2561 55, 59, 62, 66
Great Yarmouth TG5307 237, 239
Green Island, Carlingford J2411 208, 210
Greenland 37, 38, 118, 126, 183, 259, 270, 280
Green Table—Ousdale Burn ND0517 88
Grimsay 38, 74
Gronant SJ0682 238
Gruinard NG9494 88
Gruney, Ramna Stacks HU3897 71, 72
Guernsey 64
Gugh SV8908 66, 187
Gulf of Guinea 145, 205, 217, 235
Gulf of St Lawrence 74, 80, 259, 265, 280
Gull Rock, Nare Head SW9337 262
Gulland Rock SW8879 67, 78
Gun's Island J6041 162, 167
Gunna NH1051
Gweedore Bay B7726 67

Haaf Gruney HU6398 65
Handa NC1448 112, 121, 193, 247, 257, 262, 268
Hanningford Reservoir TQ7298 130
Harris 139, 262
Hartlepool Dock NZ5935 184

Hascosay HU5592 65
Havergate TM4147 149, 199
Helgoland 183, 279
Helmsdale Cliffs ND0517 273
Hermaness HP6118 81, 113, 121, 123, 285, 287, 291
High Island L5057 59, 66
Hirta, St Kilda NF0999 38, 43, 48, 121, 262, 285
Holborn Head ND1171 112
Holkham TF8943 128, 237
Holm of Papa HY5152 65, 273
Holy Isle, Arran NS0630 162
Holy Isle, Northumberland NU1343 47
Horn Head C0243 31, 249, 257, 262, 263, 287
Horse Island, Ayrshire NS2143 166
Horse of Burravoe HU5381 58
Howth Head O3038 45, 55, 59
Hoy ND29 112, 121, 139
Hudson Straits 38

Iberia 16, 253, 259, 264
Iceland 14, 16, 38, 47, 74, 113, 117, 126, 127, 145, 156, 183, 245, 259, 274, 279, 286
Icho Tower Reef, Channel Islands 67
Illaunamid L5141 59, 66
Illaunmaster F9343 62, 67, 284
Inchcolm NT1982 171
Inchgarvie NT1480 171
Inchkeith NT2983 158, 171
Inchmickery NT2181 171, 199, 207, 208, 210
Inchmarnock 162
Inishark L4965
Inishbeg B9040 67
Inishbofin L5366 66
Inishduff G6473 67
Inishglora F6131 64, 67
Inishkea Islands F5020
Inishkeeragh, Donegal B6812 67
Inishkerragh, Mayo F6130 67
Inishmore, Aran Islands L8508 263

Jackdaw Island, Strangford J5551 128
Jan Mayen 34, 75, 118
Japan 245
Jarlshof, Shetland HU4009 38
Jethou WV3979 54, 58
Junk, Hoy and Hoggs of Hoy HU3744 67
Jura 112, 162, 273

Kattegat 92, 245, 253, 264, 265, 270, 275
Keeragh Islands S8606 178, 210
Kent 45, 187, 193, 290
Kerry 45, 55, 286
Kintyre NR73 47
Kirton Marsh TF3737 130
Kuril Islands 38

Inishmurray G5754 67
Inishnabro, Blasket Islands V2192 59, 66, 71, 263, 287
Inishtearaght, Blaskets V1895 59, 62, 66, 69, 71, 263, 284, 287
Inishtooskert, Blaskets Q2300 55, 59, 62, 66, 174
Inishturk L6074 59, 67
Inishvickillane, Blaskets V2191 59, 62, 66, 69, 71, 174, 287
Ireland's Eye O2941 78, 81
Irish Sea 6, 137, 245, 253, 259
Islay 273
Isle of Man 26, 33, 34, 47, 103, 174, 193, 257, 276, 284
Isle of May NT6559 22, 23, 62, 84, 98, 99, 100, 103, 104, 151, 156, 157, 166, 167, 171, 246, 251, 252, 257, 260, 264, 268, 281, 284, 285, 286
Isles of Scilly 55, 62, 64, 103, 174, 187, 262, 284
Isle of Wight 45, 100
Italy 126, 235

Labrador 38, 49, 183, 259, 279, 280
Lady Island NS2729
Lady's Island Lake T1006 178, 208
Lamb NT5387 171
Lambay O3251 45, 59, 85, 88, 100, 158, 178, 188, 249, 263, 286
Lamb Hoga HU6188 58, 65
Lamb Island, Valencia V4279
Langstone Harbour SU7103 239
Larne Lough J4399
Larrybane Head D0545 263, 286
Leith Docks NT2678 220
L'Etac de Serk, Channel Islands WV4546 66
Les Etacs, Alderney, Channel Islands WA5406 76, 81
Lewis 140, 262, 276
Liberia 228
Lincolnshire 290
Linga, Shetland HU59 65
Lion's Head NJ8366 264
Little Cumbrae NS1451 146, 162, 174
Little Orme SH8183 85, 193
Little Sark WV4573 54, 58
Little Skellig V2762 78, 81
Little Skerry C8642 263
Llanddeiniol SN5472 85
Lochaber 89, 276
Loch an Tomain NF9261 88
Loch of Strathbeg NK0859 128, 199, 200
Lochtyn SN3155 257
Lofoten Islands 74, 80, 279
Longa NG7378 67, 121
Lough Conn G11 139
Lough Corrib M23/M14 149
Lough Cutra T4898 85
Lough Erne H23 149, 176
Lough Neagh J09 130
Lough Scannie L7044 85
Lowestoft TM5493 184, 186
Lundy SS1346 47, 54, 57, 58, 78, 80, 193, 249, 257, 268
Lunga, Treshnish Islands NM2741 67
Lye Rock SX0690 262, 286

Madeira 34, 205, 211
Maggy's Leap J3928 263
Magharee Islands Q6222 66
Main Bench Cliff SZ3185 88
Maine 91, 280
Marsden Rock NZ4164 47, 85
Marwick Head HY2225 256
Massachusetts 54
Mattle Island Q9873 66, 88, 89
Mauretania 145, 217
Mayo 45, 130, 139, 287
Meall A'Choire Odhair NN7914 149
Meall Mor NC1238 65
Mediterranean 53, 61, 75, 97, 118, 131, 145, 259
Men-a-Vaur, Tresco SV8917 187
Mexico 69
Middleton Island, Alaska 183
Midland SM7509 55, 59, 66, 174
Minch 23, 245
Mingulay NL5683 43, 262
Minsmere TM4766 199, 238
Mochrum Loch NX3053 90
Monach Islands NF6362 47, 67, 88, 270, 273
Moray Firth 187, 259
Morecambe Bay NY1557 90
Morocco 228, 235, 259
Mortlach Hills NJ33 137, 139
Mousa HU4624 65, 69
Muck NM4180 58, 262
Muck Island, Portmuck Bay D4602 286
Muckle Green Holm HY5327 67
Muckle Skerry, Orkney ND4678 67
Mull NM63 219
Mull of Galloway NX1530 83, 262
Mullion Island SW6618 174
Mutton Island, Clare Q9774 66
Mykinesholmur 75

Needle-Sron Mhor ND0919 89
Needs Ore Point SZ4299 128, 132, 217, 237, 290
Ness, Lewis NB5163 79

Netherlands 90, 91, 92, 145, 156, 205, 216, 235
Newfoundland 3, 22, 38, 49, 54, 74, 118, 125, 165, 183, 253, 265, 280, 287
Newborough Warren NNR SH4263 174
New Quay Head SN3759 257
Nigeria 206
Norfolk 46
Normandy 98
North Bull O2539 237, 238
Northern Rocks, Scilly Isles SV8614 66
North Rona HW8132 47, 62, 65, 71, 72, 173, 174
North Sea 6, 19, 23, 24, 39, 75, 83, 98, 109, 118, 123, 156, 165, 189, 245, 252, 253, 259, 280
North Shields NZ3668 22, 184, 189
North Sutor of Cromarty NH8370 85, 174
Northumberland 47
Norway 15, 21, 74, 80, 83, 97, 103, 104, 118, 126, 136, 156, 165, 217, 245, 253, 259, 265, 274, 286, 287
Noss HU5440 65, 75, 81, 113, 123
Nova Scotia 183
Novaya Zemlya 37

Orfordness TM4449 141, 146, 149, 150, 161, 162, 164, 167, 237
Orkney 7, 11, 15, 26, 28, 33, 39, 40, 47, 57, 69, 87, 103, 110, 112, 113, 118, 119, 121, 122, 139, 140, 146, 158, 173, 184, 187, 193, 196, 197, 208, 228, 230, 252, 257, 259, 268, 271, 274, 276, 287
Ortac, Alderney, Channel Islands WA5207 81
Out Skerries HU6871 273

Papa Stour HU1661 67
Papa Westray HY4952 31, 197, 230, 274

Peel Hill SC2484 273
Pennington—Keyhaven SZ3393 128
Pentland Skerries ND4678 62, 65
Plymouth SX45
Point of Ayre NX4605 4
Point of Stoer NC0236 121
Poland 90, 91, 156
Portacloy—Porturlin F8644
Porthtowan SW6747 262
Portland Breakwater SY6977
Portland 145, 183, 205, 217, 235
Portugal
Priest Island NB9202 62, 65
Puffin Island V3468 55, 59, 66, 284, 287
Putrainez, Hern WV4079 67

Rathlin D1352 47, 59, 140, 158, 188, 193, 249, 257, 262, 273, 284, 286
Rathlin O'Birne G4680 67, 69, 71
Ravenglass SD0795 131, 199
Redhead Cliffs NO7048 167
Redhythe Point NJ5767 273
Rigg Bay NX4844 90
Rhode Island 54
Rhum NM39 54, 55, 58, 262
Roaninish, Gweebara Bay B6503 67
Rockabill O3262 206, 207, 208, 210, 213
Rockcliffe Marsh NY3163
Ross and Cromarty 47, 89, 119, 173, 276
Røst, Norway 9
Rosyth NT1183 150, 162
Rothiesholm Head HY6222 174
Round and Spartina Island, Poole Harbour SY9887 128
Round Island, Scilly Isles SV9116 58
Rouzic 75
Rubha Shois NC1445 112
Runde, Norway 74
Rusk Holm, Eday HY5136 65

St Abb's Head NT9169 171, 193, 257, 268

St Agnes, Bow and Cow SV8808 58, 66

St Andrews NO5117 47

St Bees Head NX9414 262

St Cyrus NO7564 237

St David's Head SM7830 174

St Fergus Gas Terminal NK0954

St Helens, Round and Tean SV9116 187

St Ives, Cornwall NW5140 163

St Kilda NF19 xiv, 11, 14, 15, 22, 38, 40, 42, 43, 44, 47–48, 49, 52, 55, 58, 65, 69, 71, 72, 74, 78, 79, 81, 281, 282, 284

St Margaret's Island SS1297 90, 174

Saltee (Great and Little) X99 46, 55, 59, 78, 81, 174, 178, 257, 263, 268, 284, 286

Salvage Islands 34, 60, 205, 211

Samphrey HU4676 65

Samson SV8813 187

Sanda NR7204 58, 65, 162

Sanday HY64 113

Sands of Forvie NK0327 47, 199, 200

Saxavord HP6317 118

Scariff Island V4455 55, 59, 66

Scarp NA9616 88

Scar Rocks NX2634 81

Scolt Head TF8046 128, 141, 184, 199, 200, 201, 219, 230, 237

Senegal 145, 195, 235

Sheep Island, Antrim DO546 85, 286

Sheep Island, Dyfed SM8402 90

Shetland xiii, 7, 9, 11, 12, 22–24, 26, 28, 33, 43, 45, 47, 69, 80, 87, 90, 98, 103, 110, 112, 113, 114, 118, 119, 121, 122, 140, 146, 150, 158, 165, 173, 183, 189, 193, 196, 197, 219, 221, 228, 230, 231, 251, 252, 257, 259, 262, 264, 268, 269, 270, 271, 274, 276, 284, 287

Shiants NG4298 67, 78, 81, 100, 174, 257, 262, 268, 284, 285

Shillay NF8891 67

Shipman Head, Bryher SV8716 58

Siccar Point—Broadhaven NT8671 171

Skagerrak 252

Skea Skerries HY4440 67

Skelbo NH7896 47

Skelligs V2561 284, 287

Skokholm SM7305 47, 54, 55, 58, 62, 66, 178, 249, 257, 268, 284

Skomer SM7309 45, 54, 55, 58, 66, 146, 174, 178, 257, 262, 268, 284, 290

Skye 262, 271, 273, 276

Sligo 130

Soay, St Kilda NA0601

Solent 128

Somerset 45

Sound Gruney HU5896 65

South Africa 228

South Ascrib Island NG3063 67

South Binness SU7003 237

South Shields NZ3866 164

South Stack SH2182 249

South Walney SD2261 146, 148–149, 151, 199, 230

Spain 61, 97, 104, 126, 145, 165, 183, 205, 217, 235, 253

Stac an Armin, St Kilda NA1506 79

Stac Lee NA1405 79

Stack Rocks SM8113 174

Staffa NM3235 174

Stags of Broadhaven F8448 67, 69, 72, 78

Stiffkey Binks TF9743

Stornoway NB4534

Strangford Lough J56 128, 140, 167, 199, 200, 208, 210

Stroma ND3577 67, 112

Stronsay HY62 113

Strumble Head SM8941 174

Suffolk 45, 290

Sula Sgeir HW6230 14, 43, 65, 71, 72, 79, 80, 81, 262

Sule Skerry HX6224 62, 65, 71, 72, 284

Sule Stack HX5617 81

Sullom Voe HU57 275
Sumburgh Head HU4008 67, 244
Summer Isles NB9705 65, 121
Sunbiggin Tarn NY6707 130
Sutherland 47, 89, 119, 276
Svalbard 14, 34, 47, 118, 156, 173, 183, 279
Swan Island, Larne Lough J4299 208, 210
Sweden 136, 145, 183, 253, 274, 279
Switha ND3791 65
Switzerland 156
Swona ND3984 286
Syltefjordstawan 74

Tantallon NT5985 47
Tern Island, Wexford O9521 199, 208, 211, 219
Terrington Offshore Bund TF5129 131
Tetney TA3704 237
The Mouls SW9482 262
The Needles SZ2985
The Skerries SH2795 210
Tipperary (Co.) 130
Tiree NI0144 139, 174
Tormore 263, 287
Tory Island B8546 67, 262, 287
Treshnish Islands NM24 58, 162
Trevose Head SW8576 262
Troup Head NJ8266 78, 81, 193, 257, 264, 268
Tunisia 212
Turkey 60

Uists 276
Unst HP60 110, 121
Urie Lingey HU6096 65
USSR 156, 183, 270, 280

Wadden Sea 221
Walney ND1866
Wart Holm, Westray HY4818 67
Wash 130, 131
Waterford (Co.) 189, 193, 276
Western Isles 69, 88, 112, 118, 119, 121, 140, 146, 158, 173, 271
Western Rocks, Scilly Isles SV8306 65
West Germany 126, 131, 145, 156, 205, 217, 235, 253, 259
Westmann Islands 38, 74, 80
Westray HY44 31, 273
Wexford Harbour TO923 199, 208, 211, 219
Weybourne—Sheringham TG1344 46
Wiay, Skye NG2936 273
Wicklow Head T3492 47
Woody Bay, Martinhoe SS6650 193

Yell HU48 110, 121
Ynys Gwylan Bach/Fawr SH1824 284
Youghal X0979 47

Index

Arctic Skua 7, 22, 108–115, 119, 122,
  123
international distribution 108–109,
  115
distribution away from colonies 109
census methods 109–110, 118–119
in Scotland 110–112, 115
reasons for change in numbers 112–
  114
Arctic Tern 7, 9, 22, 23, 32, 108, 113,
  166, 196, 197, 207, 217, 219, 221,
  225, 226–233
international distribution 226–228,
  231–232
distribution outside breeding
  season 227–228
census methods 196–197, 228
in Britain and Ireland 225, 228–230,
  232–233
reasons for change in numbers 230–
  231

Blackbird 3
Black-browed Albatross 290–291
Black Guillemot xiii, 7, 11, 16, 22, 26,
  28, 32, 33, 269–277
international distribution 270, 275
census methods 270–271
in Britain and Ireland 271–273
reasons for change in numbers 273–
  275
Black-headed Gull 3, 6, 7, 11, 15, 21,
  125–135, 178, 194, 201, 207, 296
international distribution 125–127,
  132–133
census methods 127–128
in Britain and Ireland 128–131,
  133–135
reasons for change in numbers 131–
  132
Black Tern 206, 290

Blenny 269
Botulism 131, 150, 164, 178
Breeding failures
in Norway 9, 21–22, 103
in Shetland xiii, 9, 22–24, 114, 122–
  123, 189, 230–231
Brown Trout 91
Butterfish 269

Calanus 6
Capelin 22, 80, 243
Carrion Crow 238
Cat 16, 69, 149, 274
Census methods 25–34, 39–40, 54,
  61–62, 69, 75–76, 83–85, 98–100,
  109–110, 118–119, 127–128, 137,
  146, 157–158, 173, 183–184, 196–
  197, 206–207, 217, 228, 235, 245–
  247, 260, 270–271, 280–282
Chemical pollution 17–18, 80, 92, 104,
  122, 216, 253, 265
Cod 21
Common Gull 3, 6, 7, 15, 136–143,
  290
international distribution 136–137,
  141
census methods 137
in Britain and Ireland 137–140,
  142–143
reasons for change in numbers 140–
  141
Common Tern 7, 166, 196, 197, 206,
  207, 210, 212, 216–225, 228, 230,
  231
international distribution 216–217,
  221–222
distribution outside breeding
  season 216–217
census methods 196–197, 217
in Britain and Ireland 217–220,
  223–224, 225

Common Tern – *contd*
reasons for change in numbers 220–
221
Cormorant xiii, 5, 6, 7, 10, 11, 21,
82–95, 96, 103, 104
international distribution 92–93
distribution away from colonies 83
census methods 82–85
in Britain and Ireland 85–90, 94–95
reasons for change in
numbers 90–92
inland nesting 90

Dab 91
Diet 18, 37, 49, 53, 60, 68, 73, 82, 96,
103, 113, 116, 122, 125, 136, 144,
150, 155, 164–165, 172, 176, 182,
194, 204, 216, 226, 234, 243, 258,
269, 278
Distribution at sea xii, 39, 69, 75, 80,
98, 109, 118, 122, 156, 183, 245,
258, 259, 280
Dog 69, 149
Drowning in fishing nets xiii, 11, 15,
16–17, 80, 90, 91–92, 104, 253, 264,
287

EC Bird Directive xvi, 205, 216, 235

Ferret 16
Fishery xiii, 6, 11, 18–24
Fishery discards 6, 19–21, 73, 80, 114,
116, 123, 150, 155, 164–165, 172,
177
Food and foraging 4–6, 18–24, 37, 60,
73, 75, 80, 82, 96, 103, 108, 113–
114, 116, 122–123, 125, 131, 136,
144, 150, 155, 164–165, 172, 176–
178, 182, 189, 194, 204, 216, 221,
226, 234, 239, 243, 258, 264, 269,
273–274, 278, 287
Fox 16, 131, 151, 200, 211, 238
Fulmar 3, 4, 5, 7, 9, 10, 11, 12, 13, 14,
20, 22, 23, 28, 37–52, 79

distribution away from colonies 39
history in North Atlantic 38–39
international distribution 37–39, 50
census methods 39–40
in Britain and Ireland 40–48, 51, 52
reasons for change in
numbers 48–49
nest sites 47

Gannet xv, 3, 4, 5, 6, 11, 14, 19, 21,
22, 23, 28, 47, 73–81, 116, 123, 150,
165, 290
as food for humans 74–75, 79, 80
international distribution 73–75, 81
census methods 75–76
in Britain and Ireland 77–79, 81
reasons for change in
numbers 79–80
distribution away from colonies 75

Goat 287
Great Auk xiv, 15
Great Black-backed Gull 7, 15, 19, 22,
80, 150, 157, 165, 172–181
international distribution 172–173,
179
census methods 157–158, 173
in Britain and Ireland 174–176,
180–181
reasons for change in numbers 176–
179
Great Skua xv, 19, 22, 109, 110, 112,
113, 114, 116–124, 150, 165
international distribution 116–118,
123
distribution away from colonies 118
census methods 118–119
in Scotland 119–120, 124
reasons for change in numbers 121–
123
Ground predators xiv, 11, 16, 57, 64,
69, 131, 149, 208, 211, 221, 231,
238–239, 270, 274, 287
Guillemot 3, 10, 11, 12, 13, 14, 15, 17,
21, 22, 23, 28, 33, 78, 243–257, 258,
260, 263, 265, 287
international distribution 244–245,
254–255

Guillemot – *contd*
distribution away from colonies 245
census methods 247
in Britain and Ireland 247–251,
  255–257
reasons for change in numbers 251–
  253, 255–257
Gull-billed Tern 290
Gull culling 148, 150, 151, 156, 165–
  167, 178–179

Habitat change 112–113, 122, 149,
  166, 208, 216, 220
Haddock 241
Hedgehog 231, 274
Herring 6, 18, 19, 21, 22, 23, 24, 49,
  73, 80, 103, 104, 189, 231, 243, 278
Herring Gull xiii, 7, 15, 28, 47, 145,
  146, 148, 149, 150, 151, 155–171,
  178, 211
international distribution 155–156,
  167–168
movements away from colonies 156
census methods 157–158
in Britain and Ireland 158–163,
  169–171
reasons for change in numbers 163–
  165, 171
control measures 165–167
Hooded Crow 47
Human persecution/egg collecting xiv,
  11, 13–15, 47–48, 79, 80, 83, 90–91,
  104, 114, 118, 121–122, 131, 149,
  156, 165, 178, 183, 189, 200–201,
  211, 212–213, 239, 252, 253, 259,
  264, 265, 287

Inland nesting 7, 47, 83, 85, 88, 90,
  110–111, 121, 125–126, 128, 130–
  131, 135, 136, 137, 139, 144, 149–
  150, 155, 163, 164, 168, 172, 174,
  176, 194, 216, 226

Kestrel 238
Kittiwake 3, 5, 6, 7, 9, 11, 12, 15, 21,
  22, 23, 28, 47, 108, 113, 114, 116,
  182–193

Kittiwake – *contd*
international distribution 182–183,
  189–190
distribution away from colonies 183
census methods 183–184
in Britain and Ireland 184–189,
  191–193
reasons for change in numbers 189

Leach's Petrel 5, 68–72, 116
international distribution 68–69, 72
census methods 69
in Britain and Ireland 69–72
Legal protection xvi, 118, 131, 178,
  200, 237, 264
Lesser Black-backed Gull xv, 7, 15, 21,
  144–154, 157, 158, 162, 165, 166,
  167, 178
international distribution 144–146,
  151–152
movements 145–146
census methods 146, 157–158
in Britain and Ireland 147–150,
  152–154
reasons for change in numbers 150–
  151, 154
Lesser Crested Tern 290
Lifespan 9–10, 39
Little Gull 290
Little Shearwater 290
Little Tern 6, 149, 196, 234–242
international distribution 234–235,
  240–241
distribution outside breeding
  season 235
census methods 196–197, 235
in Britain and Ireland 235–237,
  241–242
reasons for change in numbers 237–
  239
Lumpsucker 269

Mackerel 19, 73, 80
Manx Shearwater xv, 6, 10, 16, 53–59,
  64
international distribution 53–54, 57

Manx Shearwater – *contd*
  census methods 54
  in Britain and Ireland 55–59
Mediterranean Gull 290
Mink 16, 131, 221, 231, 270, 274
Monitoring of seabirds xii–xiii, 11–12, 23, 24, 46–47, 188–189, 199, 208, 249, 251, 257, 264, 268, 284–286

Nesting – on buildings 3, 7, 11, 47, 90, 137, 150, 155, 158, 160, 162, 163, 164, 168, 176, 182, 186, 205, 220
Non-annual nesting 84, 99–100, 103–104
Norway Lobster 19
Norway Pout 19

Offal 5, 19–21, 37, 49, 53, 60, 68, 164, 172, 177, 189
Oil pollution xiii, 11, 15, 17, 104, 252–253, 264–265, 270, 274–275, 280, 287
Operation Seafarer (background) xi, xv, 11–12, 25, 31–32, 307–316
Otter 274
Oystercatcher 238

Perch 91
Peregrine 210, 211
Pike 91
Plaice 19
Plankton 5, 6, 21, 37, 49, 53, 60, 68
Poor Cod 150
Puffin xiii, 9, 10, 11, 14, 15, 16, 17, 21, 22, 33, 54, 64, 71, 104, 113, 165, 263, 278–289
  international distribution 279–280, 288
  distribution outside breeding season 280
  census methods 280
  in Britain and Ireland 282–289
  reasons for change in numbers 287

Rabbit 54, 166
Rat xiv, 11, 16, 57, 64, 69, 211, 274, 287

Raven 47, 48
Razorbill xv, 9, 10, 11, 12, 15, 16, 17, 21, 22, 28, 33, 249, 258–268, 287
  international distribution 259–265
  distribution away from colonies 259
  census methods 260
  in Britain and Ireland 260–264, 266–268
  reasons for change in numbers 264–265
Regulation of numbers 9, 10, 13
Reintroduction of seabirds 57, 210
Ringing xiii, 10, 12, 39, 54, 75, 80, 89–90, 98, 104, 109, 118, 126–127, 151, 156, 162, 173, 183, 195–196, 201, 205–206, 212, 216–217, 235, 245, 259, 280, 286
Roach 91
Robin 10
Roseate Tern 3, 196, 197, 201, 204–215, 217
  international distribution 204–206, 214
  distribution outside breeding season 205–206
  census methods 205–206
  in Britain and Ireland 208–211, 215
  reasons for change in numbers 211–213
Rubbish tips 125, 150, 155, 156, 164, 172, 177, 178

Saithe 82, 103
Salmon 17, 91, 287
Sandeel xiii, 6, 18, 19, 22, 23, 24, 49, 73, 80, 91, 104, 108, 113, 114, 116, 122, 123, 189, 194, 204, 230, 231, 243, 258, 269, 278, 287
Sand Martin 275
Sandwich Tern 7, 166, 194–203, 206, 207, 212, 219, 290
  international distribution 194–196, 202
  distribution outside breeding season 195–196
  census methods 196–197

Sandwich Tern – *contd*
in Britain and Ireland   197–199,
   202–203
reasons for change in numbers   199–
   201
Seabirds
as food   14, 38, 42, 47–48, 57, 74, 79,
   80, 117–118
as predators   6, 108, 113, 114, 116,
   122–123, 144, 165, 172, 178
Sea Eagle   47
Sea Trout   91
Shag   xv, 6, 7, 9, 10, 15, 22, 23, 47, 83,
   84, 85, 90, 96–107
international distribution   96–98, 105
distribution away from colonies   98
census methods   98–100
in Britain and Ireland   100–103,
   106–107

Shag – *contd*
reasons for change in numbers   103–
   105
Sheep   69
Sprat   18, 19, 22, 23, 49, 73, 204, 243,
   258, 278
Starling   274
Stoat   16, 239, 274
Storm Petrel   xv, 5, 16, 60–67, 69
international distribution   60–61, 64
census methods   61–62
in Britain and Ireland   62–67

Tree Mallow   207

Whiting   19, 22, 82, 150
Wrasse   82, 91